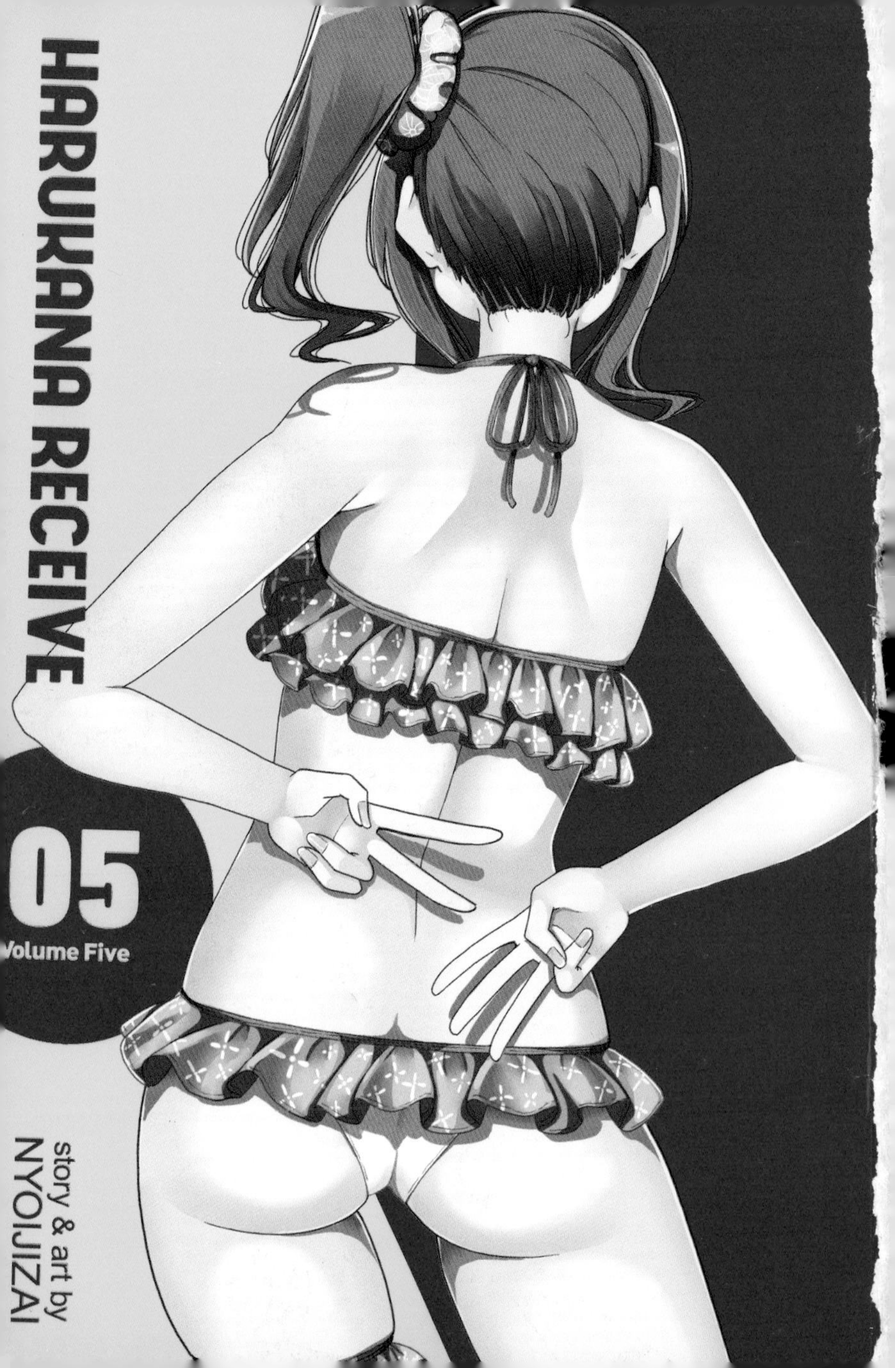
HARUKANA RECEIVE
05
Volume Five
story & art by
NYOIJIZAI

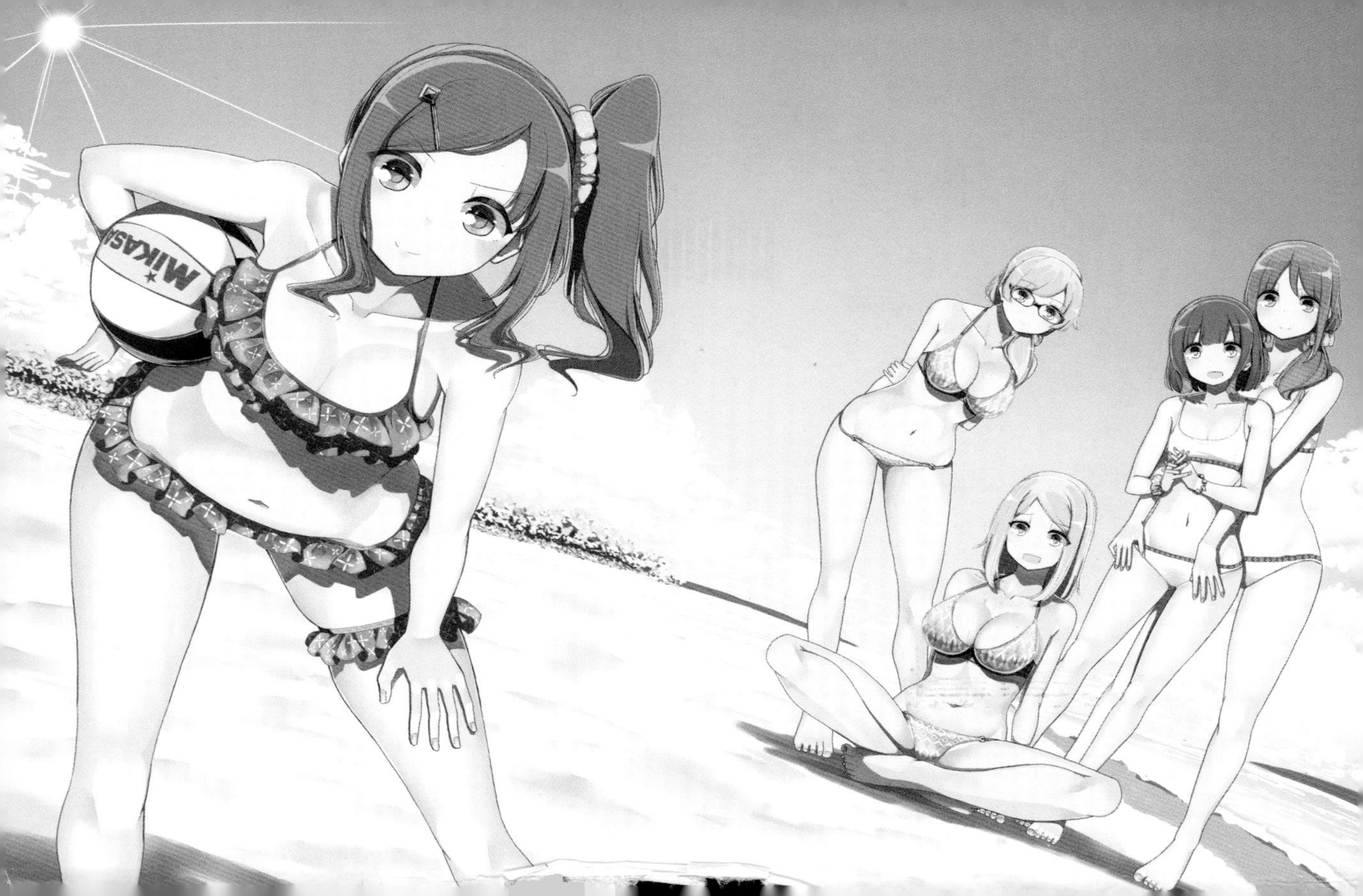
MIKASA

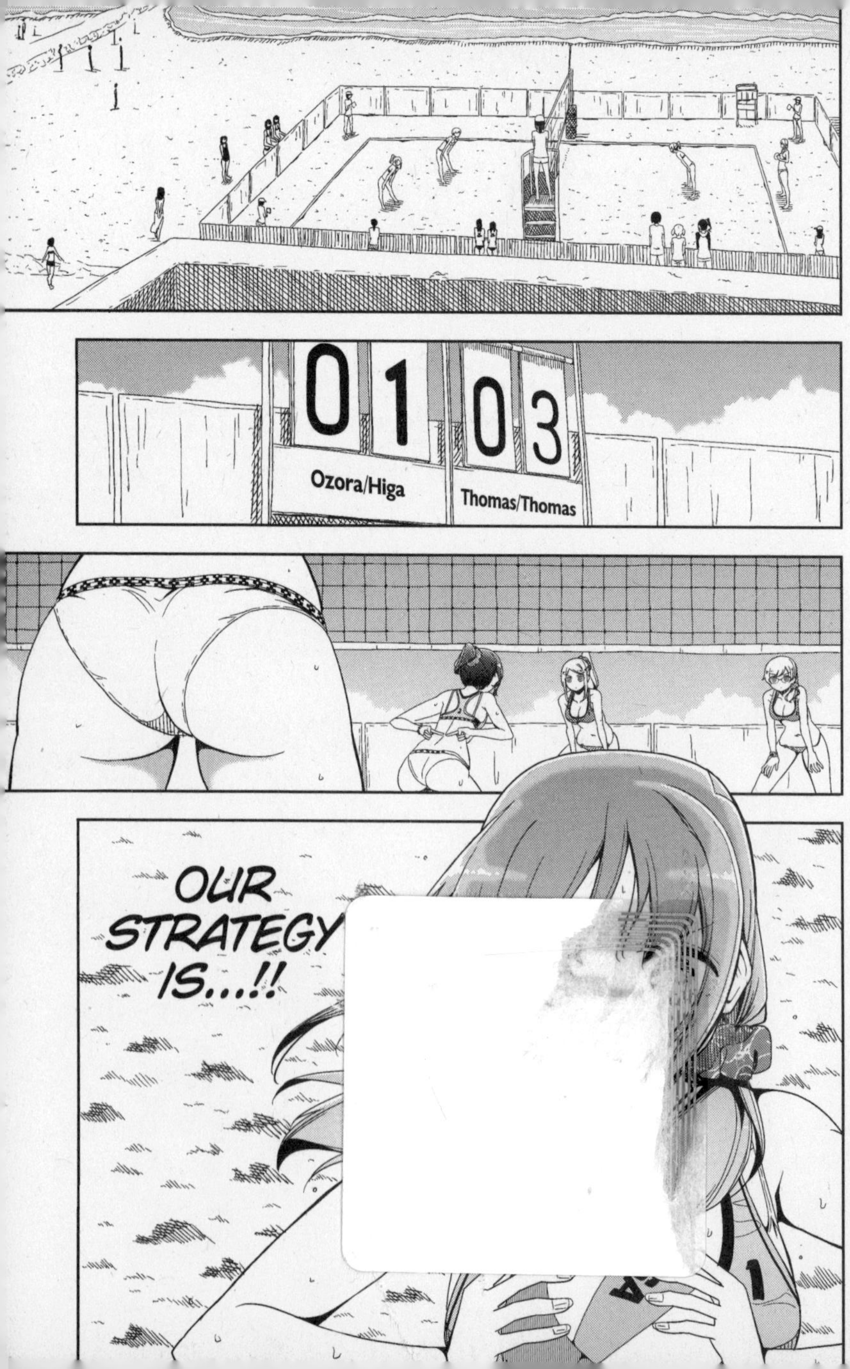
01
03
Ozora/Higa
Thomas/Thomas
OUR STRATEGY IS...!!

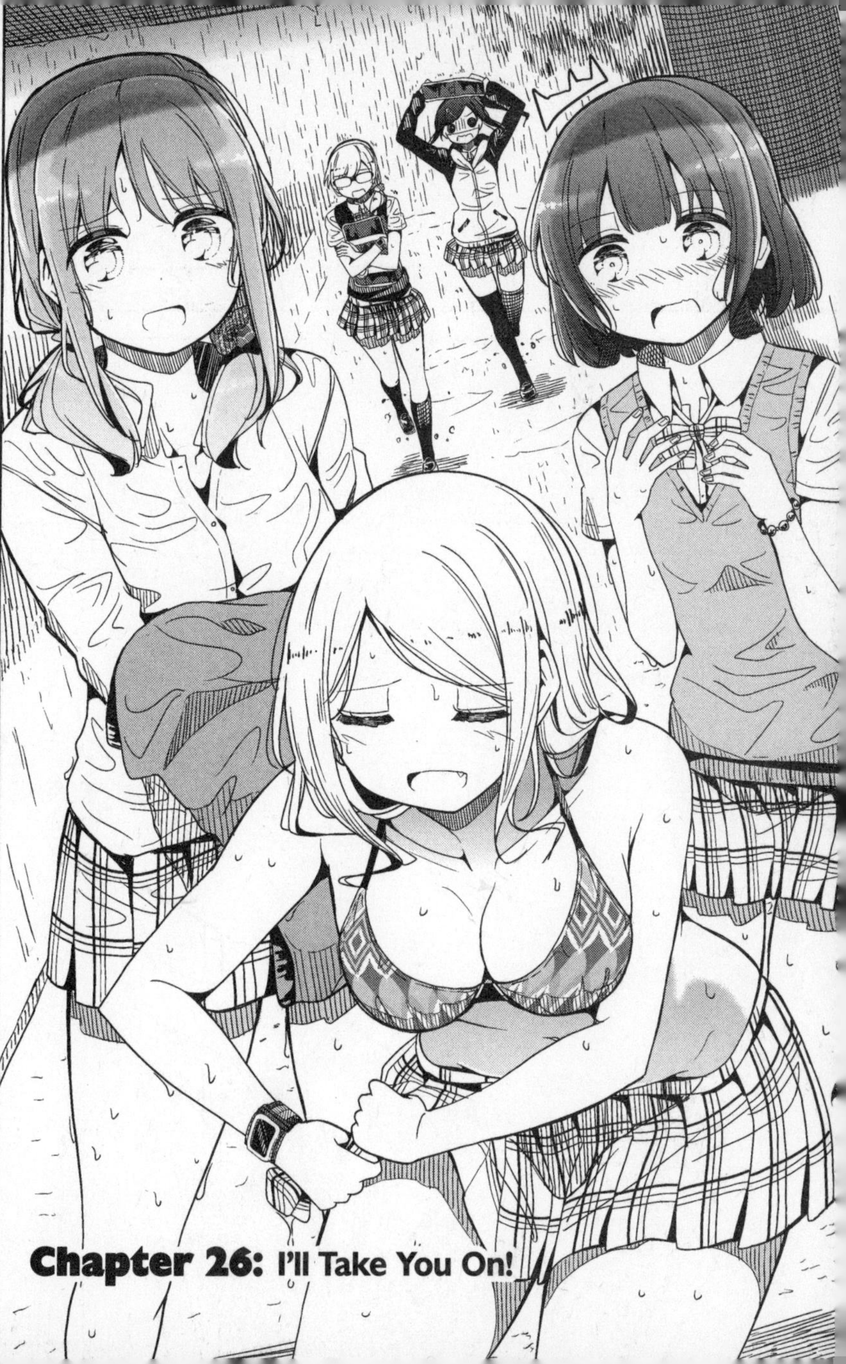
Chapter 26: I'll Take You On!

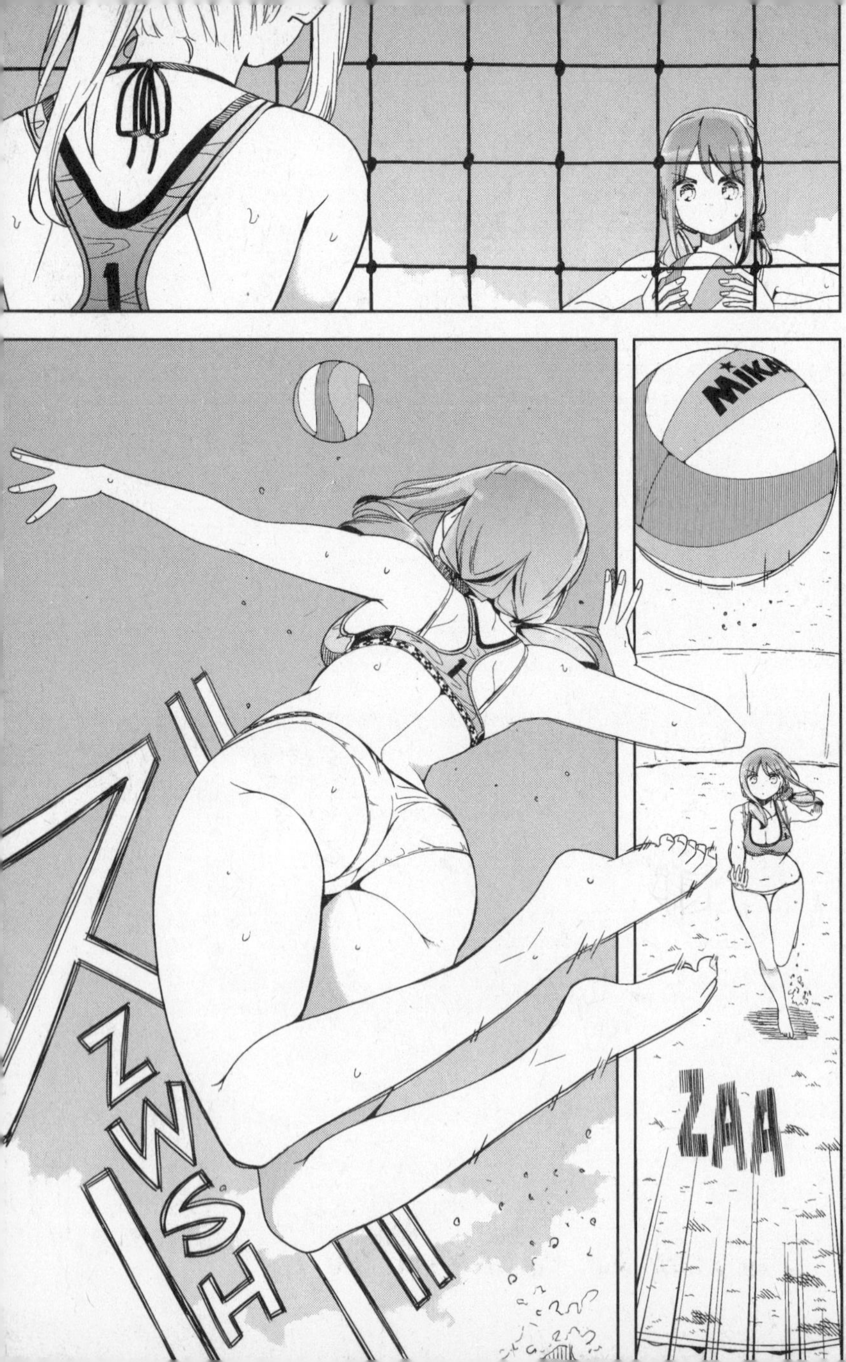
MIKA
ZAA

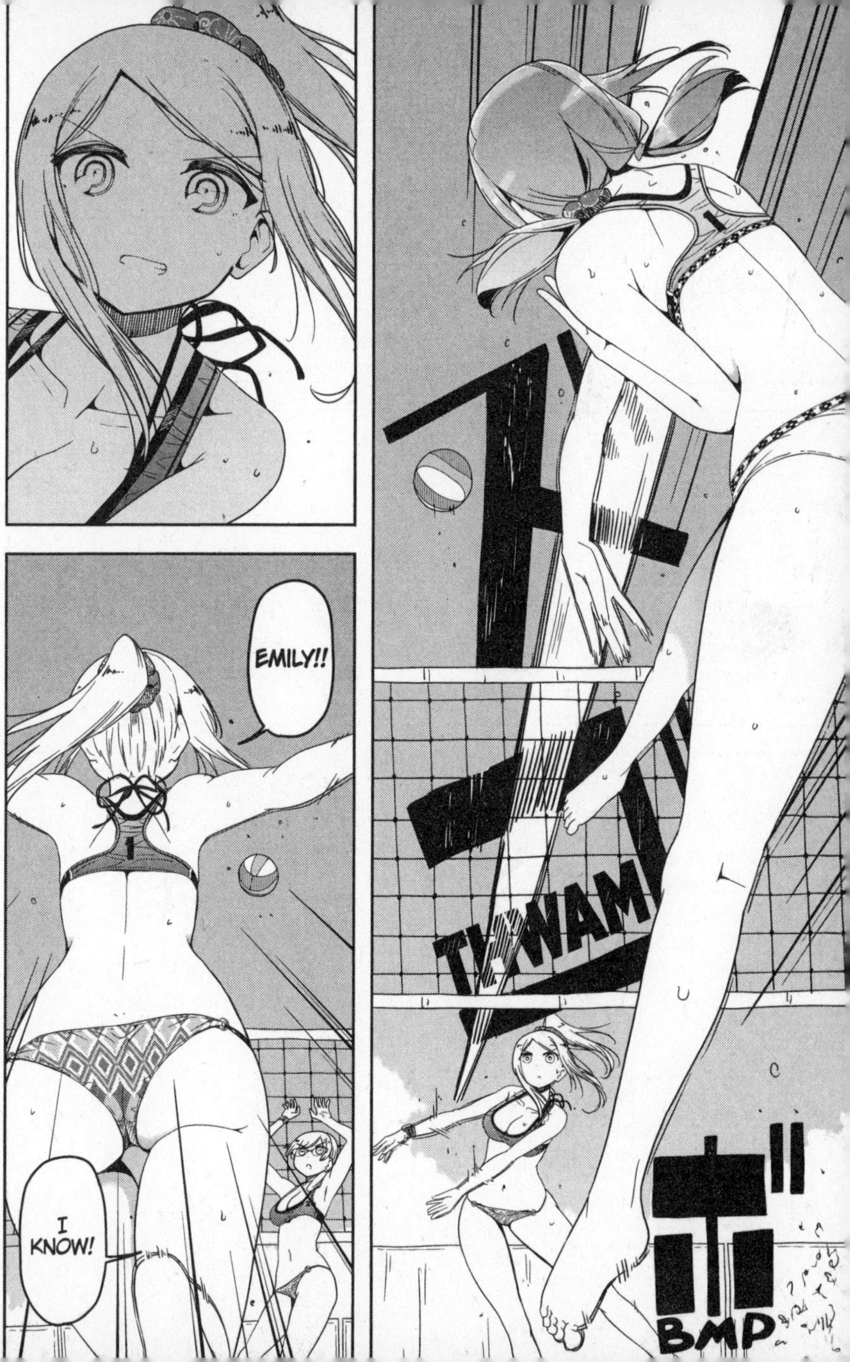
THWAM
BMP
EMILY!!
I KNOW!

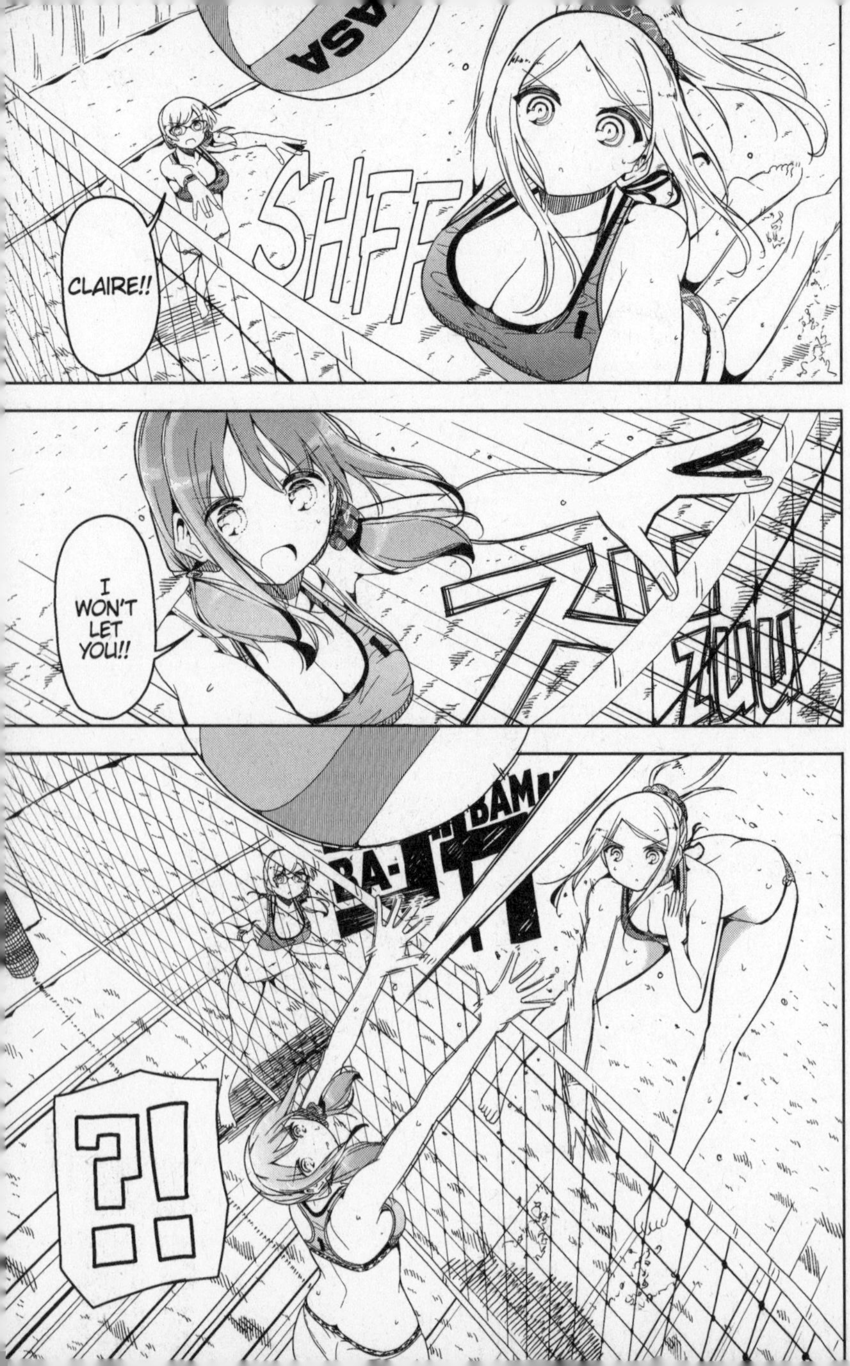
SHFF
CLAIRE!!
ZUUU
ZUU
I WON'T LET YOU!!
BA-
BAM!!
?!

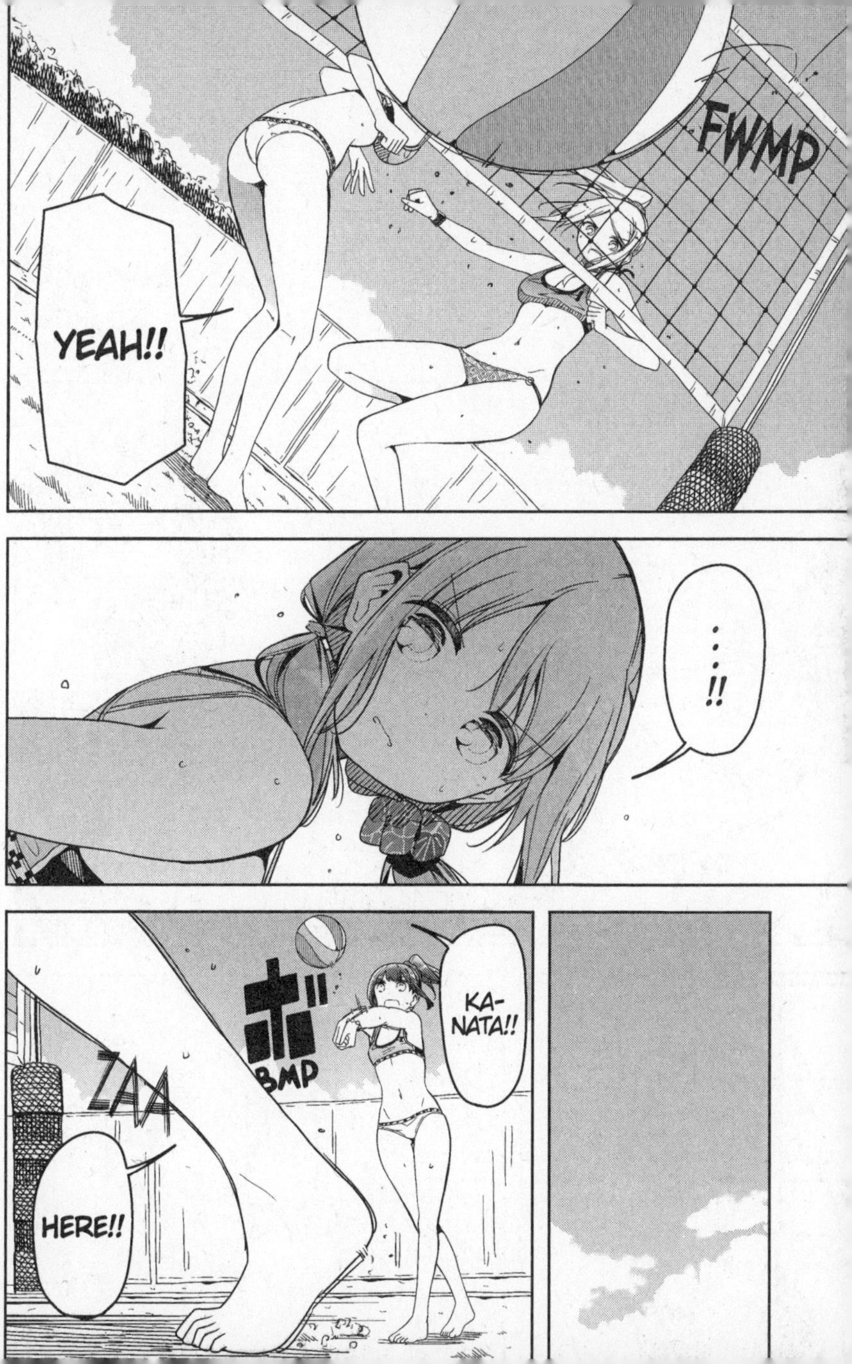
FWMP
YEAH!!
...!!
KA-NATA!!
BMP
ZAA
HERE!!

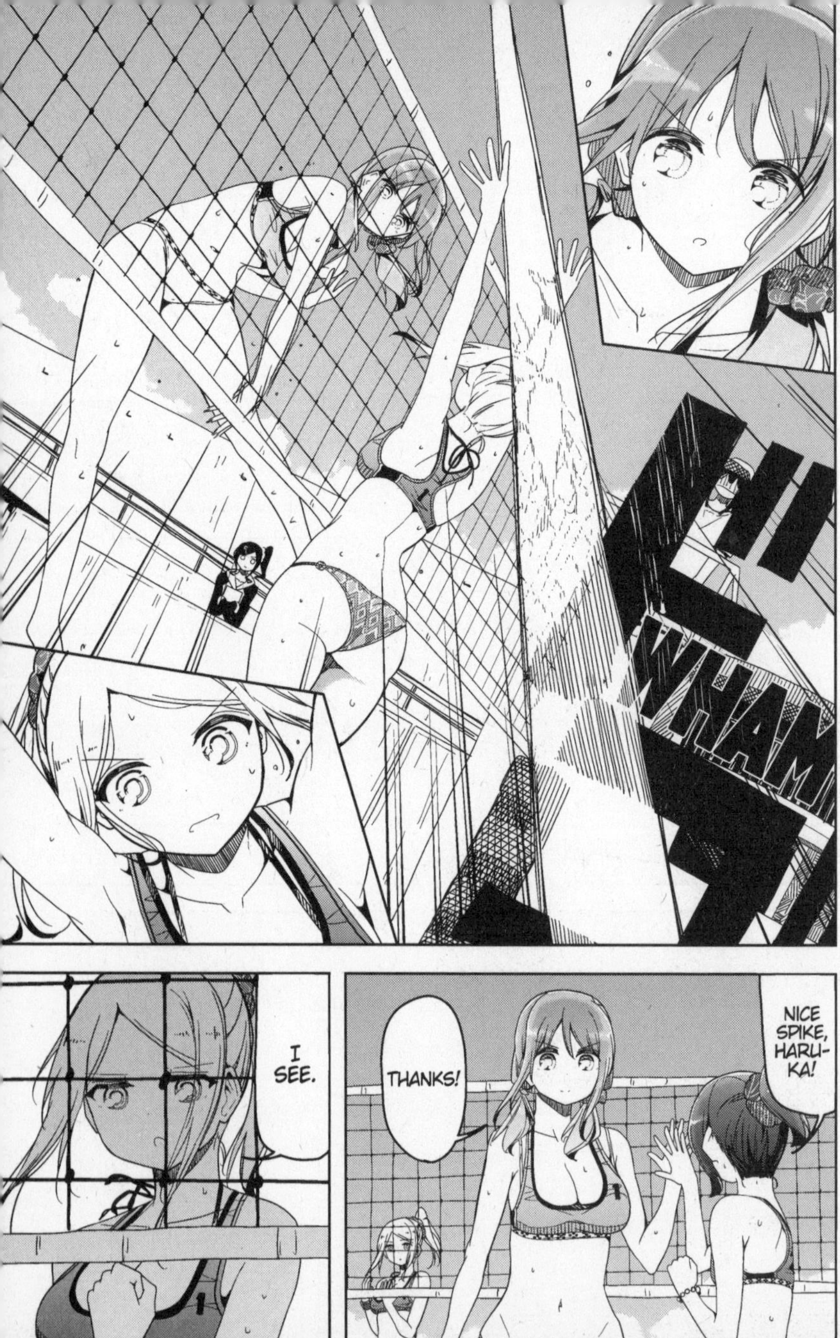
WHAM
NICE SPIKE, HARU-KA!
THANKS!
I SEE.

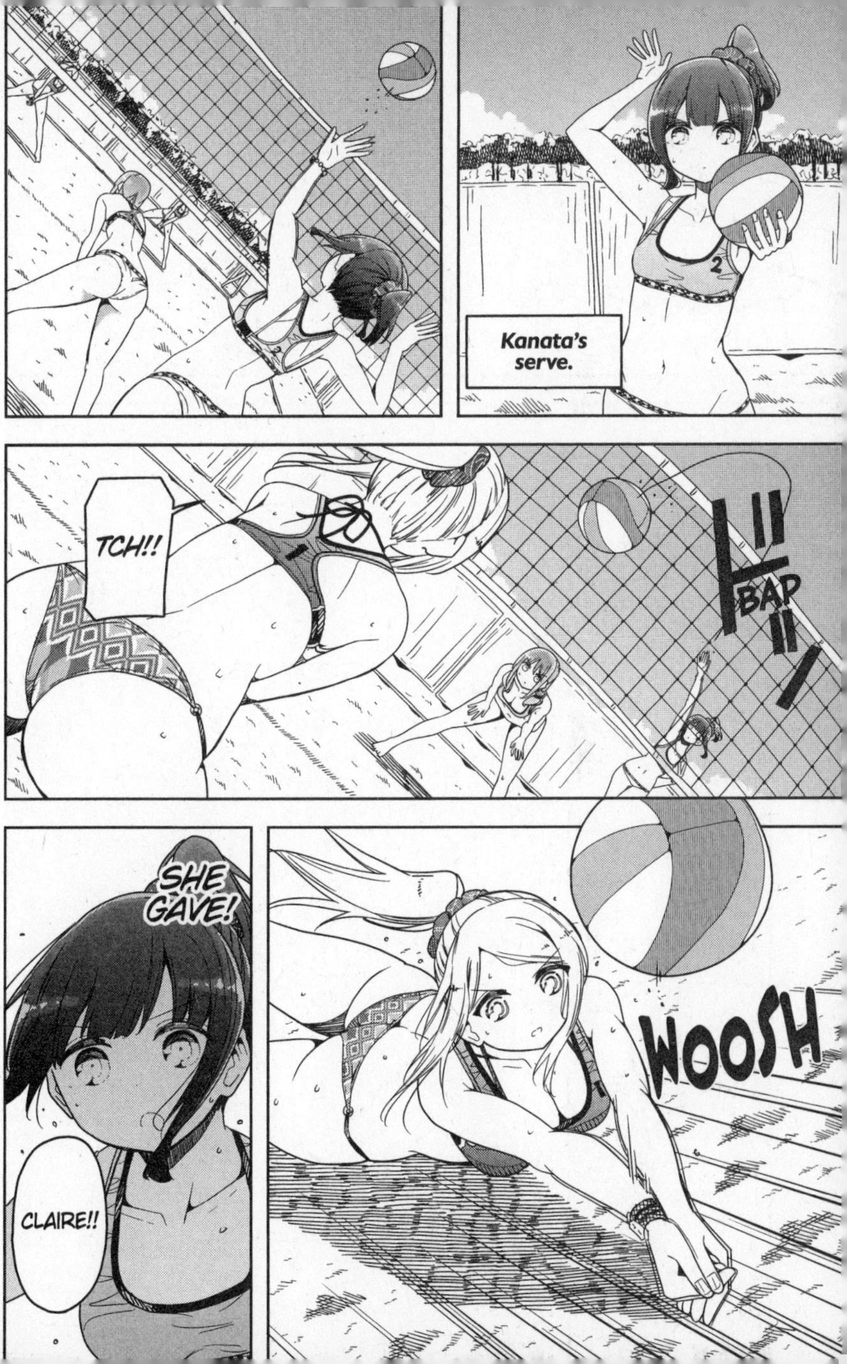
Kanata's serve.
BAP
TCH!!
WOOSH
SHE GAVE!
CLAIRE!!

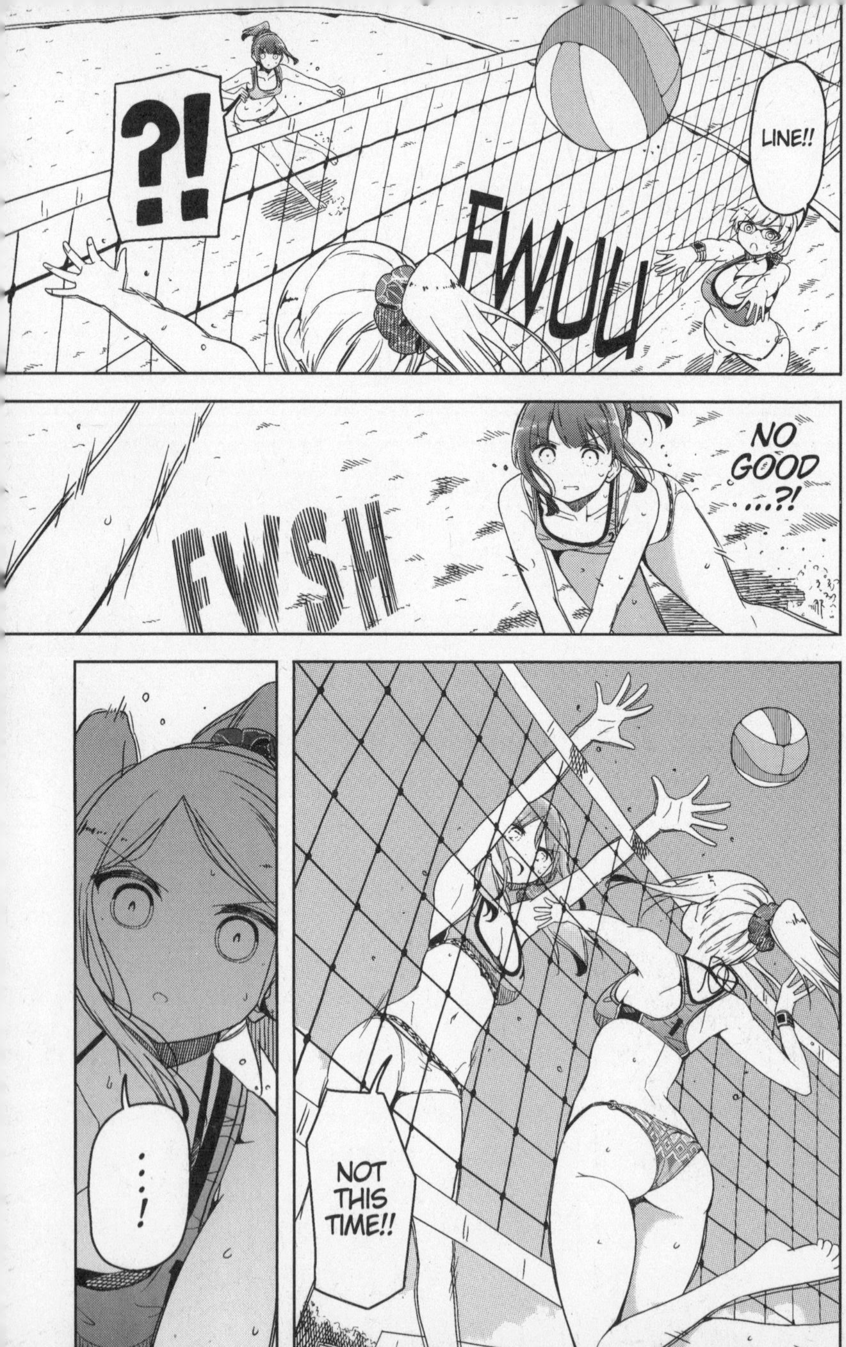
LINE!!
FWUU
?!
NO GOOD ...?!
FWSH
NOT THIS TIME!!
...!

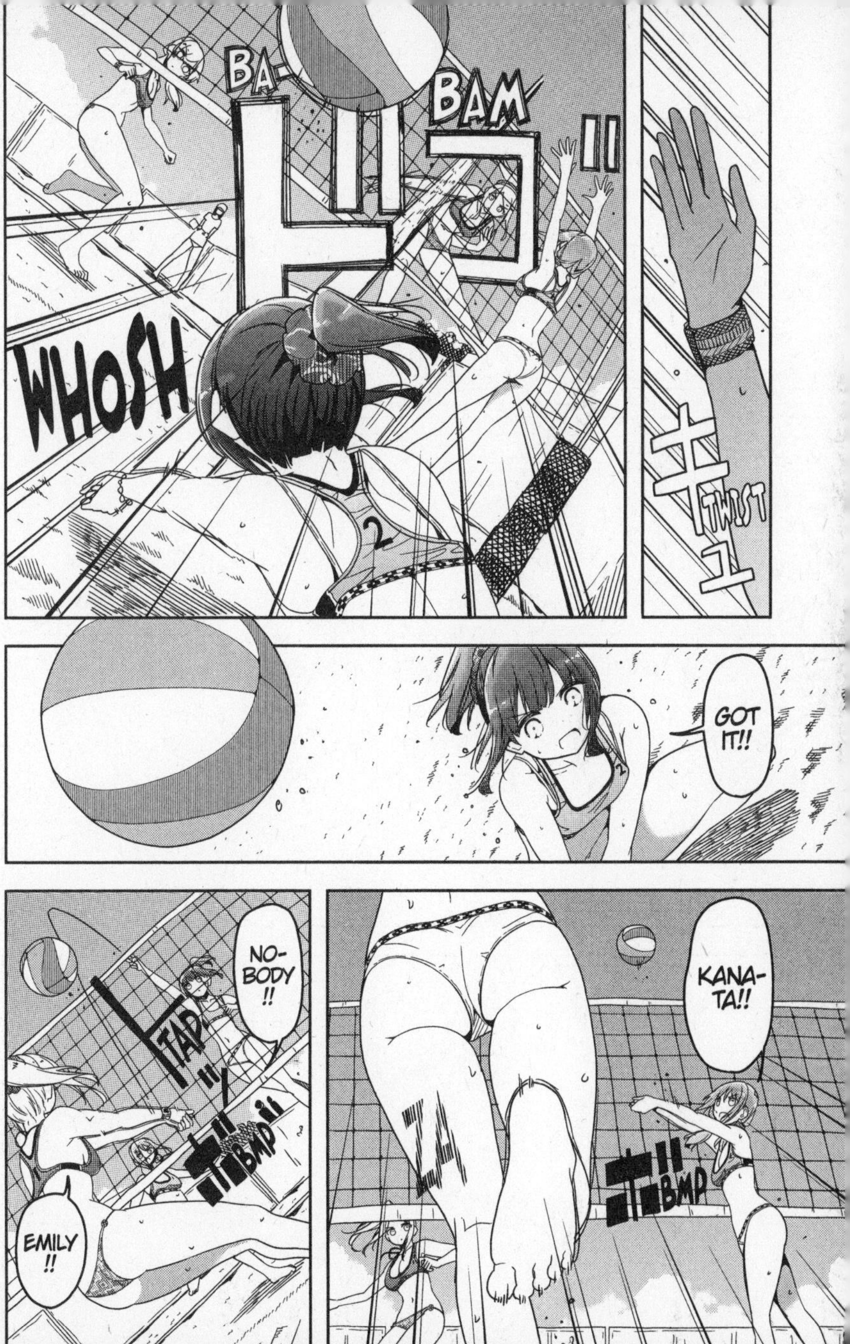
TWIST
BA-
BAM
WHOSH
GOT IT!!
KANA-TA!!
BMP
NO-BODY!!
TAP
BMP
EMILY!!

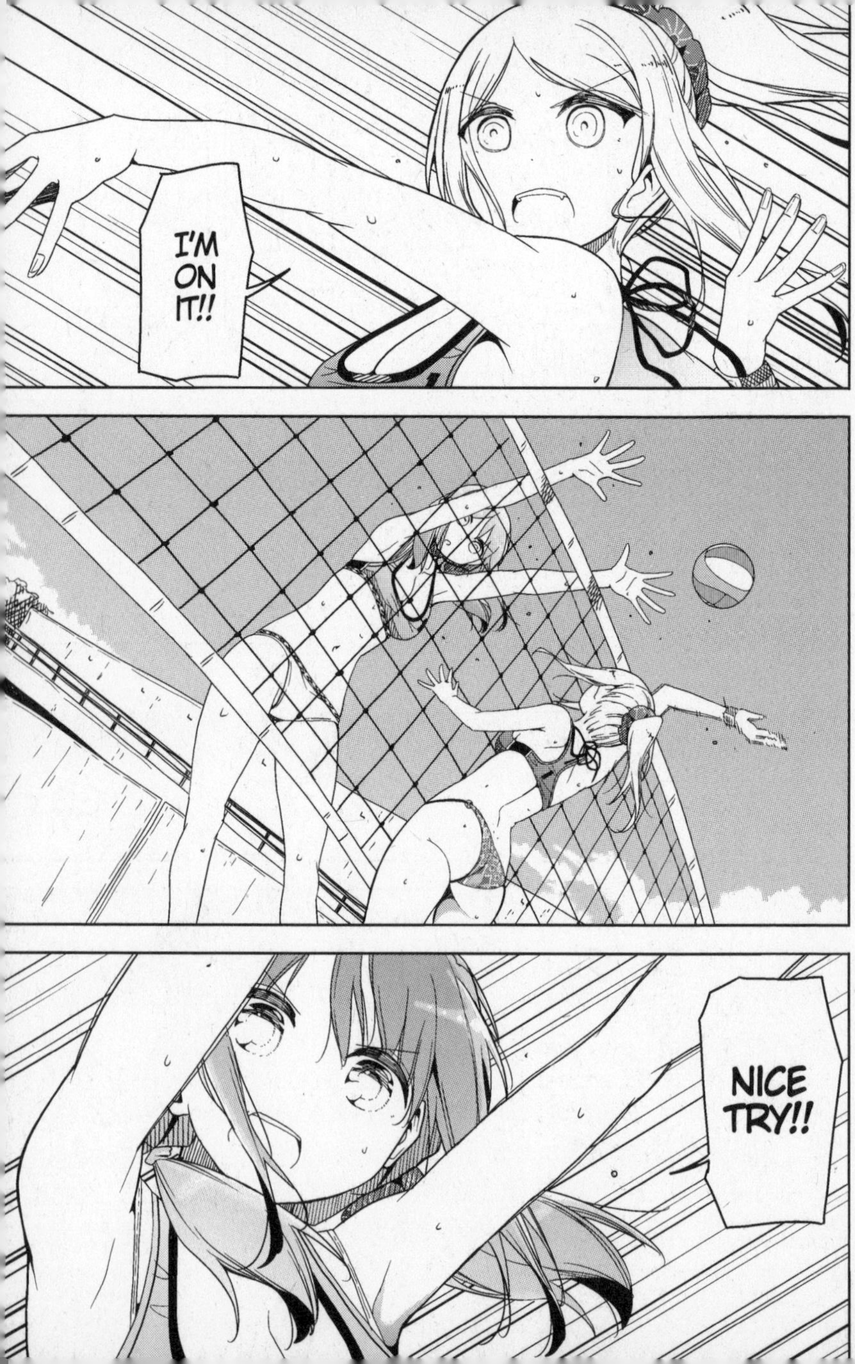
I'M ON IT!!
NICE TRY!!

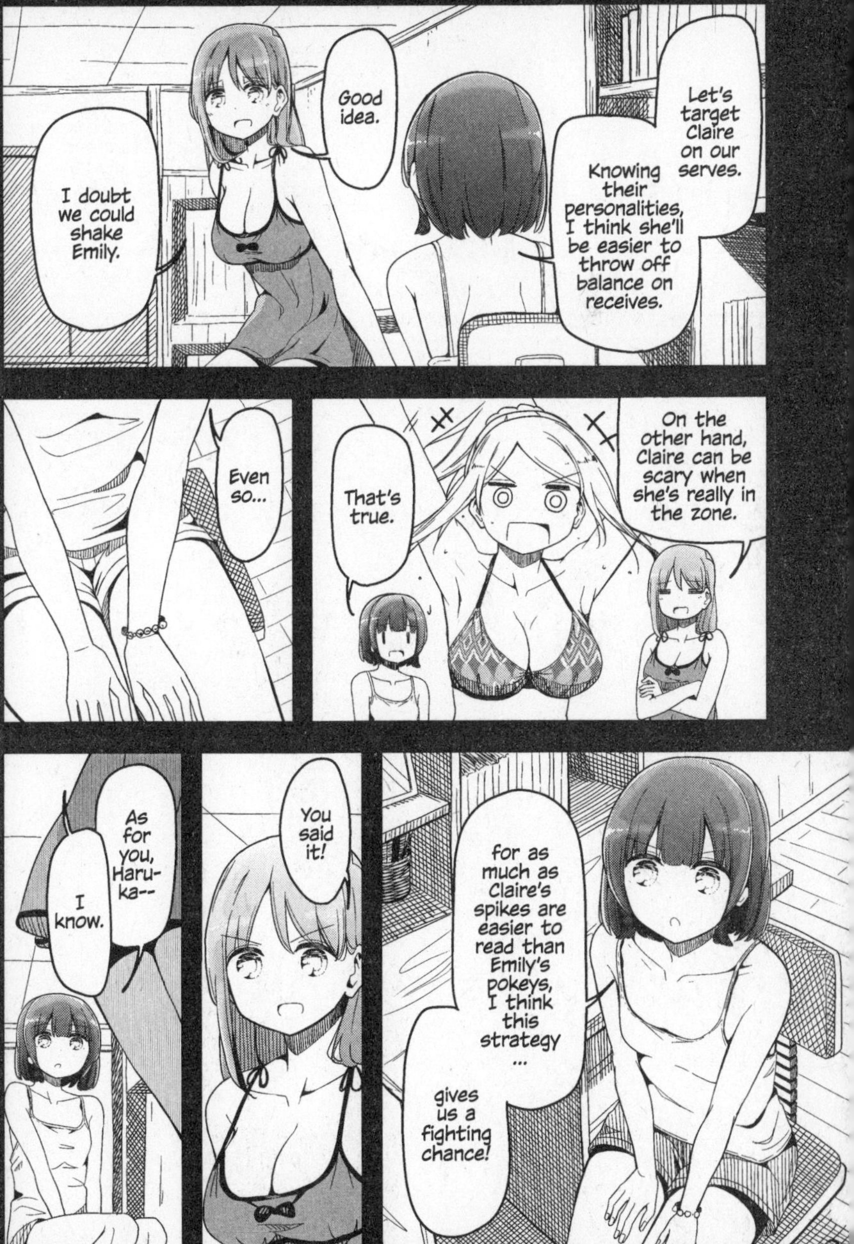
Let's target Claire on our serves.
Knowing their personalities, I think she'll be easier to throw off balance on receives.
Good idea.
I doubt we could shake Emily.
On the other hand, Claire can be scary when she's really in the zone.
That's true.
Even so...
for as much as Claire's spikes are easier to read than Emily's pokeys, I think this strategy ...
gives us a fighting chance!
You said it!
As for you, Haru-ka--
I know.

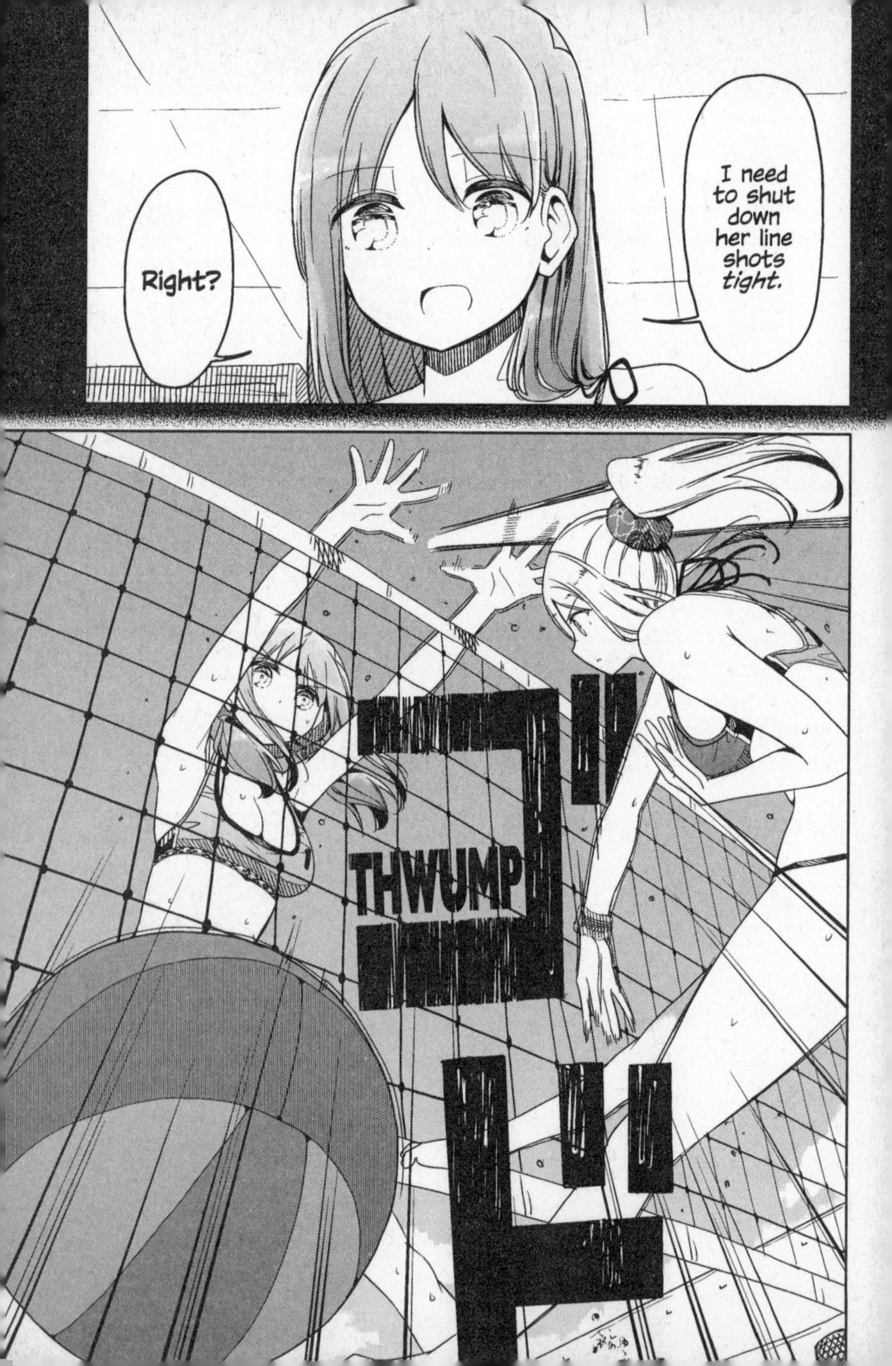
I need to shut down her line shots *tight*.
Right?
THWUMP

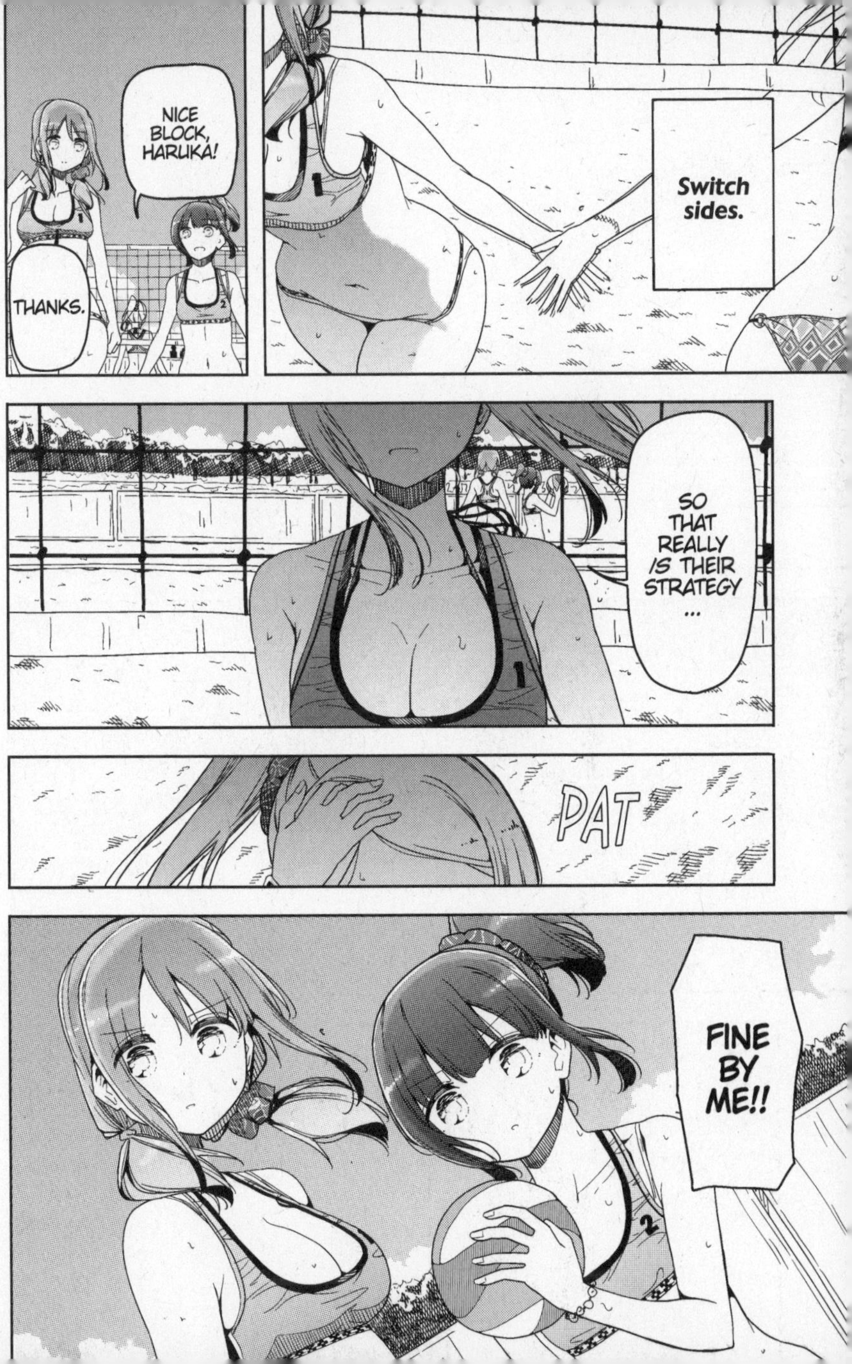
Switch sides.
NICE BLOCK, HARUKA!
THANKS.
SO THAT REALLY *IS* THEIR STRATEGY ...
PAT
FINE BY ME!!

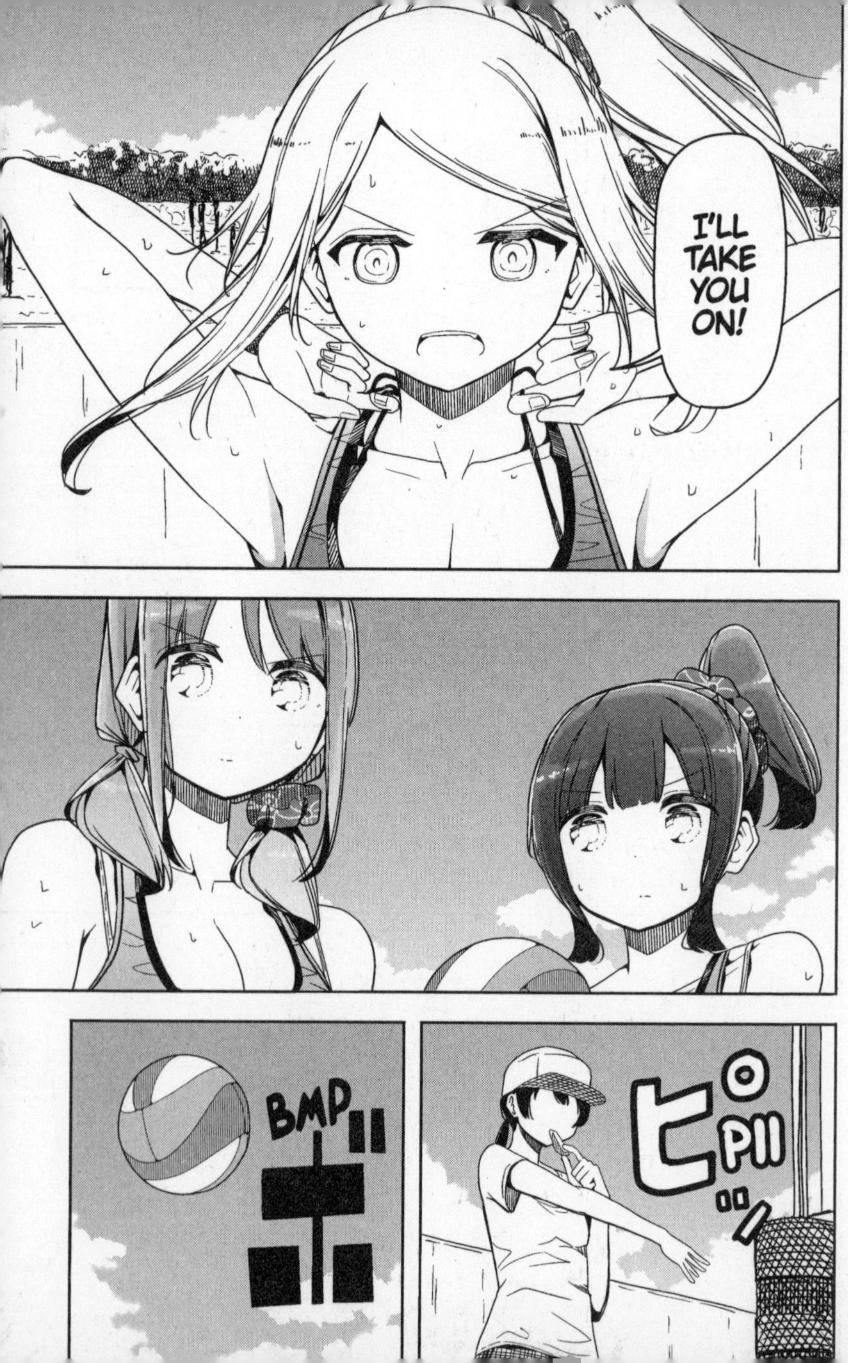
I'LL TAKE YOU ON!
PII
BMP

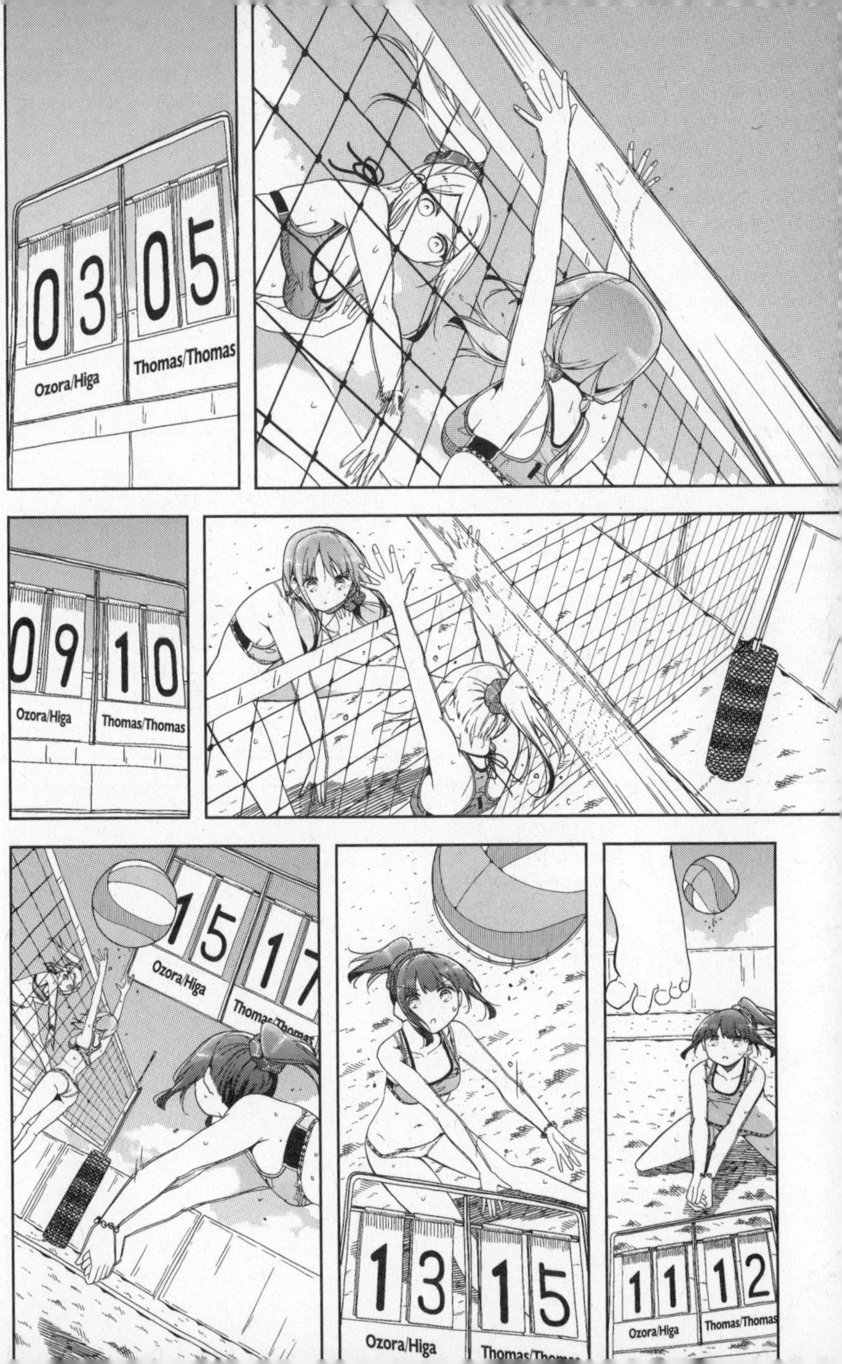

03 05
Ozora/Higa
Thomas/Thomas
09 10
Ozora/Higa
Thomas/Thomas
11 12
Ozora/Higa
Thomas/Thomas
13 15
Ozora/Higa
15 17
Ozora/Higa

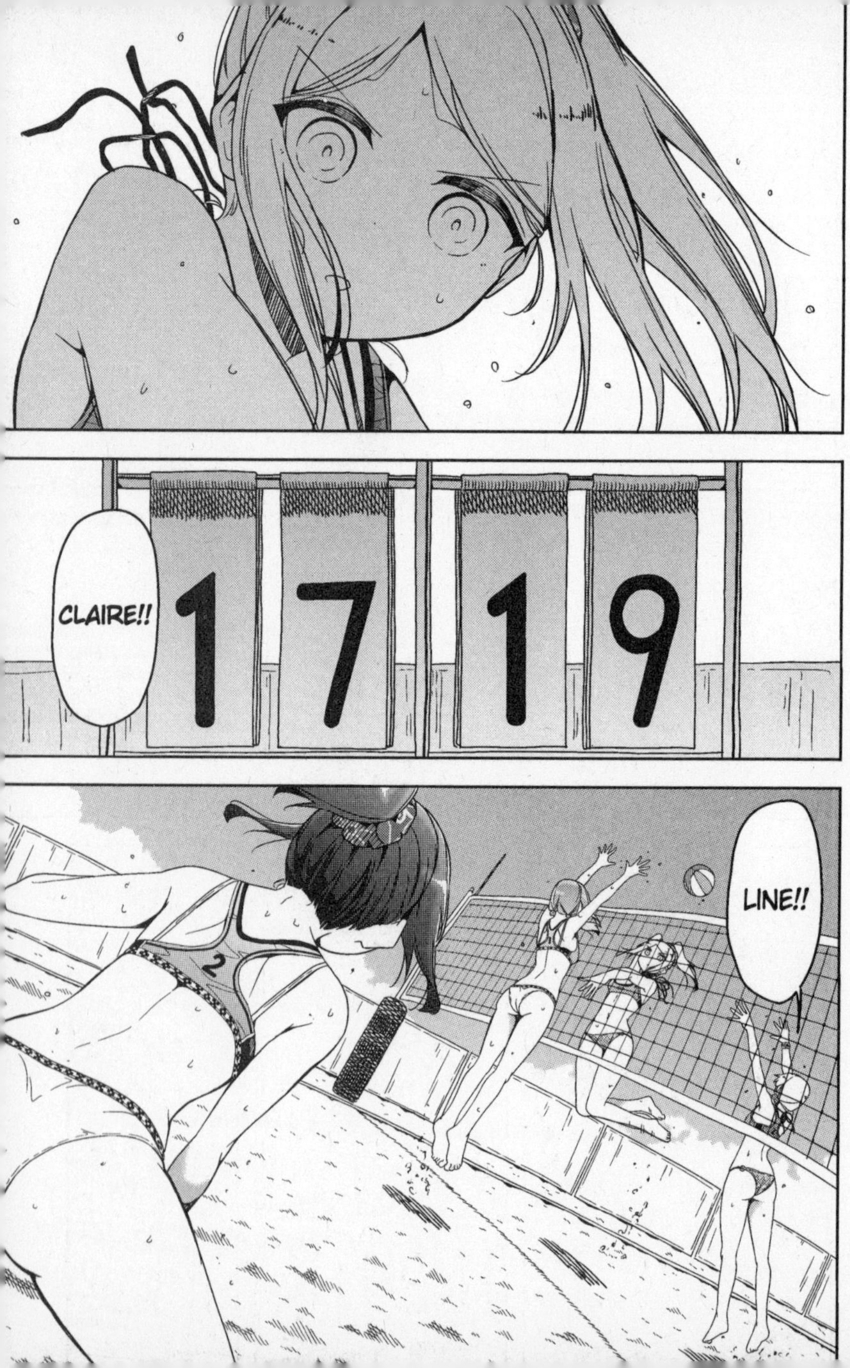
CLAIRE!!
17
19
LINE!!

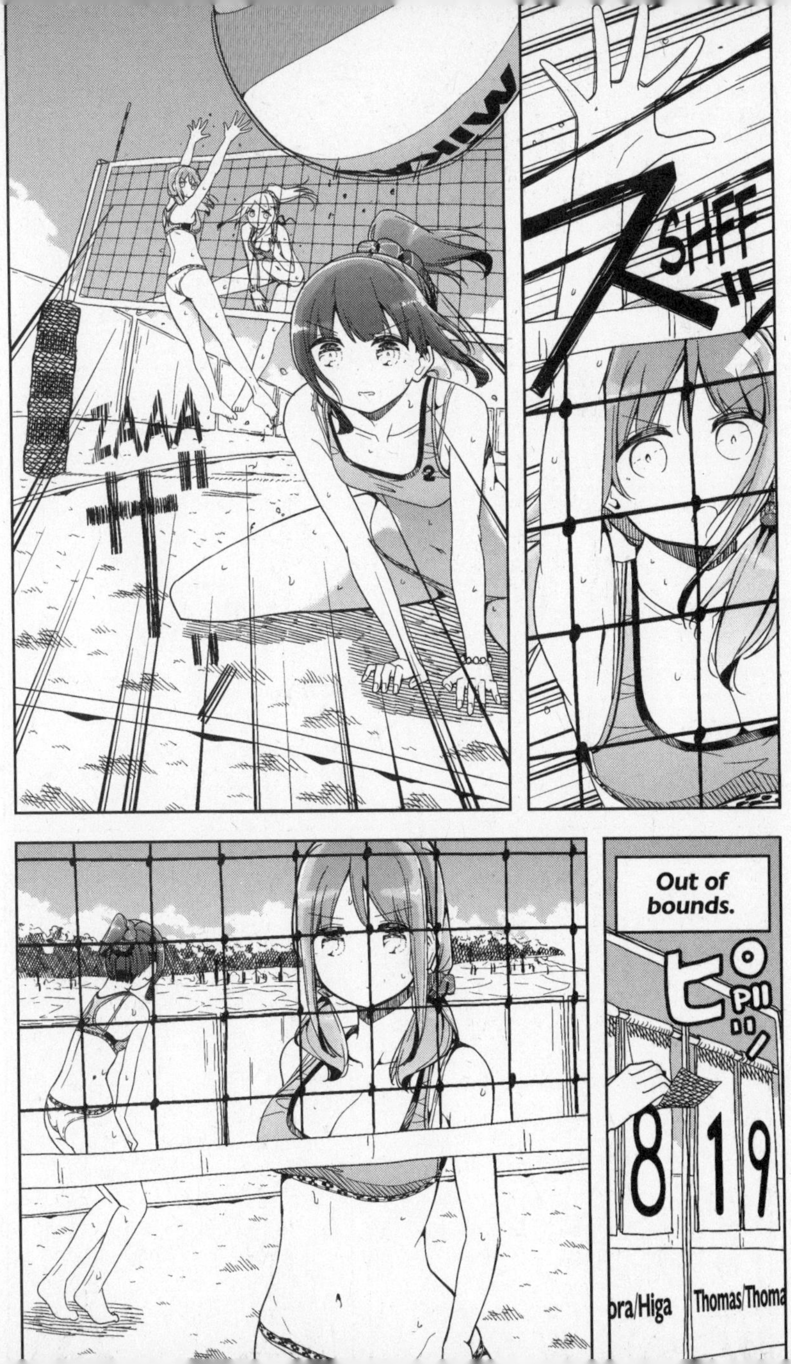
SHFF
ZAAA
Out of bounds.
PII
8
19
ora/Higa
Thomas/Thoma

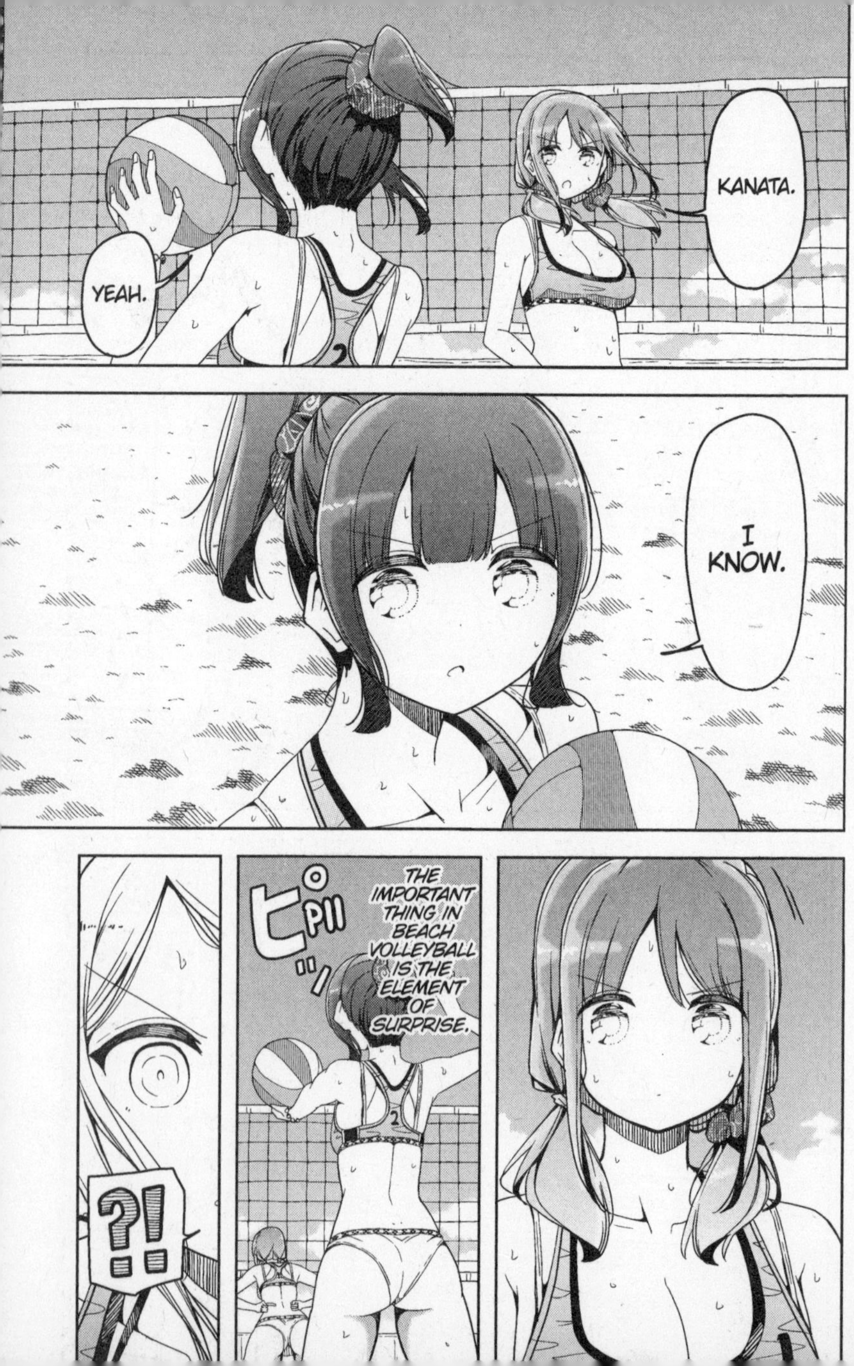
KANATA.
YEAH.
I KNOW.
PII
THE IMPORTANT THING IN BEACH VOLLEYBALL IS THE ELEMENT OF SURPRISE.
?!

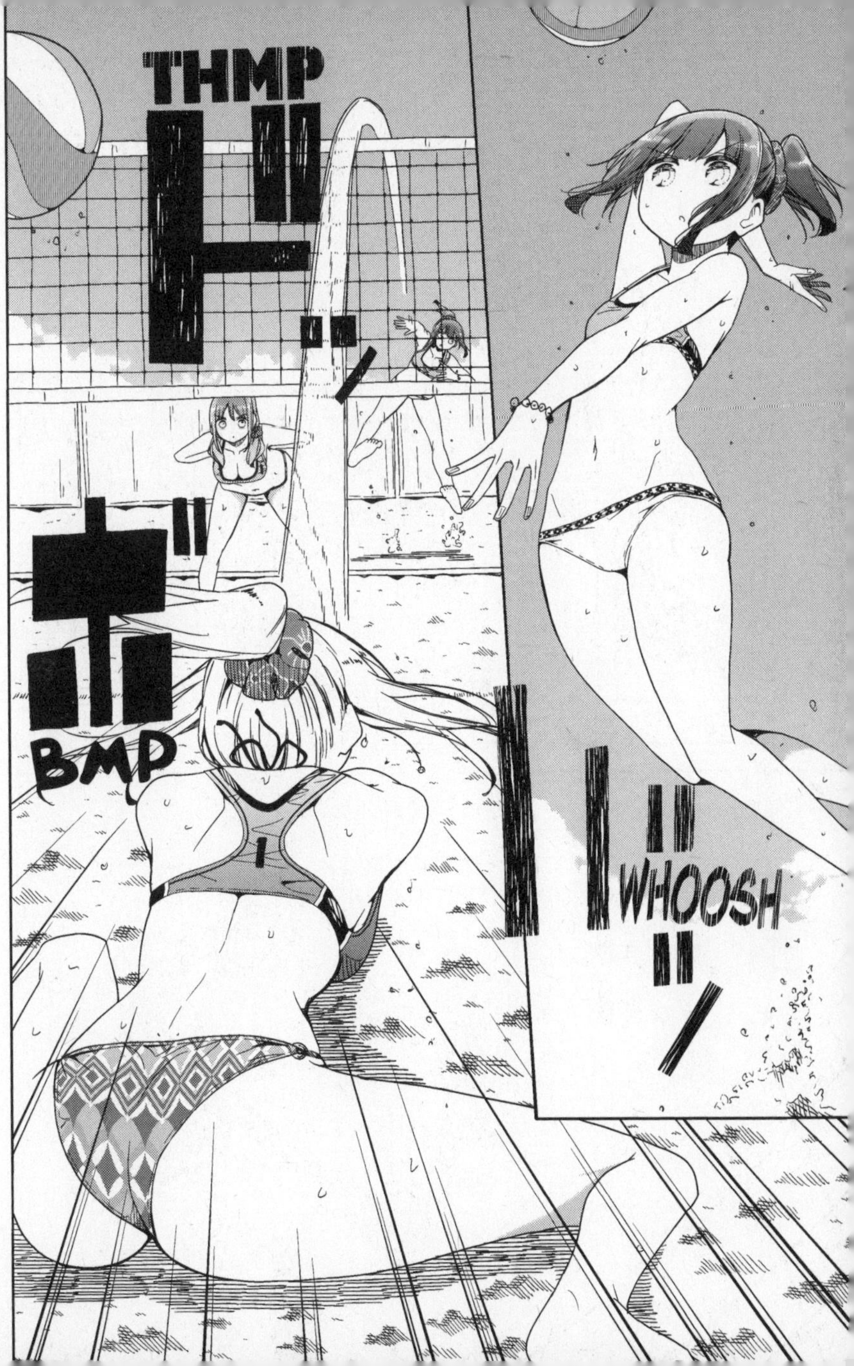
WHOOSH
THMP
BMP

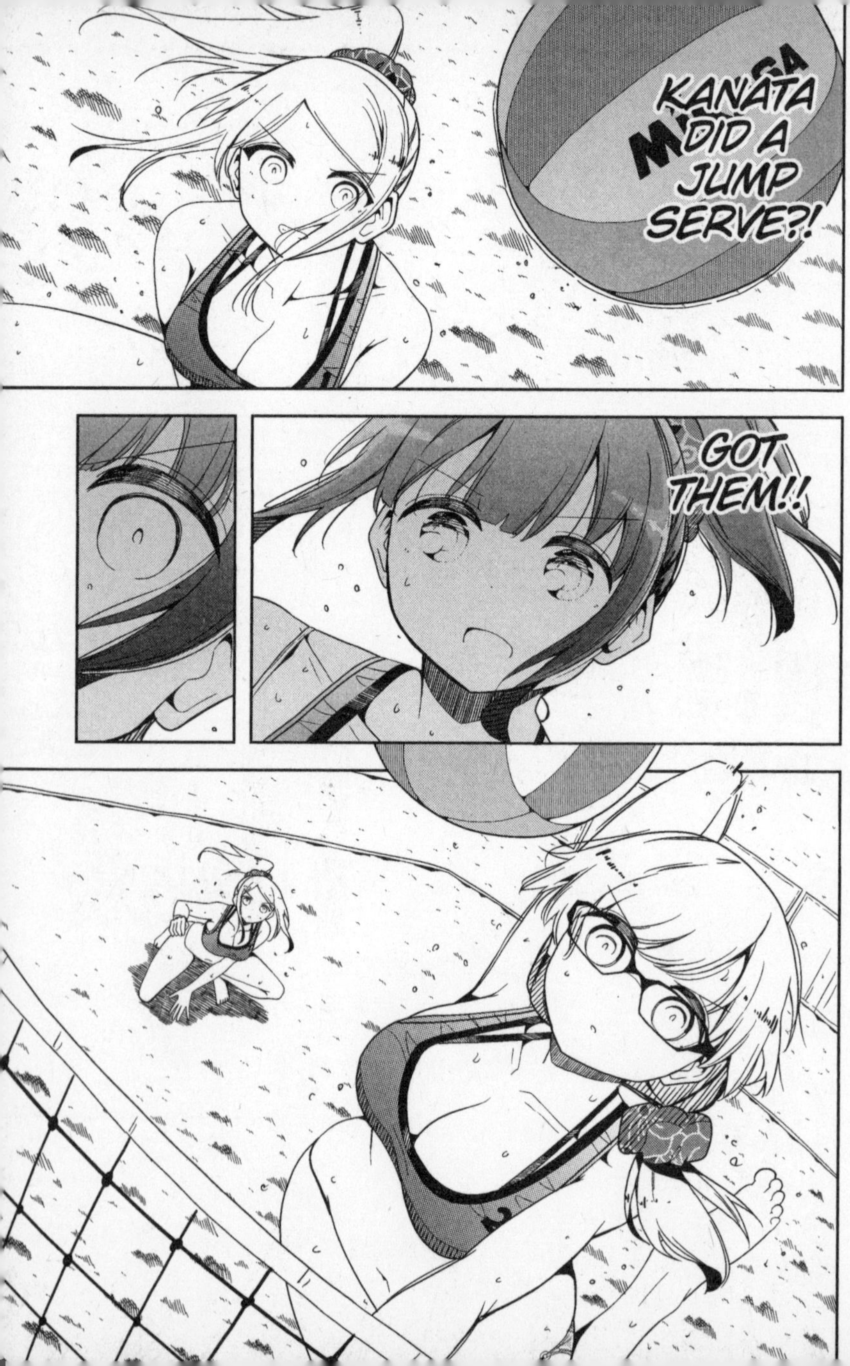
KANATA DID A JUMP SERVE?!
GOT THEM!!

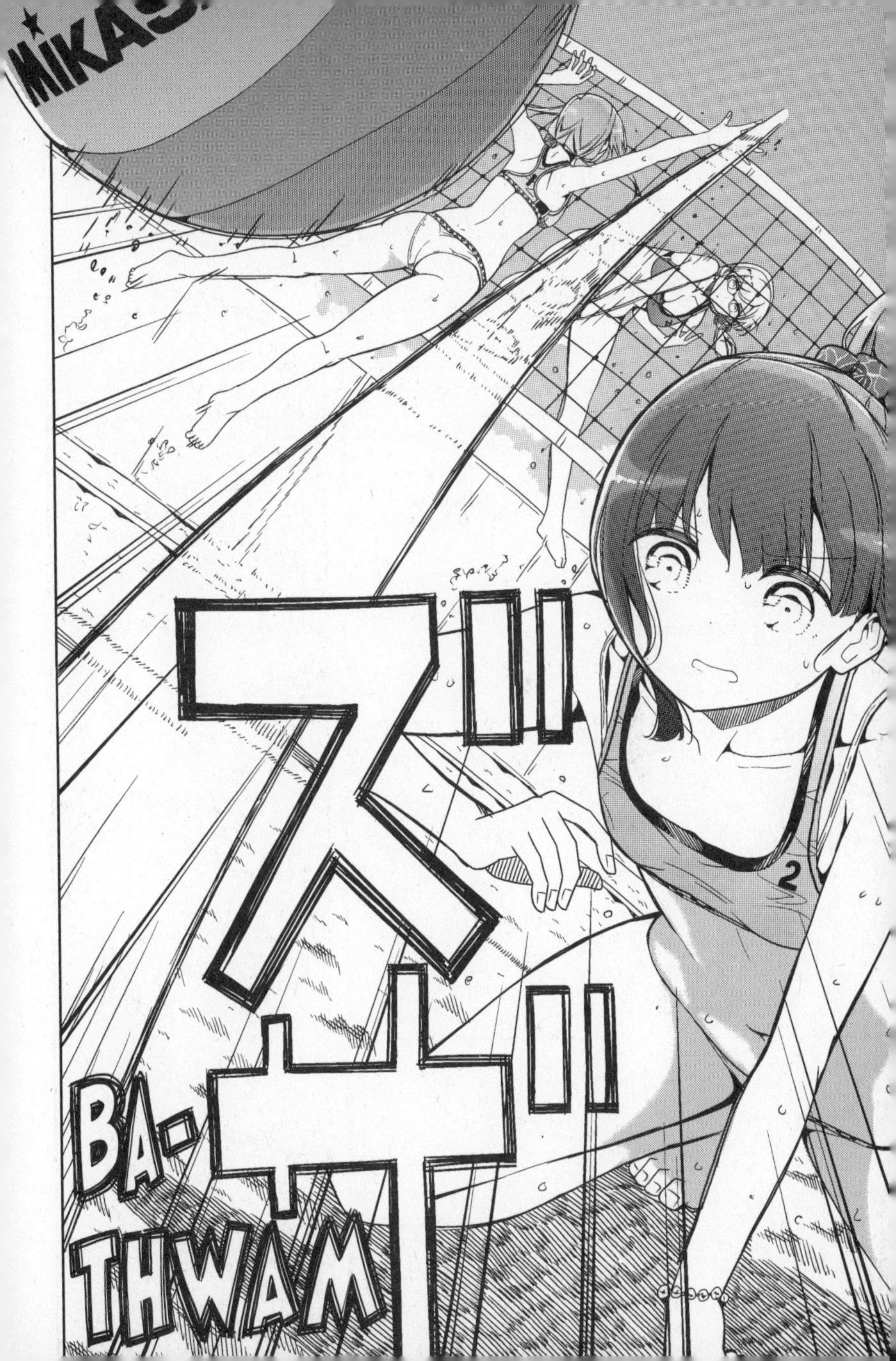

BA-THWAM

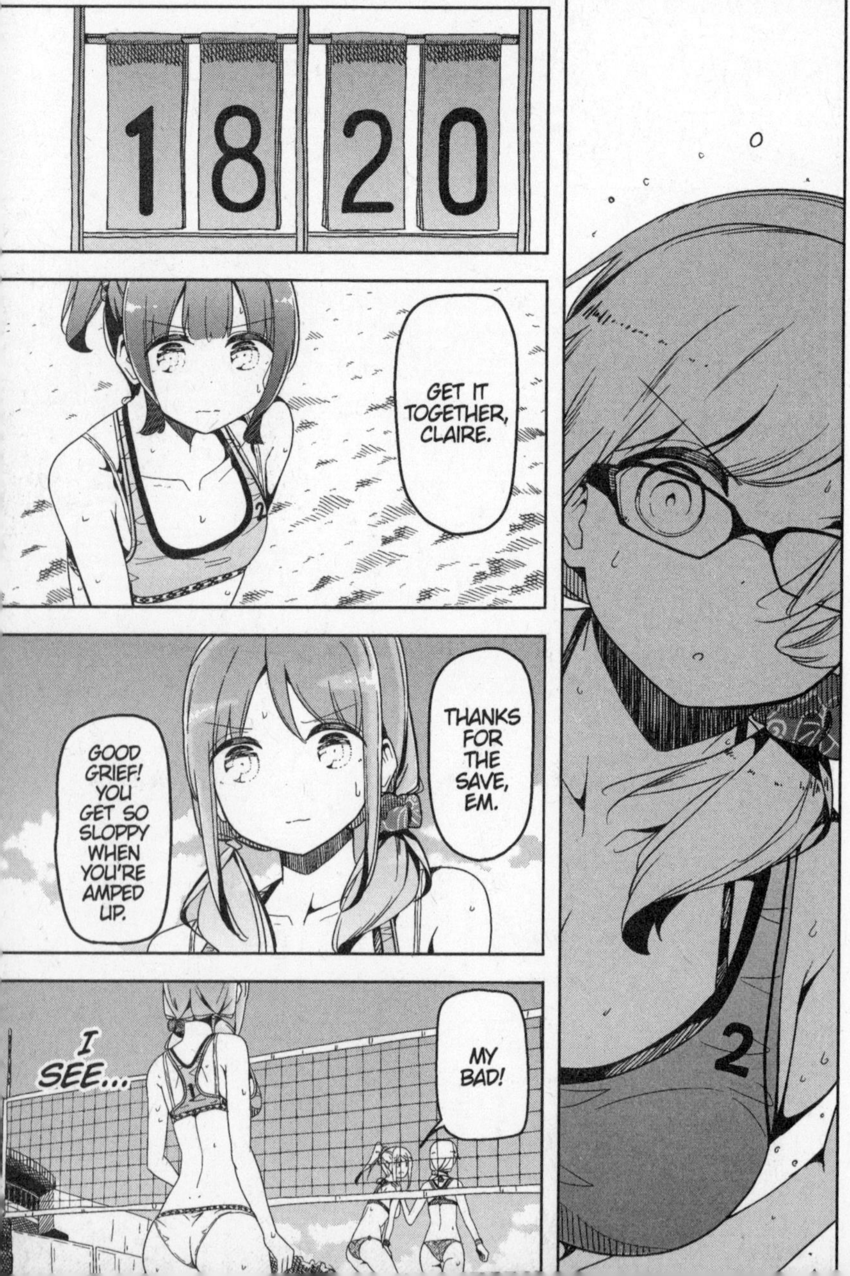
18 20
GET IT TOGETHER, CLAIRE.
THANKS FOR THE SAVE, EM.
GOOD GRIEF! YOU GET SO SLOPPY WHEN YOU'RE AMPED UP.
MY BAD!
I SEE...

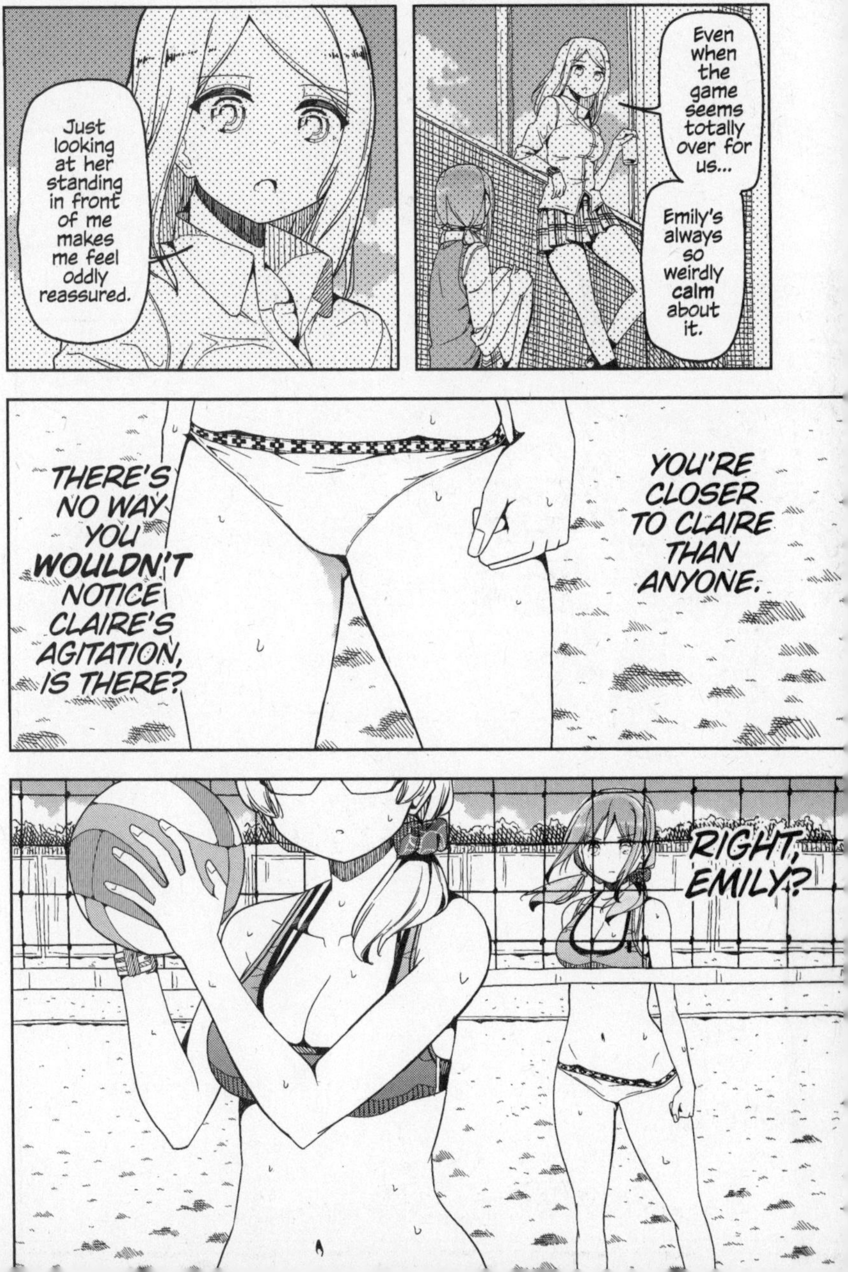
Even when the game seems totally over for us...
Emily's always so weirdly calm about it.
Just looking at her standing in front of me makes me feel oddly reassured.
YOU'RE CLOSER TO CLAIRE THAN ANYONE.
THERE'S NO WAY YOU WOULDN'T NOTICE CLAIRE'S AGITATION, IS THERE?
RIGHT, EMILY?

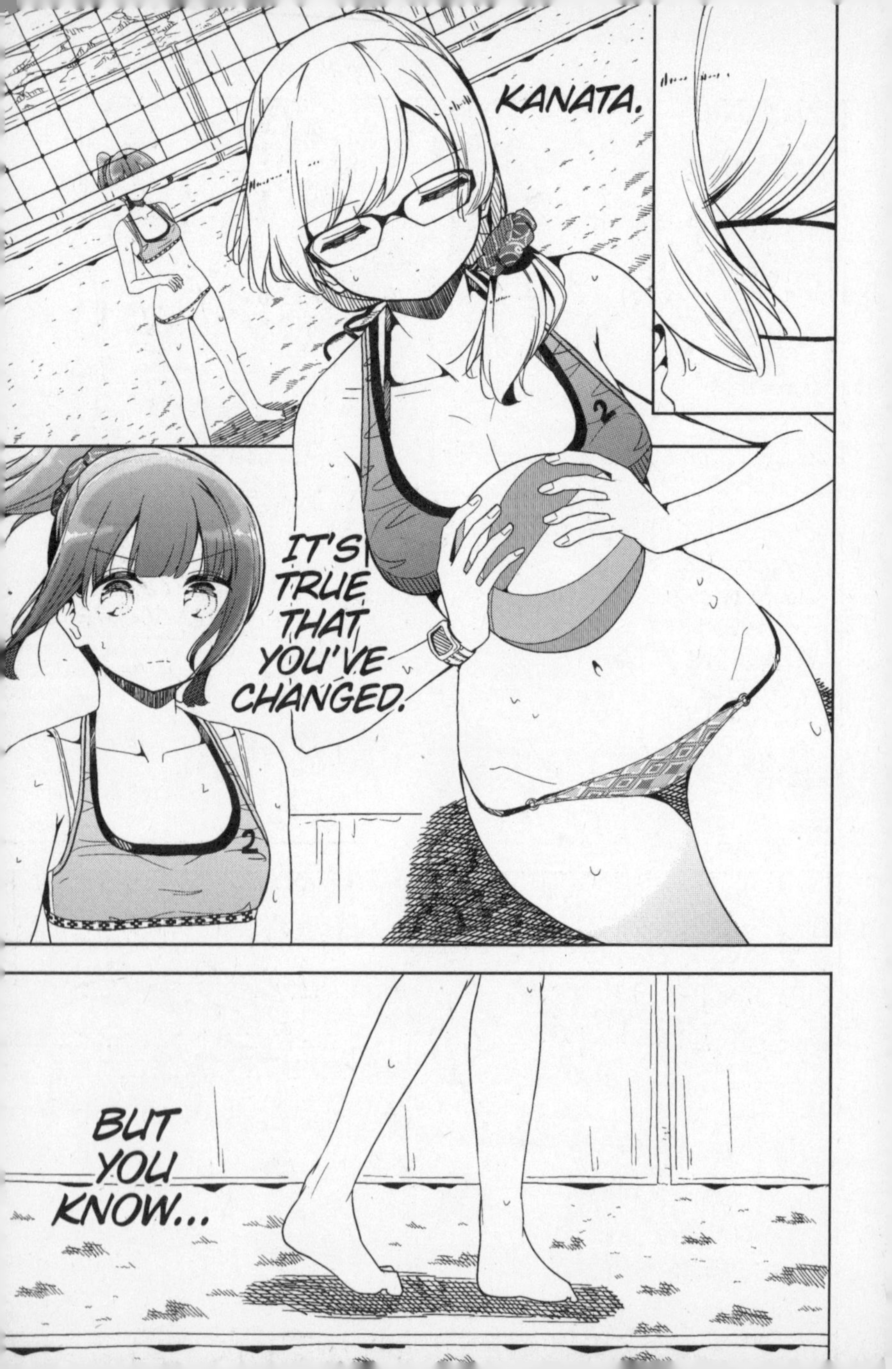
KANATA.
IT'S TRUE THAT YOU'VE CHANGED.
BUT YOU KNOW...

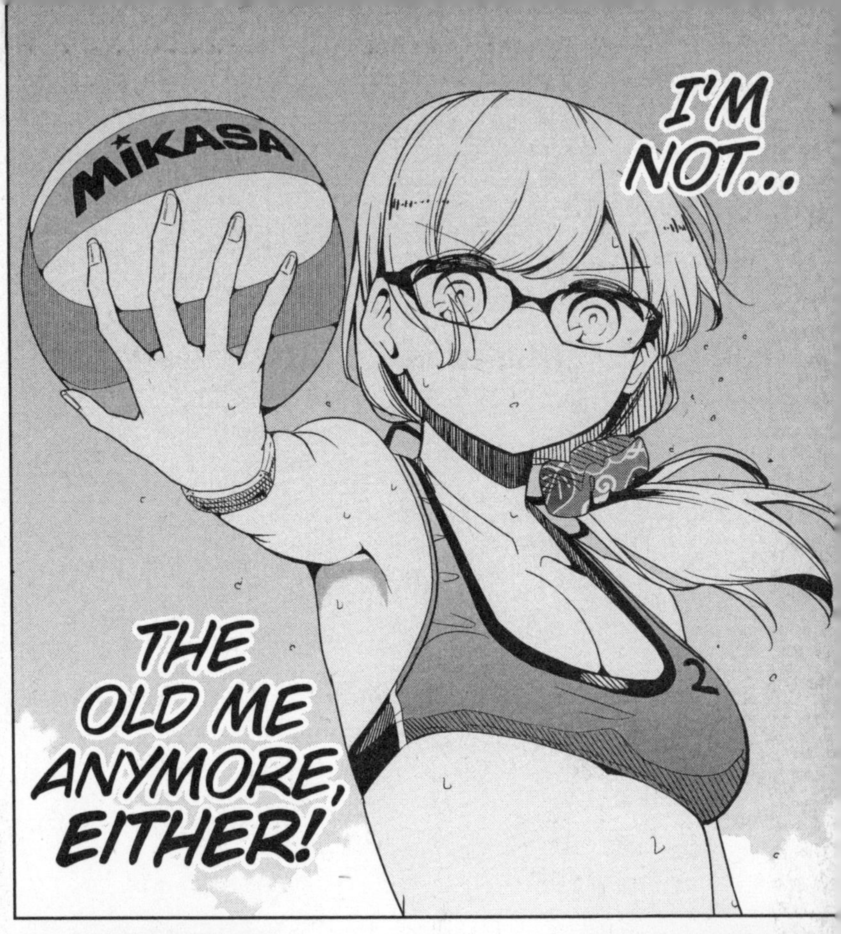

I'M NOT...
THE OLD ME ANYMORE, EITHER!

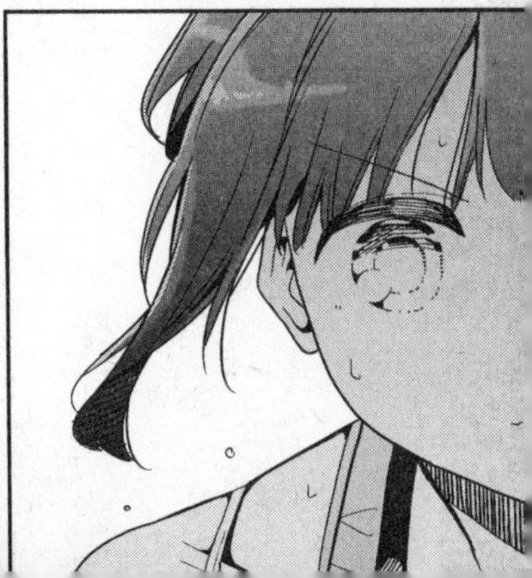
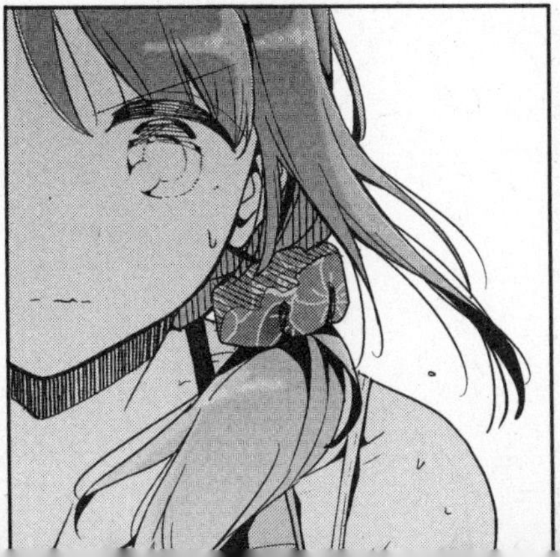

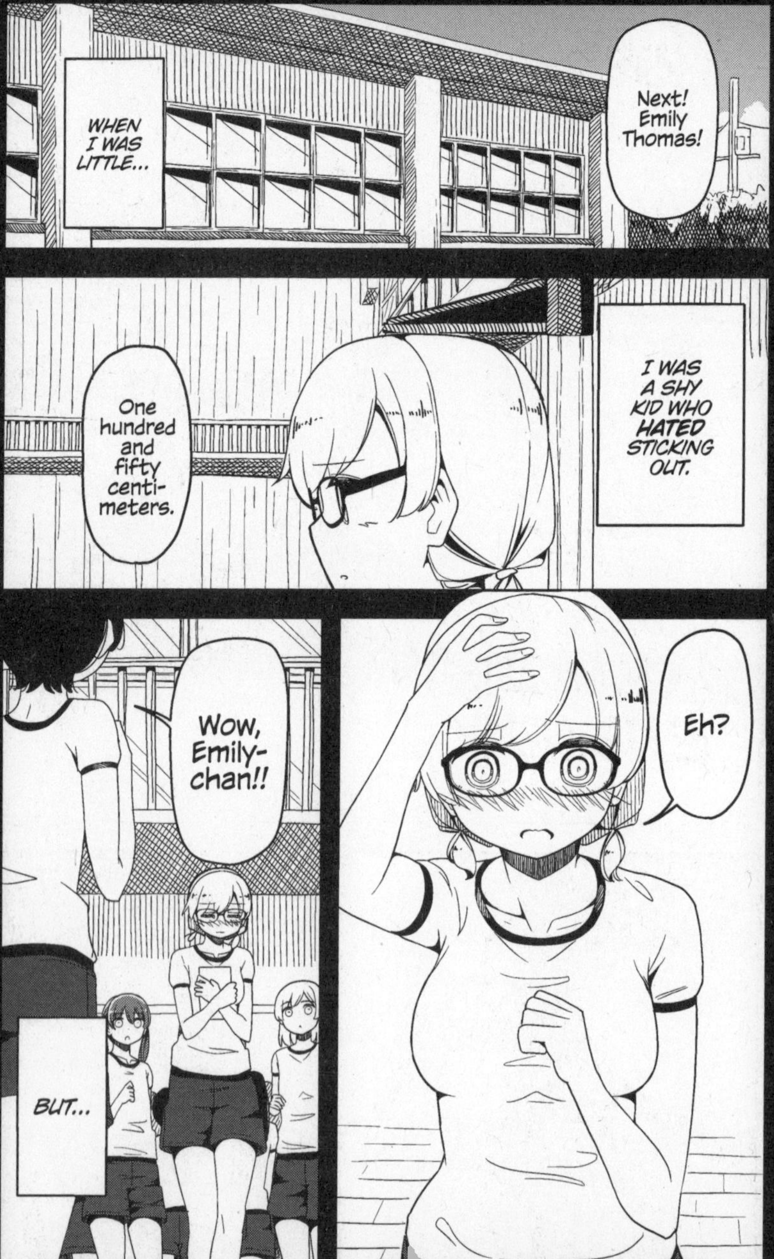
Next! Emily Thomas!
WHEN I WAS LITTLE...
I WAS A SHY KID WHO HATED STICKING OUT.
One hundred and fifty centimeters.
Eh?
Wow, Emily-chan!!
BUT...

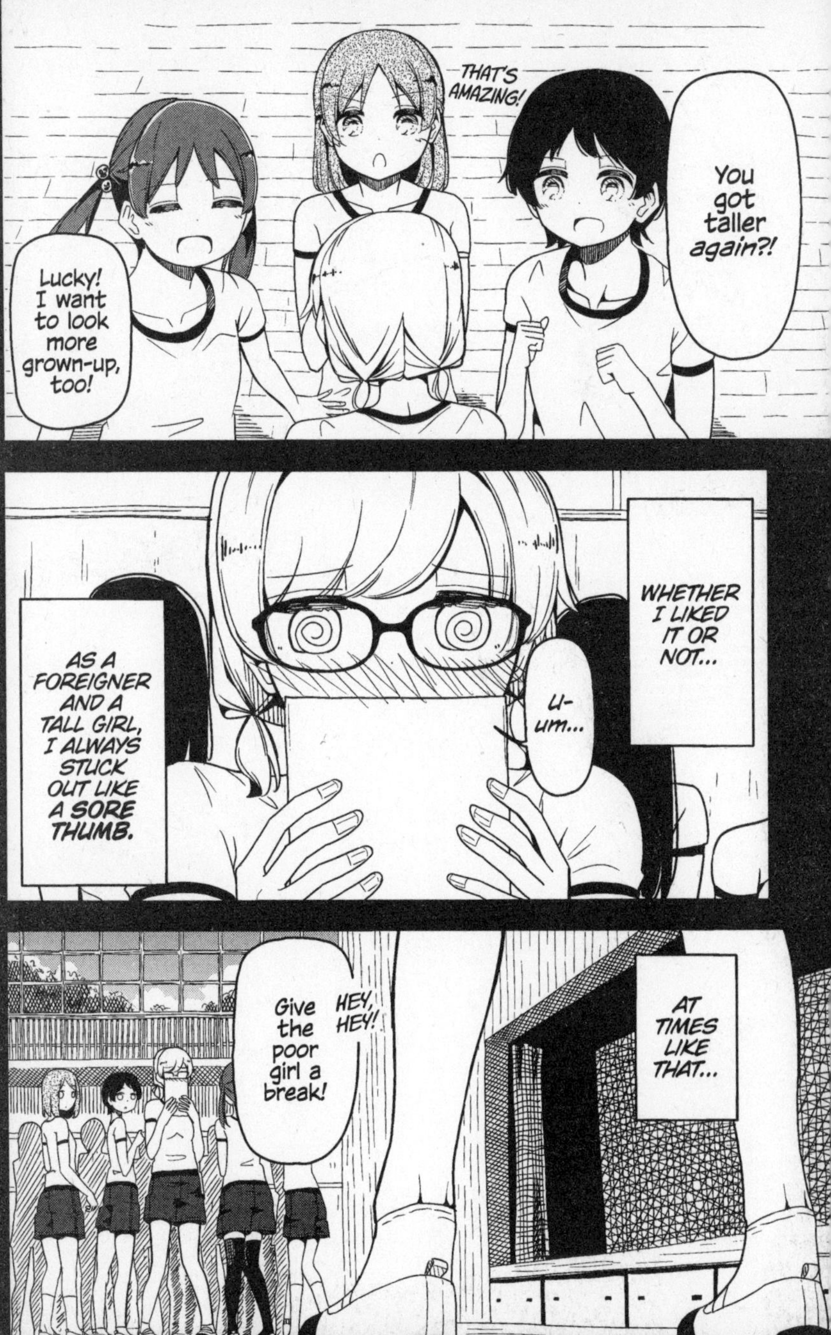
You got taller again?!
THAT'S AMAZING!
Lucky! I want to look more grown-up, too!
WHETHER I LIKED IT OR NOT...
U-um...
AS A FOREIGNER AND A TALL GIRL, I ALWAYS STUCK OUT LIKE A SORE THUMB.
AT TIMES LIKE THAT...
HEY, HEY!
Give the poor girl a break!

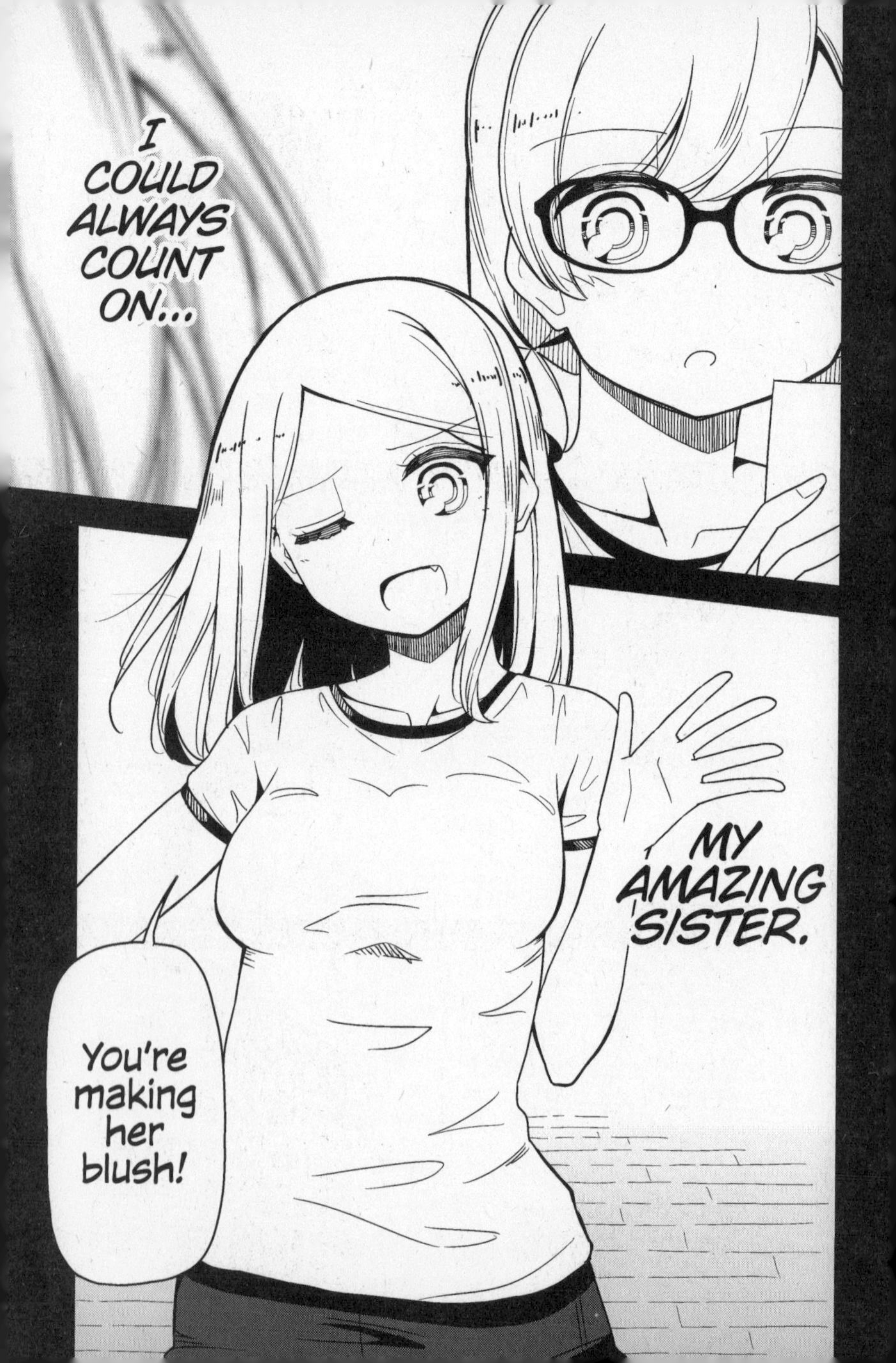
I COULD ALWAYS COUNT ON...
MY AMAZING SISTER.
You're making her blush!

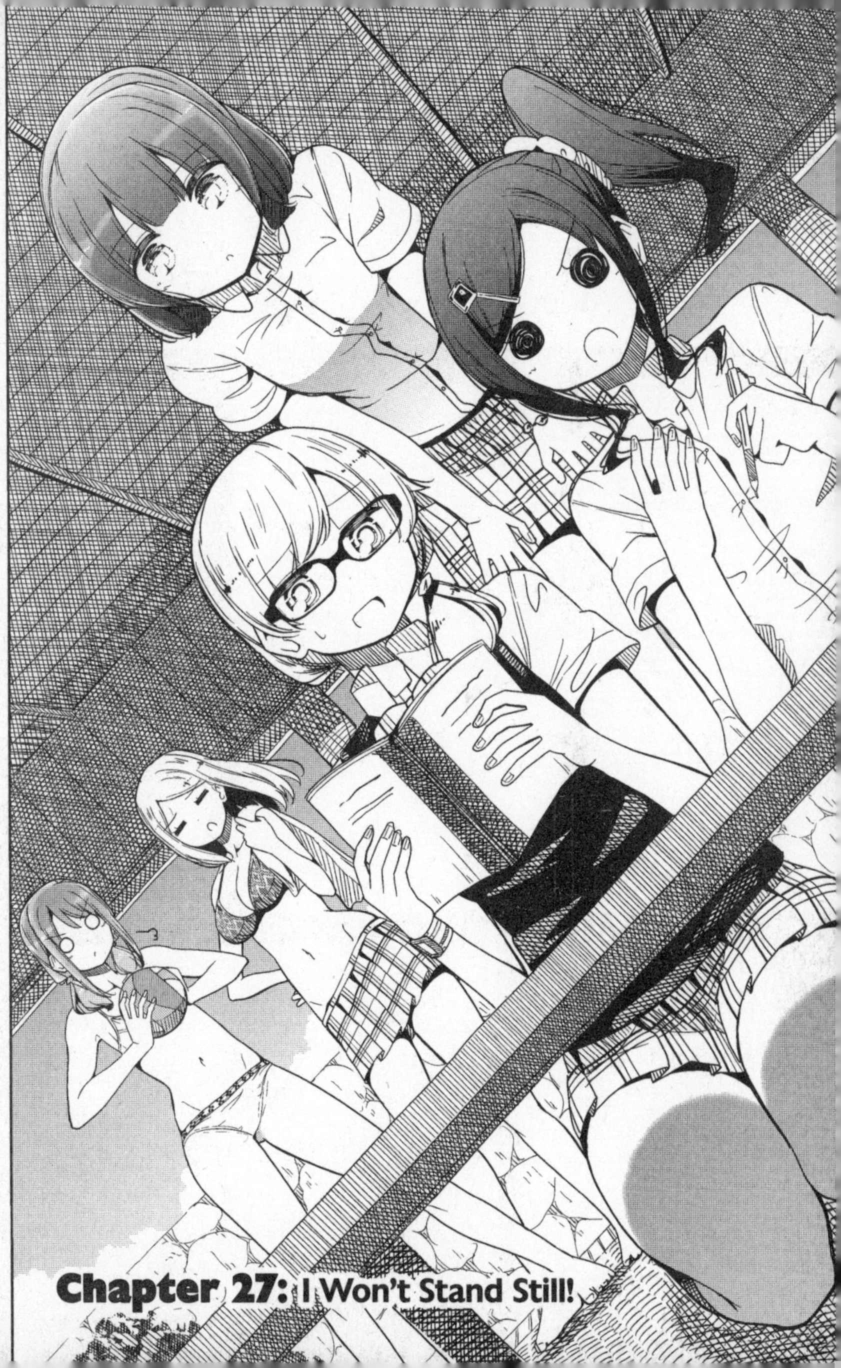

Chapter 27: I Won't Stand Still!

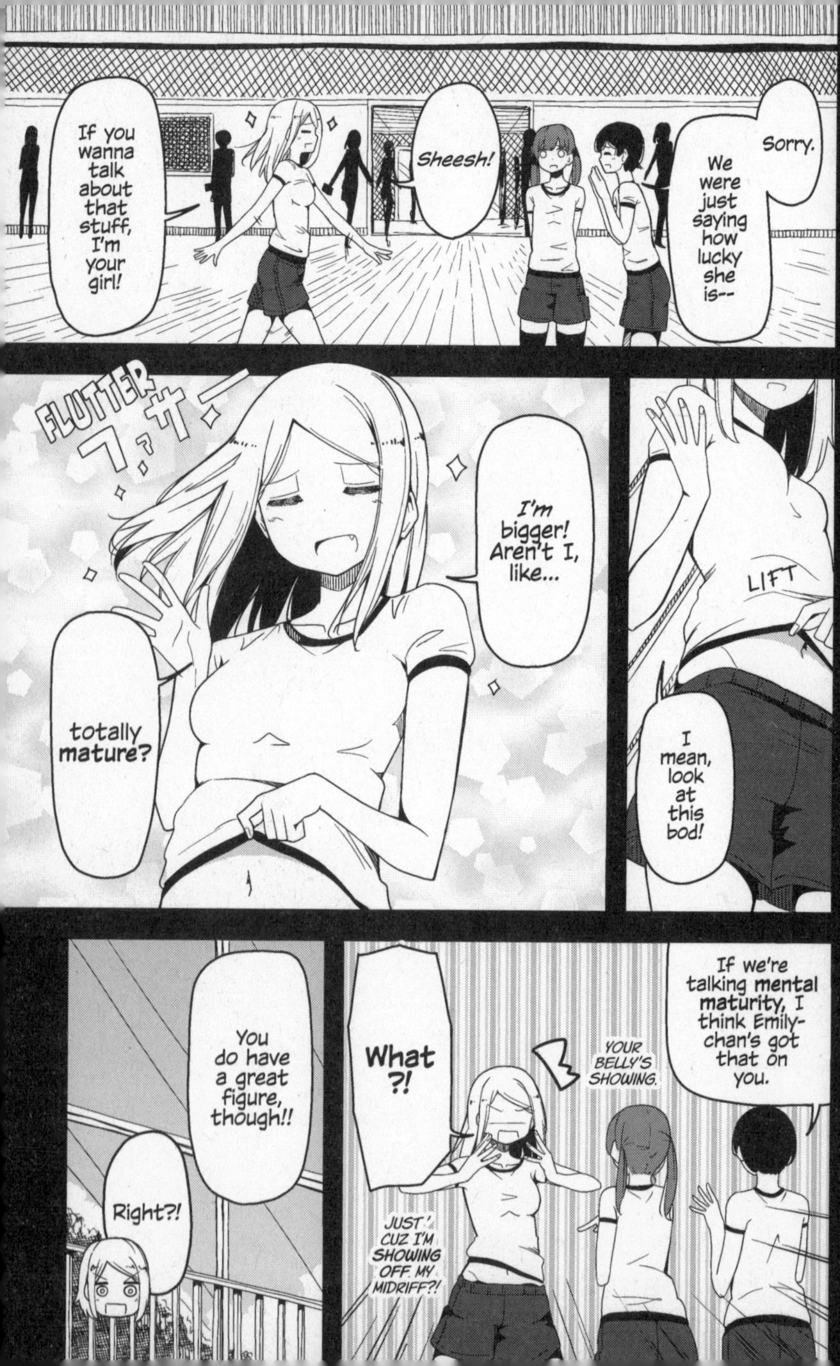

Sorry.
We were just saying how lucky she is--
Sheesh!
If you wanna talk about that stuff, I'm your girl!
LIFT
I mean, look at this bod!
FLUTTER
I'm bigger! Aren't I, like...
totally mature?
If we're talking mental maturity, I think Emily-chan's got that on you.
YOUR BELLY'S SHOWING.
What?!
JUST 'CUZ I'M SHOWING OFF MY MIDRIFF?!
You do have a great figure, though!!
Right?!

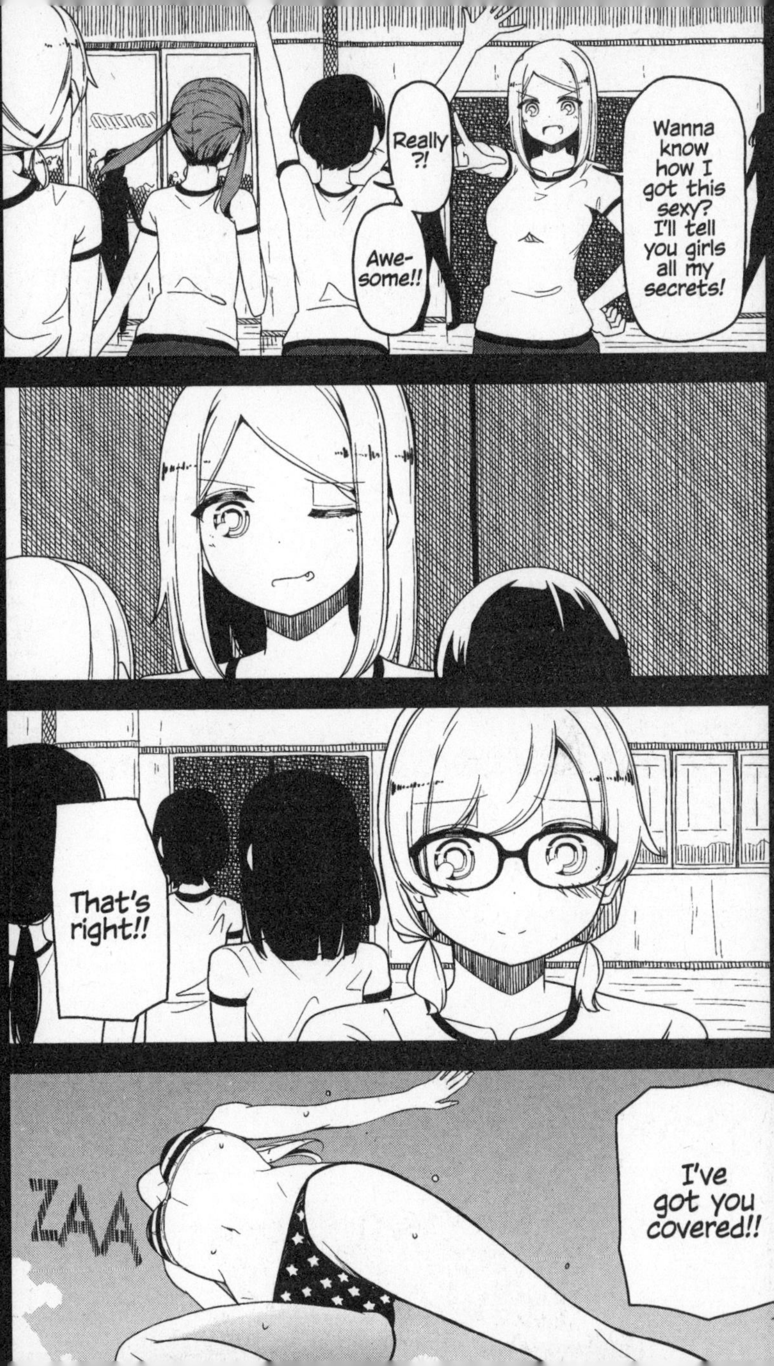
Wanna know how I got this sexy? I'll tell you girls all my secrets!
Really?!
Awe-some!!
That's right!!
I've got you covered!!
ZAA

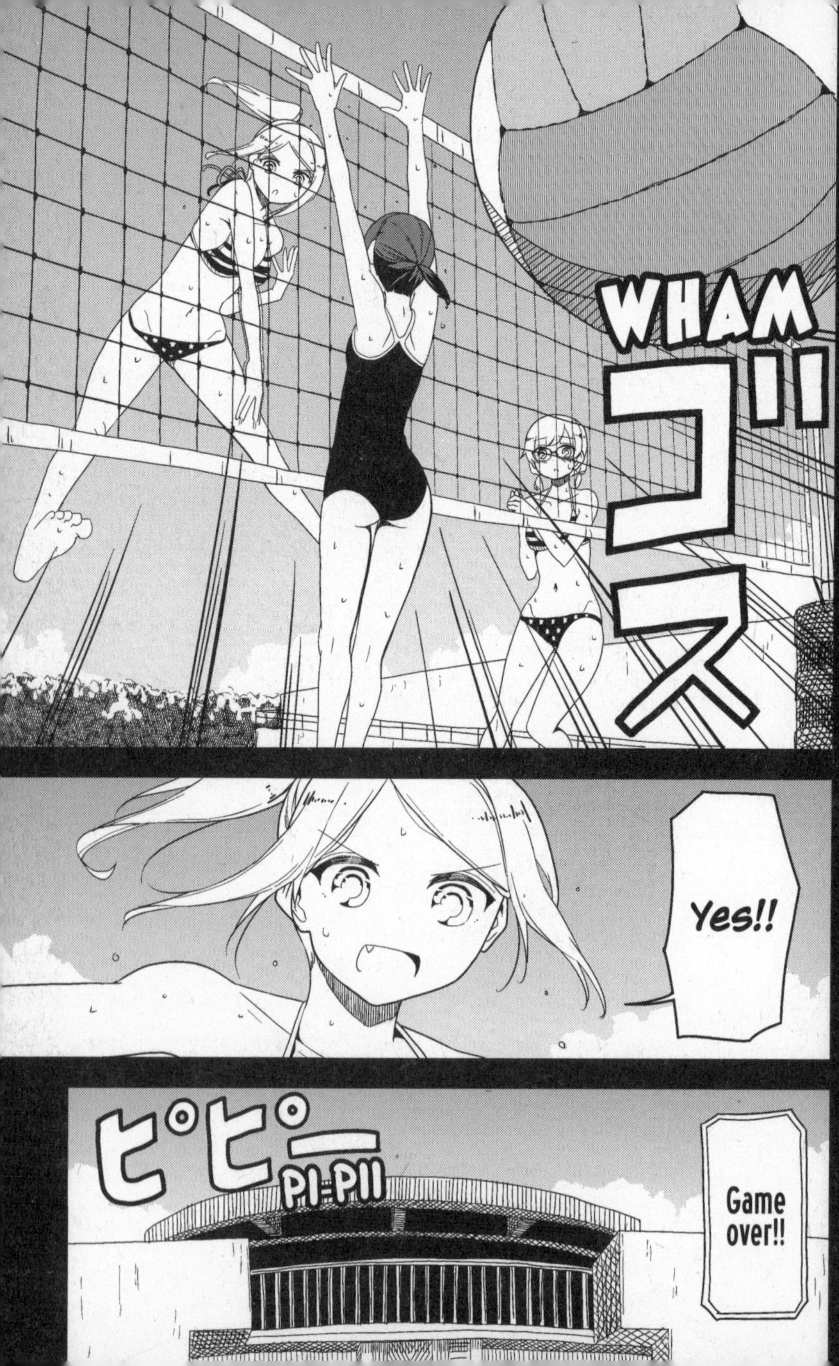
WHAM
ゴス
Yes!!
Game over!!
ピピー
PI-PII

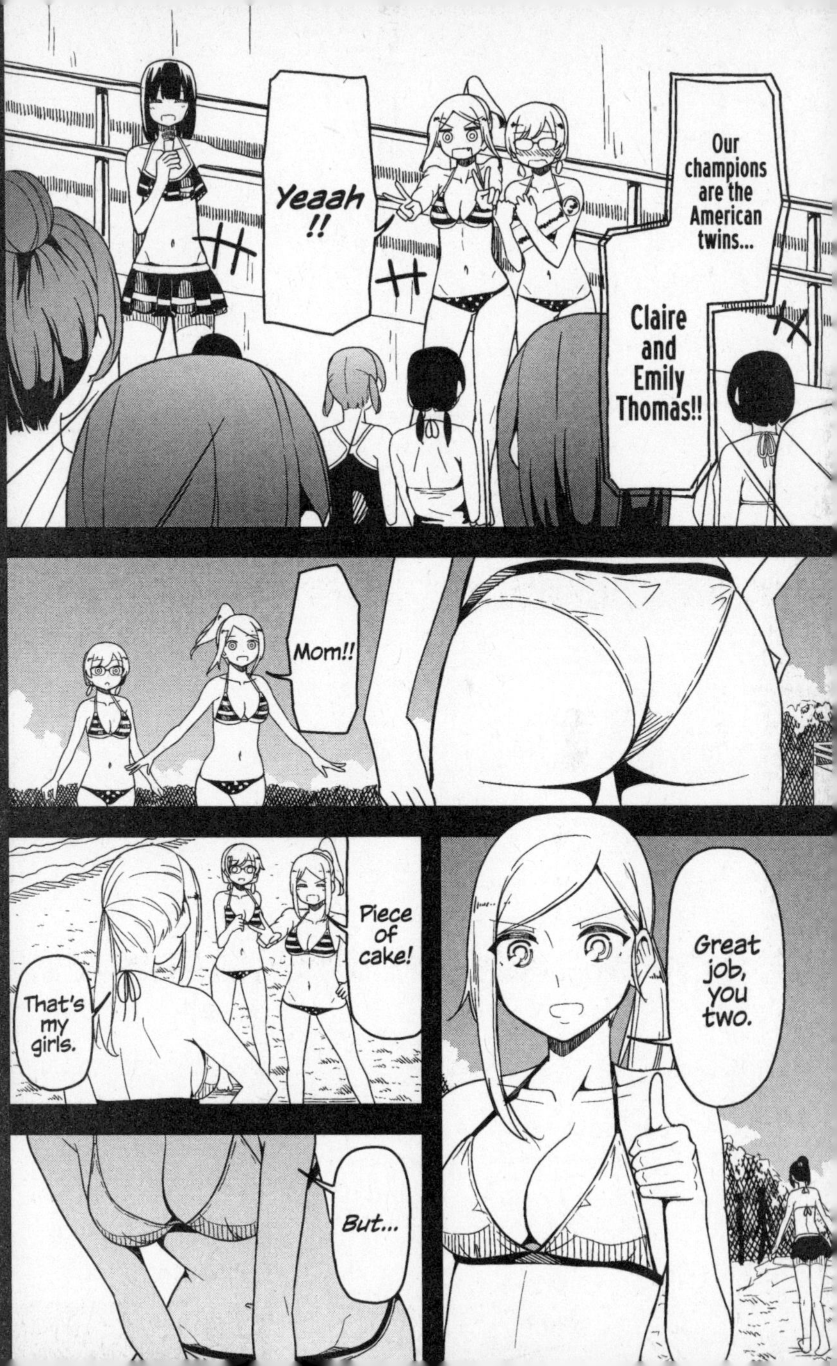
Our champions are the American twins...
Claire and Emily Thomas!!
Yeaah!!
Mom!!
Great job, you two.
Piece of cake!
That's my girls.
But...

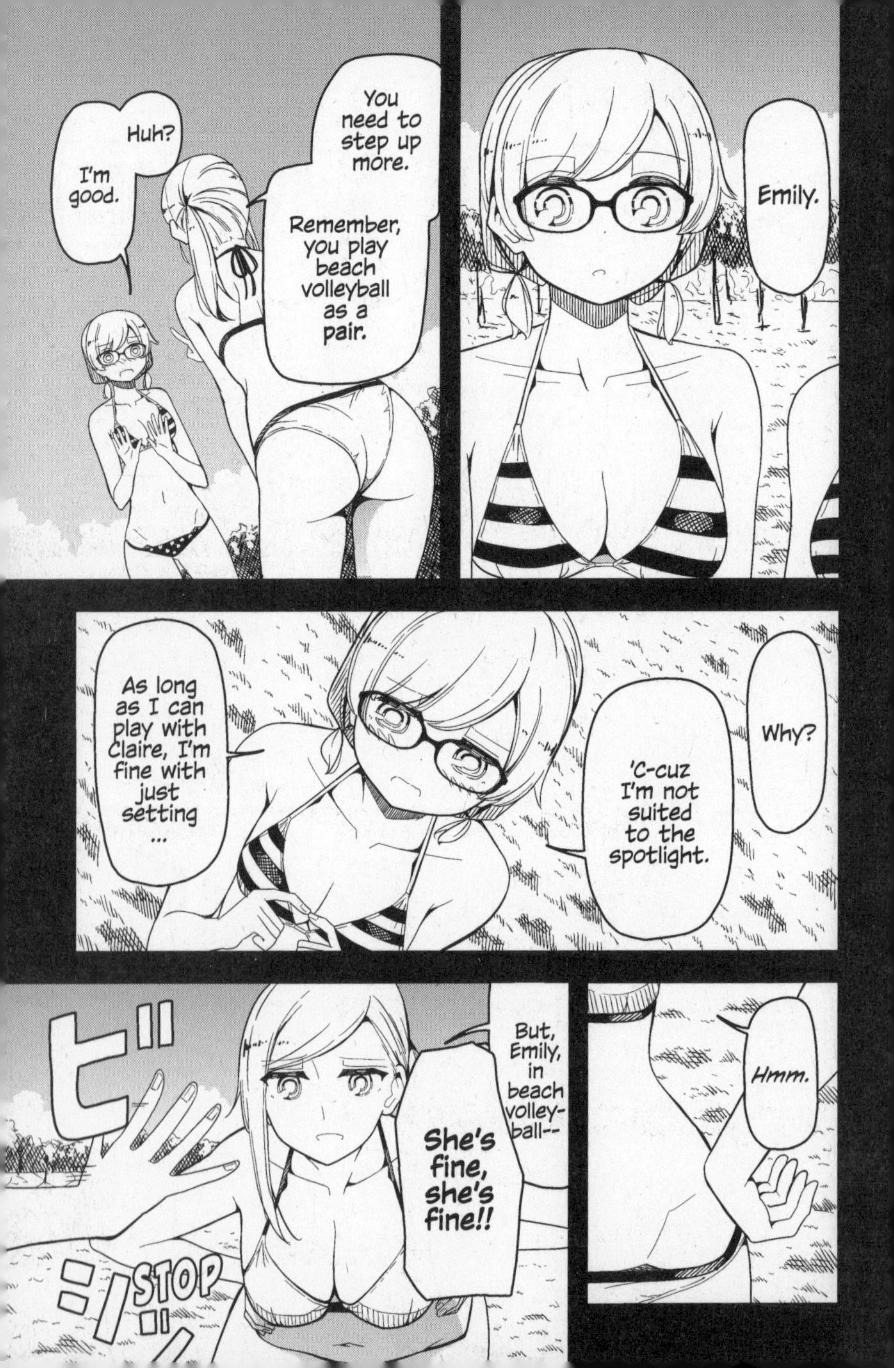
Emily.
You need to step up more.
Remember, you play beach volleyball as a pair.
Huh?
I'm good.
Why?
'C-cuz I'm not suited to the spotlight.
As long as I can play with Claire, I'm fine with just setting ...
Hmm.
But, Emily, in beach volley-ball--
She's fine, she's fine!!
STOP

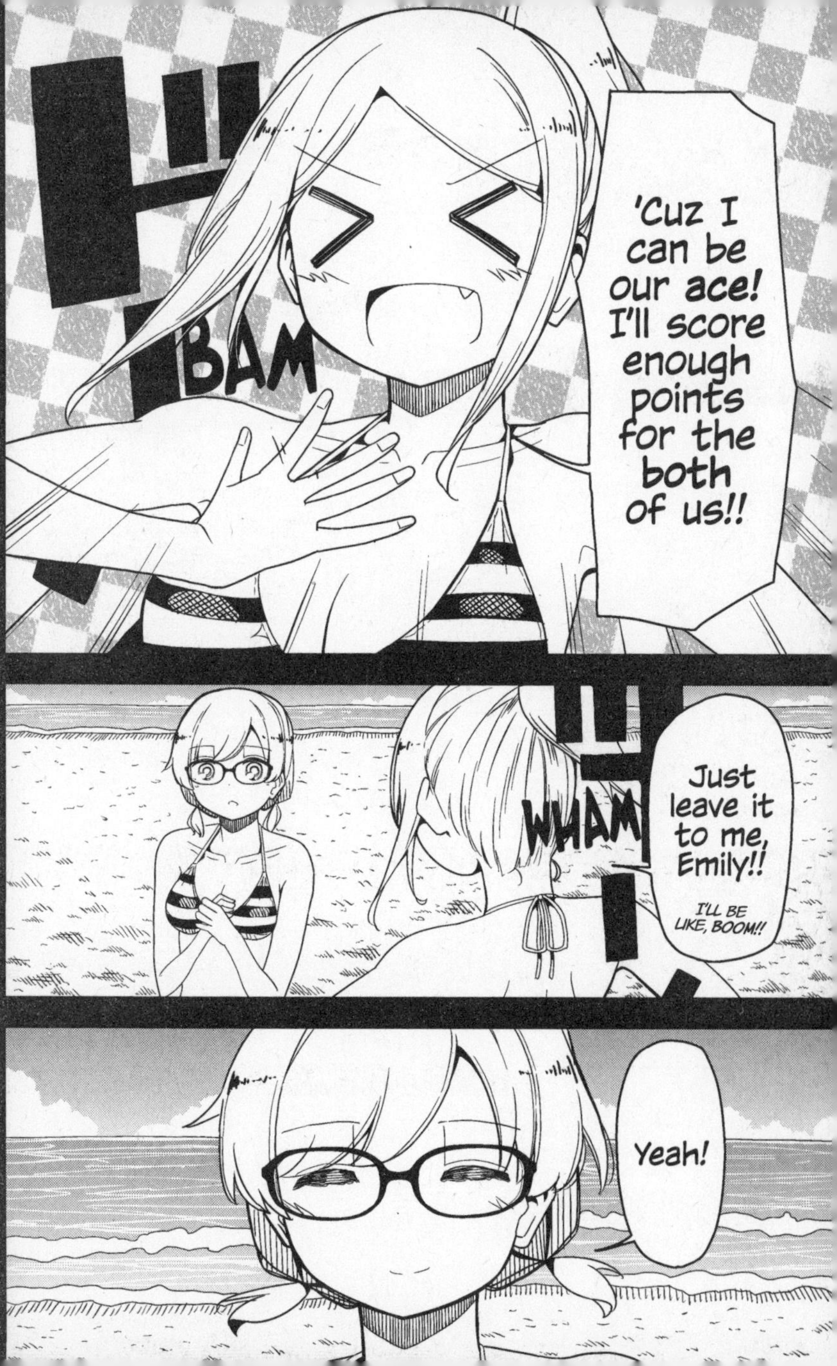
BAM
'Cuz I can be our ace! I'll score enough points for the both of us!!
WHAM
Just leave it to me, Emily!!
I'LL BE LIKE, BOOM!!
Yeah!

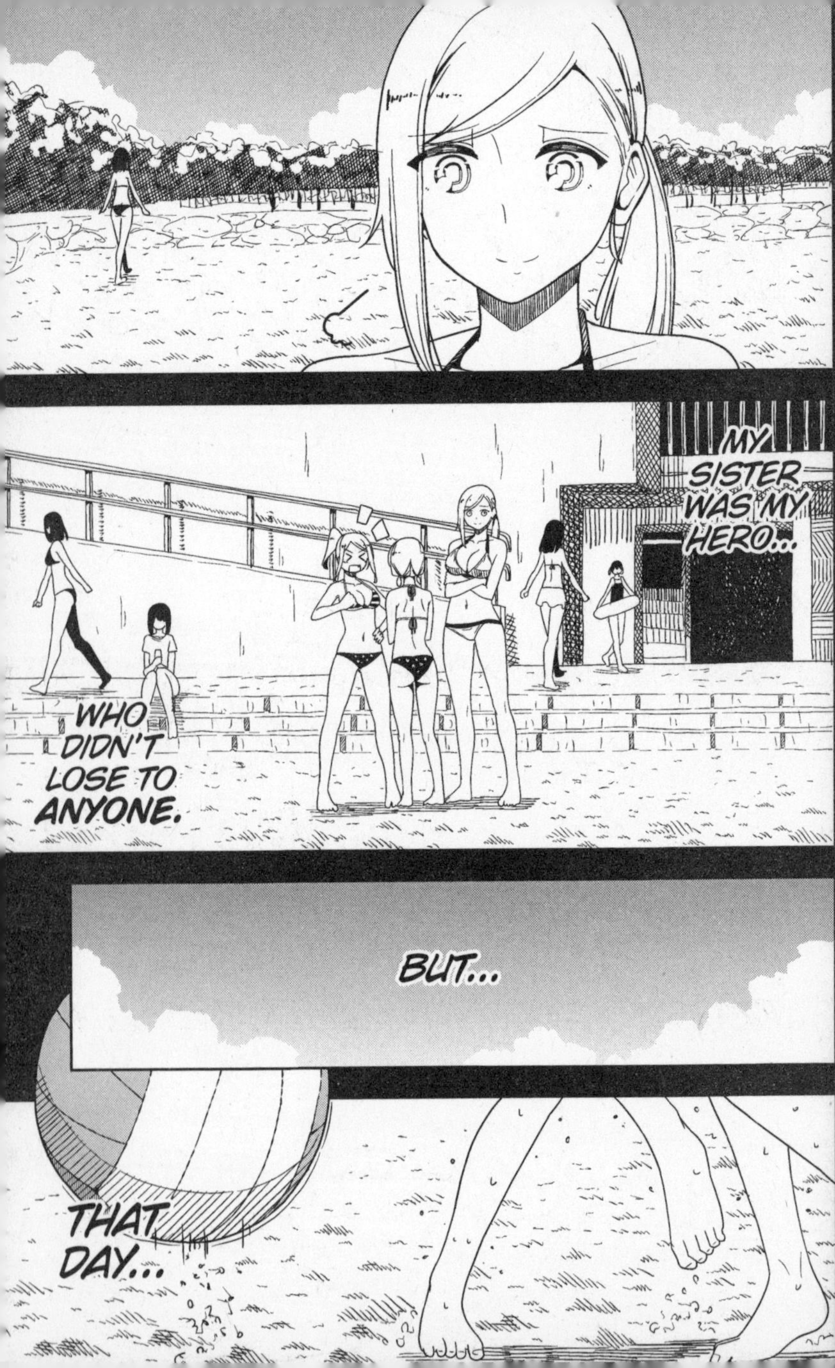
MY SISTER WAS MY HERO...
WHO DIDN'T LOSE TO ANYONE.
BUT...
THAT DAY...

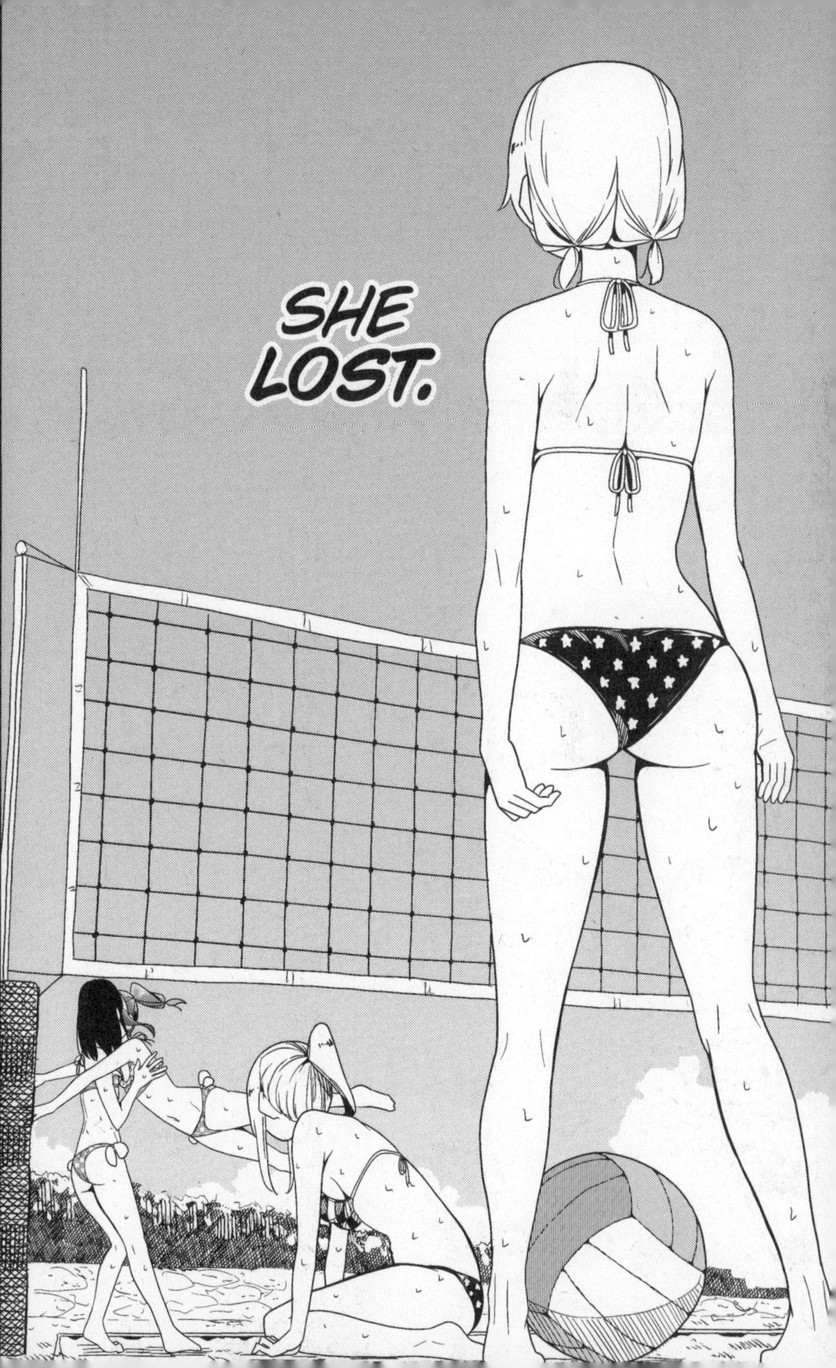
SHE
LOST.

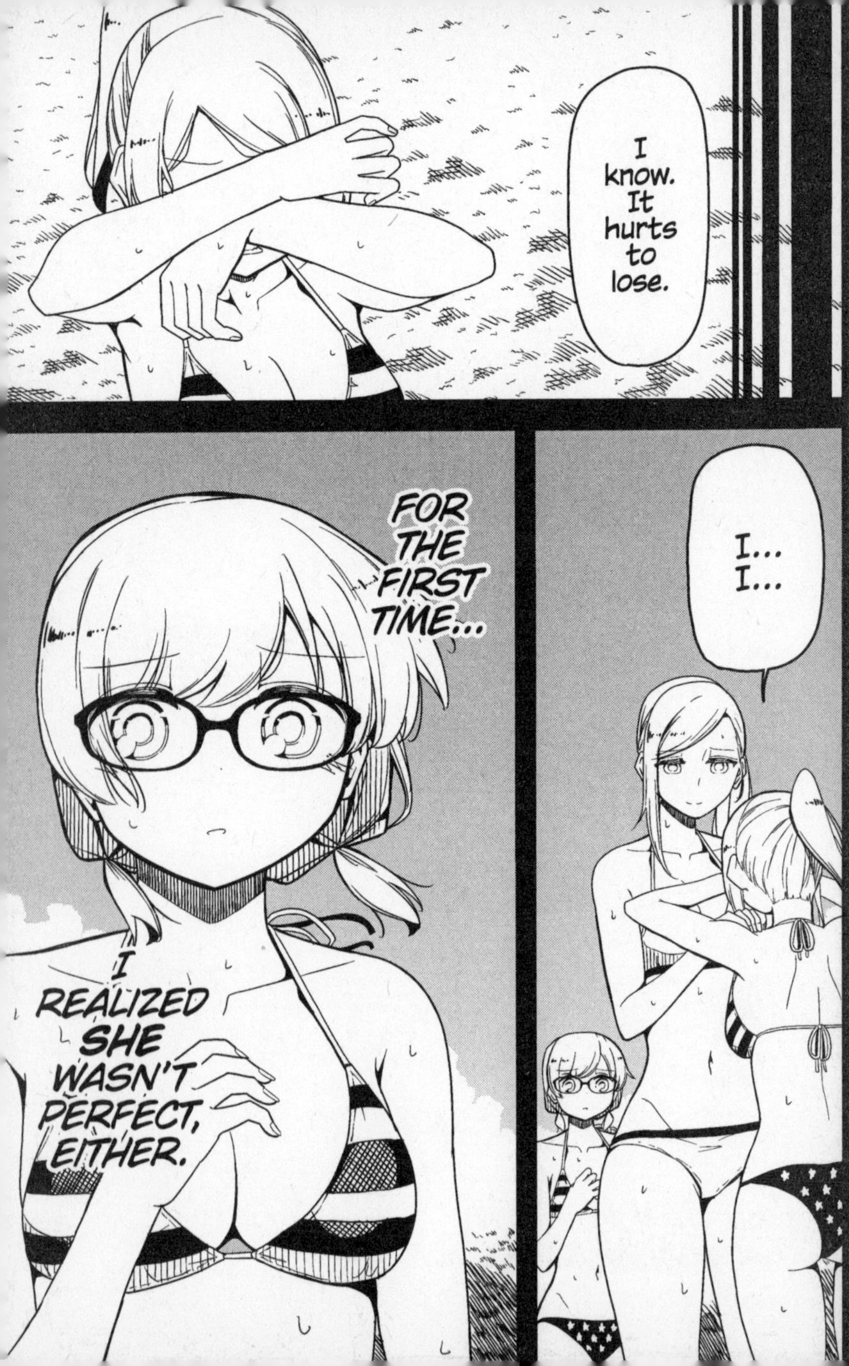
I know. It hurts to lose.
I... I...
FOR THE FIRST TIME...
I REALIZED SHE WASN'T PERFECT, EITHER.

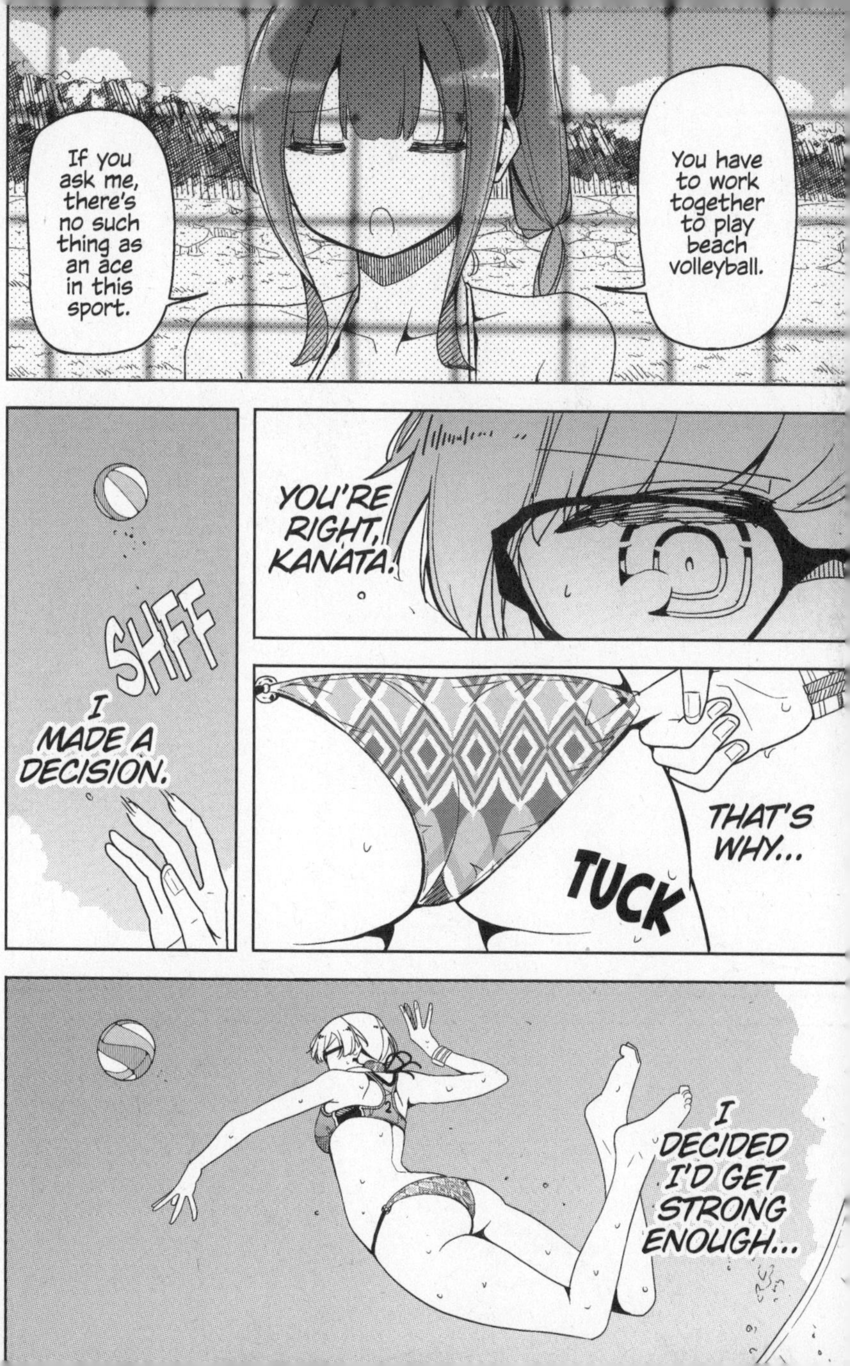
You have to work together to play beach volleyball.
If you ask me, there's no such thing as an ace in this sport.
YOU'RE RIGHT, KANATA.
THAT'S WHY...
TUCK
SHFF
I MADE A DECISION.
I DECIDED I'D GET STRONG ENOUGH...

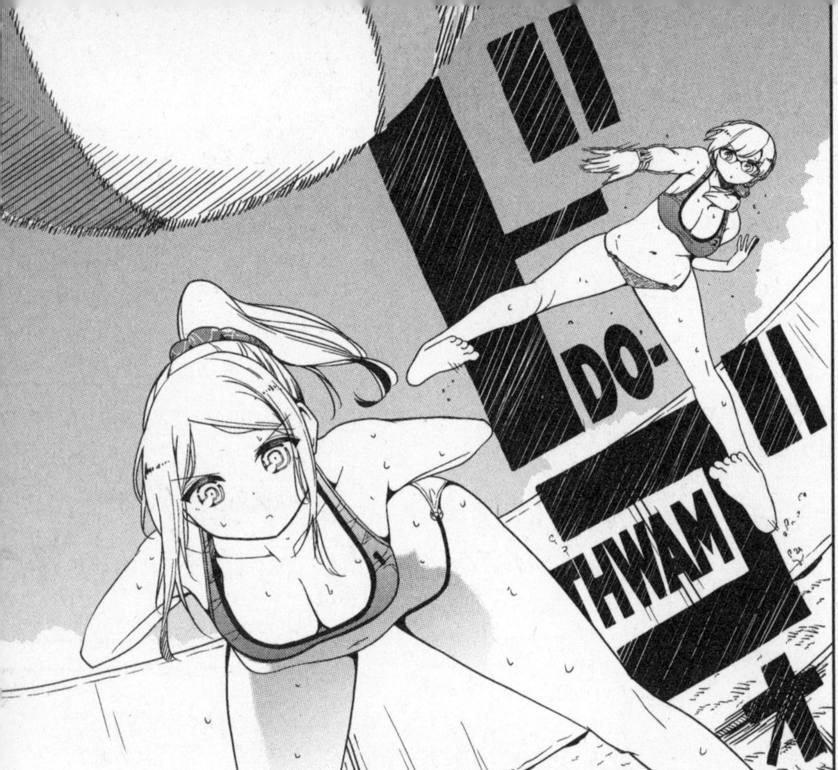
DO-
HWAM

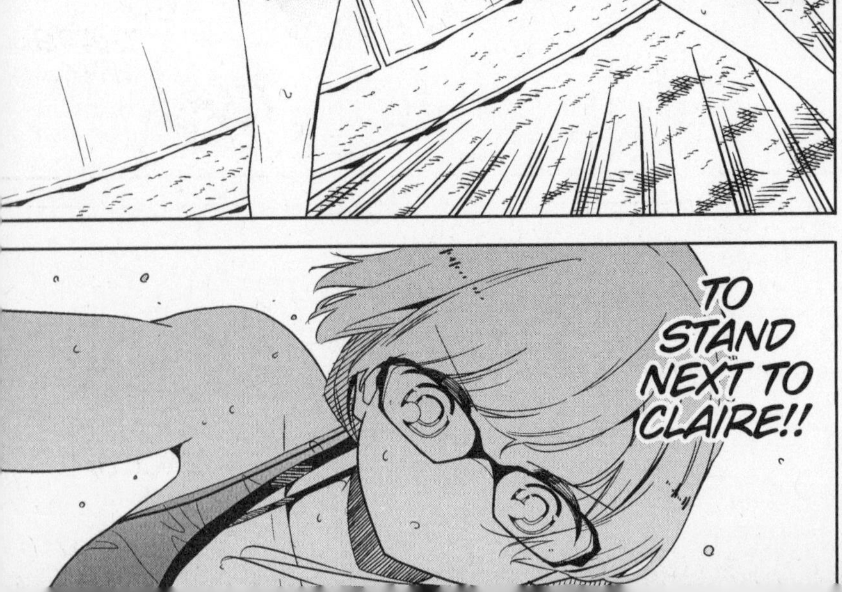
TO STAND NEXT TO CLAIRE!!

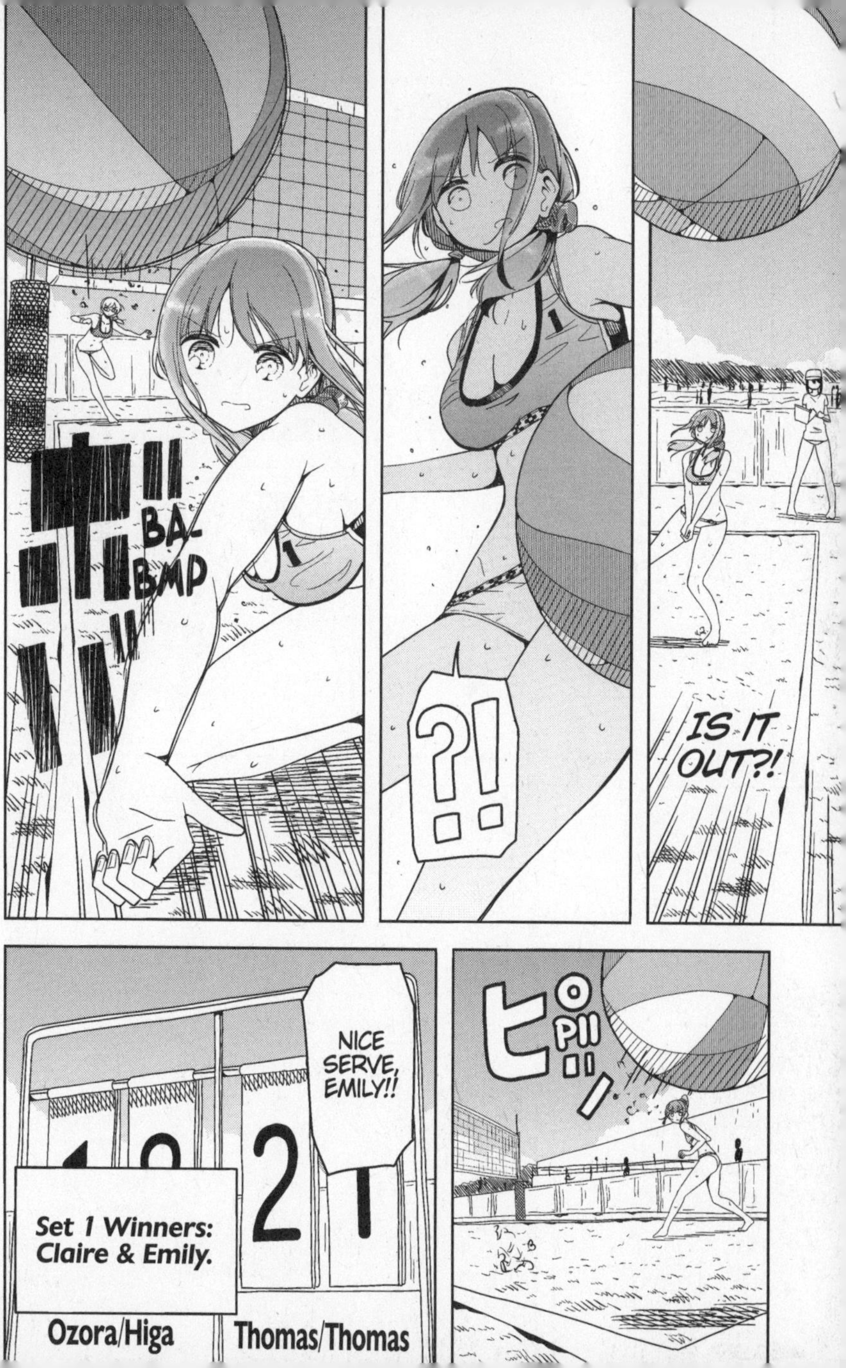
?!
BA-BMP
IS IT OUT?!
PII
NICE SERVE, EMILY!!
2
1
Set 1 Winners: Claire & Emily.
Ozora/Higa
Thomas/Thomas

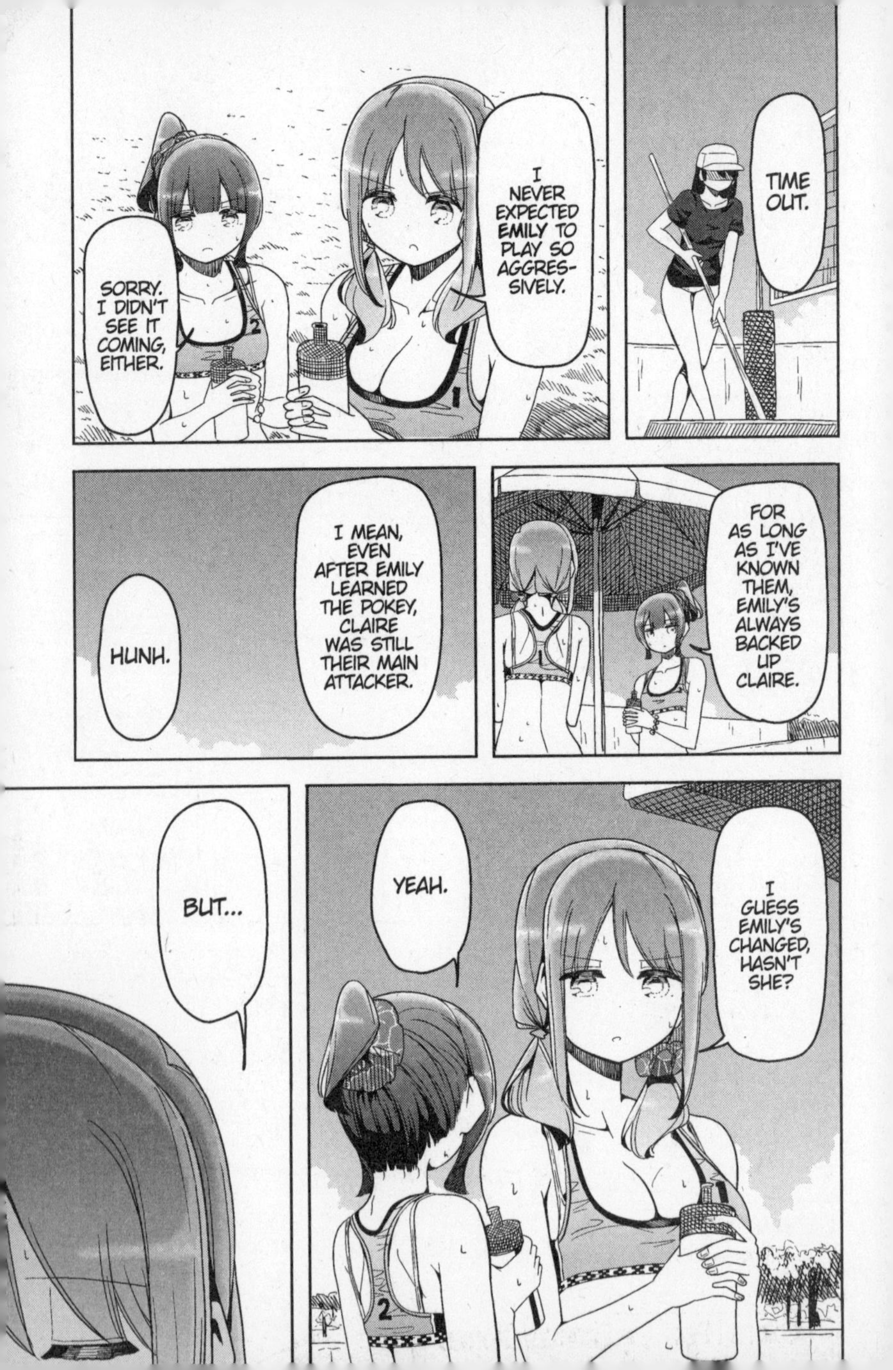
TIME OUT.
I NEVER EXPECTED EMILY TO PLAY SO AGGRESSIVELY.
SORRY. I DIDN'T SEE IT COMING, EITHER.
FOR AS LONG AS I'VE KNOWN THEM, EMILY'S ALWAYS BACKED UP CLAIRE.
I MEAN, EVEN AFTER EMILY LEARNED THE POKEY, CLAIRE WAS STILL THEIR MAIN ATTACKER.
HUNH.
I GUESS EMILY'S CHANGED, HASN'T SHE?
YEAH.
BUT...

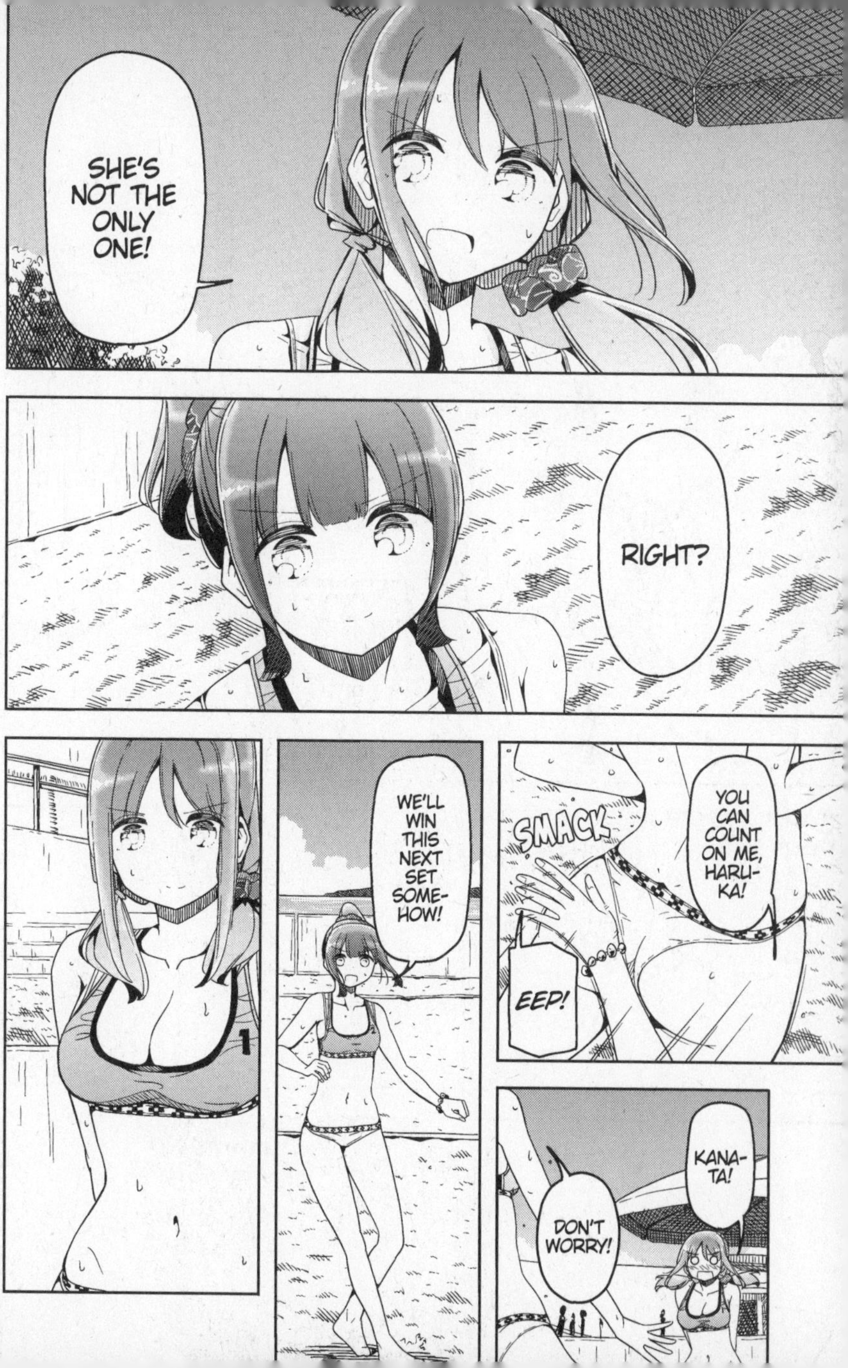
SHE'S NOT THE ONLY ONE!
RIGHT?
SMACK
YOU CAN COUNT ON ME, HARU-KA!
EEP!
KANA-TA!
DON'T WORRY!
WE'LL WIN THIS NEXT SET SOME-HOW!

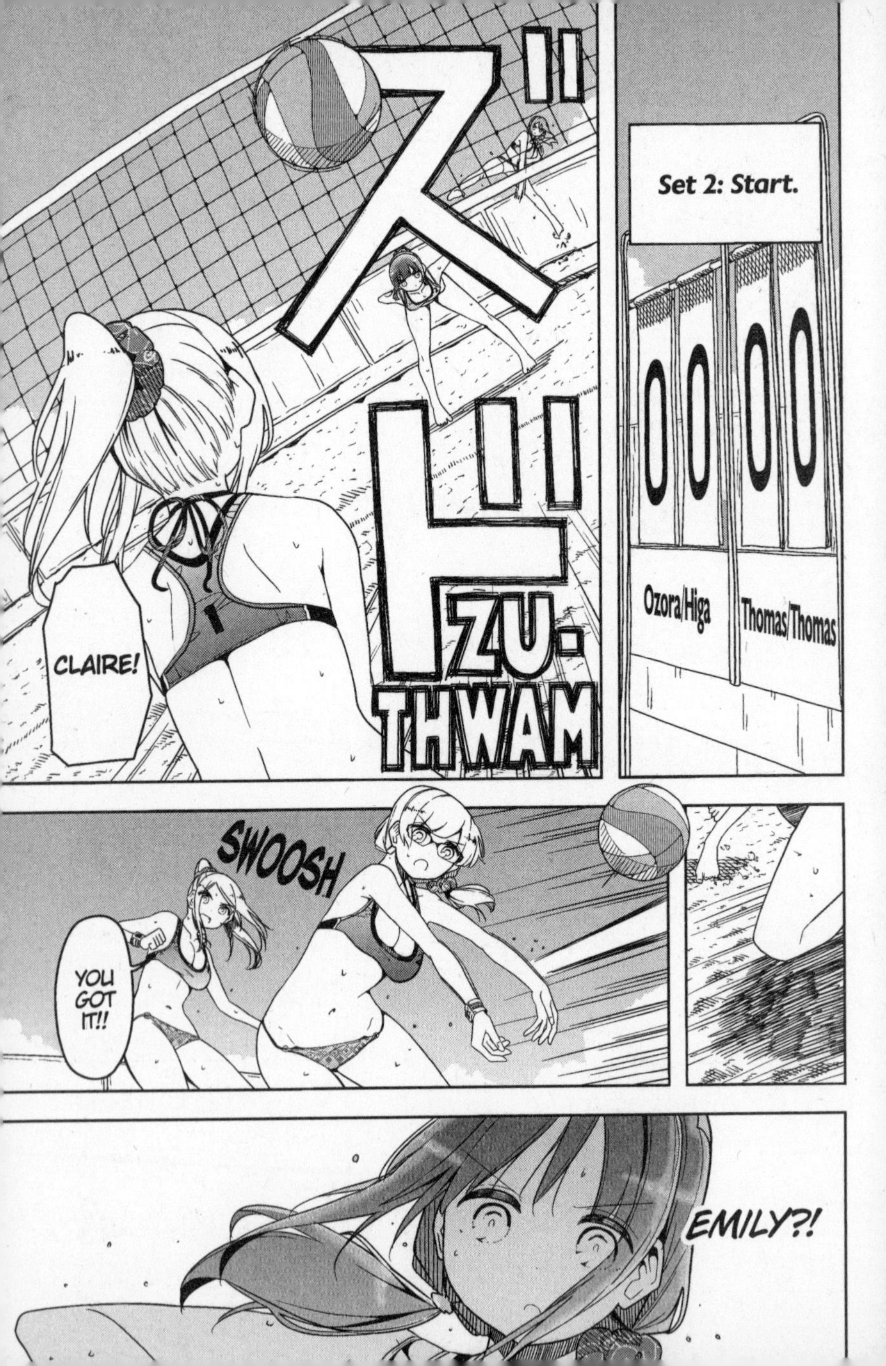
Set 2: Start.
0 0 0 0
Ozora/Higa
Thomas/Thomas
ZU-THWAM
CLAIRE!
SWOOSH
YOU GOT IT!!
EMILY?!

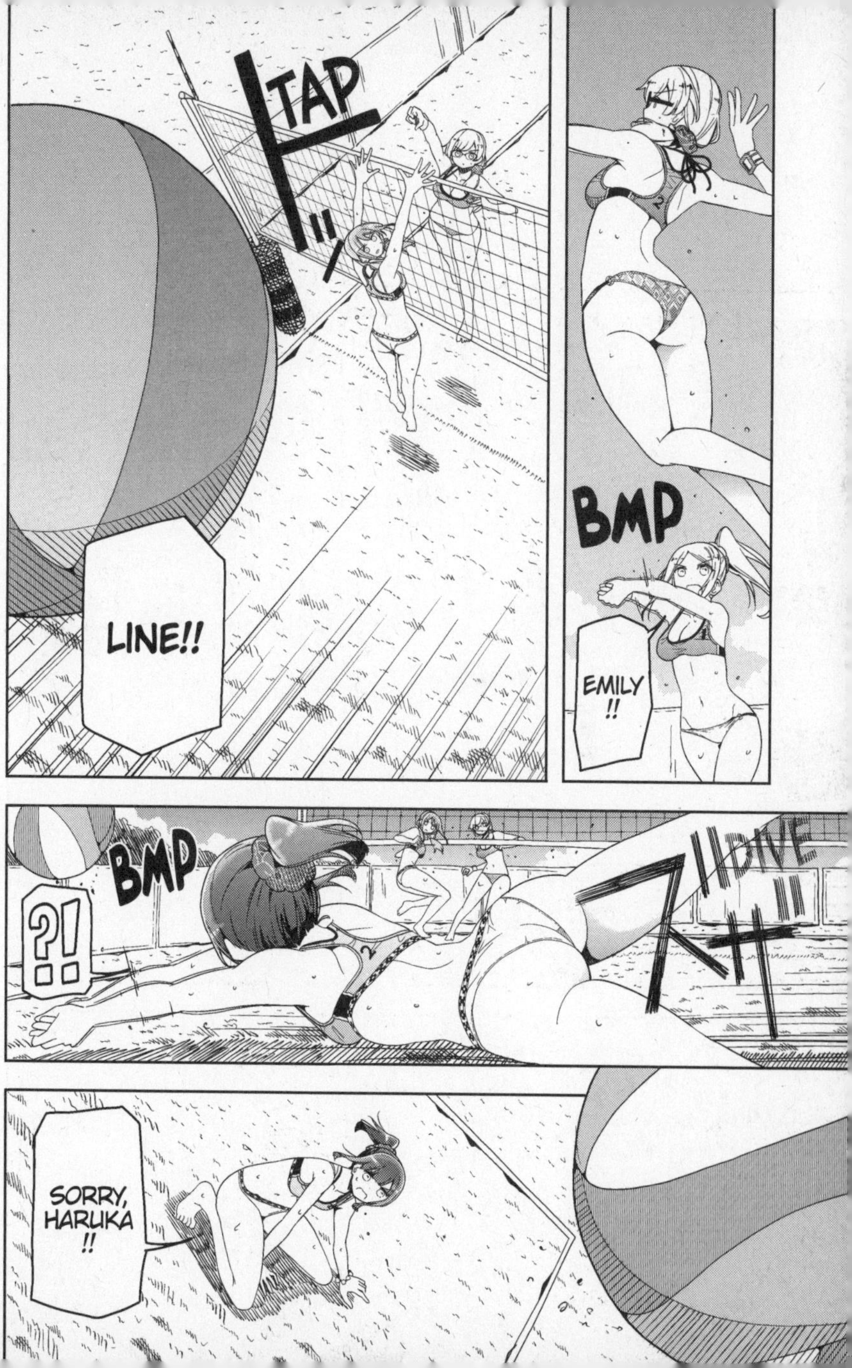
BMP
EMILY!!
TAP!!
LINE!!
DIVE!!
BMP
?!
SORRY, HARUKA!!

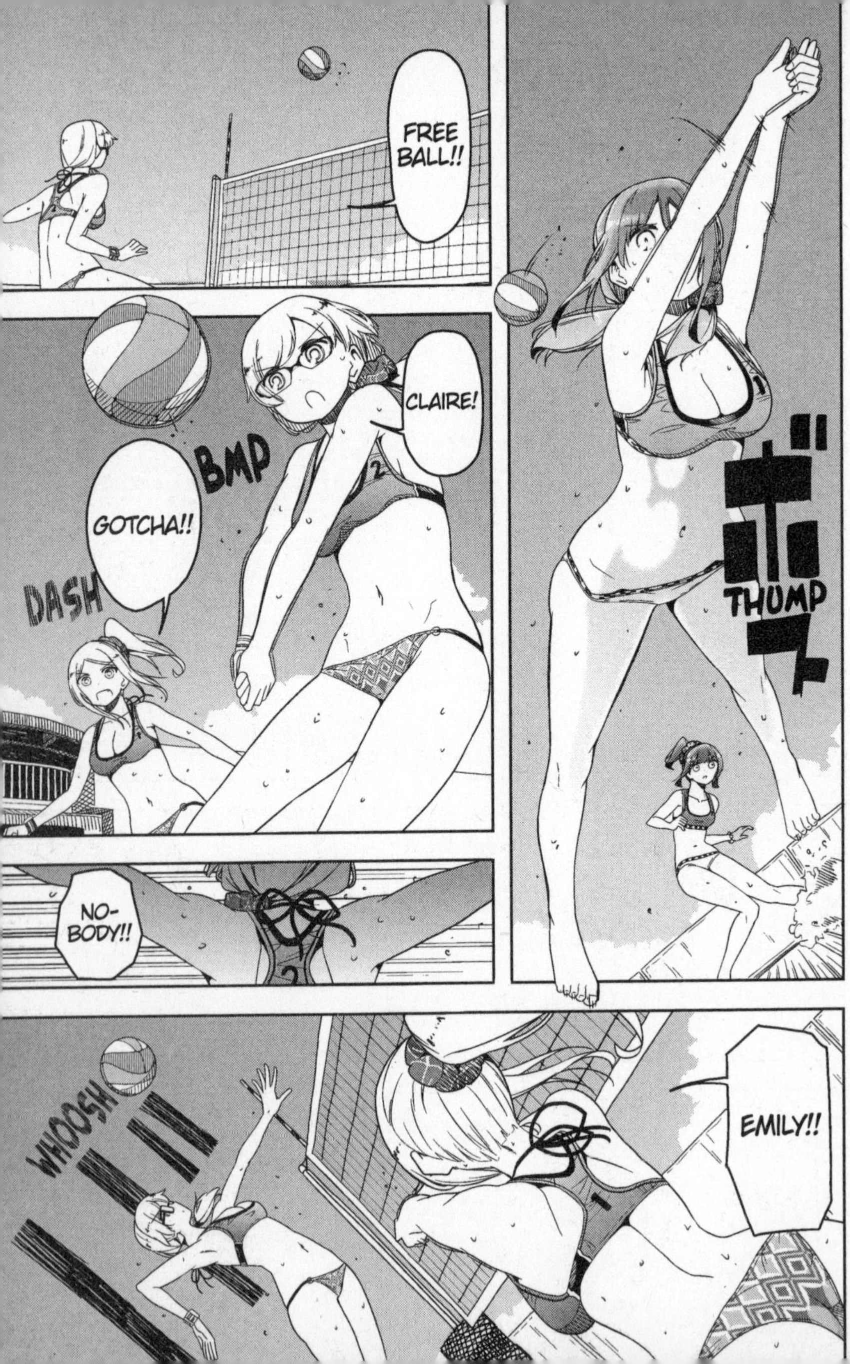

ボ
THUMP
FREE BALL!!
CLAIRE!
BMP
GOTCHA!!
DASH
NO-BODY!!
EMILY!!
WHOOSH

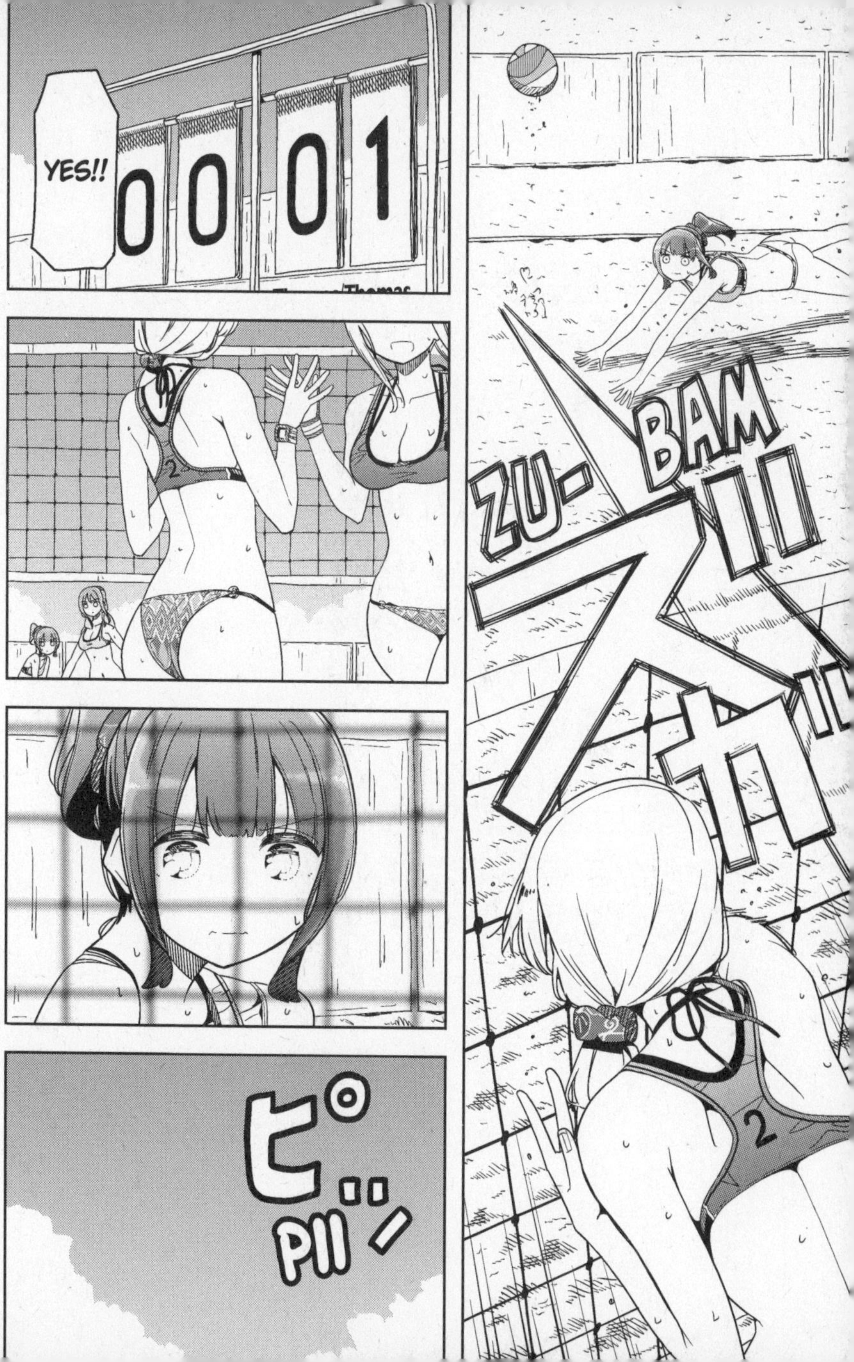
ZU-BAM
YES!!
0 0 0 1
ピ
PII

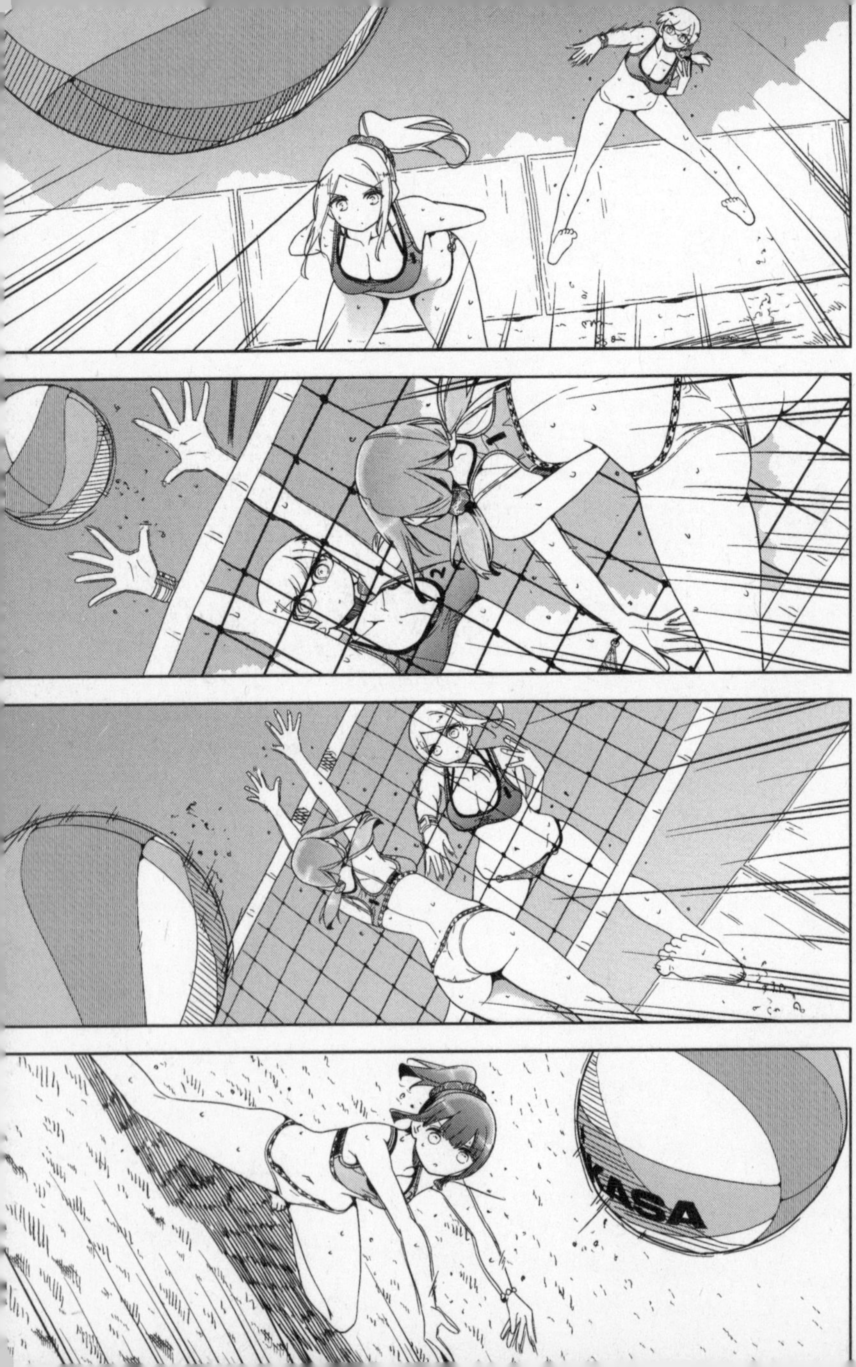
KASA

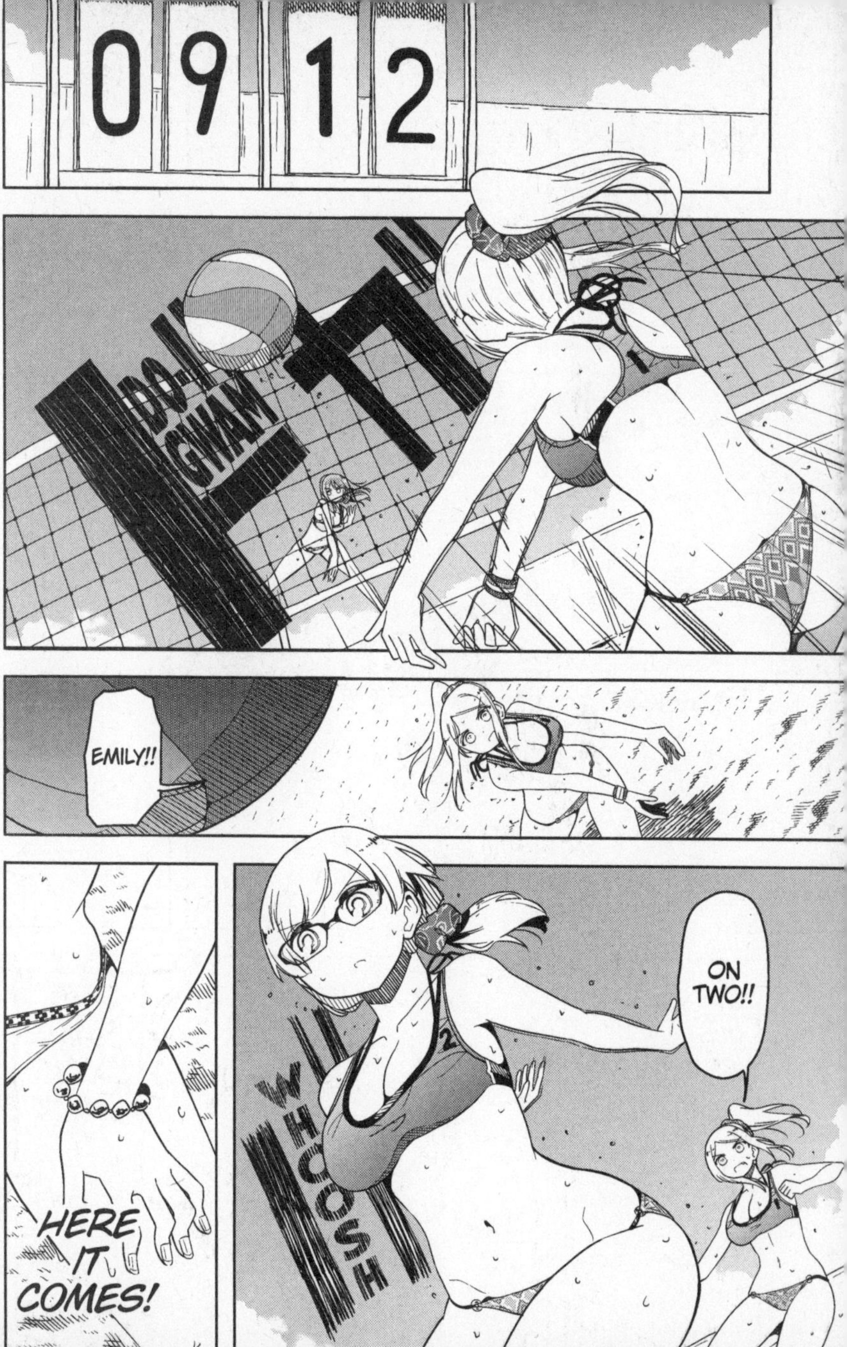
09 12
DO-
GWAM
EMILY!!
ON TWO!!
WHOOSH
HERE IT COMES!

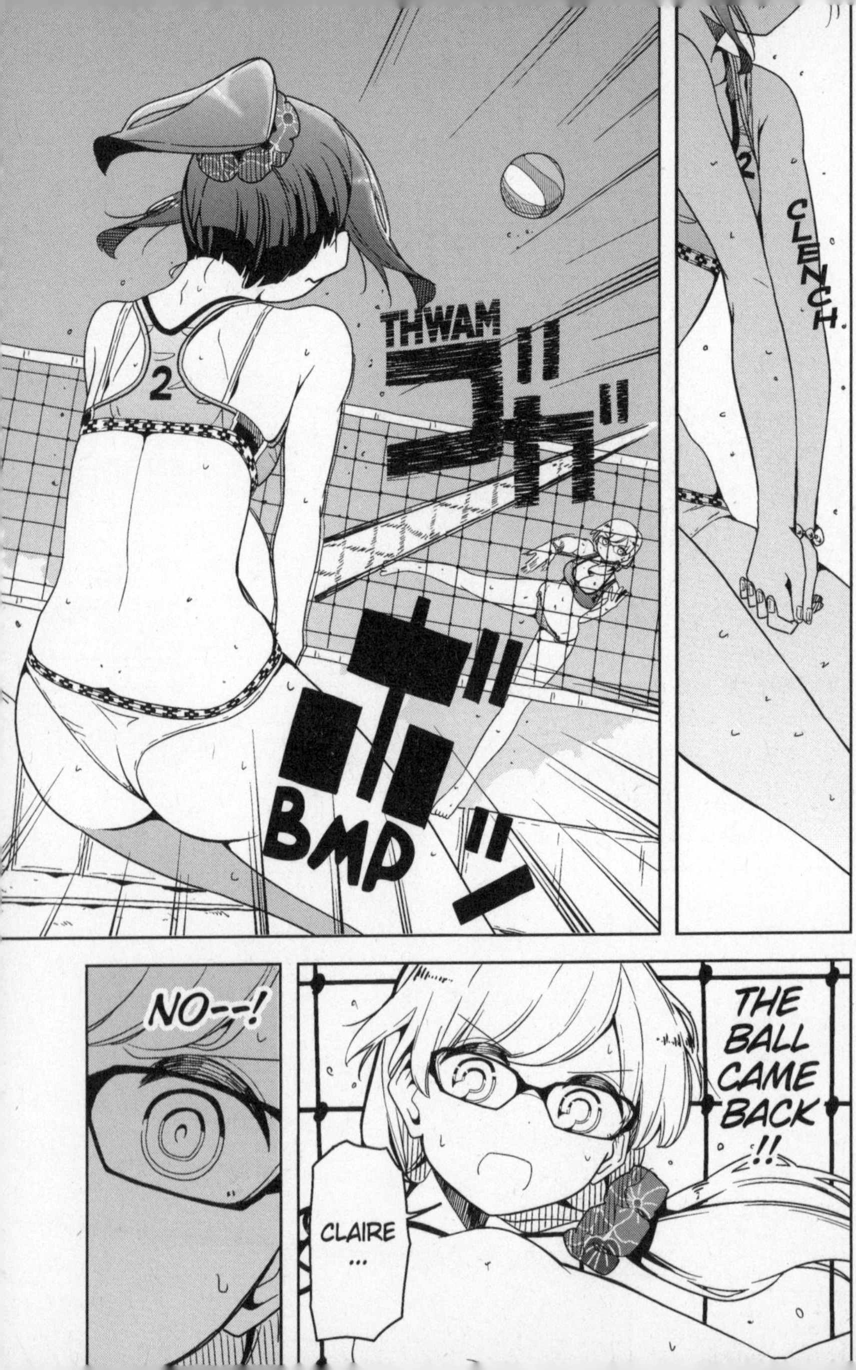
CLENCH
THWAM
BMP
THE BALL CAME BACK!!
CLAIRE ...
NO--!

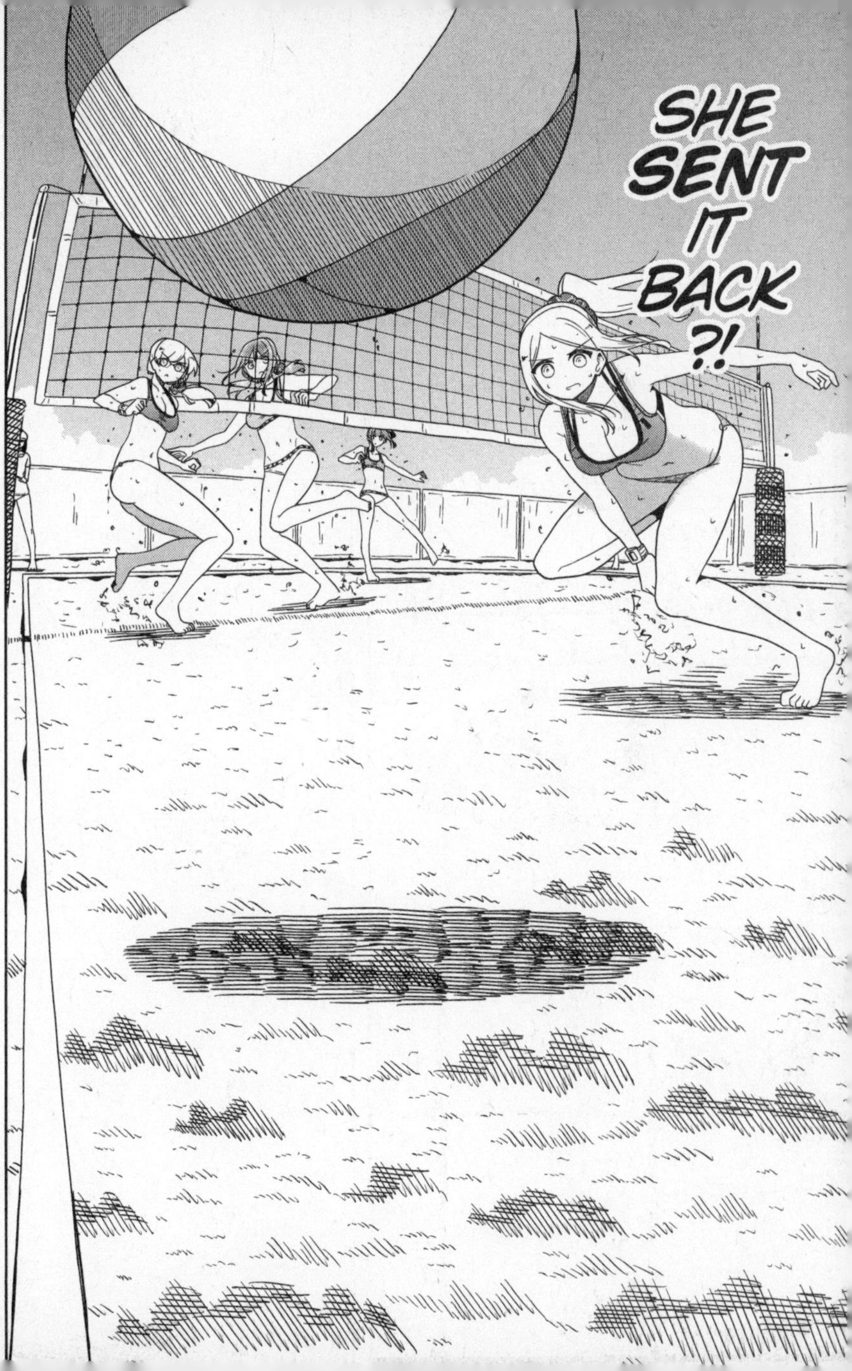
SHE SENT IT BACK ?!

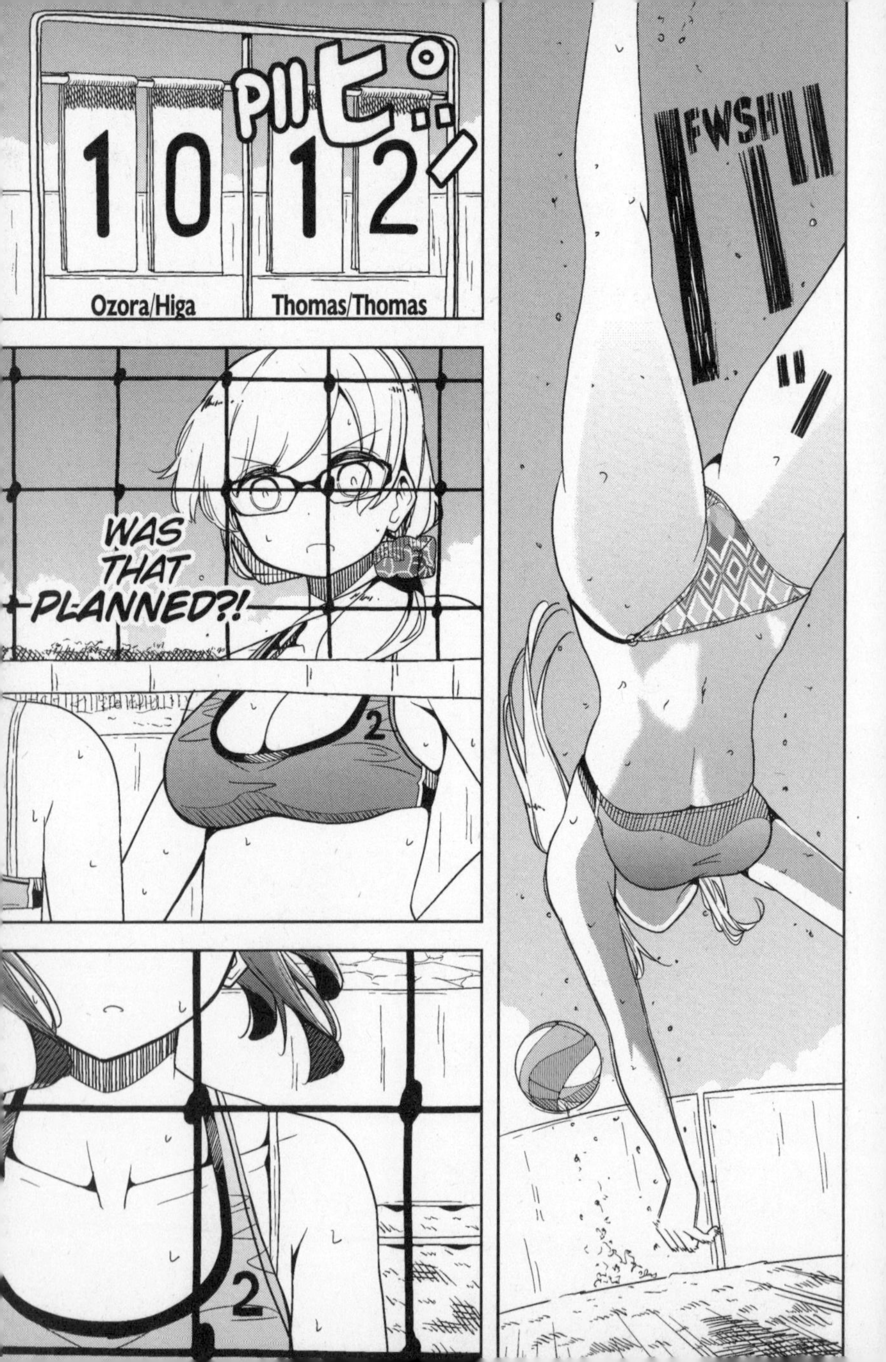
FWSH
PII
10
12
Ozora/Higa
Thomas/Thomas
WAS THAT PLANNED?!

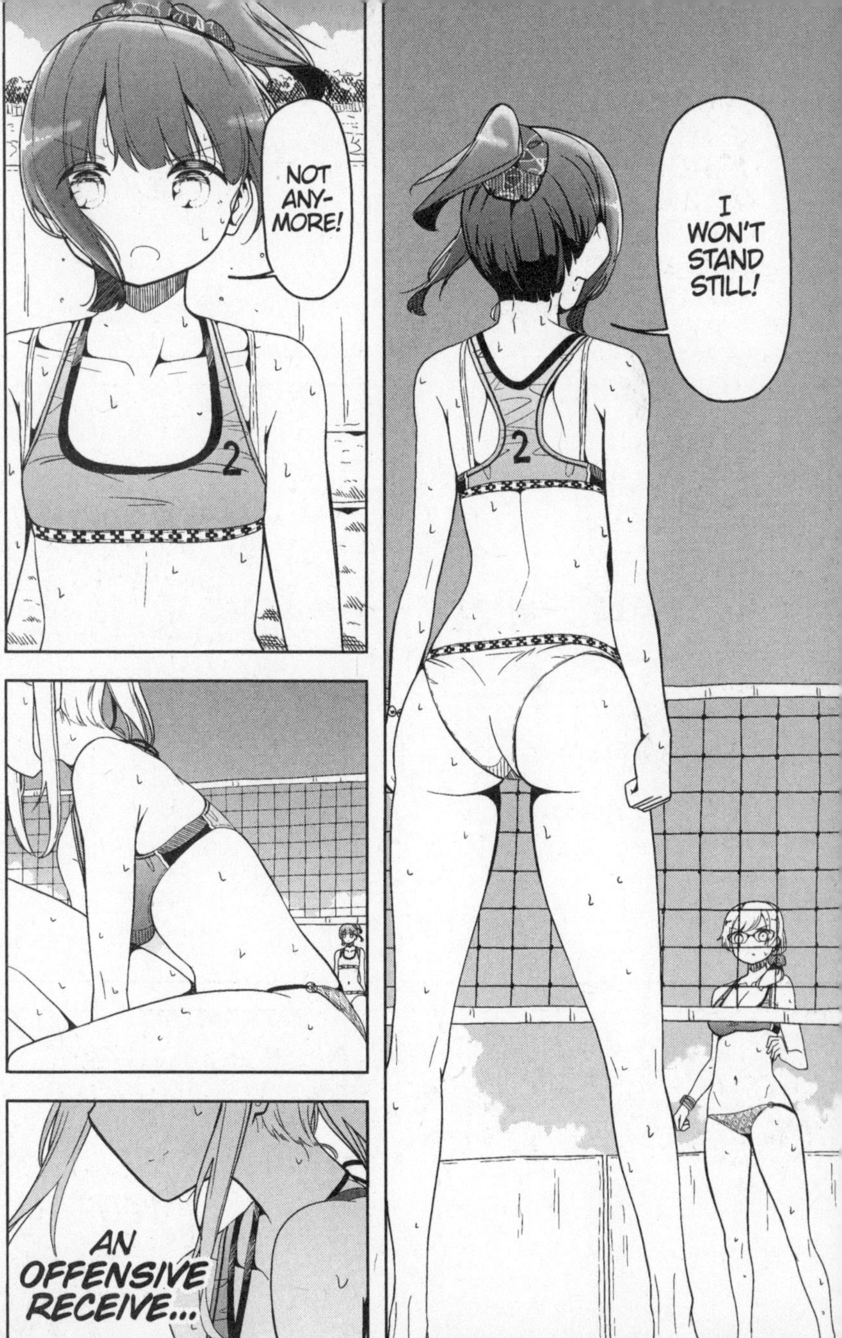
I WON'T STAND STILL!
NOT ANY-MORE!
AN OFFENSIVE RECEIVE...

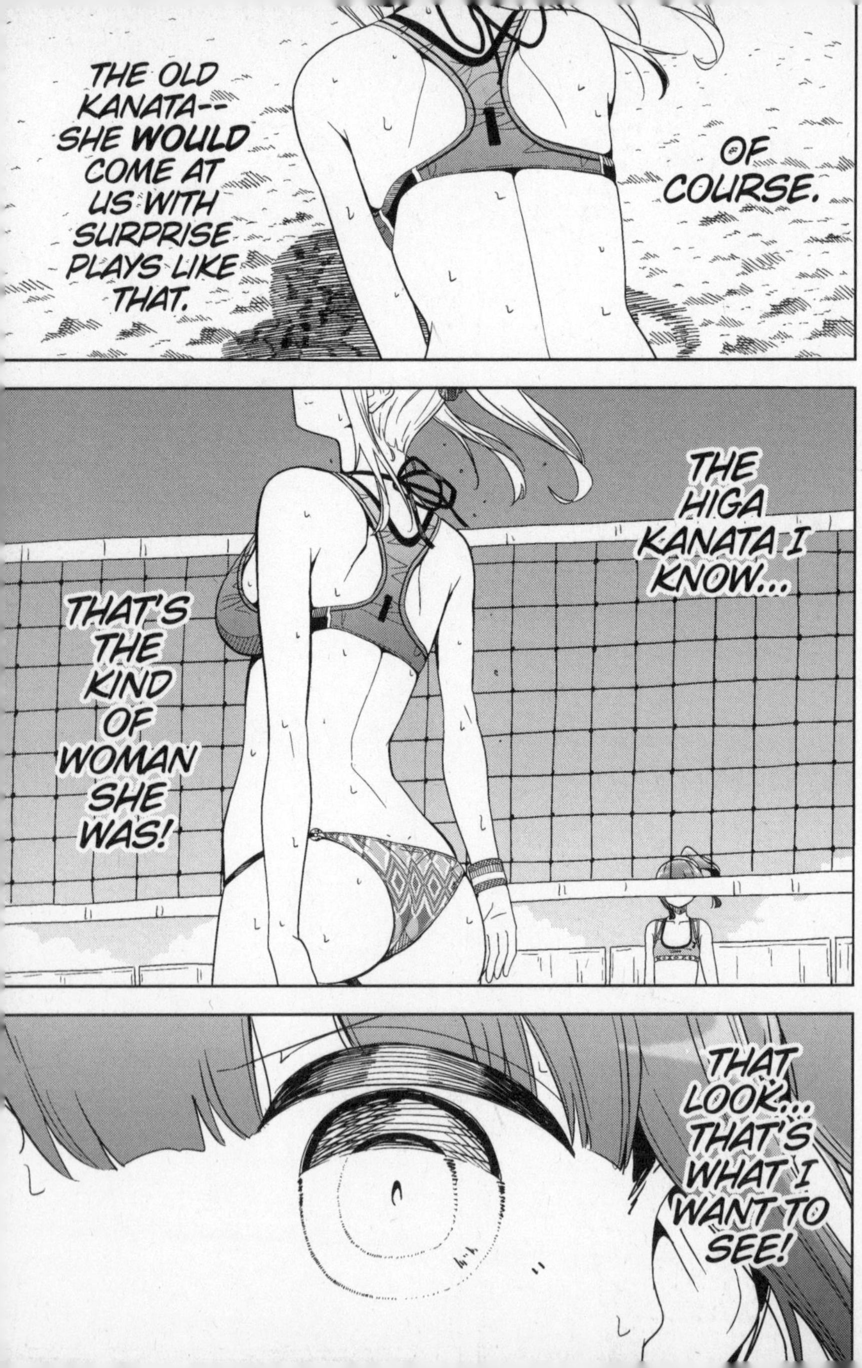
OF COURSE.
THE OLD KANATA-- SHE WOULD COME AT US WITH SURPRISE PLAYS LIKE THAT.
THE HIGA KANATA I KNOW...
THAT'S THE KIND OF WOMAN SHE WAS!
THAT LOOK... THAT'S WHAT I WANT TO SEE!

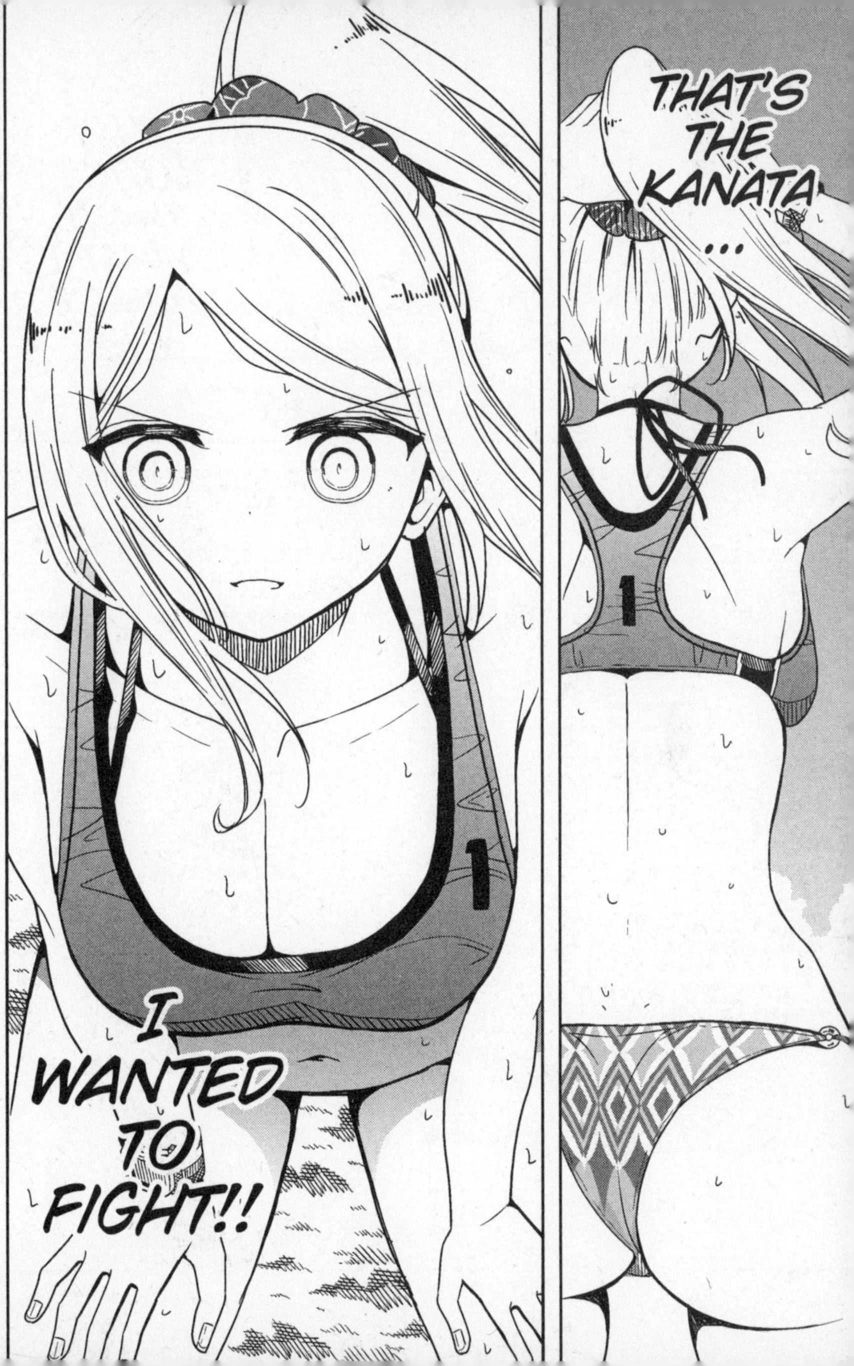
THAT'S THE KANATA...
I WANTED TO FIGHT!!

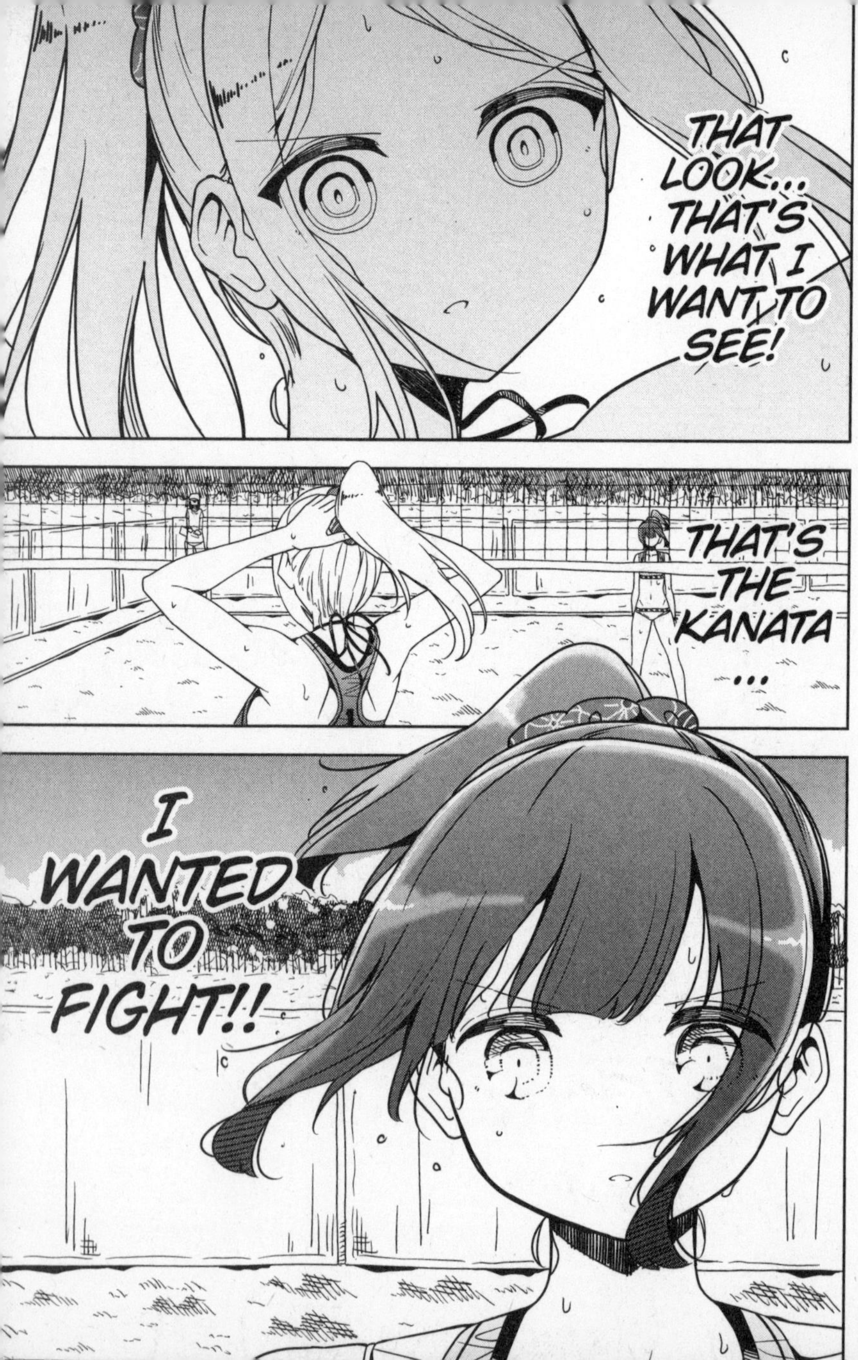
THAT LOOK... THAT'S WHAT I WANT TO SEE!
THAT'S THE KANATA...
I WANTED TO FIGHT!!

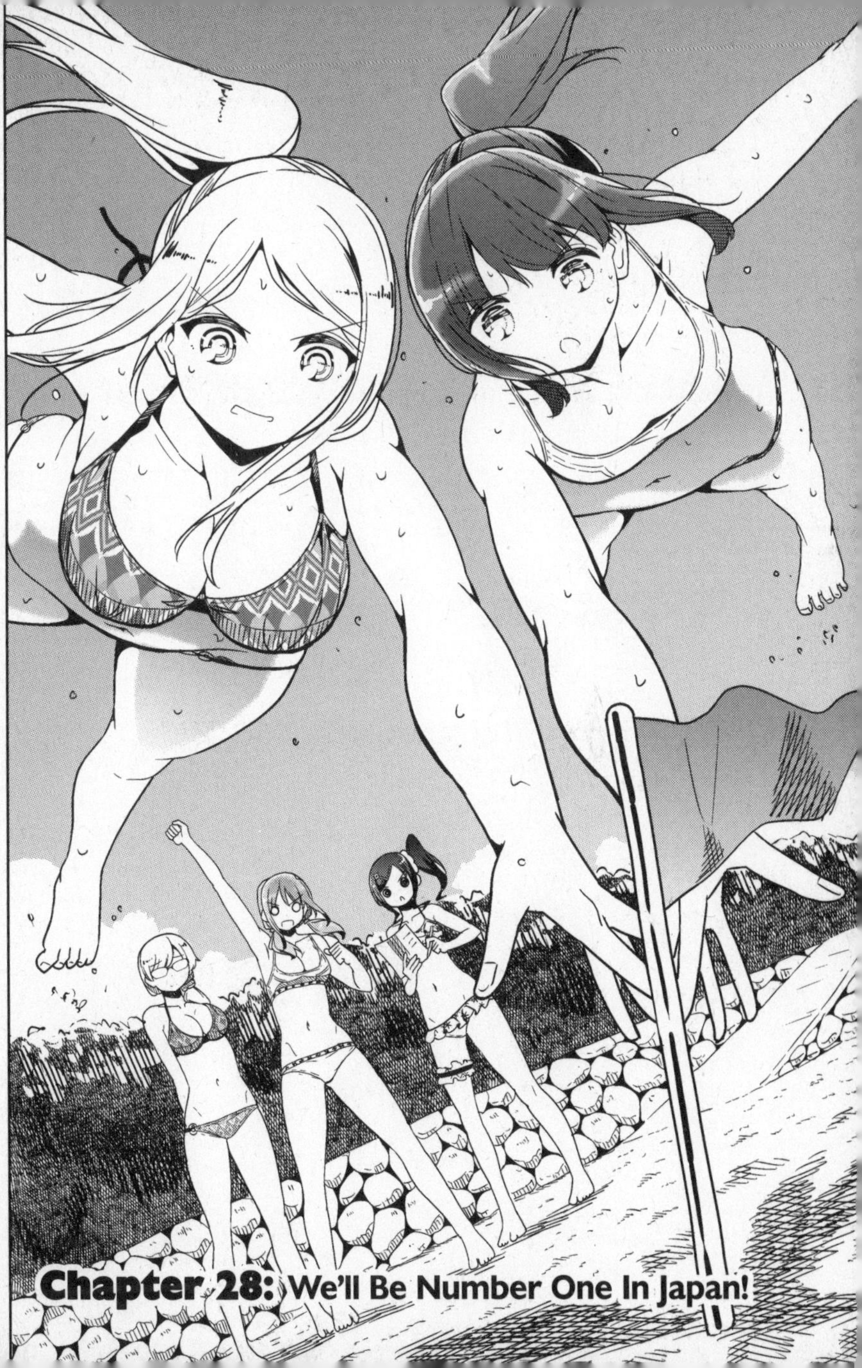

Chapter 28: We'll Be Number One In Japan!

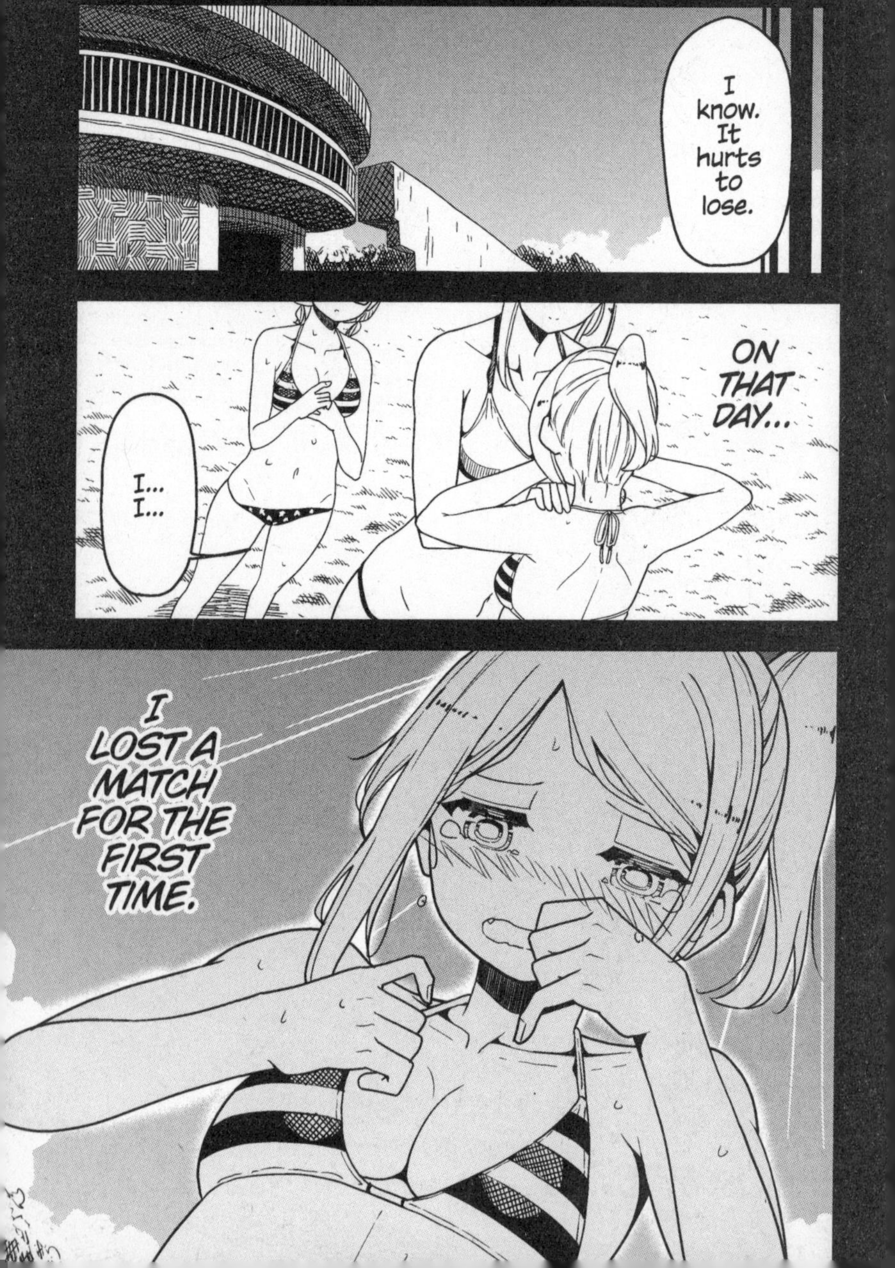
I know. It hurts to lose.
ON THAT DAY...
I... I...
I LOST A MATCH FOR THE FIRST TIME.

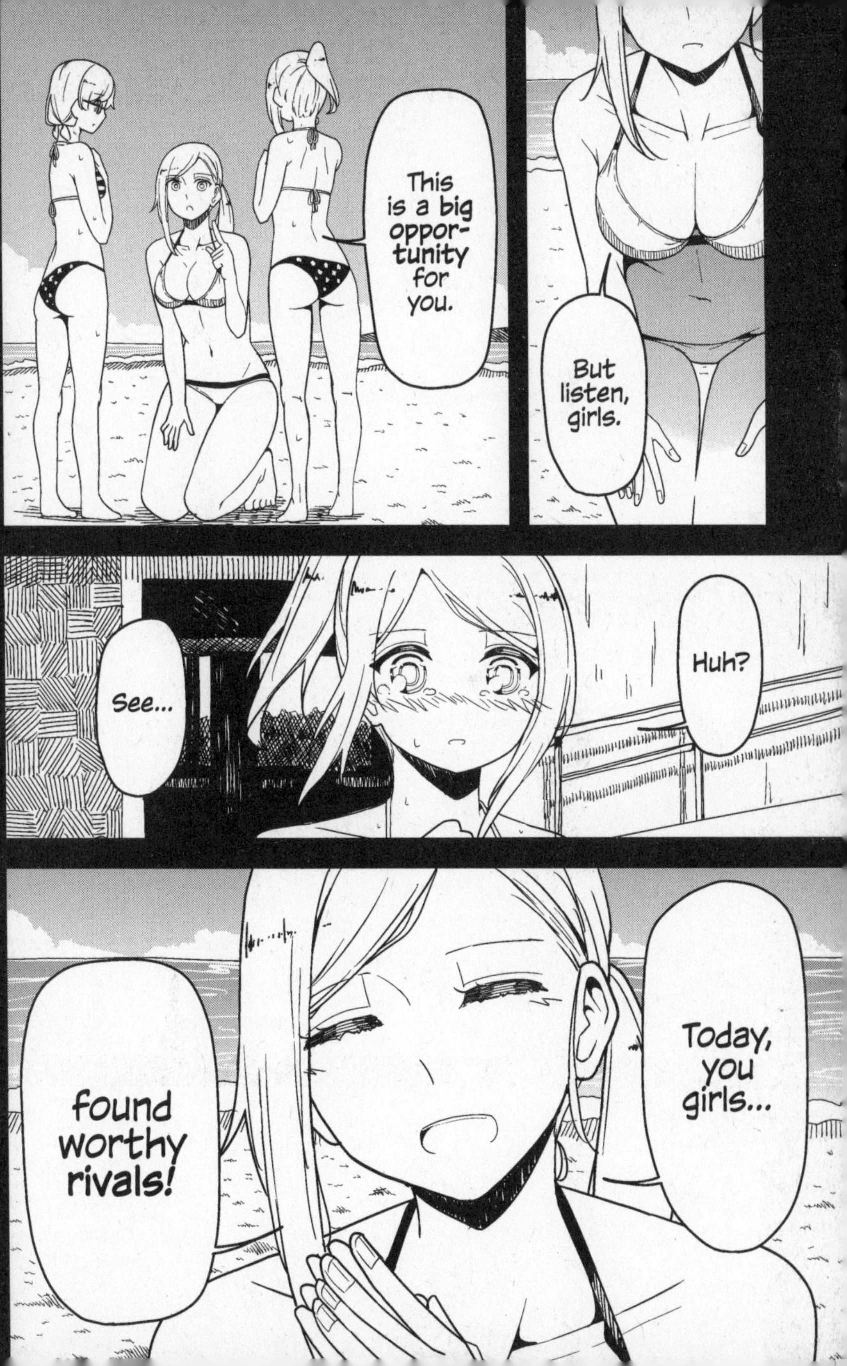
But listen, girls.
This is a big opportunity for you.
Huh?
See...
Today, you girls...
found worthy rivals!

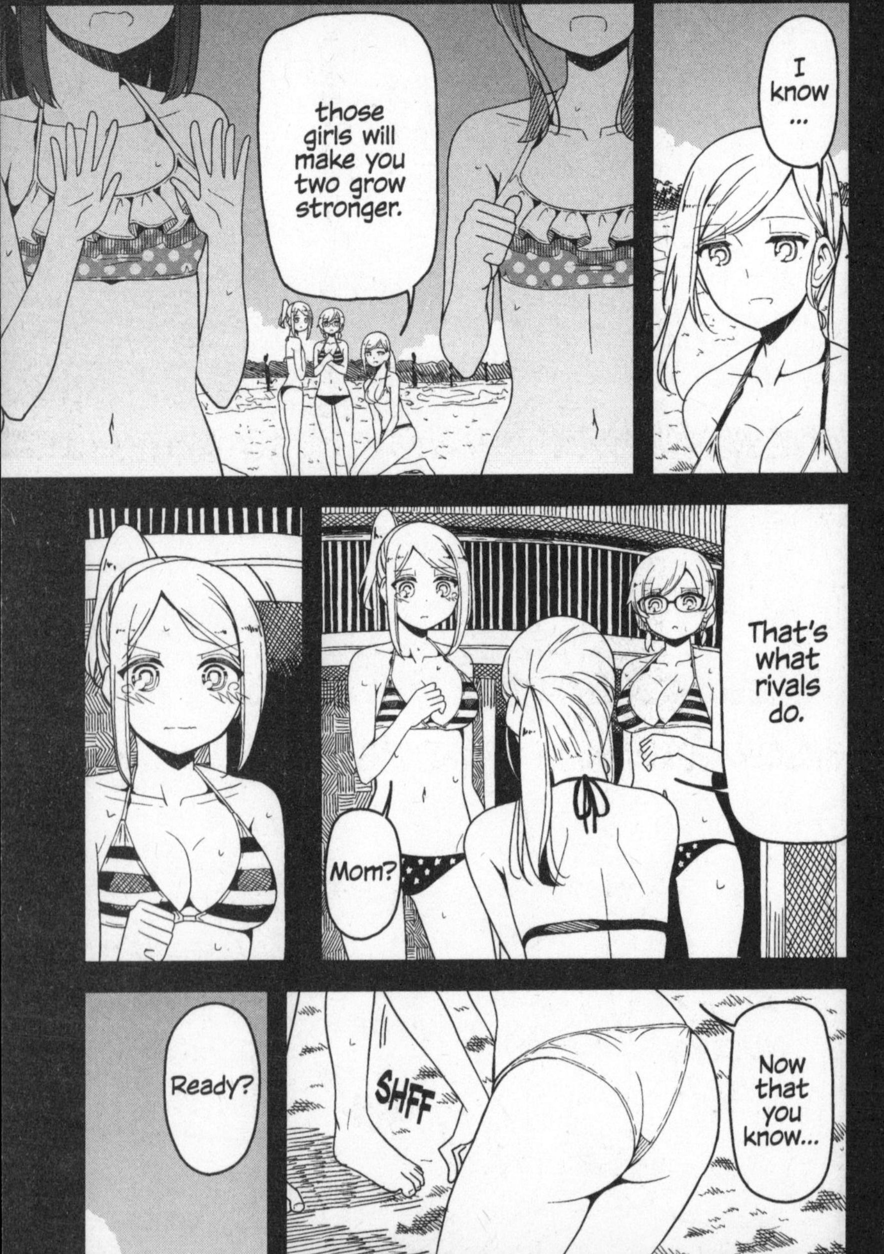
I know ...
those girls will make you two grow stronger.
That's what rivals do.
Mom?
Now that you know...
SHFF
Ready?

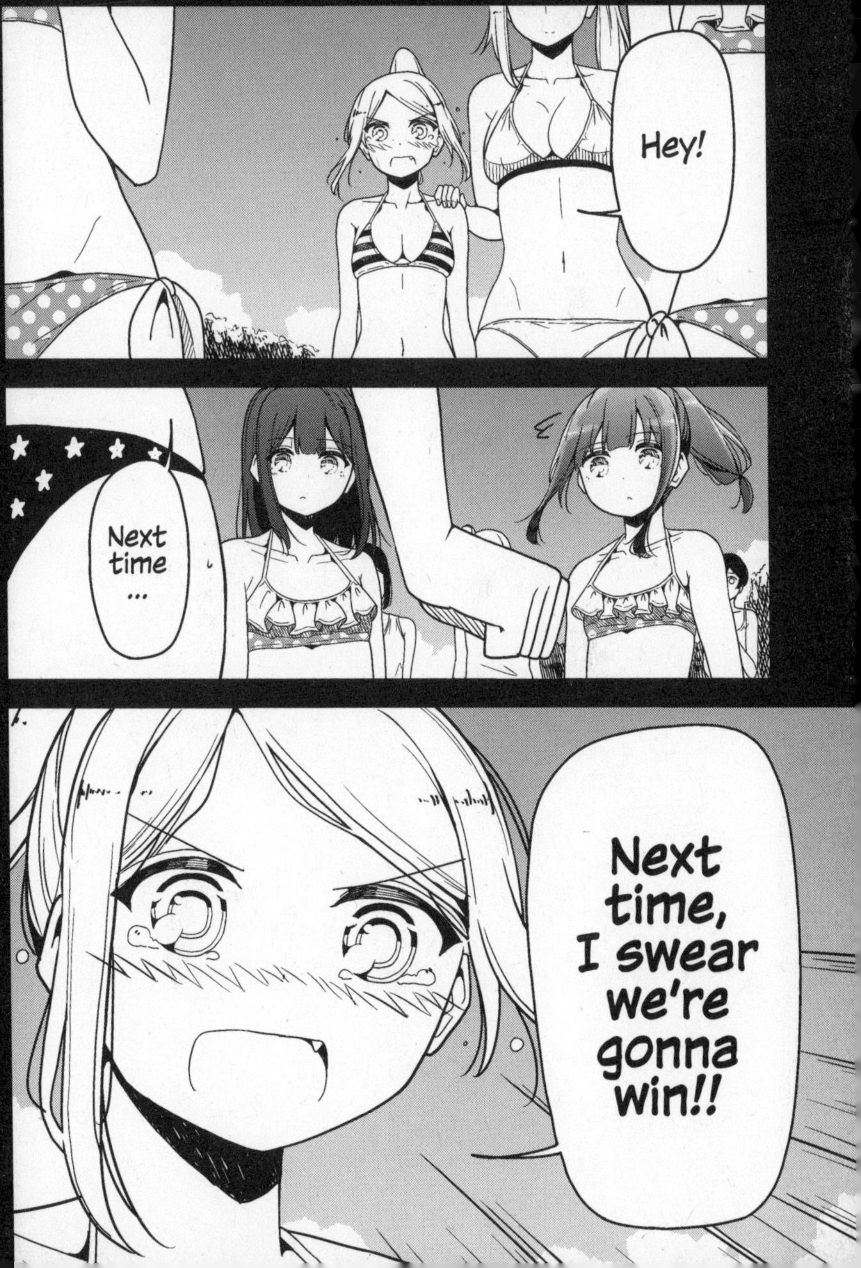
Hey!
Next time ...
Next time, I swear we're gonna win!!

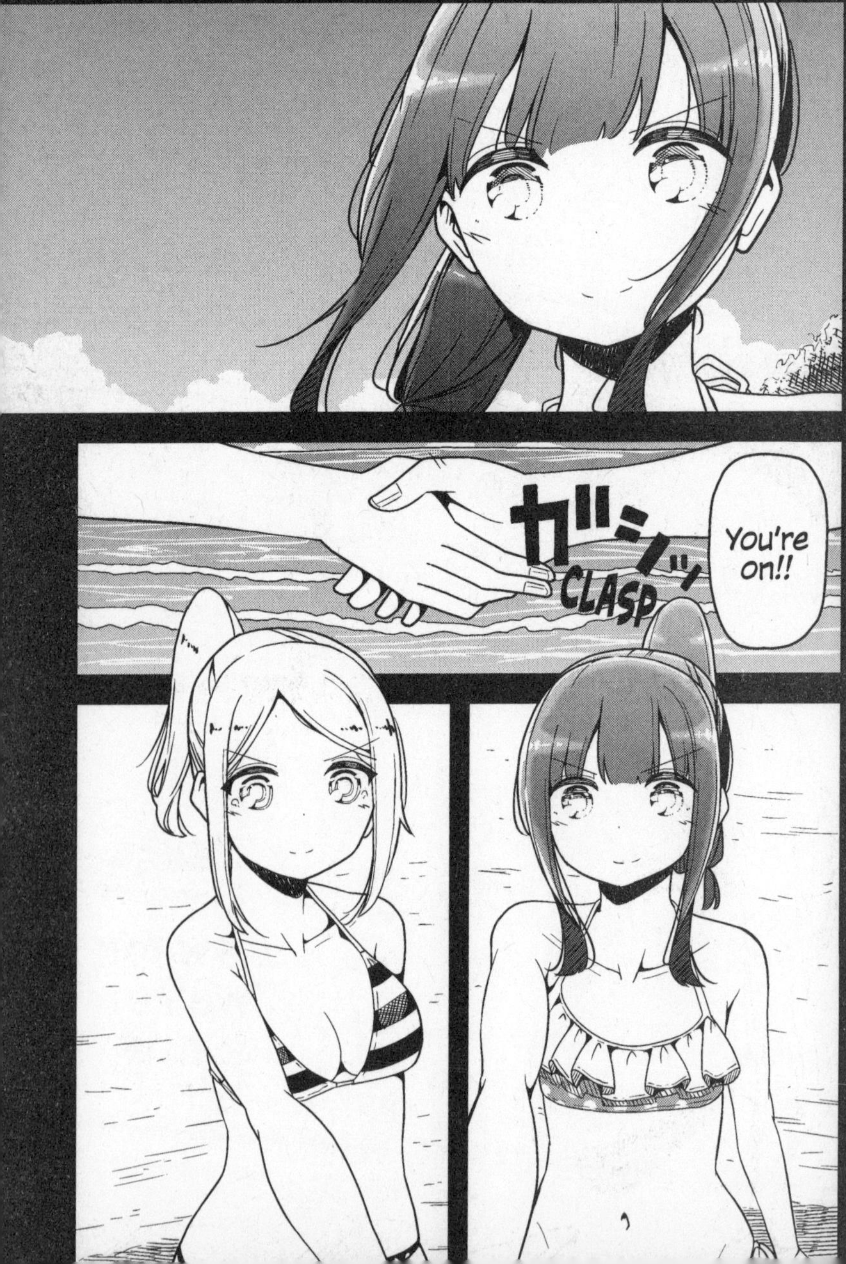
ガシッ
CLASP
You're on!!

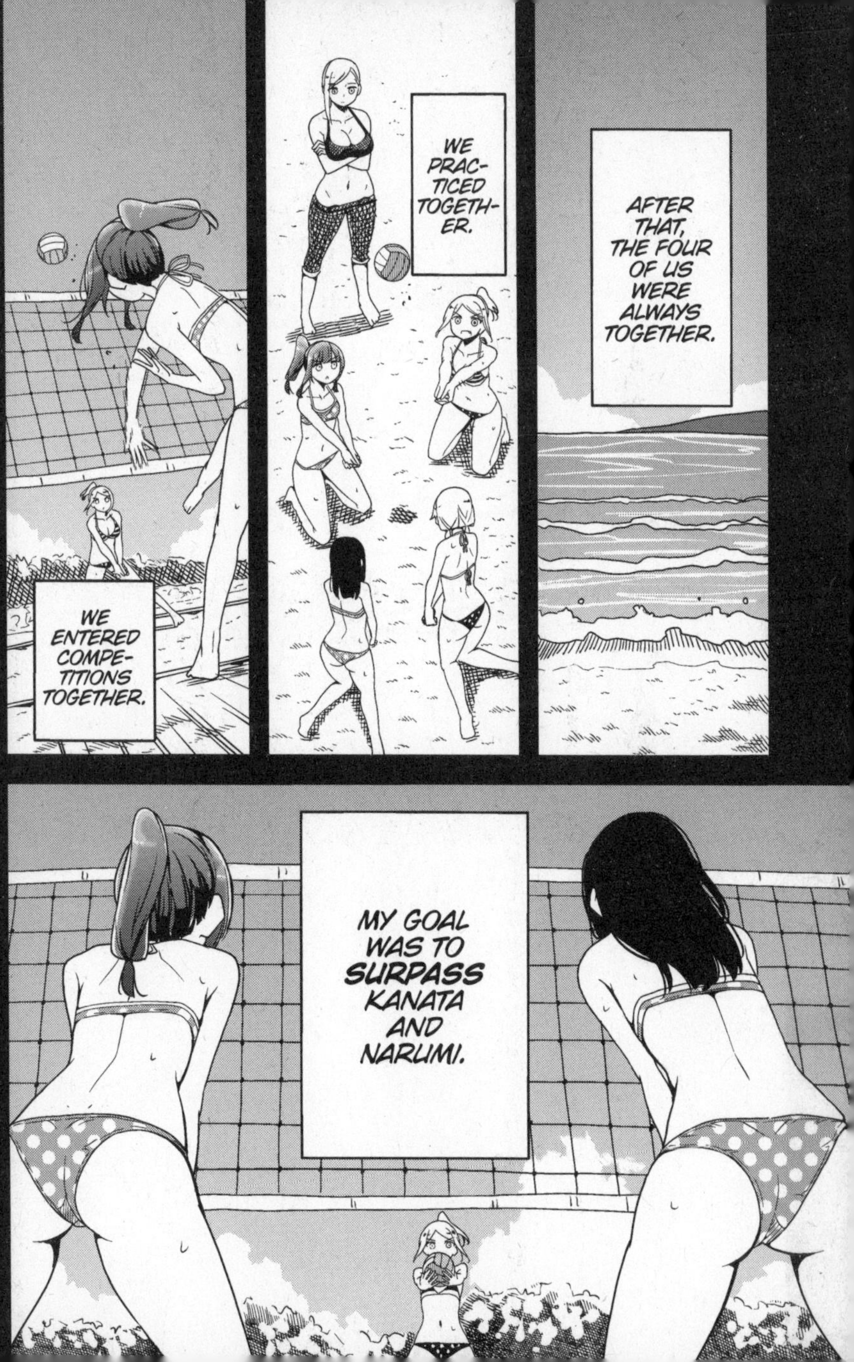
AFTER THAT, THE FOUR OF US WERE ALWAYS TOGETHER.
WE PRACTICED TOGETHER.
WE ENTERED COMPETITIONS TOGETHER.
MY GOAL WAS TO SURPASS KANATA AND NARUMI.

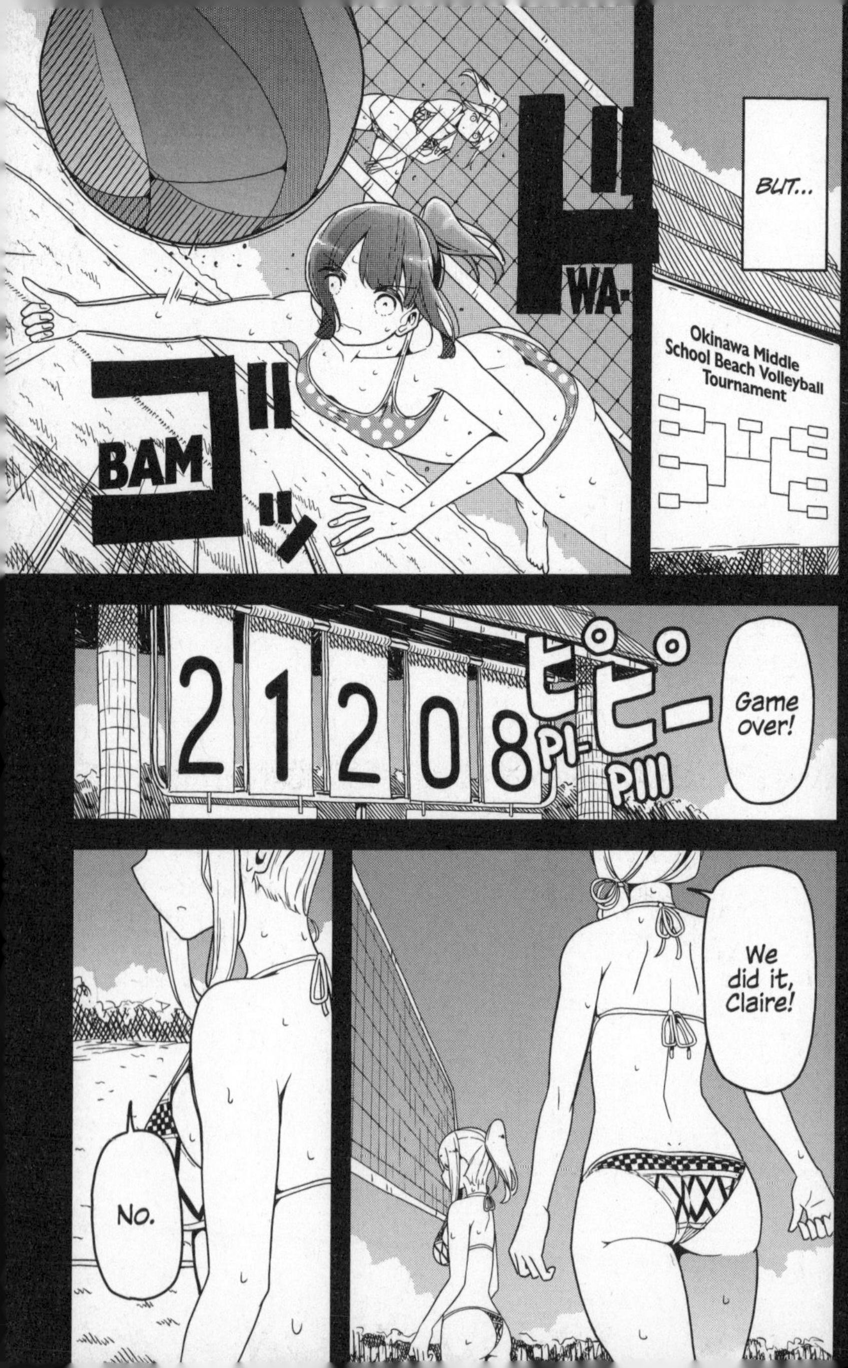
BUT...
Okinawa Middle School Beach Volleyball Tournament
WA-
BAM
Game over!
PI-
PIII
21208
We did it, Claire!
NO.

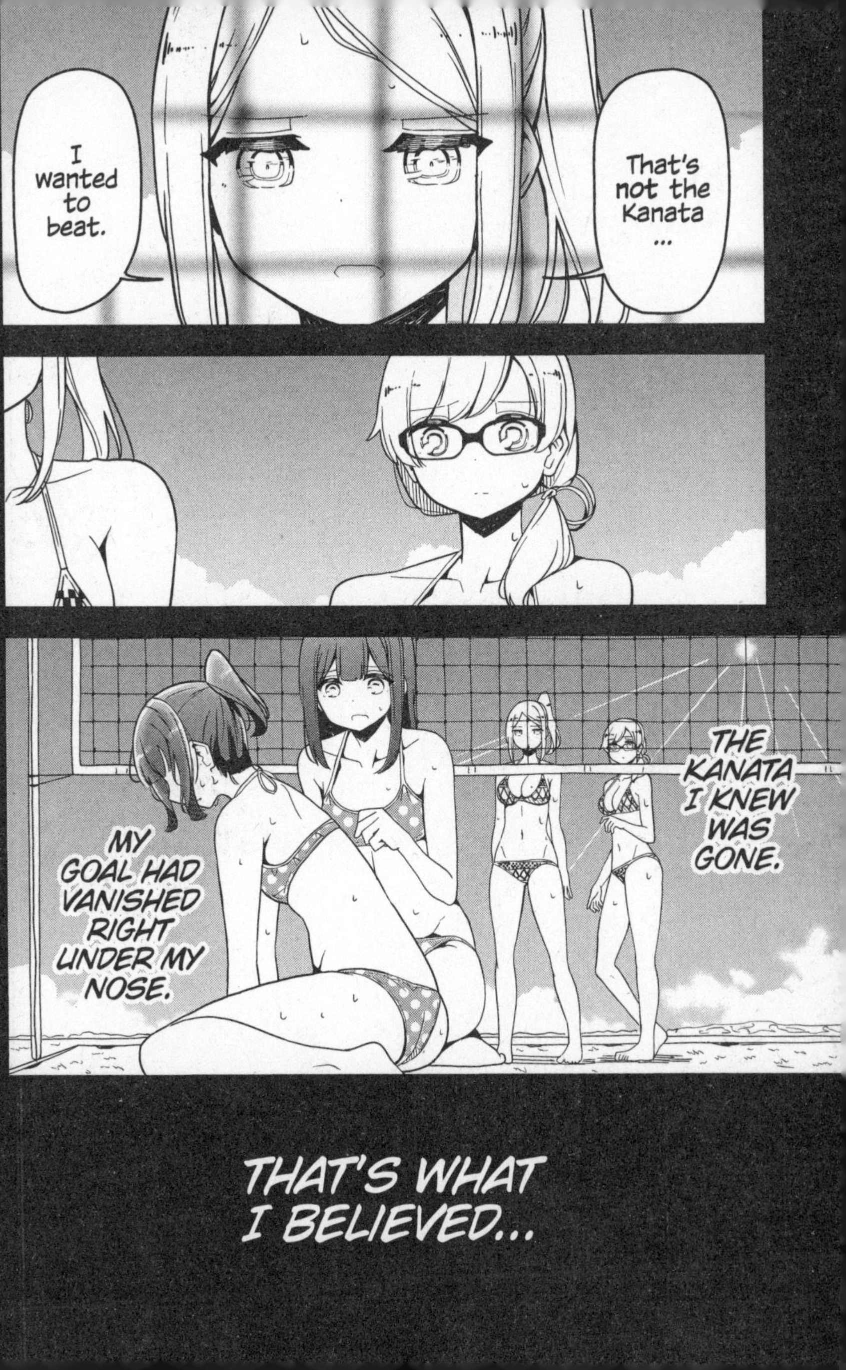
That's not the Kanata ...
I wanted to beat.
THE KANATA I KNEW WAS GONE.
MY GOAL HAD VANISHED RIGHT UNDER MY NOSE.
THAT'S WHAT I BELIEVED...

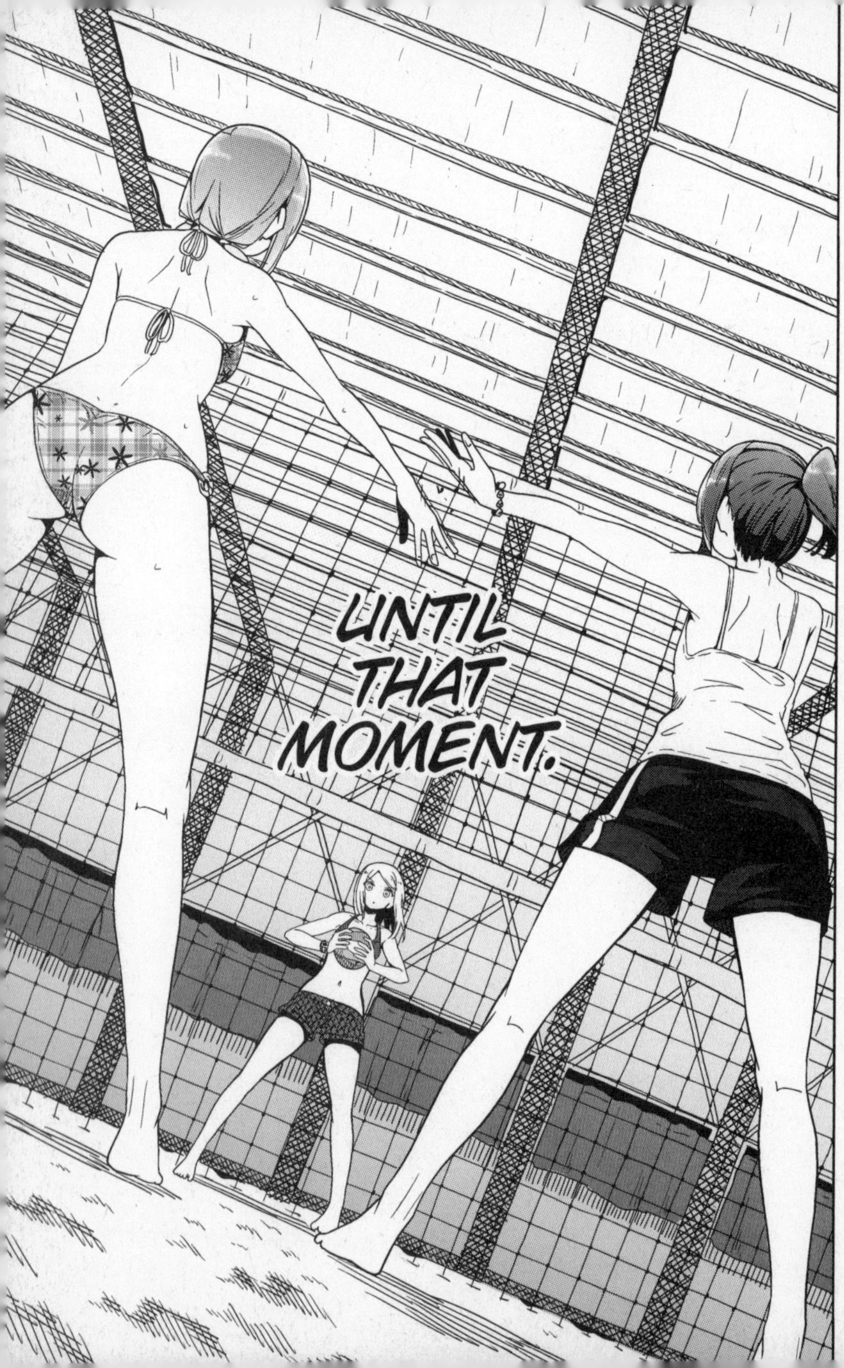
UNTIL THAT MOMENT.

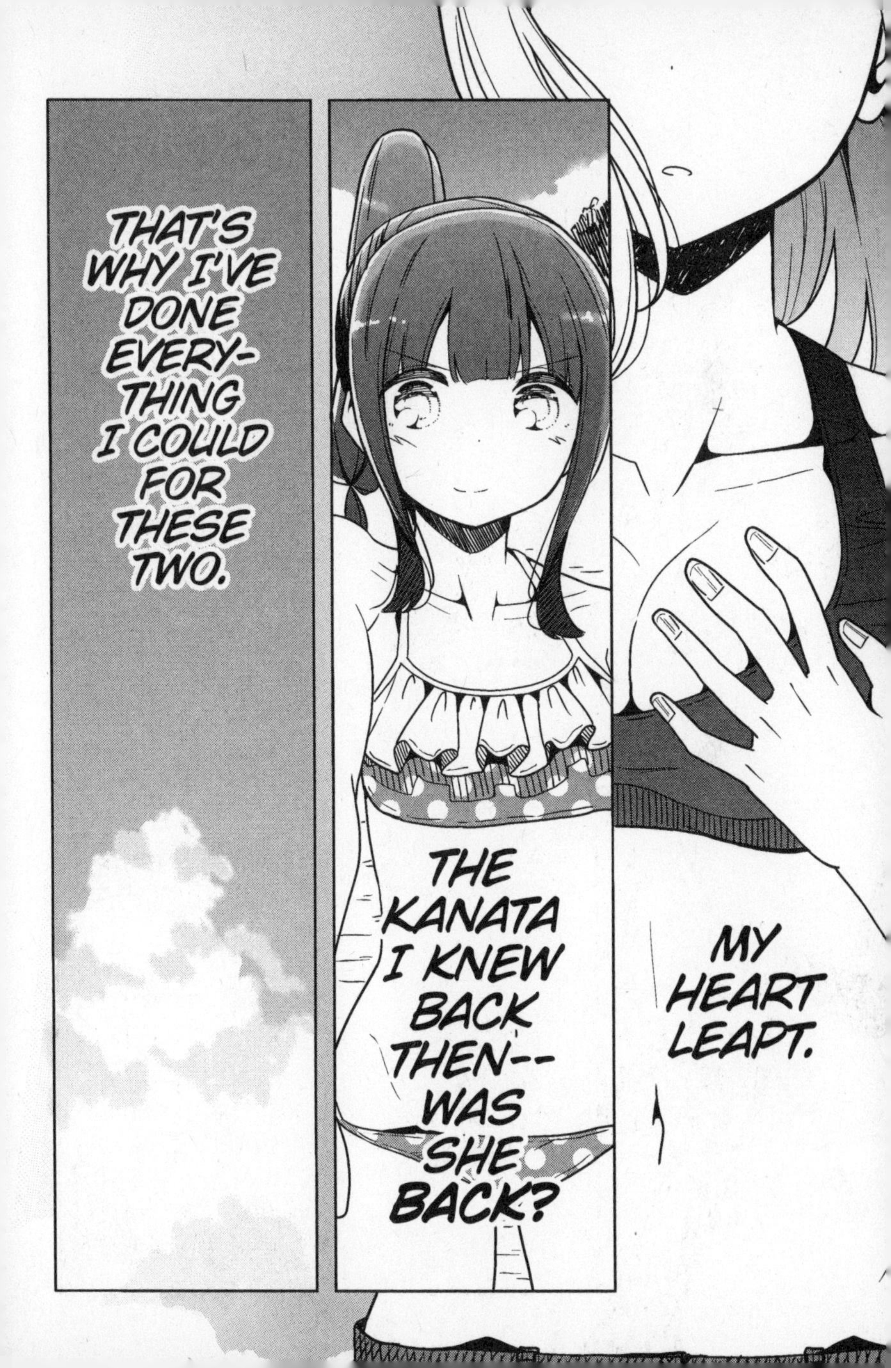
MY HEART LEAPT.
THE KANATA I KNEW BACK THEN--WAS SHE BACK?
THAT'S WHY I'VE DONE EVERYTHING I COULD FOR THESE TWO.

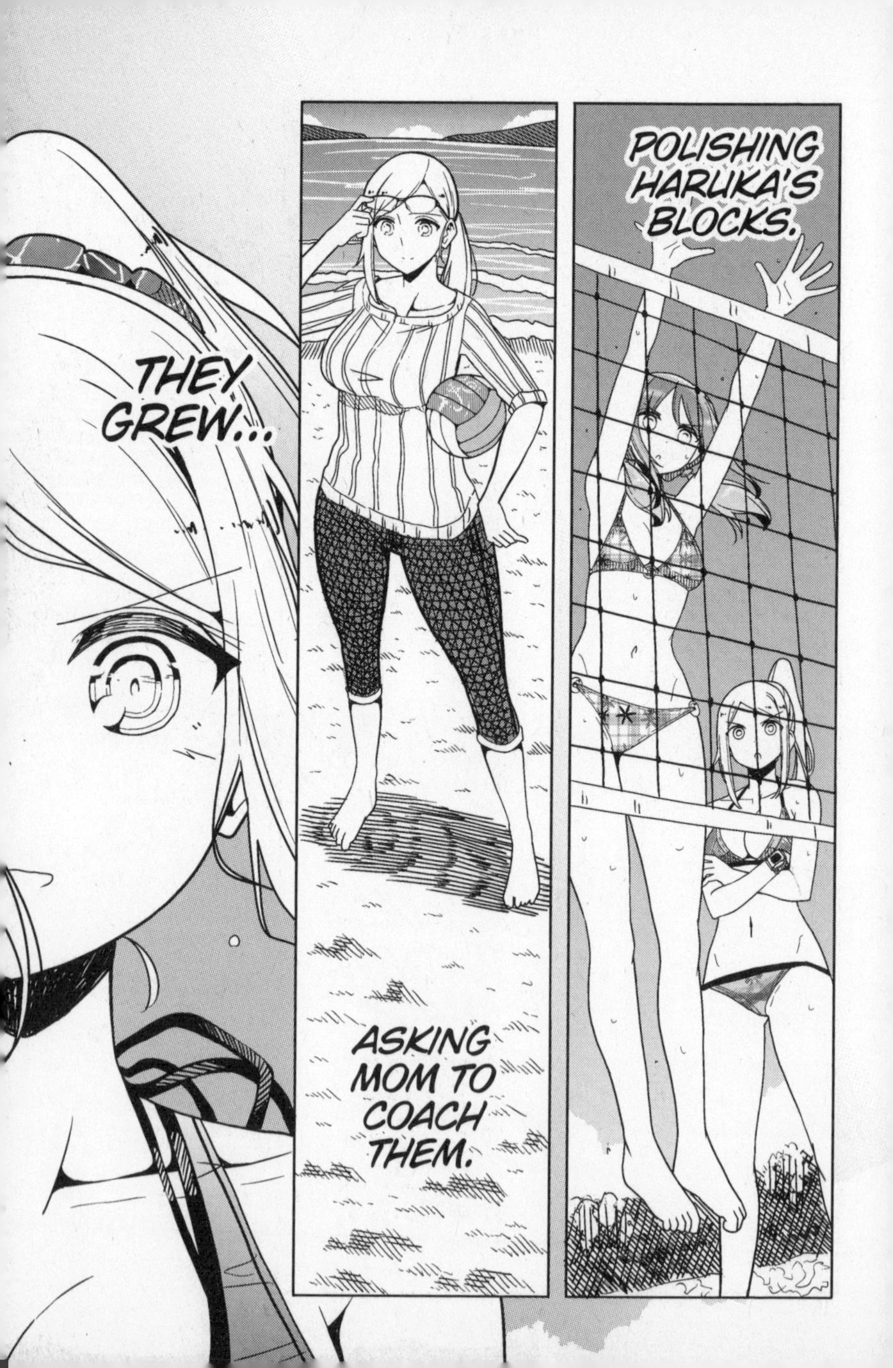
POLISHING HARUKA'S BLOCKS.
ASKING MOM TO COACH THEM.
THEY GREW...

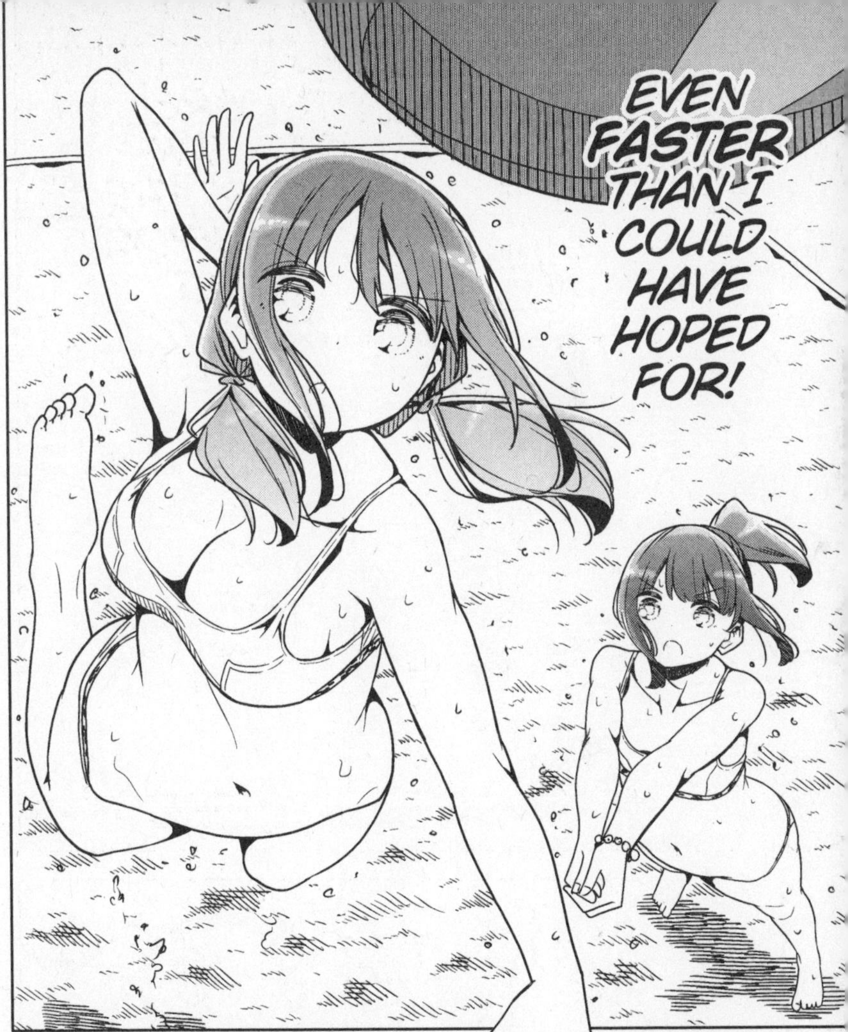
EVEN FASTER THAN I COULD HAVE HOPED FOR!
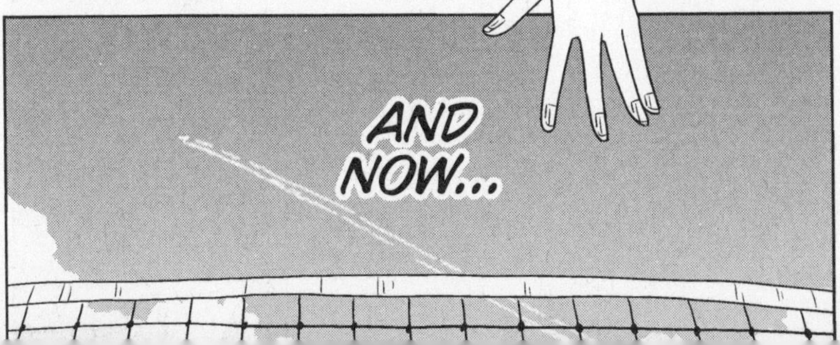
AND NOW...

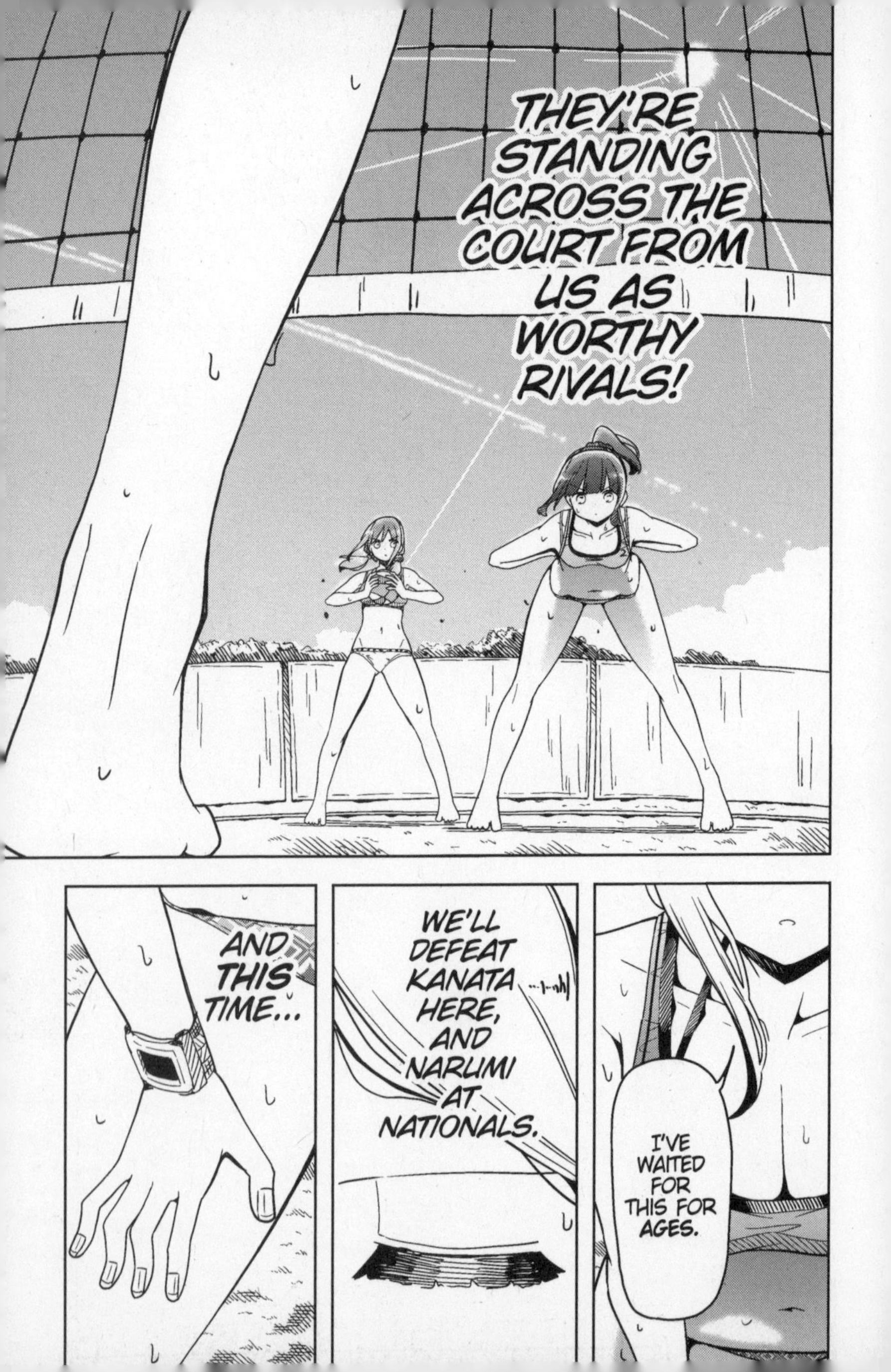
THEY'RE STANDING ACROSS THE COURT FROM US AS WORTHY RIVALS!
AND THIS TIME...
WE'LL DEFEAT KANATA HERE, AND NARUMI AT NATIONALS.
I'VE WAITED FOR THIS FOR AGES.

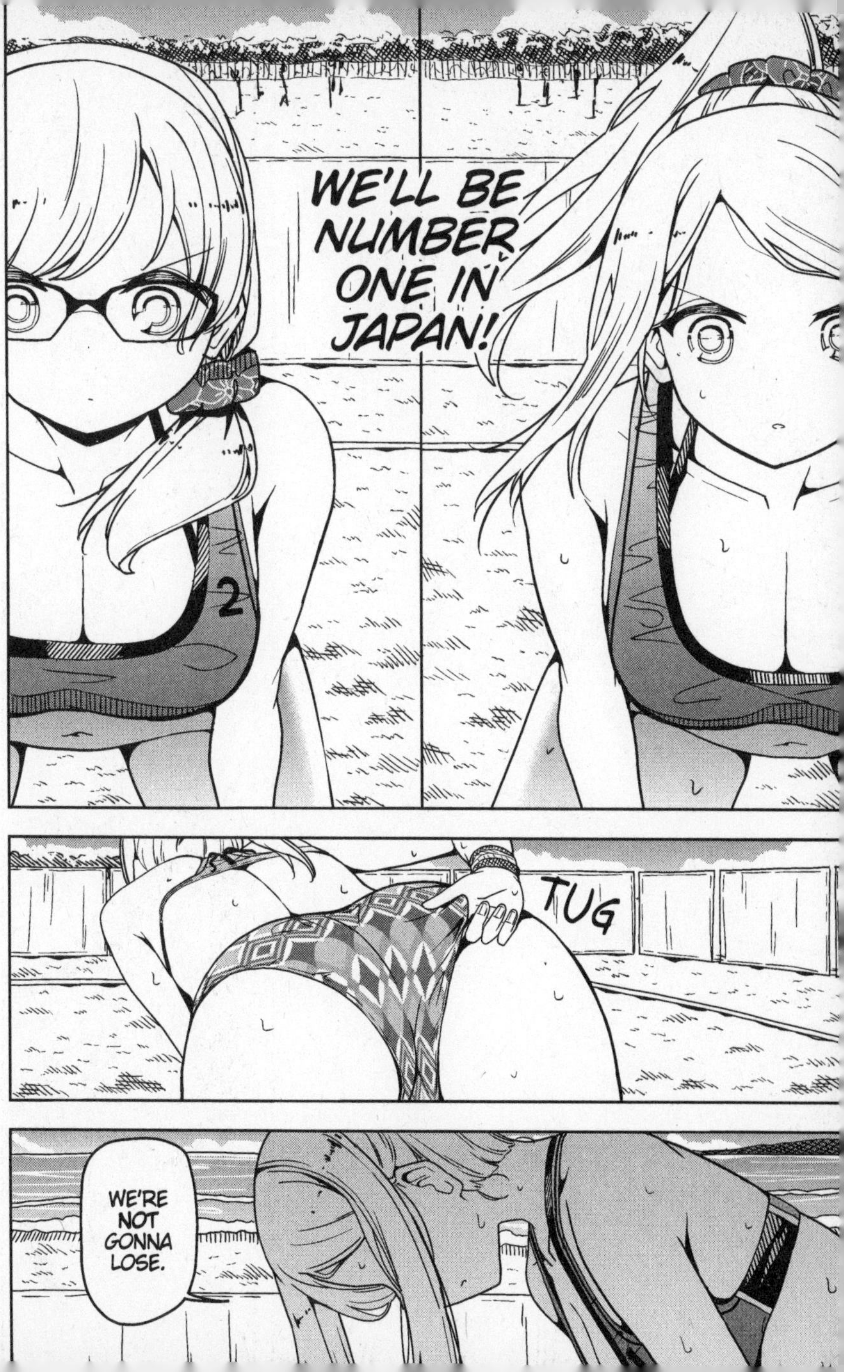
WE'LL BE NUMBER ONE IN JAPAN!
TUG
WE'RE NOT GONNA LOSE.

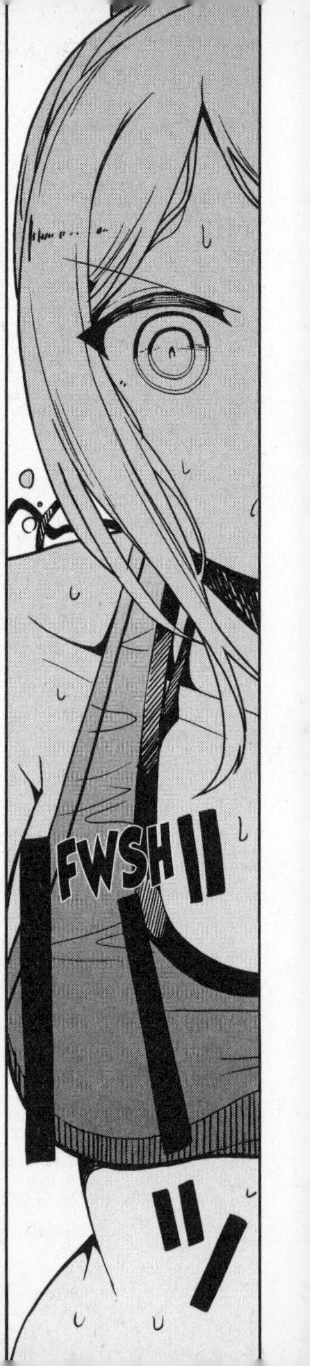
FWSH

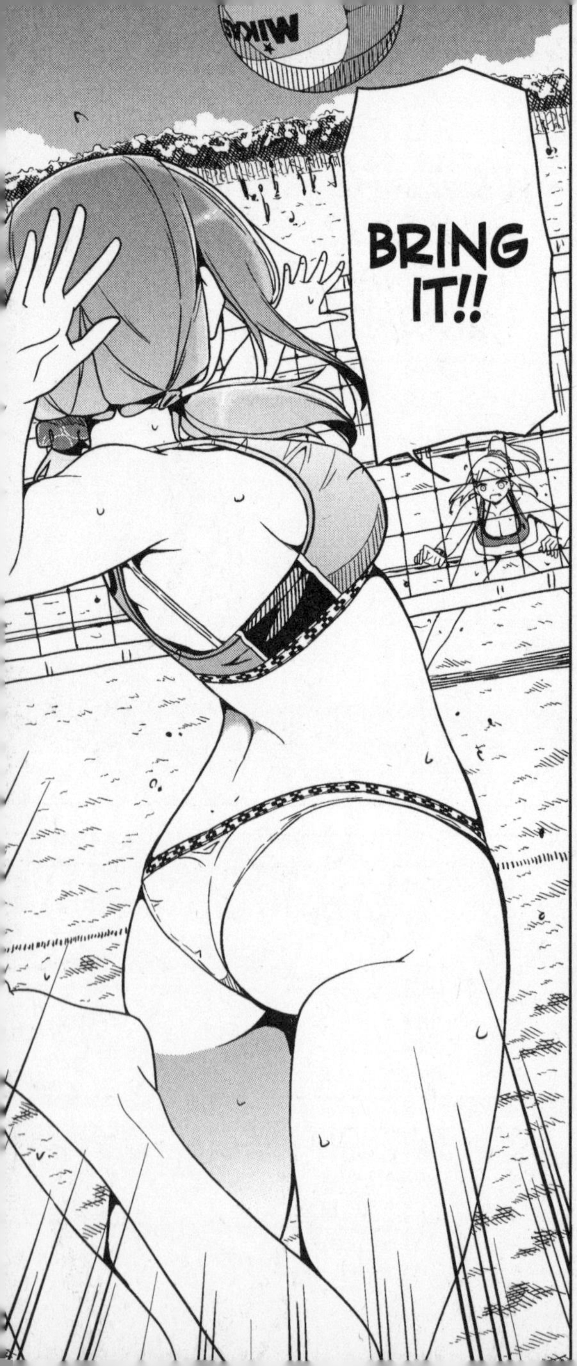
BRING IT!!

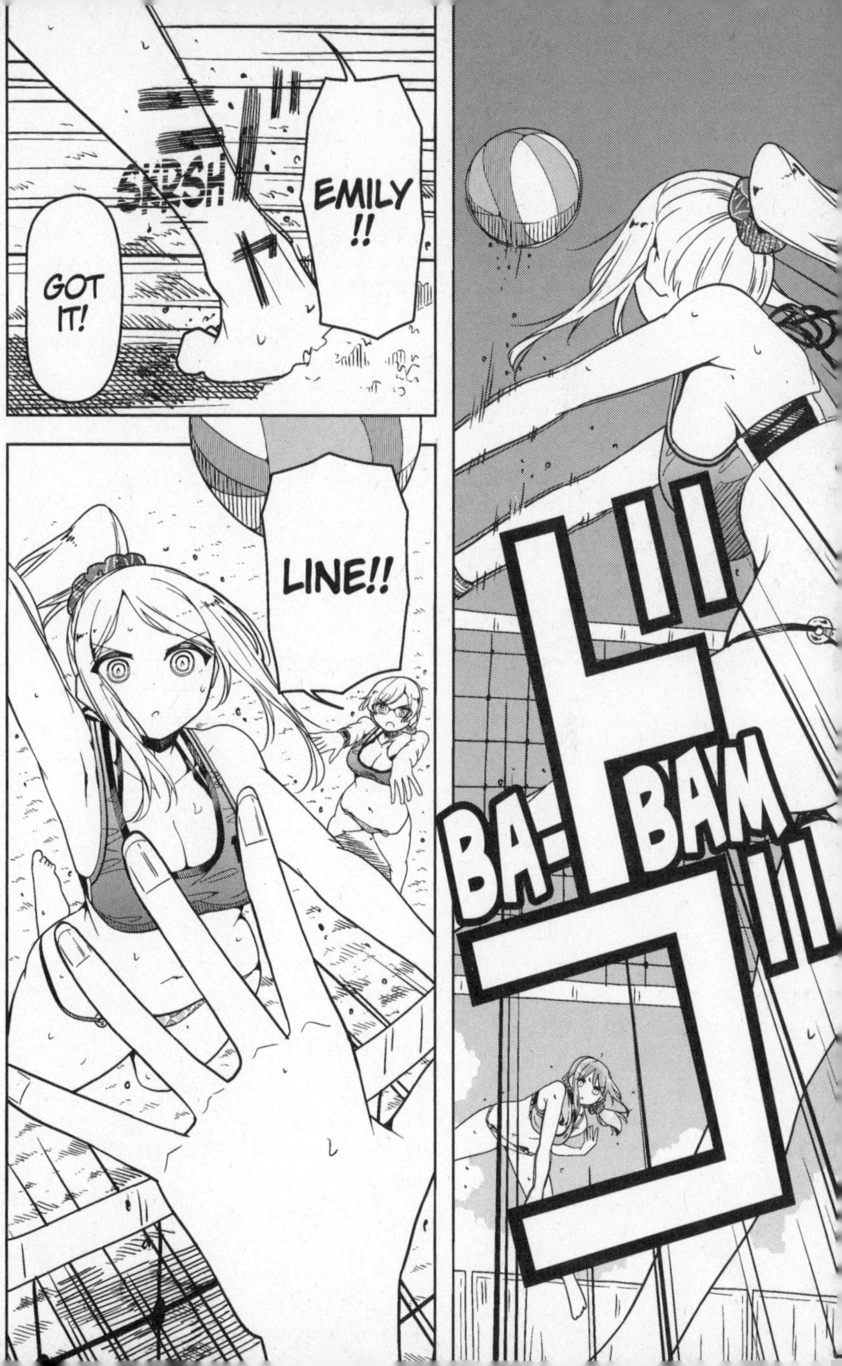
BA-BAM
EMILY!!
SKRSH
GOT IT!
LINE!!

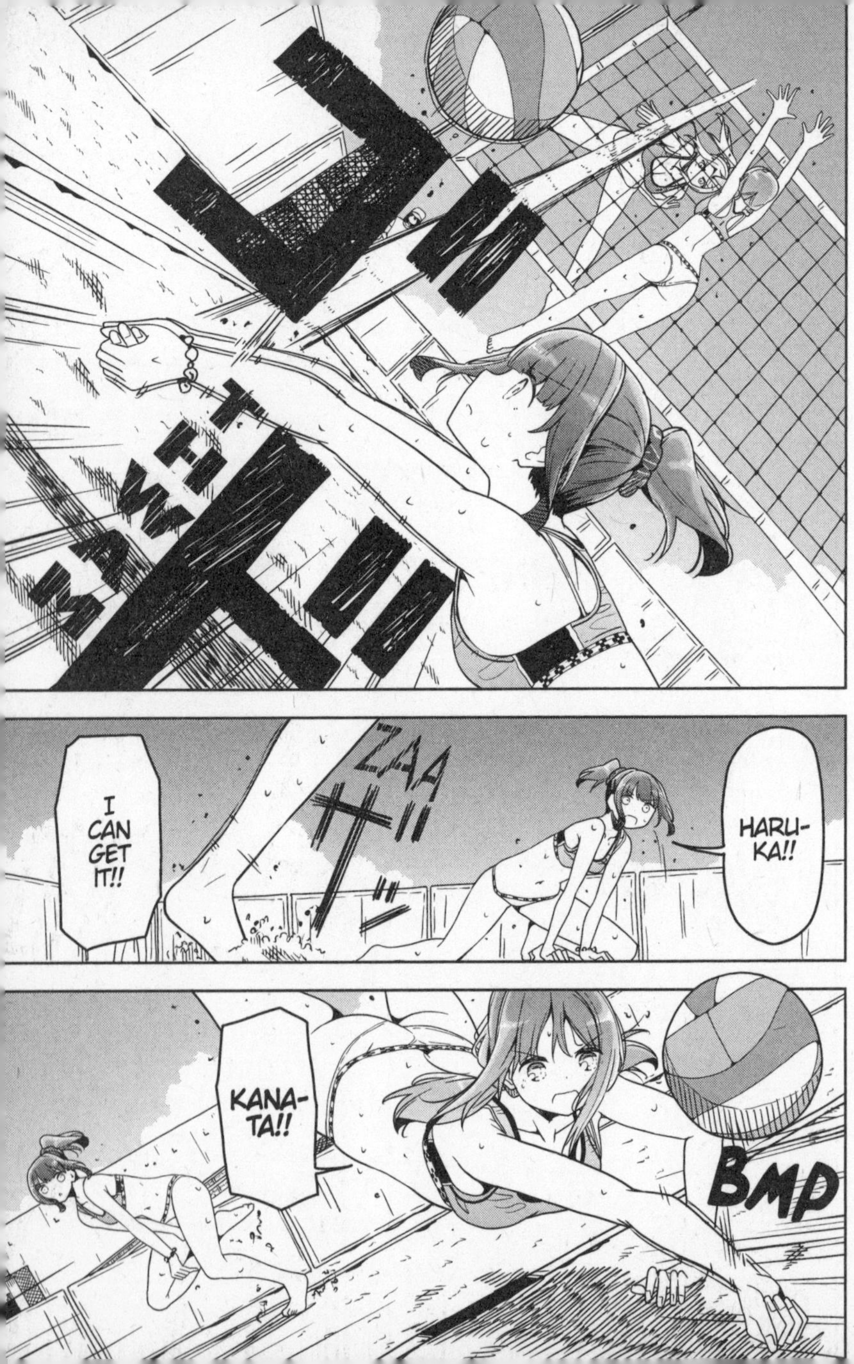
THWAM
HARU-KA!!
ZAA
I CAN GET IT!!
KANA-TA!!
BMP

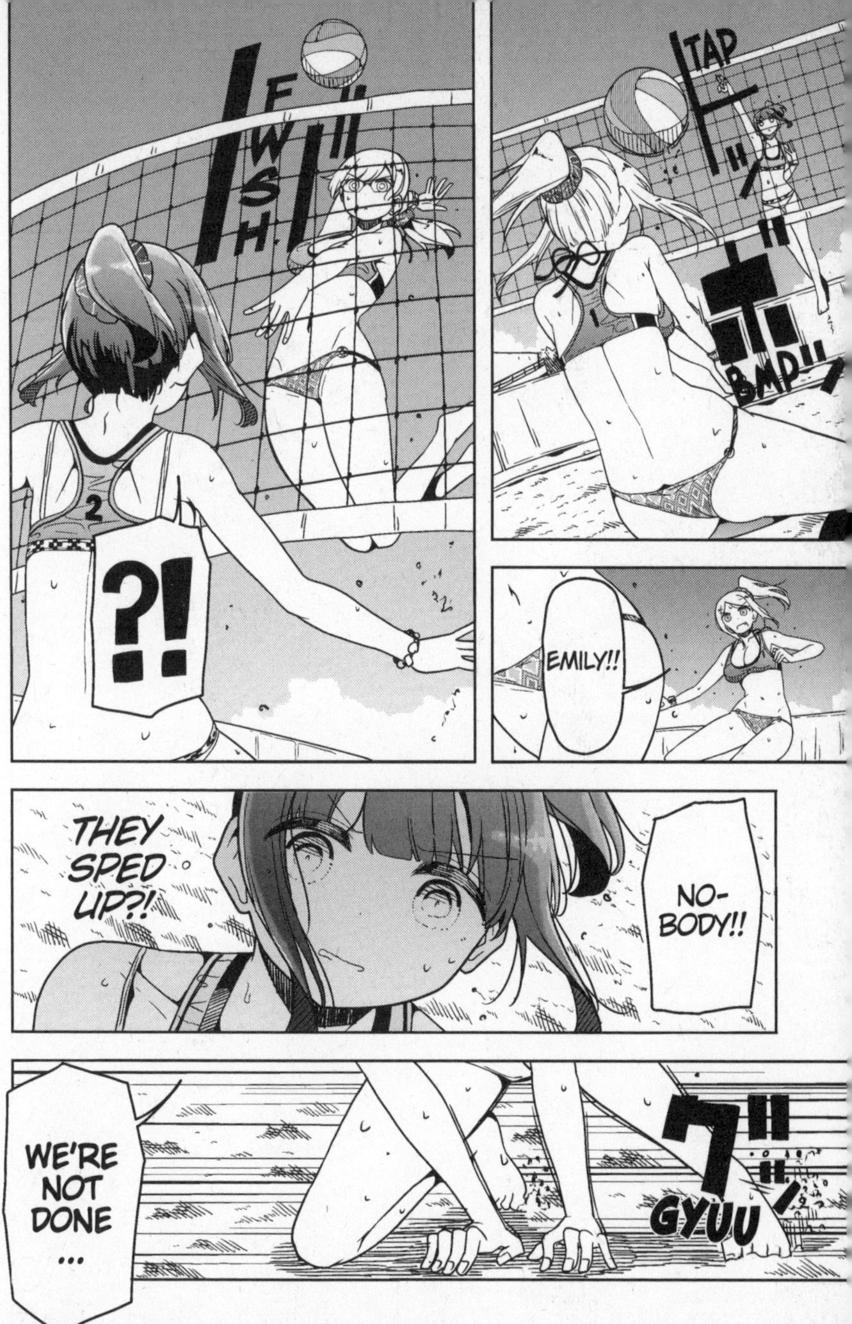
TAP
BMP!!
FWSH
?!
EMILY!!
NO-BODY!!
THEY SPED UP?!
WE'RE NOT DONE ...
GYUU

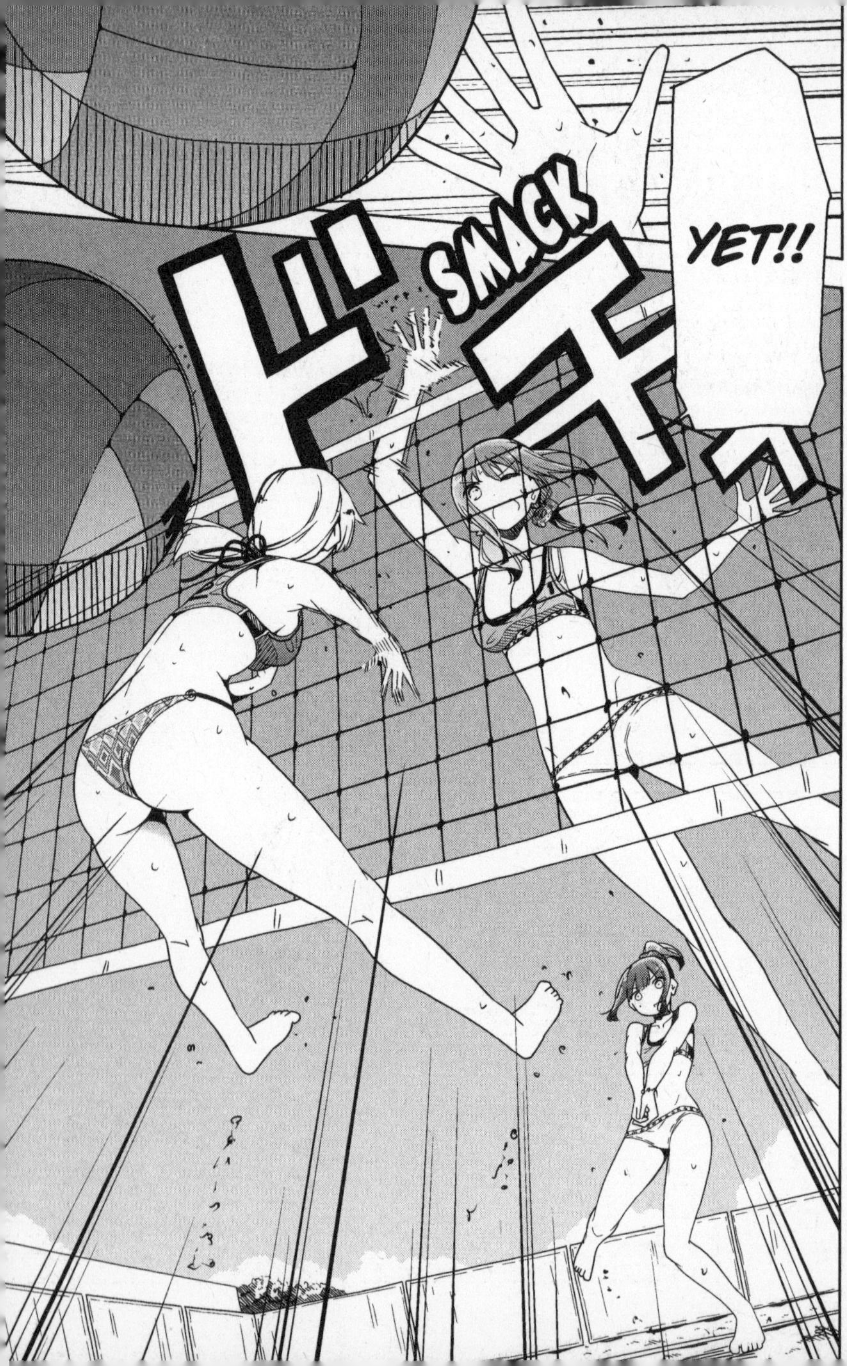
YET!!
SMACK

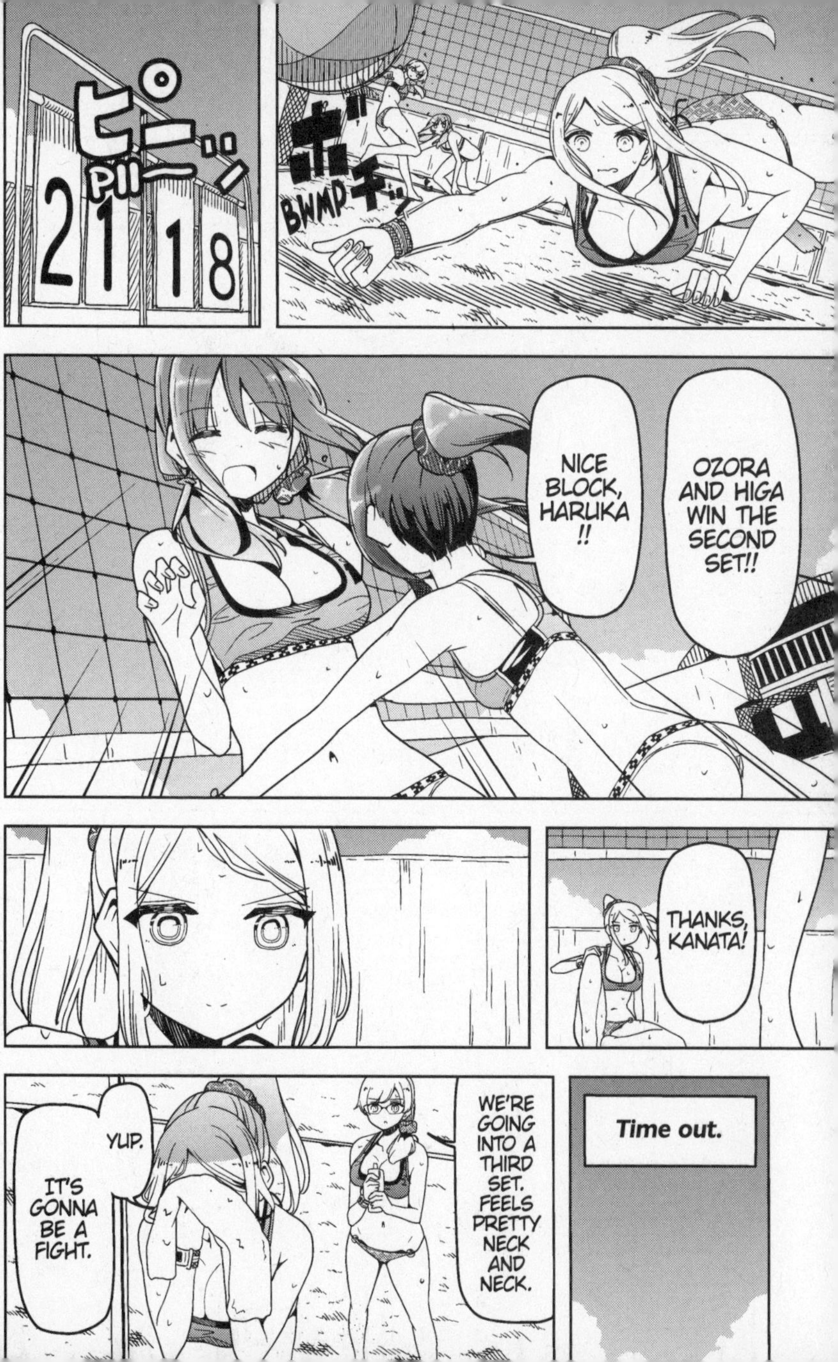
BWMP
PII—
21
18
OZORA AND HIGA WIN THE SECOND SET!!
NICE BLOCK, HARUKA!!
THANKS, KANATA!
Time out.
WE'RE GOING INTO A THIRD SET. FEELS PRETTY NECK AND NECK.
YUP.
IT'S GONNA BE A FIGHT.

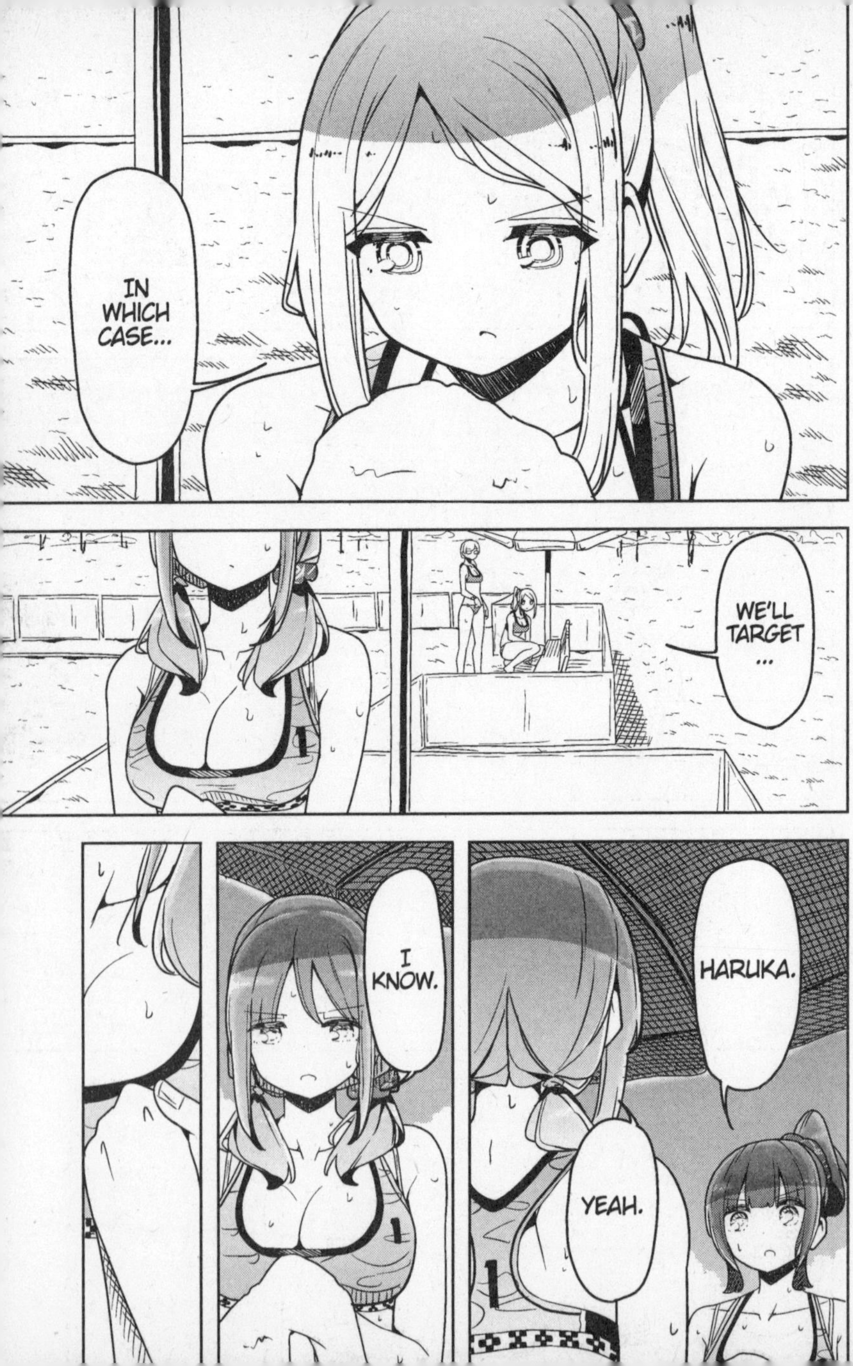
IN WHICH CASE...
WE'LL TARGET ...
HARUKA.
YEAH.
I KNOW.

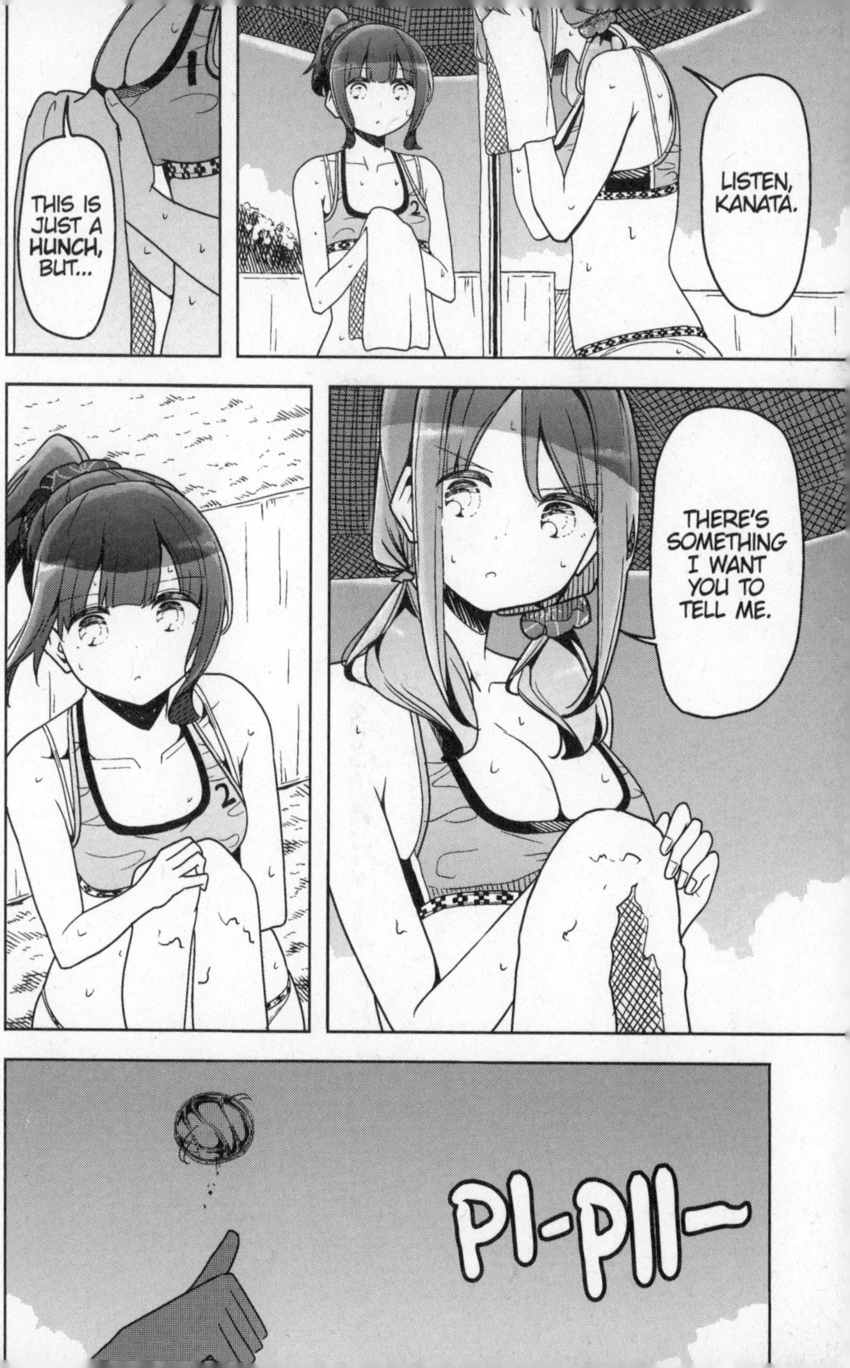
LISTEN, KANATA.
THIS IS JUST A HUNCH, BUT...
THERE'S SOMETHING I WANT YOU TO TELL ME.
PI-PII~

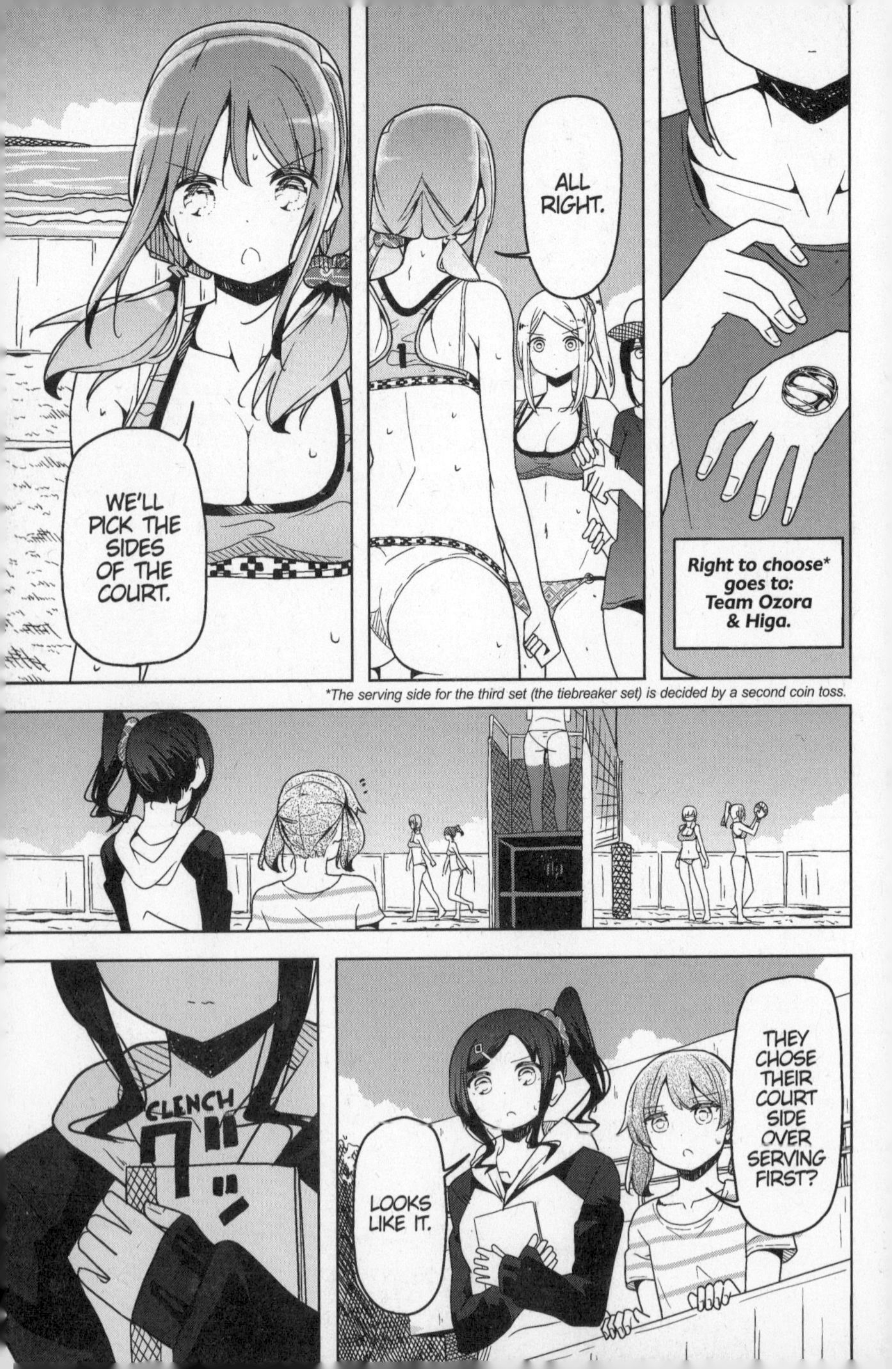
Right to choose* goes to: Team Ozora & Higa.
ALL RIGHT.
WE'LL PICK THE SIDES OF THE COURT.
THEY CHOSE THEIR COURT SIDE OVER SERVING FIRST?
LOOKS LIKE IT.
CLENCH

*The serving side for the third set (the tiebreaker set) is decided by a second coin toss.

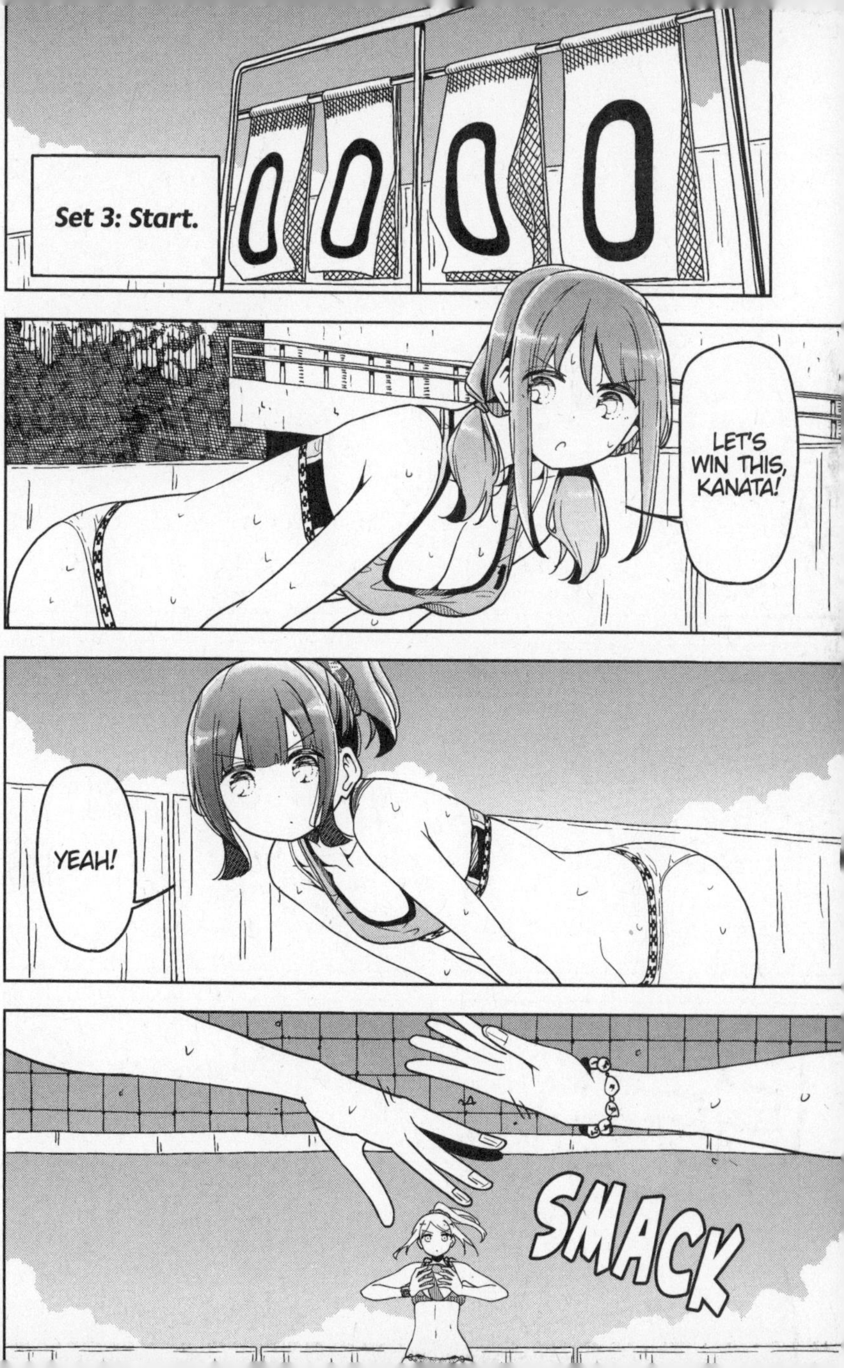
Set 3: Start.
LET'S WIN THIS, KANATA!
YEAH!
SMACK

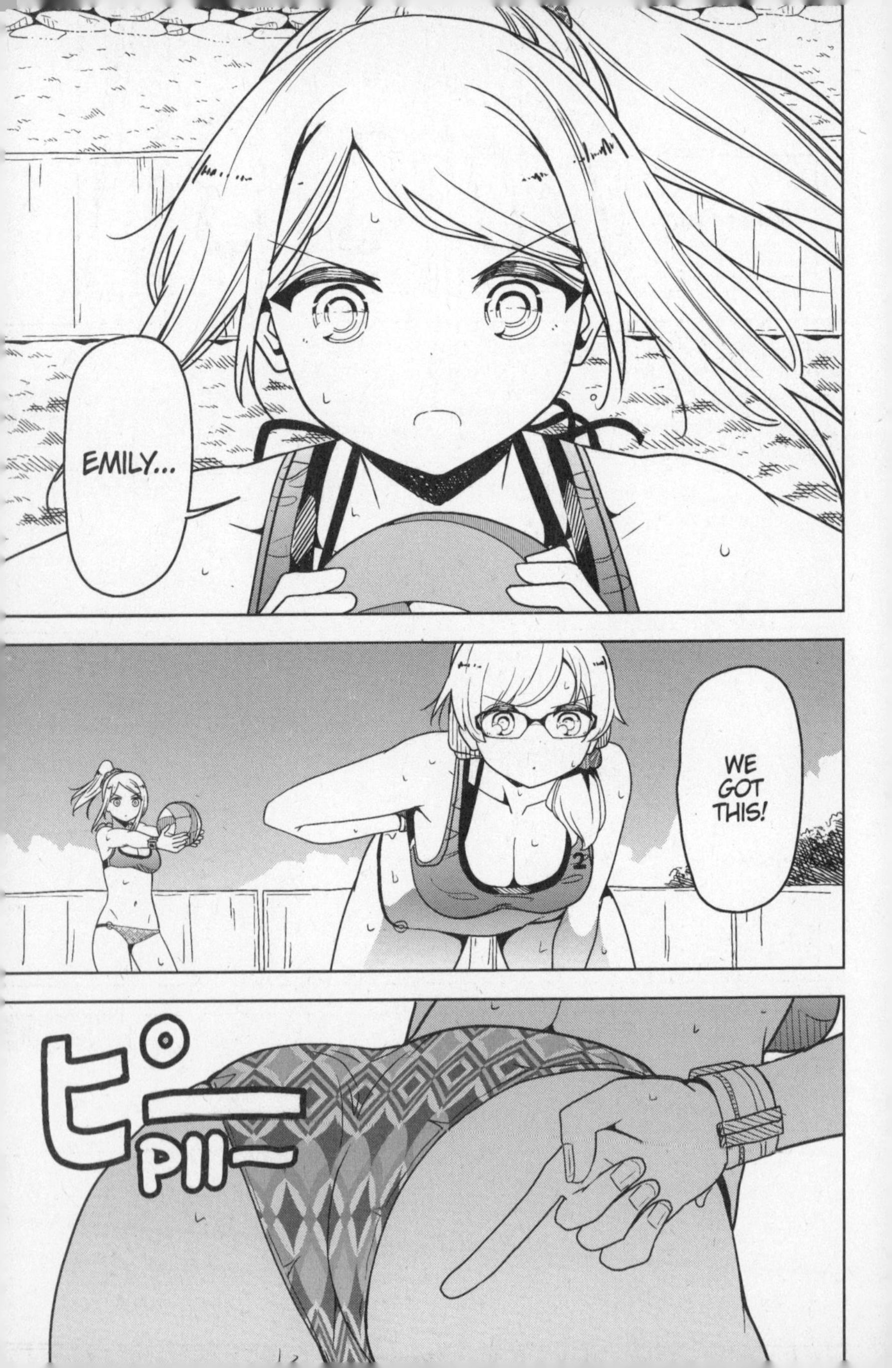
EMILY...
WE GOT THIS!
ピー
PII—

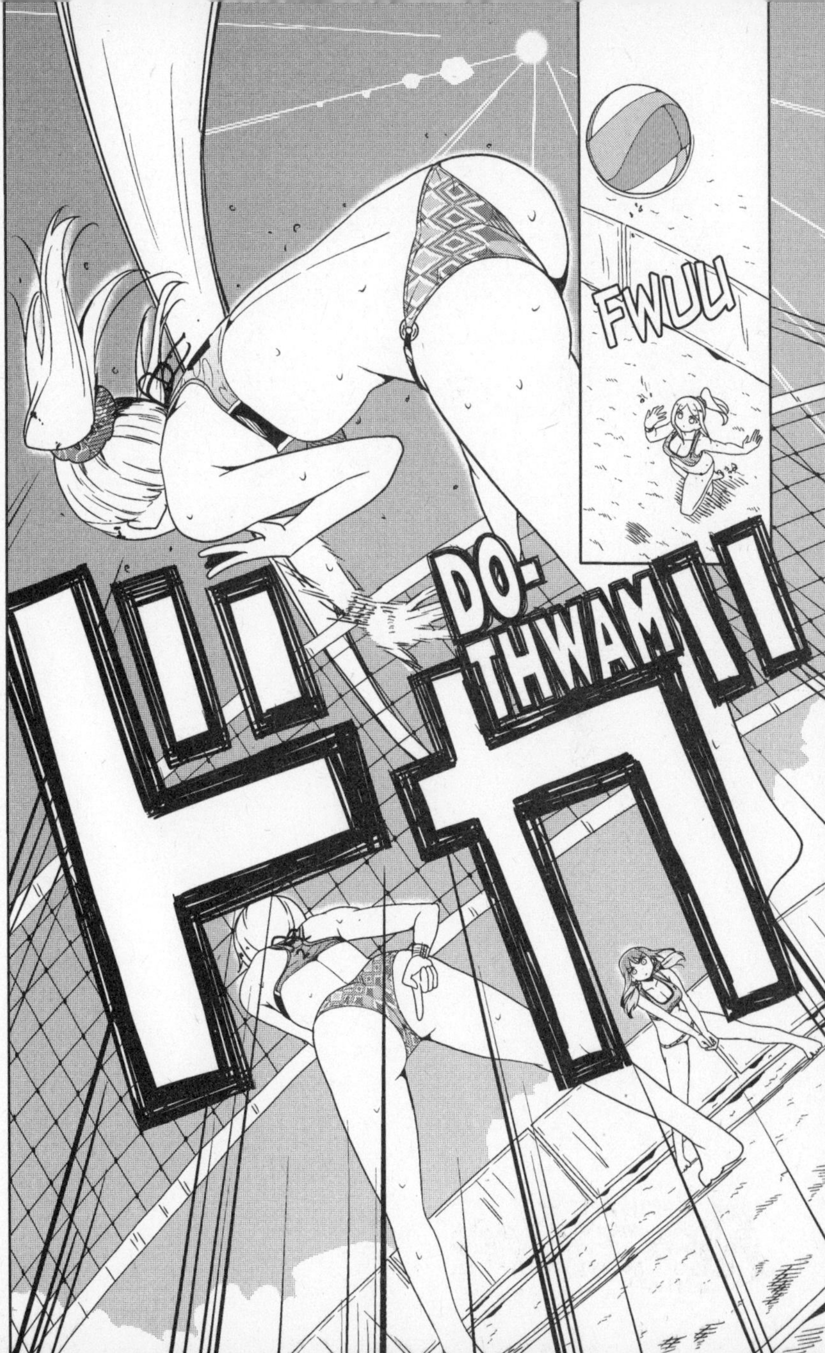
FWUU
DO-THWAM!!

Harukana★Receive

Presented by Nyoijizai

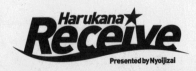

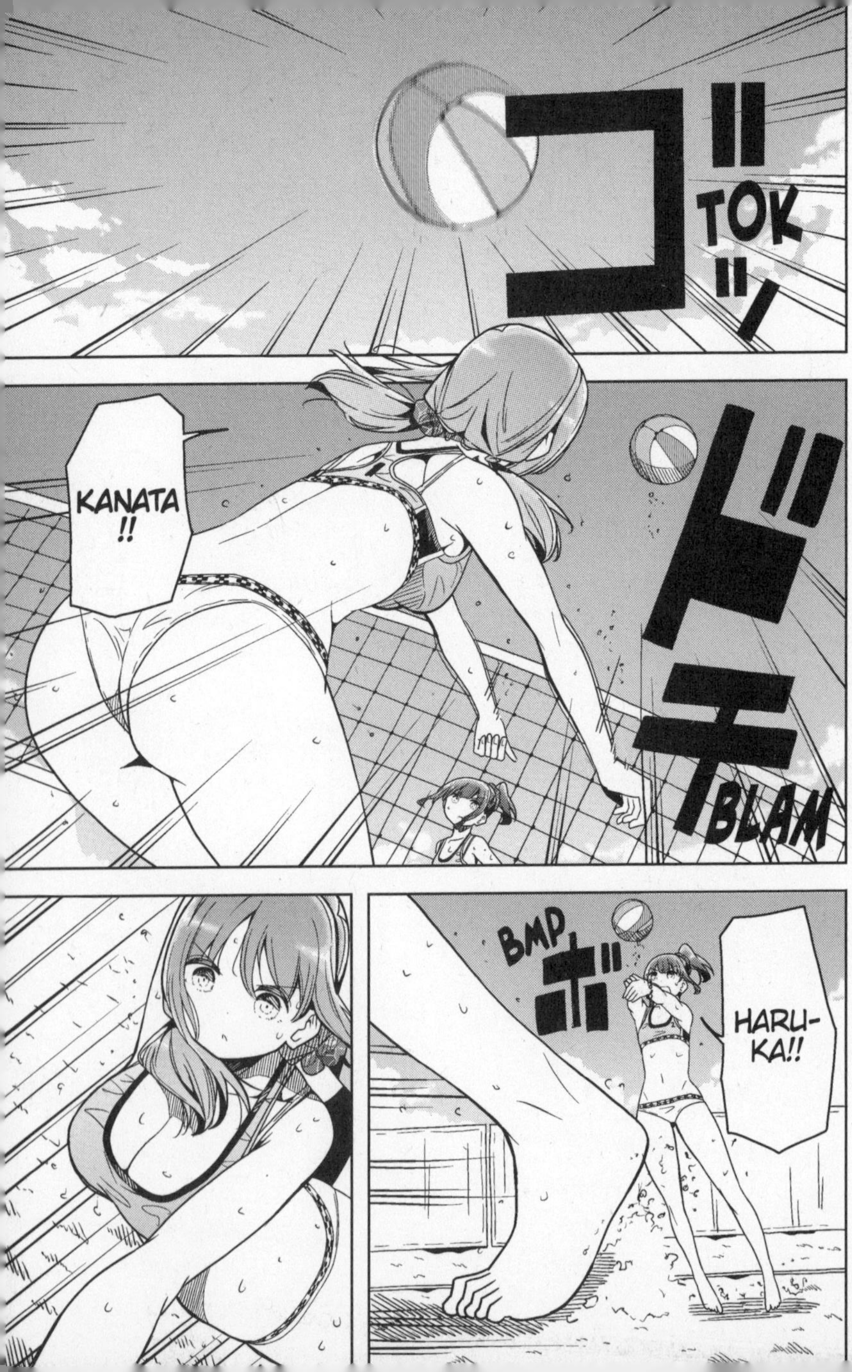
TOK
KANATA!!
BLAM
BMP
HARU-KA!!

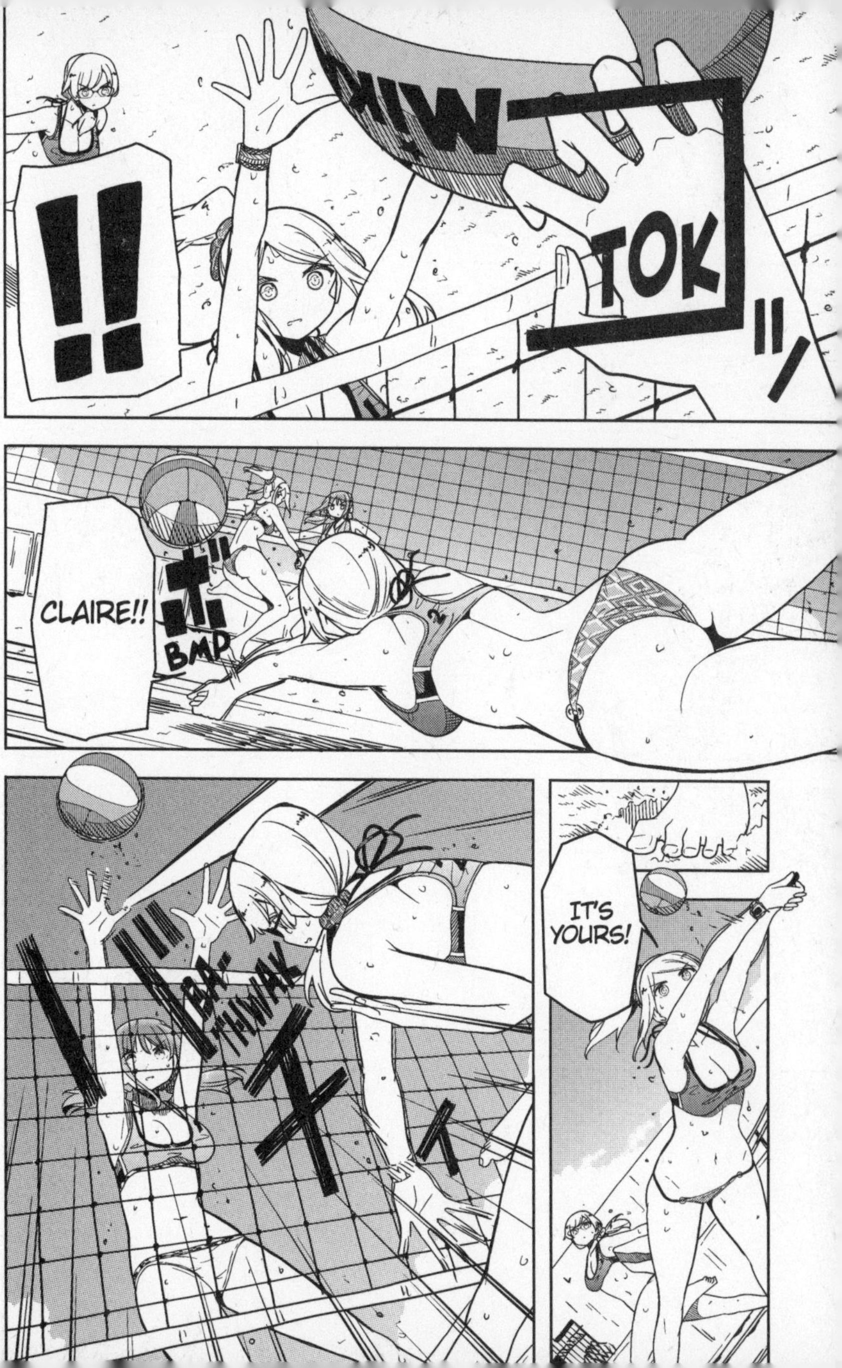
!!
TOK
CLAIRE!!
BMP
IT'S YOURS!
BA-THWAK

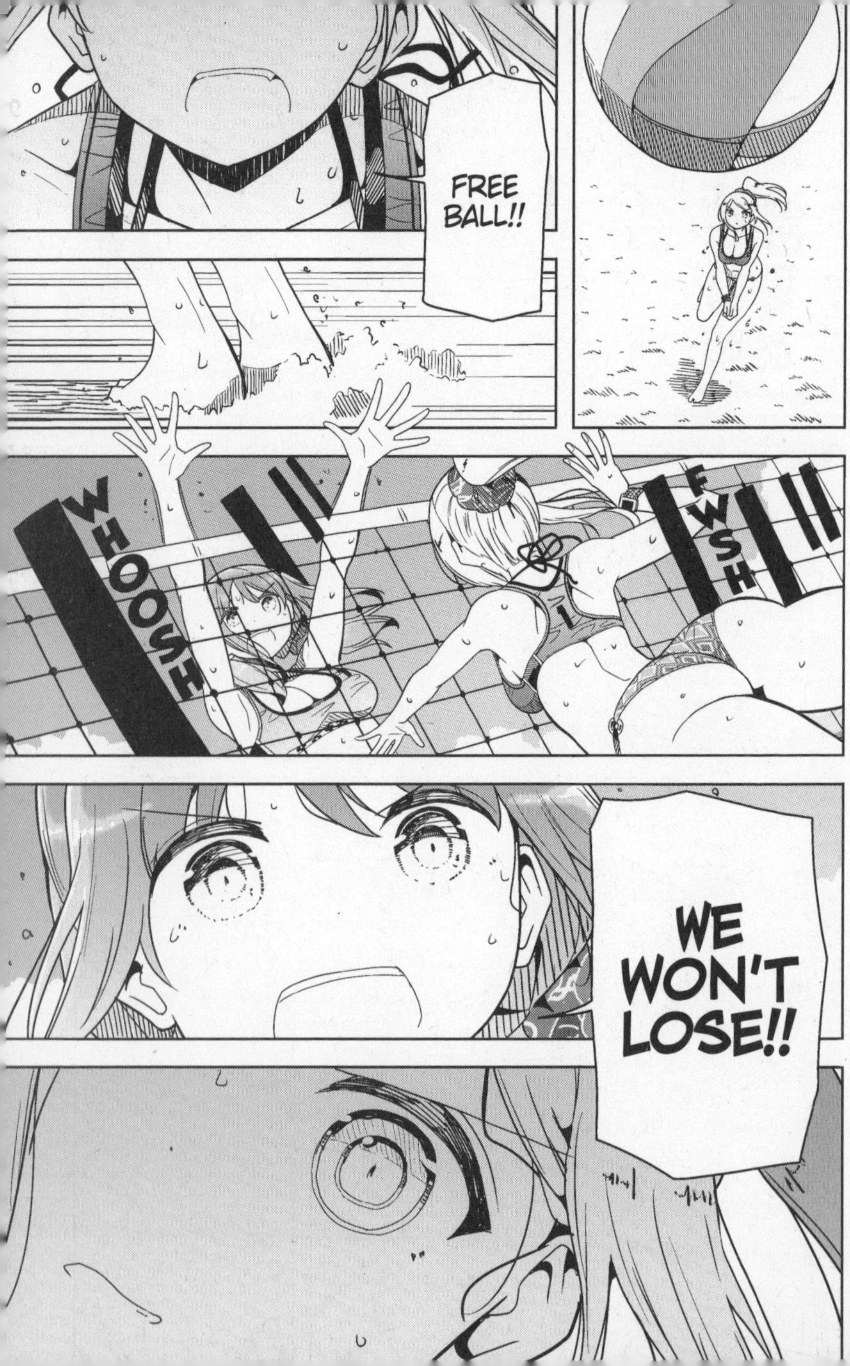
FREE BALL!!
FWSH
WHOOSH
WE WON'T LOSE!!

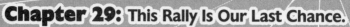

Chapter 29: This Rally Is Our Last Chance.

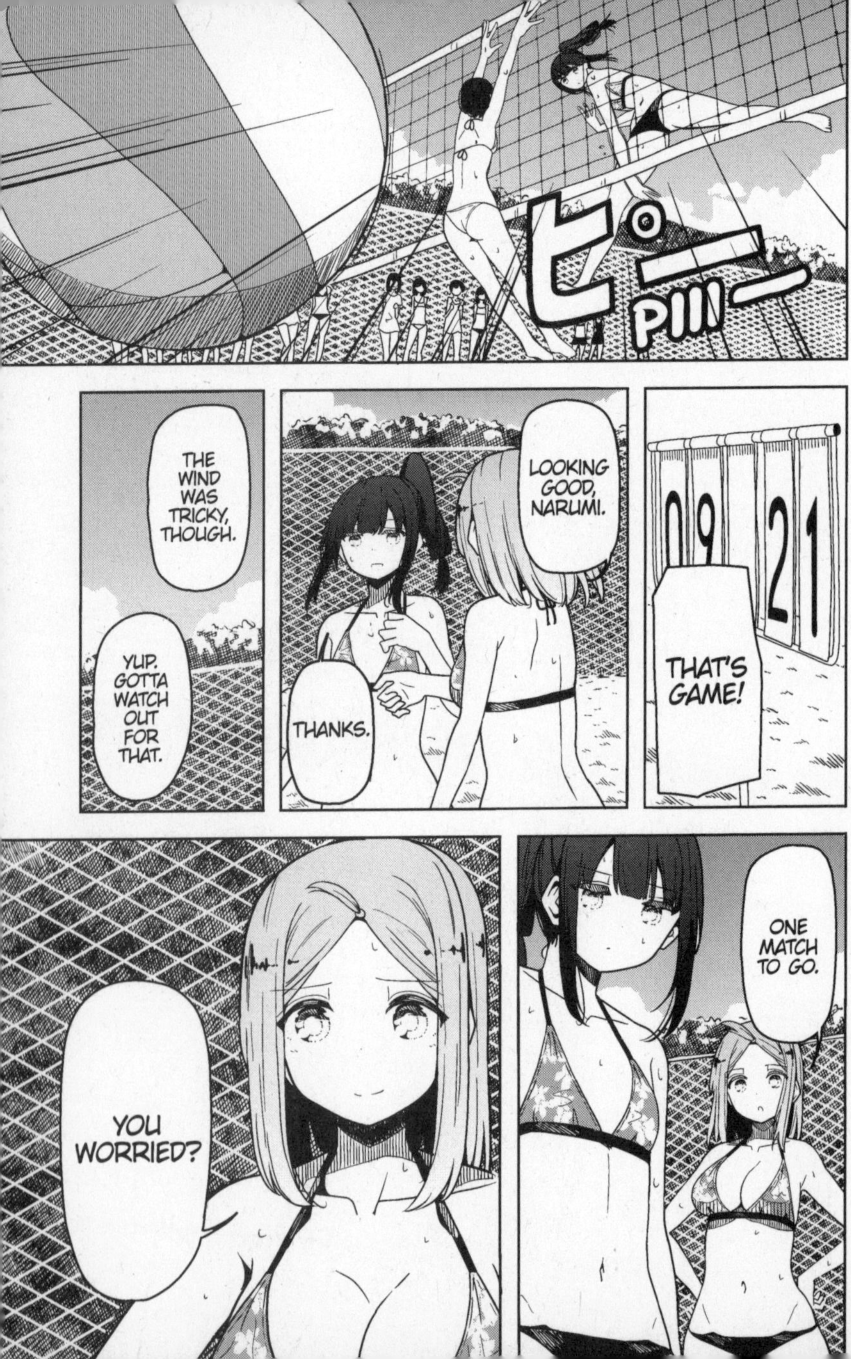
ピーー
PIII
THAT'S GAME!
LOOKING GOOD, NARUMI.
THANKS.
THE WIND WAS TRICKY, THOUGH.
YUP. GOTTA WATCH OUT FOR THAT.
ONE MATCH TO GO.
YOU WORRIED?

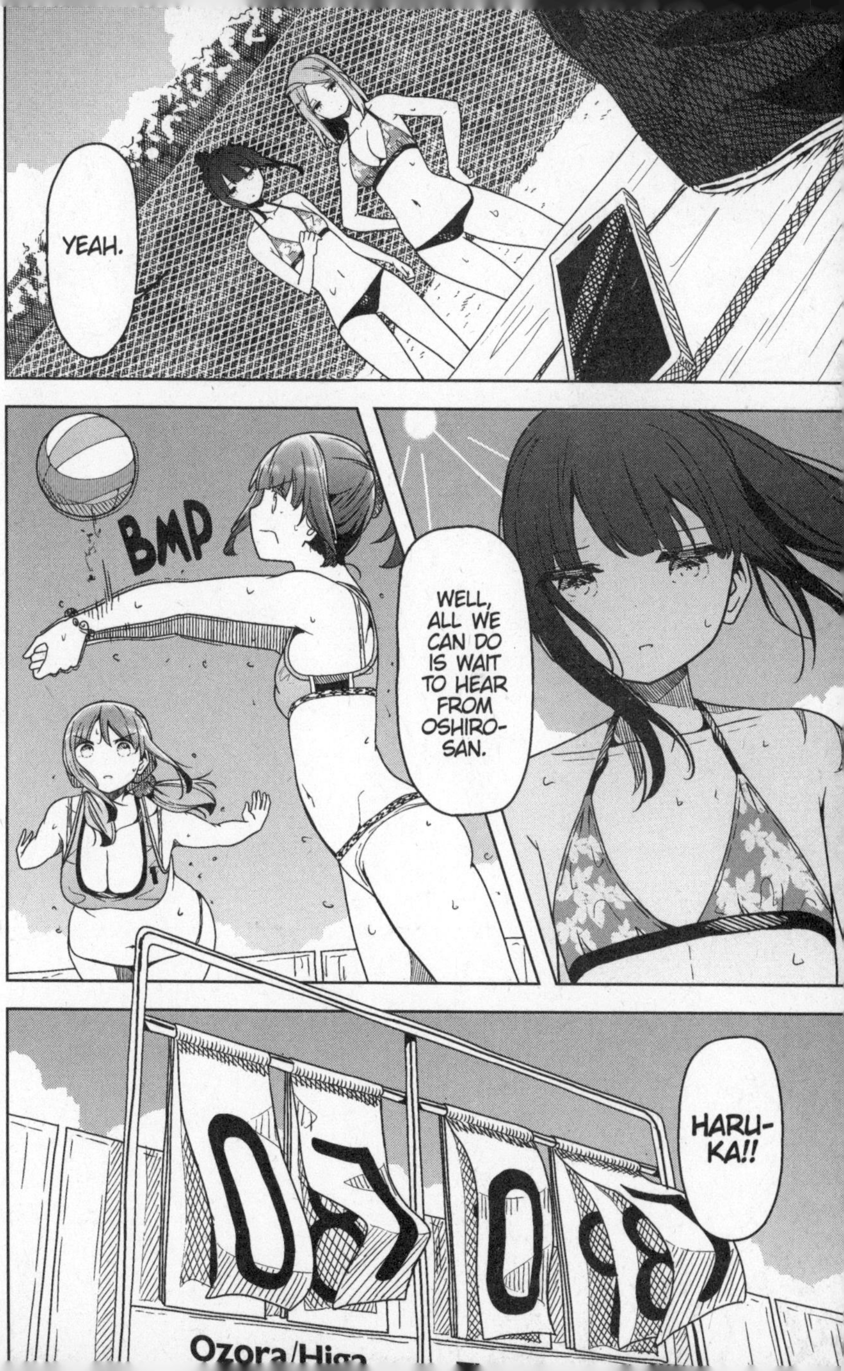
YEAH.
WELL, ALL WE CAN DO IS WAIT TO HEAR FROM OSHIRO-SAN.
BMP
HARU-KA!!
Ozora/Higa

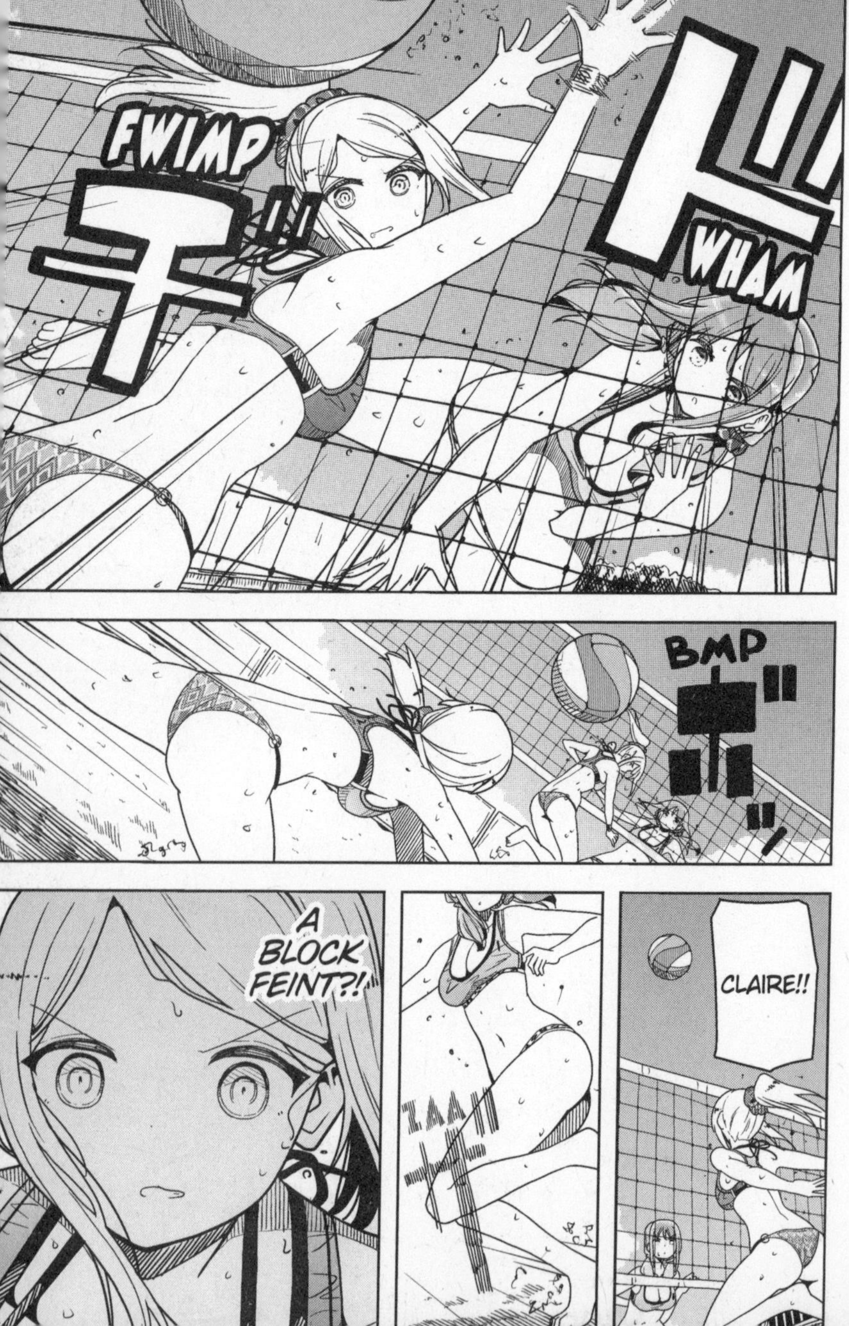
WHAM
FWIMP
BMP
CLAIRE!!
A BLOCK FEINT?!

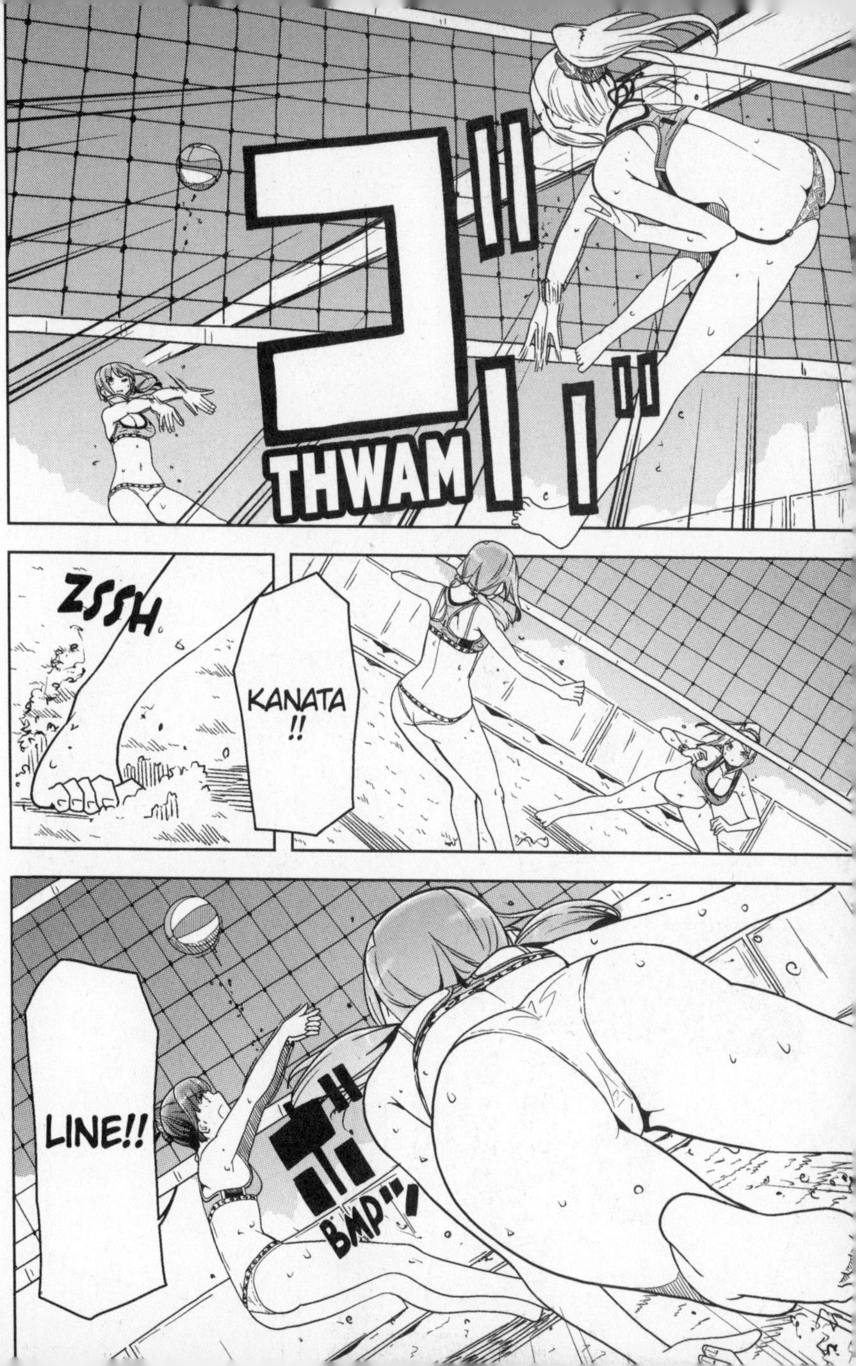
THWAM
KANATA !!
ZSSH
LINE!!
BMP!!

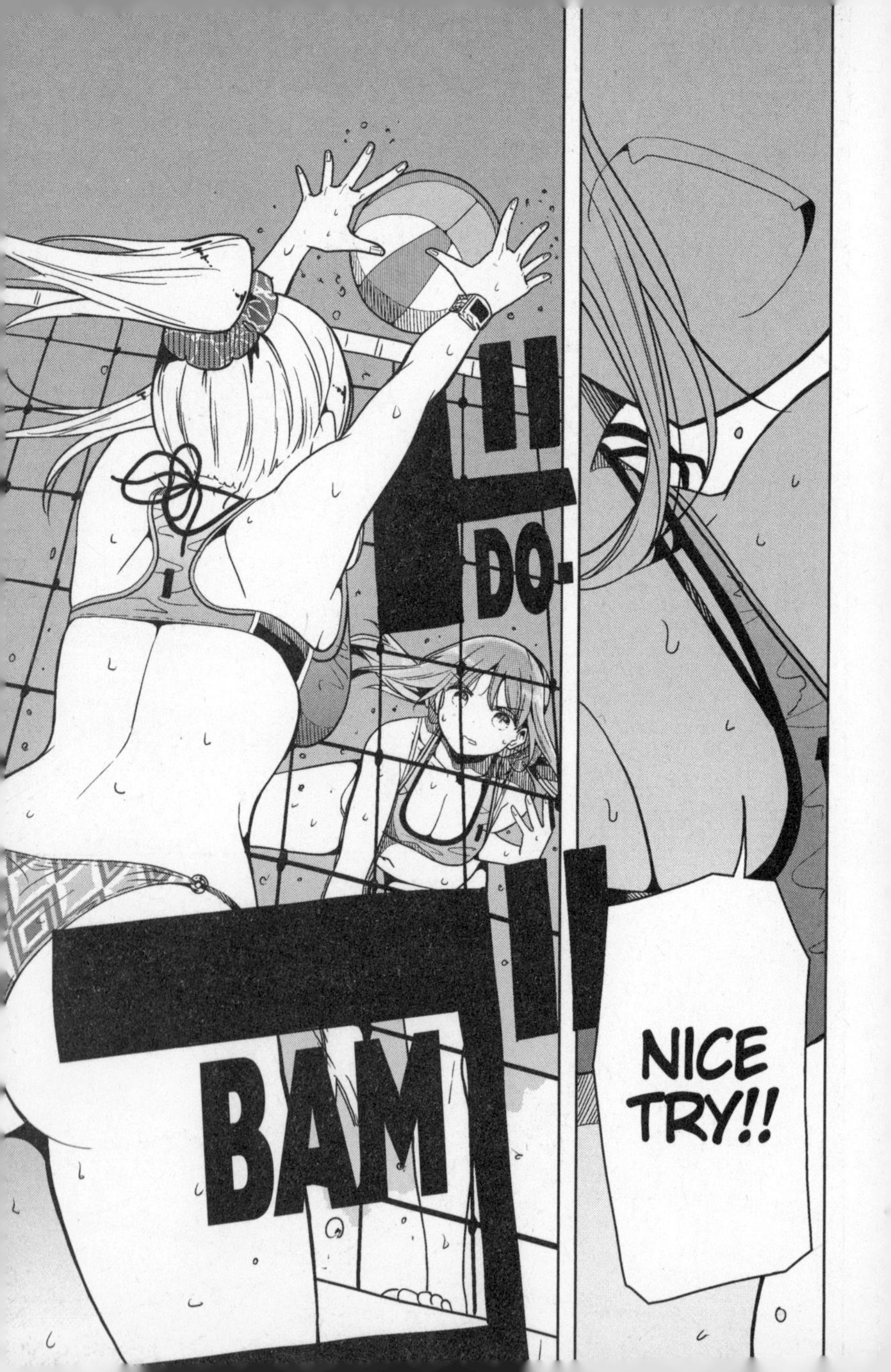
NICE TRY!!
HI-DO-!!
BAM

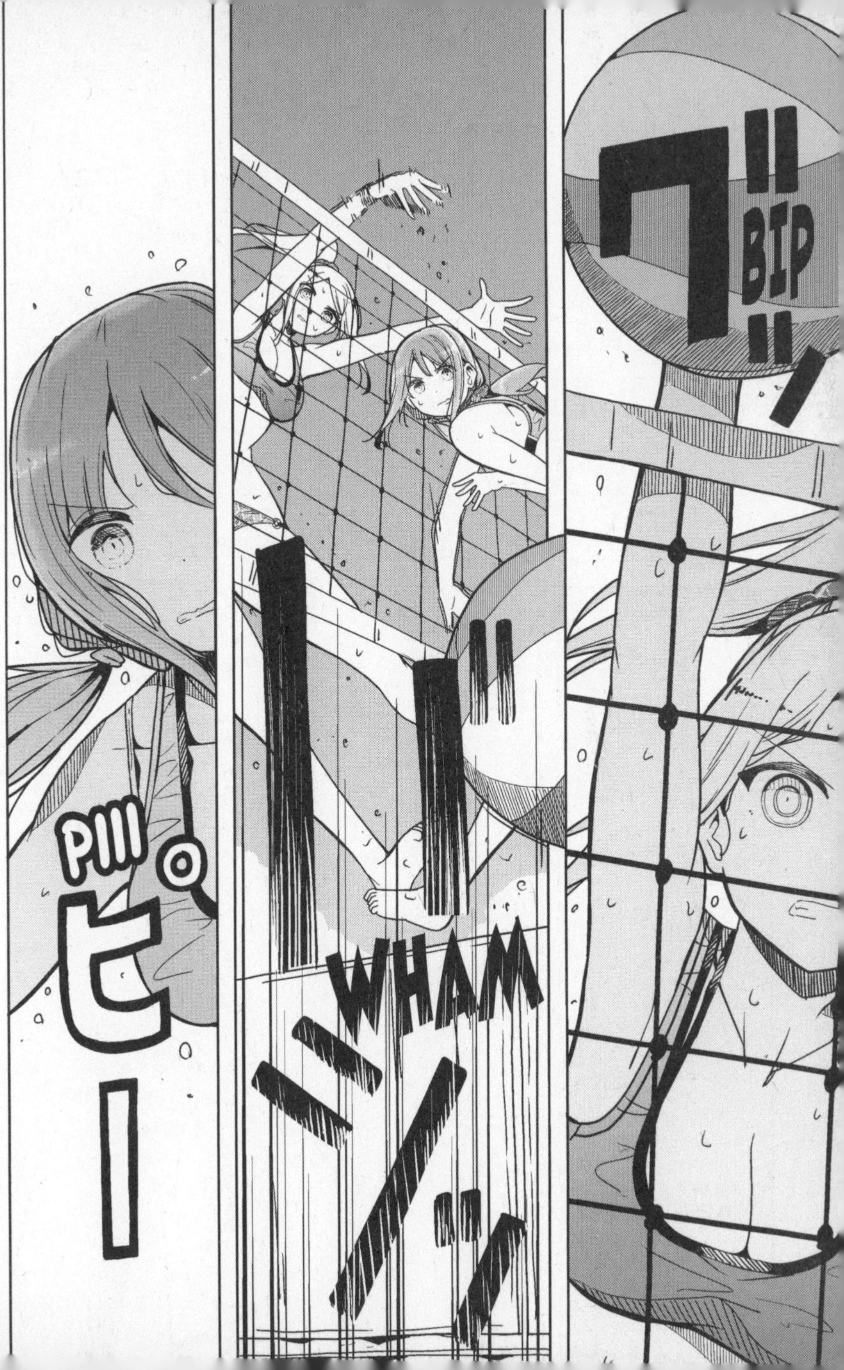
BIP
WHAM
PIII
ピー

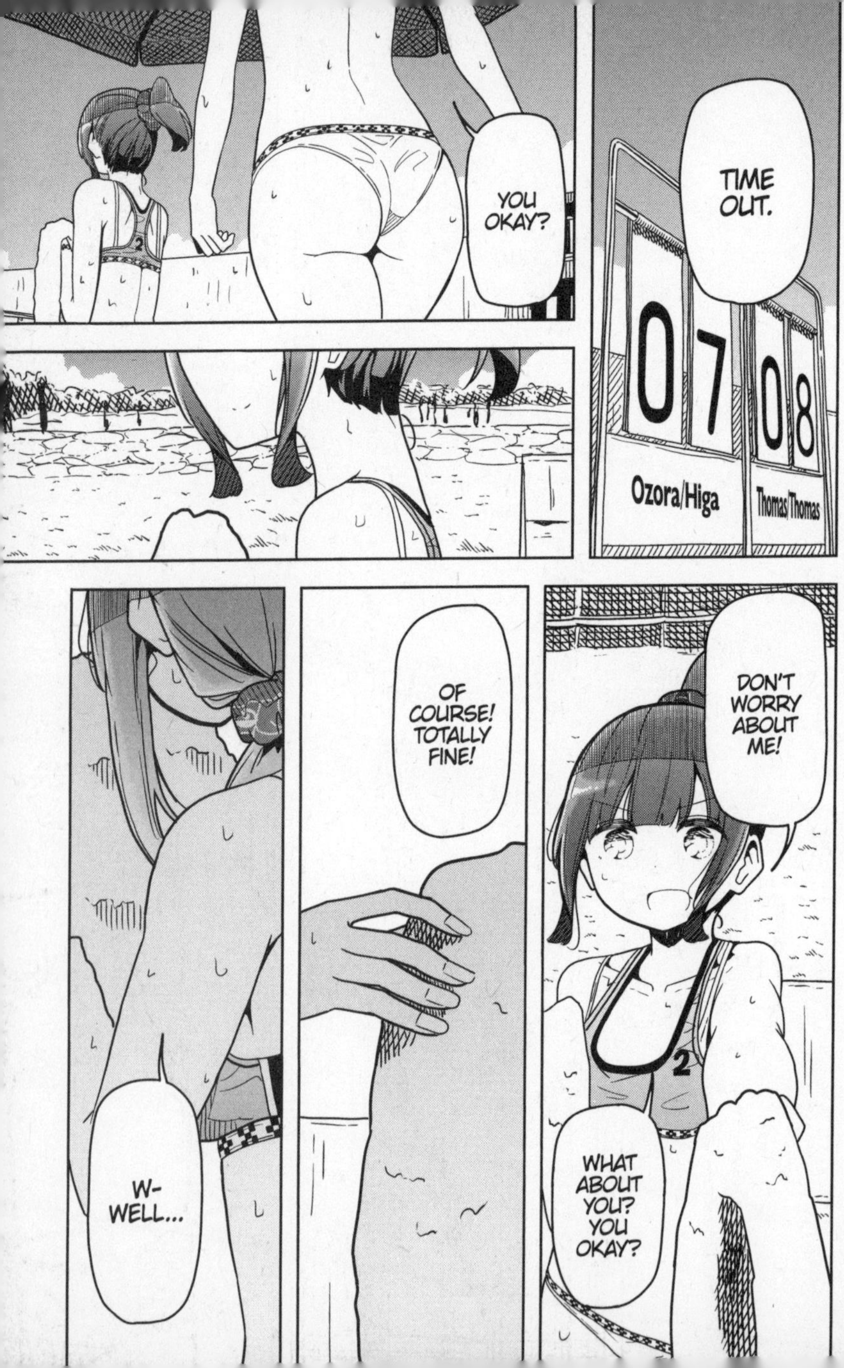
TIME OUT.
07
08
Ozora/Higa
Thomas/Thomas
YOU OKAY?
DON'T WORRY ABOUT ME!
WHAT ABOUT YOU? YOU OKAY?
OF COURSE! TOTALLY FINE!
W-WELL...

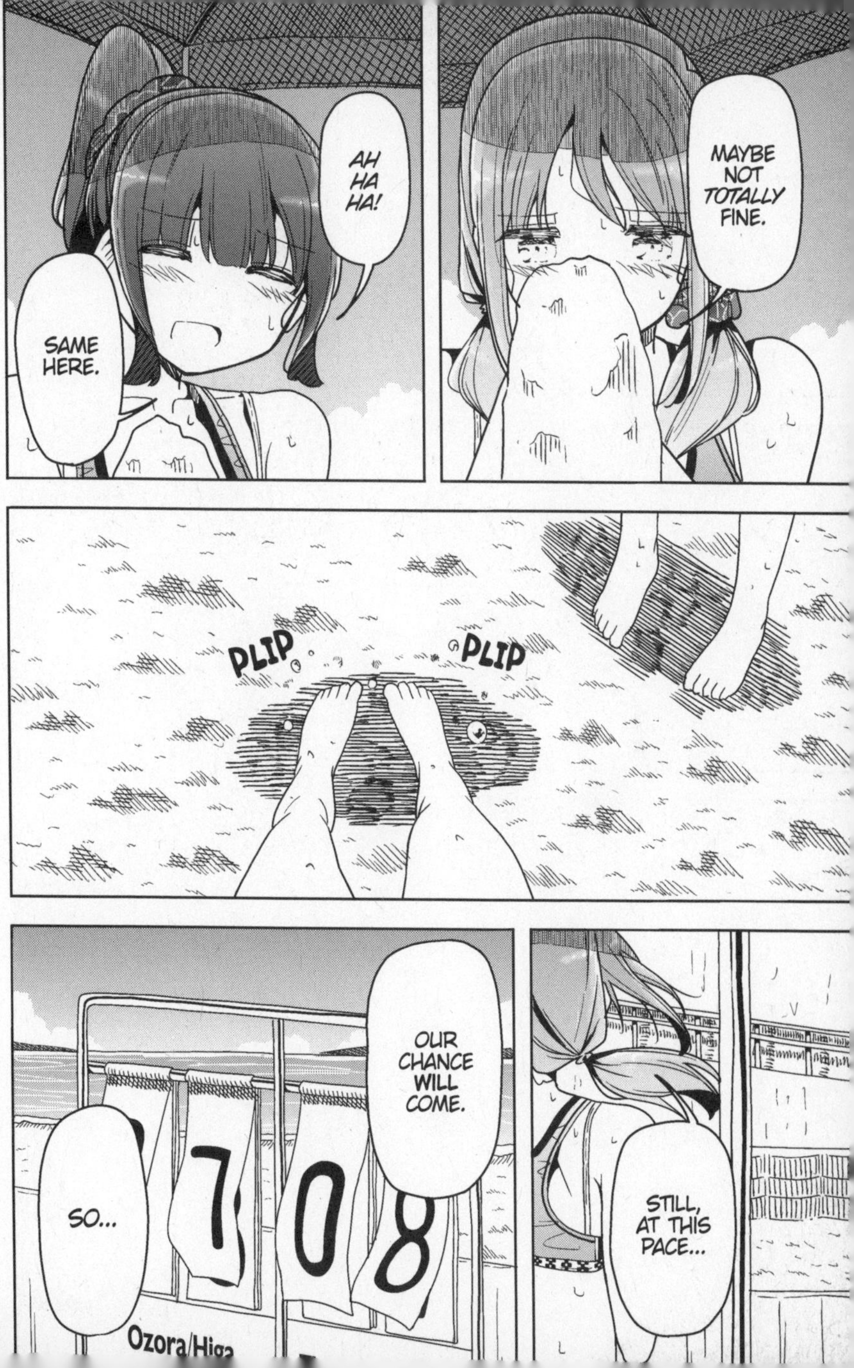
MAYBE NOT TOTALLY FINE.
AH HA HA!
SAME HERE.
PLIP
PLIP
STILL, AT THIS PACE...
OUR CHANCE WILL COME.
SO...
Ozora/Higa

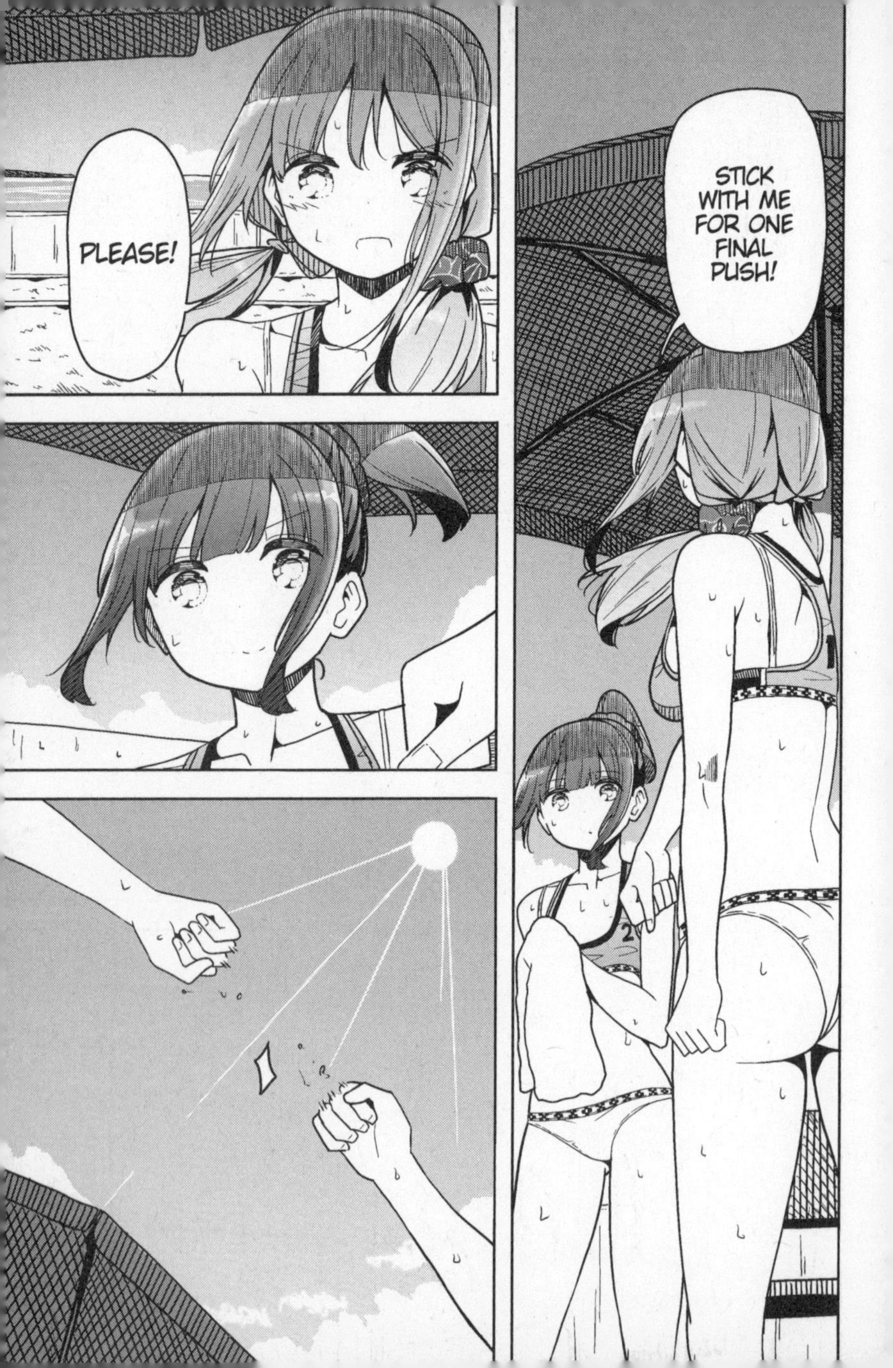
STICK WITH ME FOR ONE FINAL PUSH!
PLEASE!

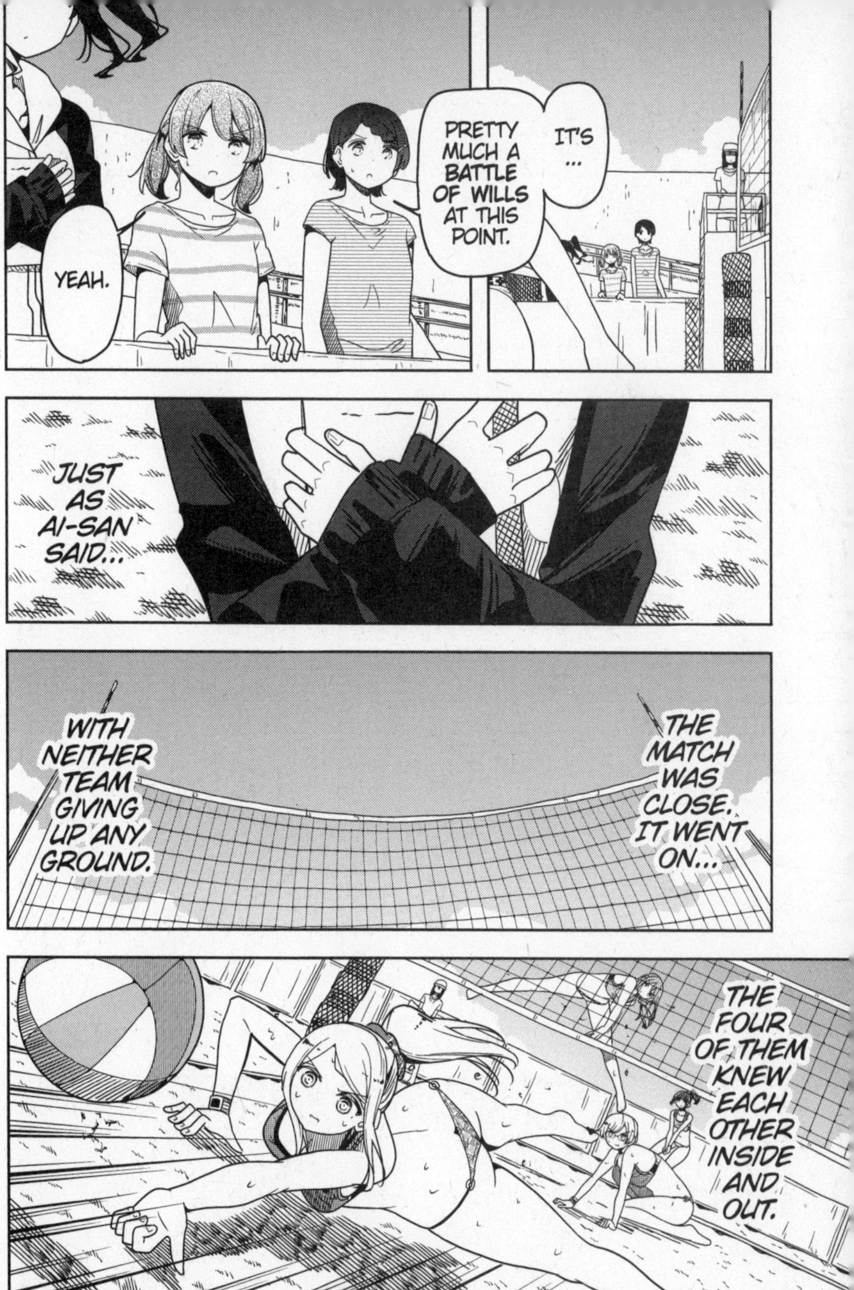
IT'S ...
PRETTY MUCH A BATTLE OF WILLS AT THIS POINT.
YEAH.
JUST AS AI-SAN SAID...
THE MATCH WAS CLOSE. IT WENT ON...
WITH NEITHER TEAM GIVING UP ANY GROUND.
THE FOUR OF THEM KNEW EACH OTHER INSIDE AND OUT.

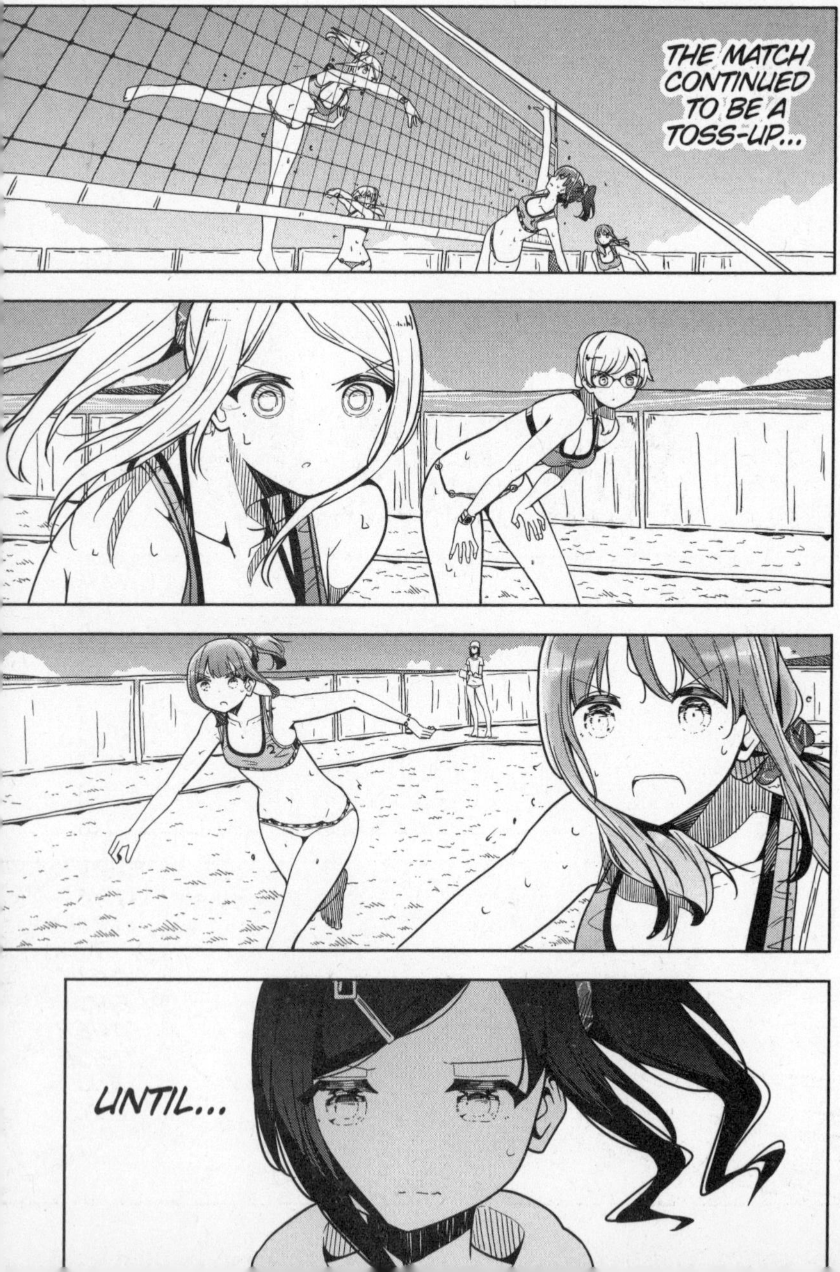
THE MATCH CONTINUED TO BE A TOSS-UP...
UNTIL...

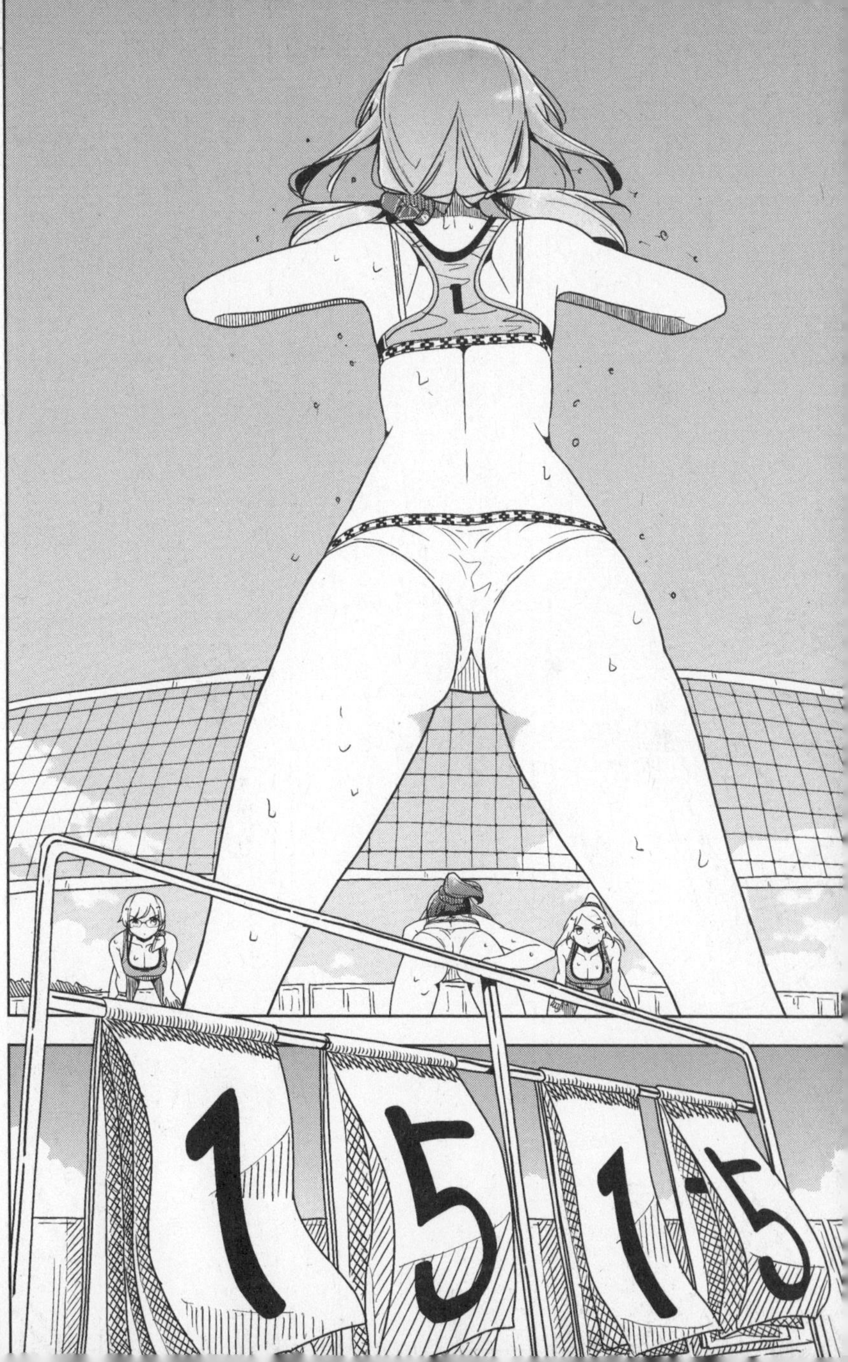
15 15

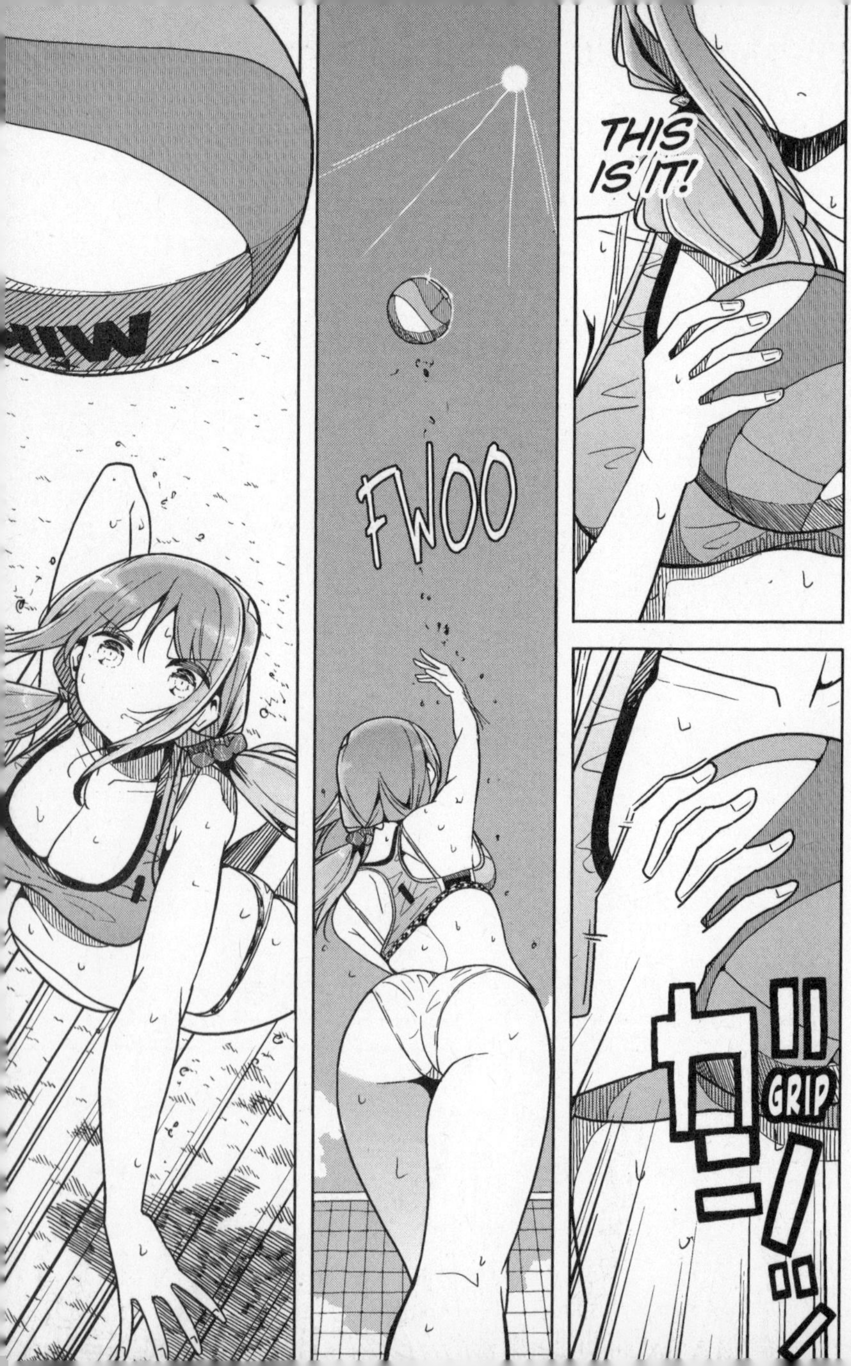
THIS IS IT!
GRIP
FWOO

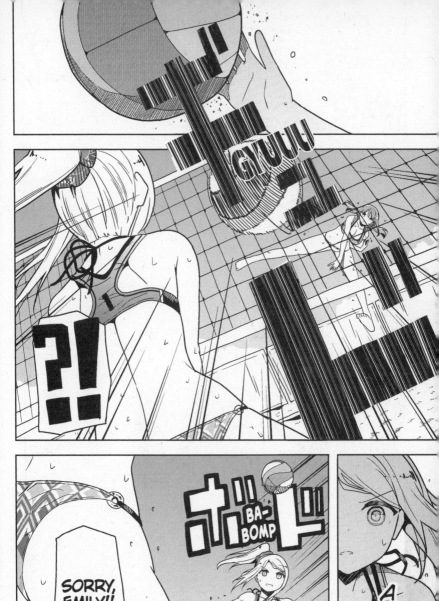

GYUUU

?!

BA-
BOMP

SORRY, EMILY!!

A DRIVE?!!

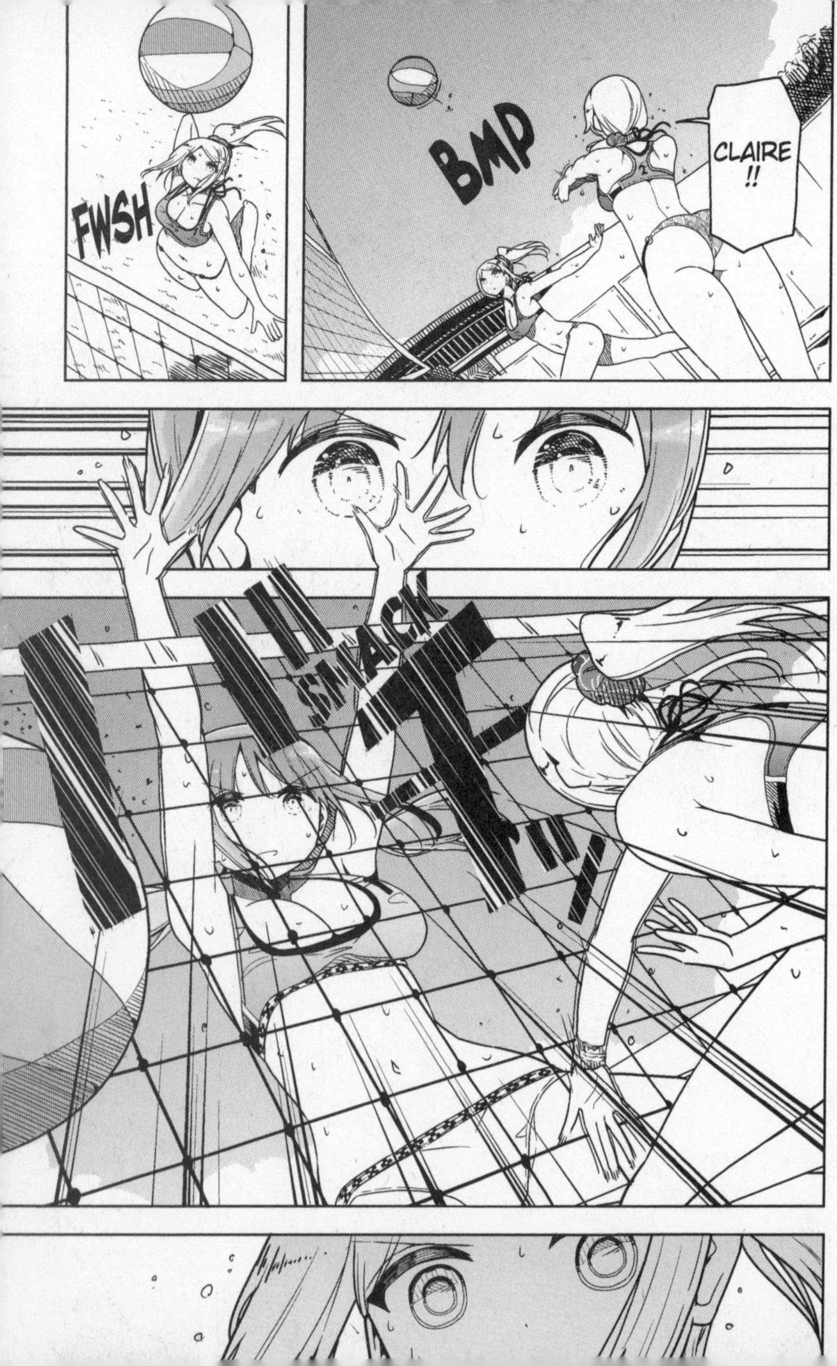
BMP
CLAIRE !!
FWSH
SMACK

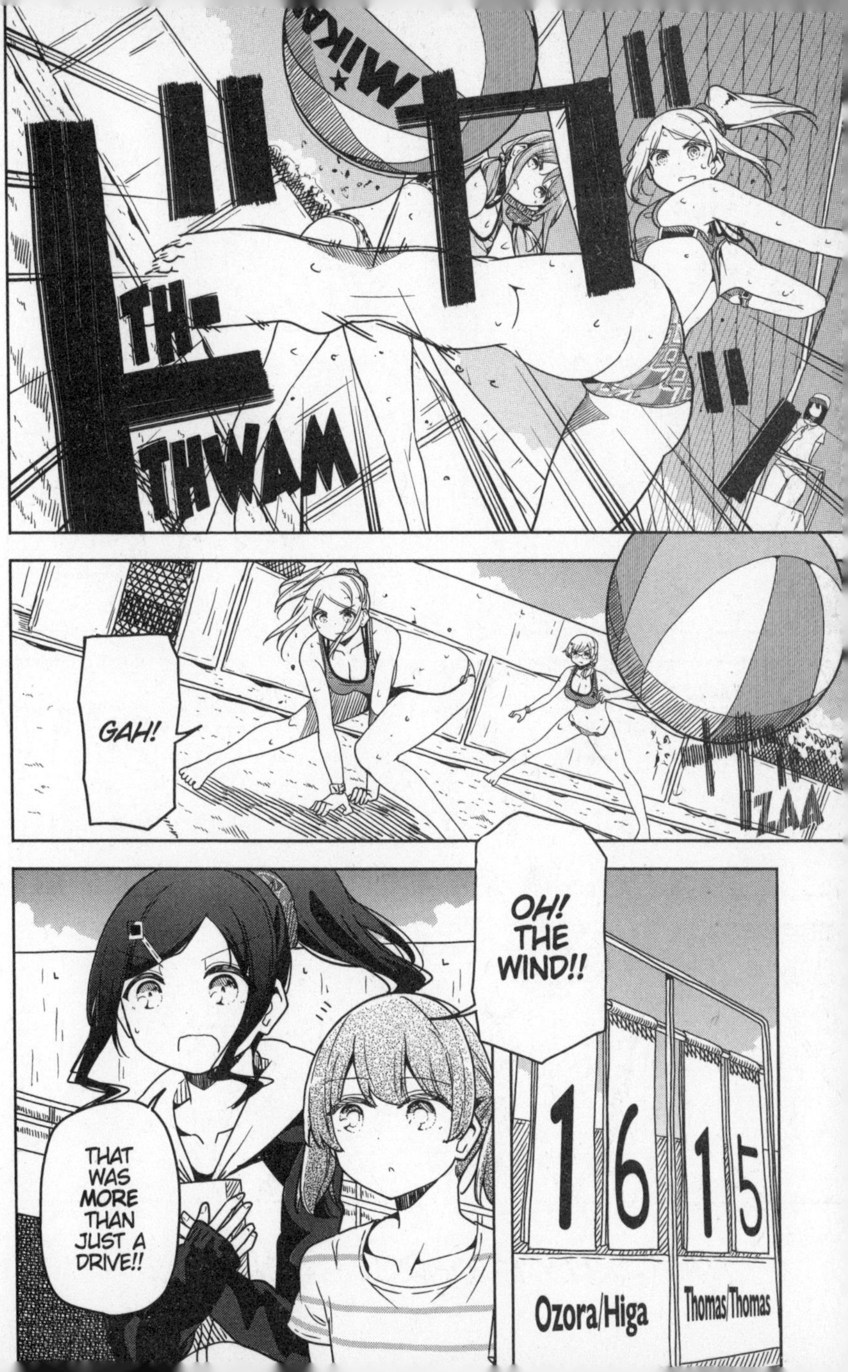
TH-
THWAM
GAH!
ZAA
OH! THE WIND!!
THAT WAS MORE THAN JUST A DRIVE!!
16
15
Ozora/Higa
Thomas/Thomas

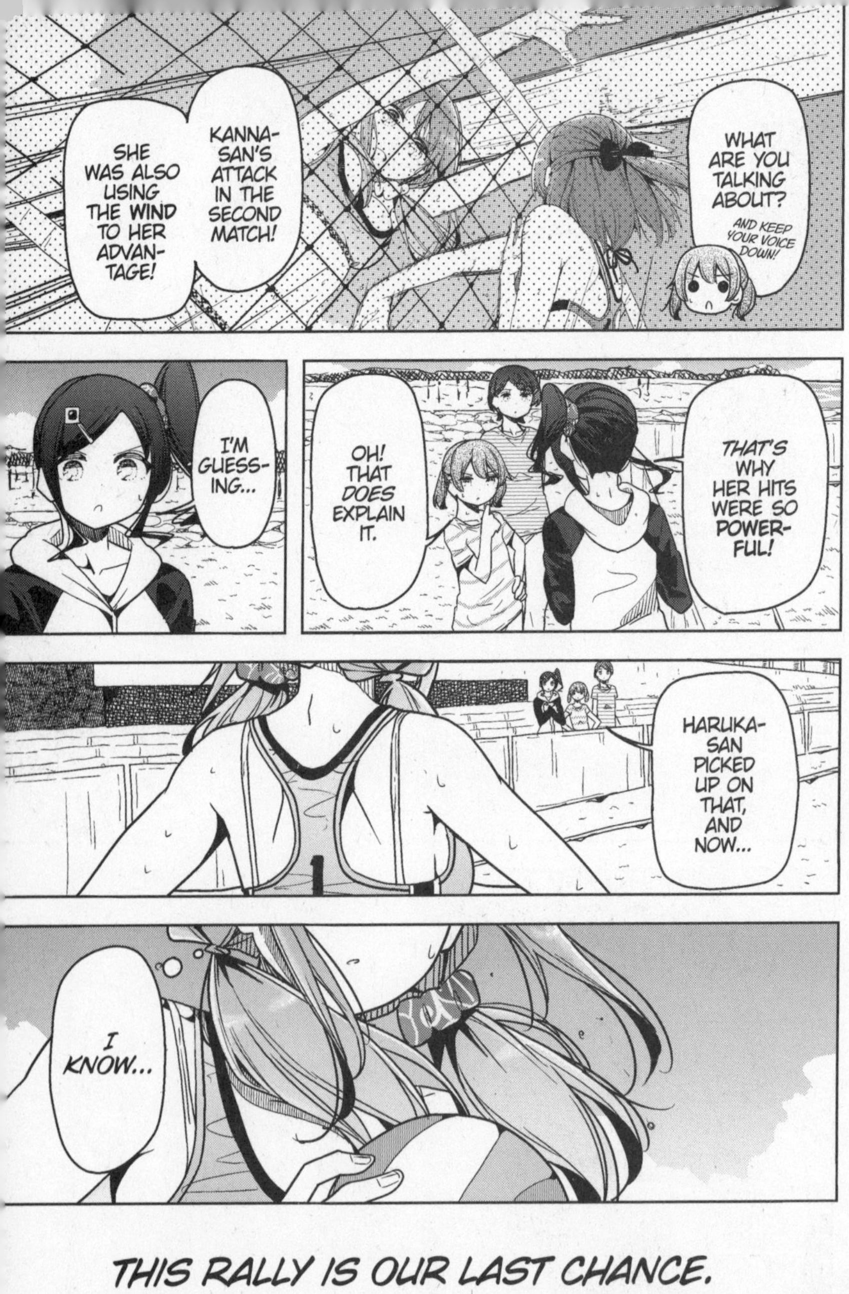
WHAT ARE YOU TALKING ABOUT?
AND KEEP YOUR VOICE DOWN!
KANNA-SAN'S ATTACK IN THE SECOND MATCH!
SHE WAS ALSO USING THE WIND TO HER ADVANTAGE!
THAT'S WHY HER HITS WERE SO POWERFUL!
OH! THAT *DOES* EXPLAIN IT.
I'M GUESSING...
HARUKA-SAN PICKED UP ON THAT, AND NOW...
I KNOW...

THIS RALLY IS OUR LAST CHANCE.

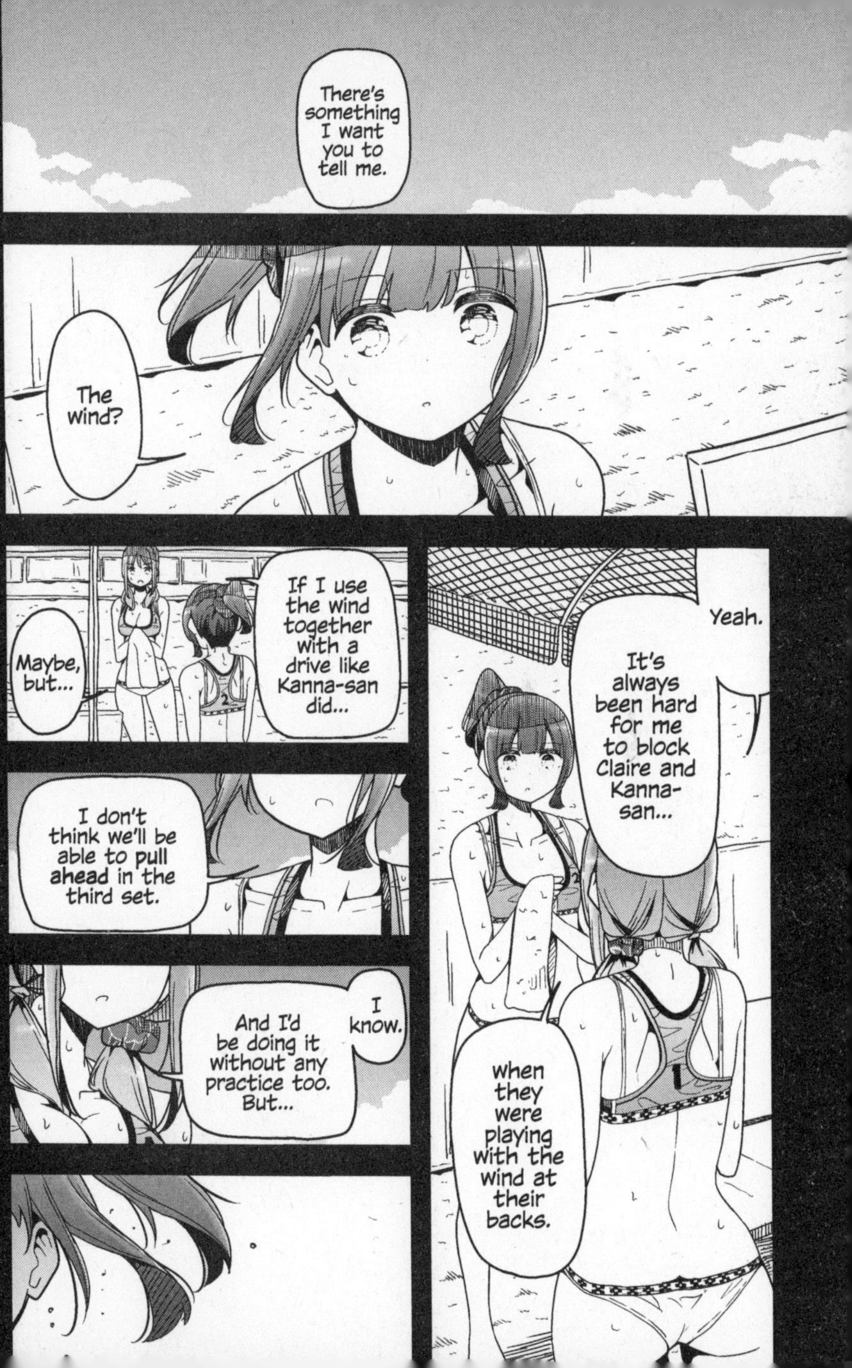
There's something I want you to tell me.
The wind?
Yeah.
It's always been hard for me to block Claire and Kanna-san...
when they were playing with the wind at their backs.
If I use the wind together with a drive like Kanna-san did...
Maybe, but...
I don't think we'll be able to pull ahead in the third set.
I know.
And I'd be doing it without any practice too. But...

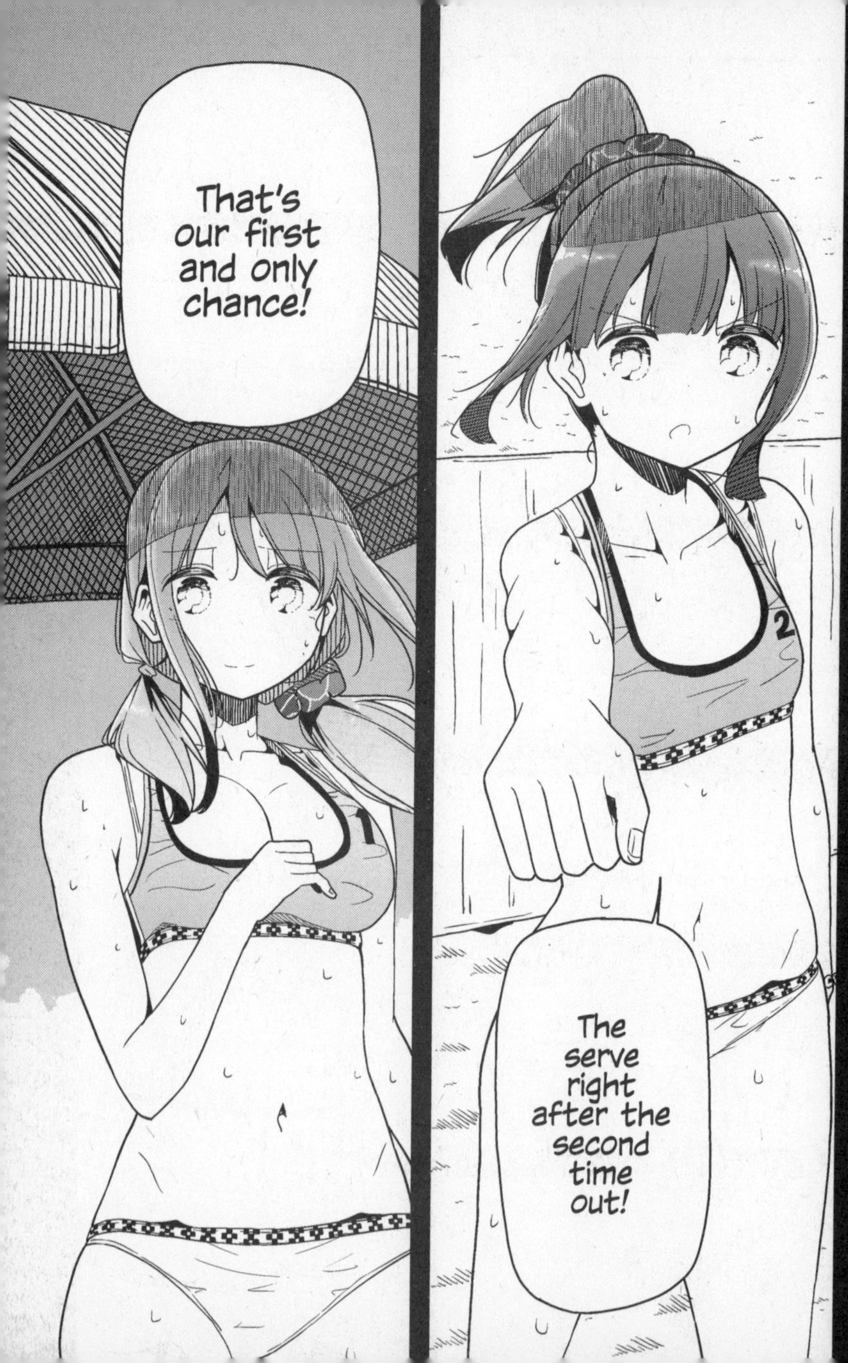
The serve right after the second time out!
That's our first and only chance!

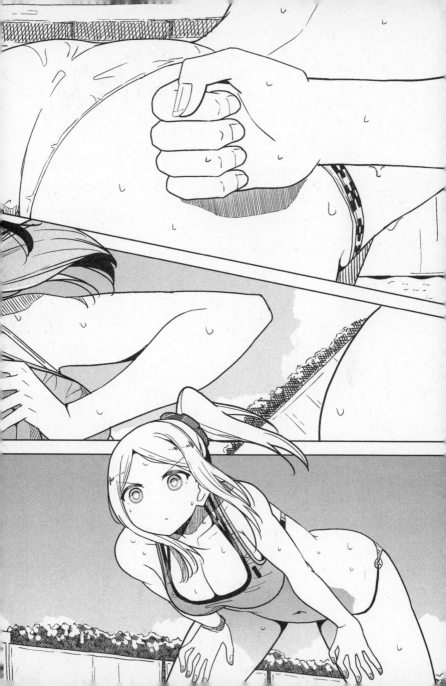

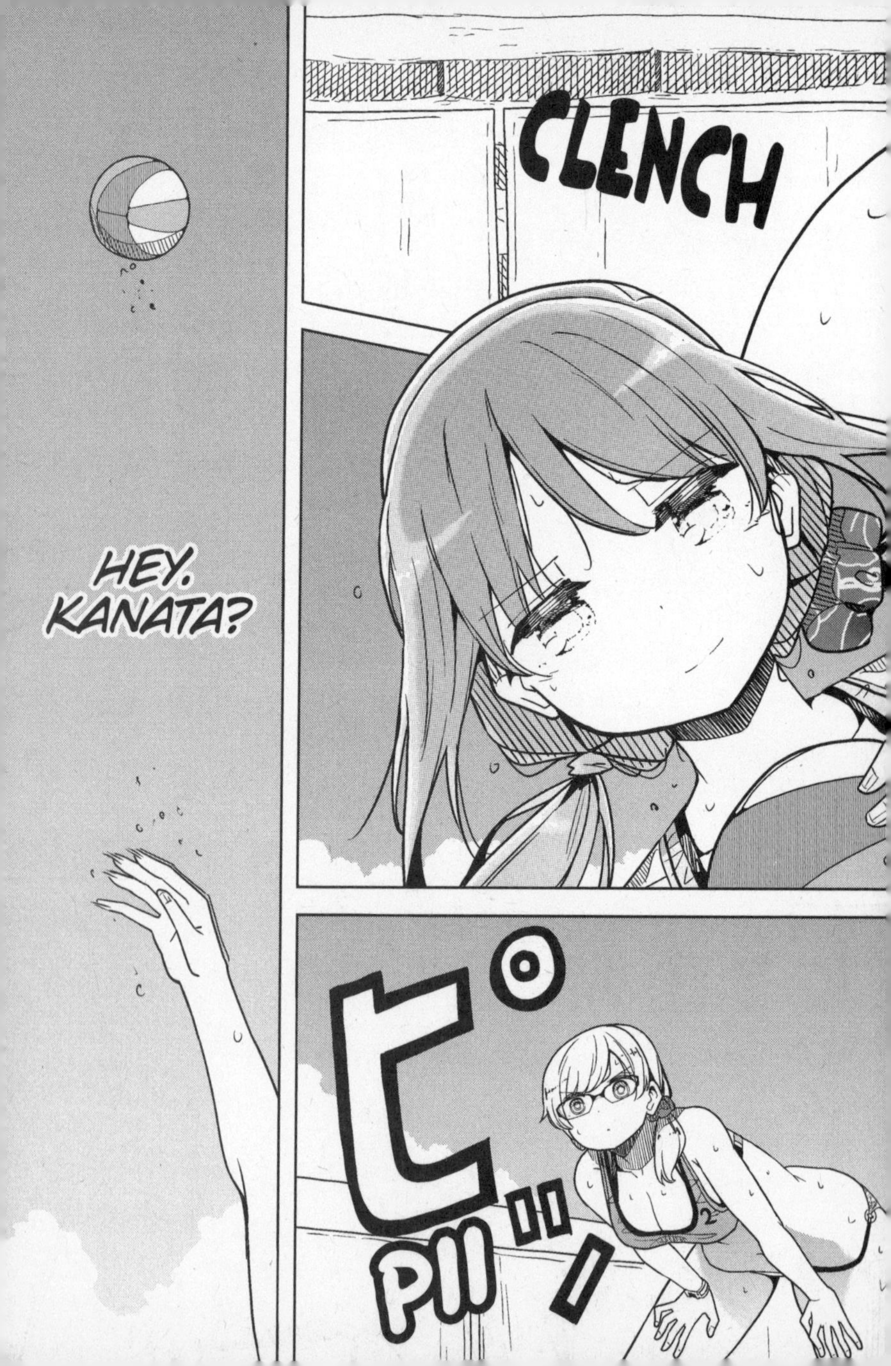
CLENCH
ピ
PII
HEY. KANATA?

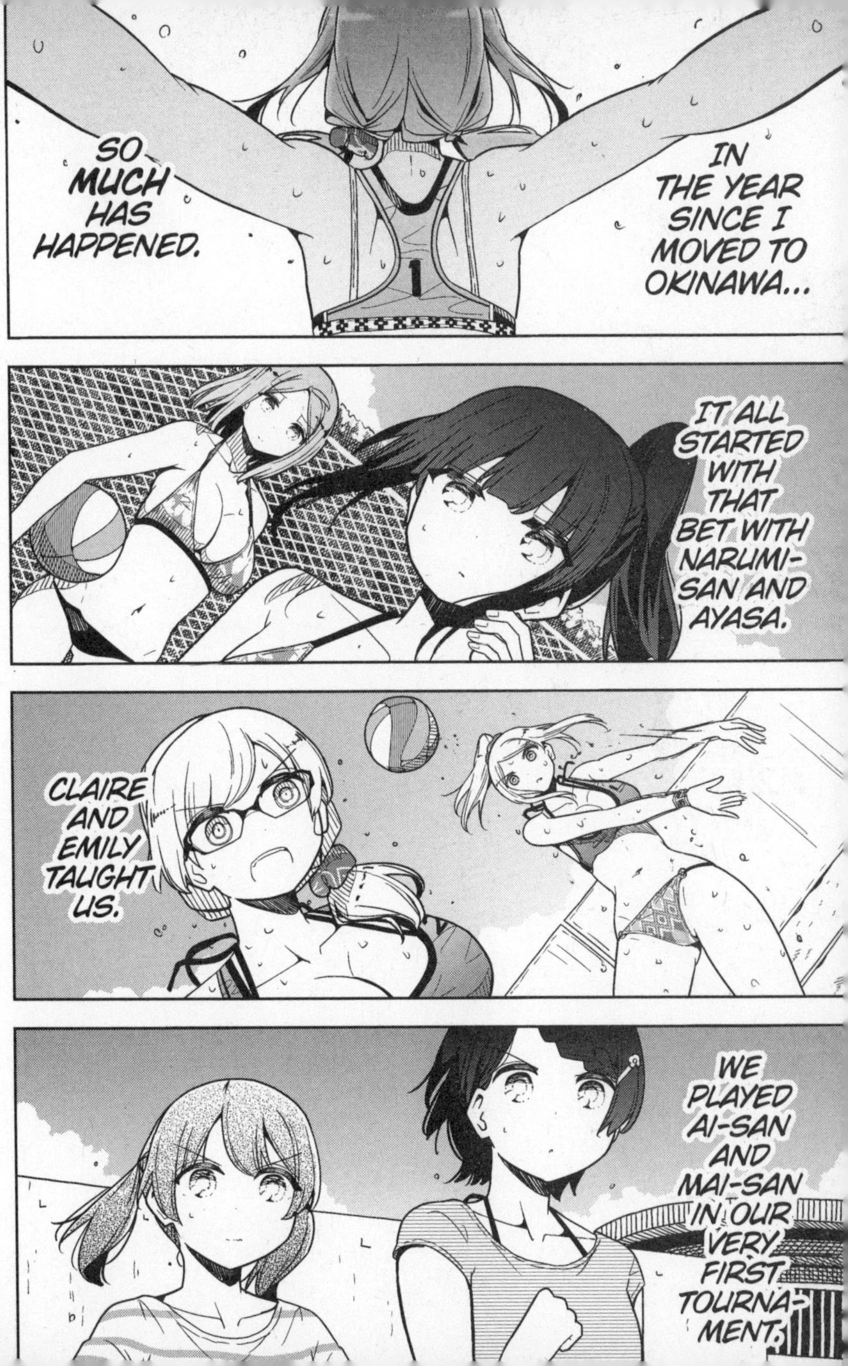
IN THE YEAR SINCE I MOVED TO OKINAWA...
SO MUCH HAS HAPPENED.
IT ALL STARTED WITH THAT BET WITH NARUMI-SAN AND AYASA.
CLAIRE AND EMILY TAUGHT US.
WE PLAYED AI-SAN AND MAI-SAN IN OUR VERY FIRST TOURNAMENT.

AND, WE BECAME FRIENDS WITH AKARI-CHAN, TOO.

MARISSA GAVE US A BEACH VOLLEYBALL BOOT CAMP.

HAD BEACH VOLLEYBALL, DIDN'T WE?

WE ALWAYS...

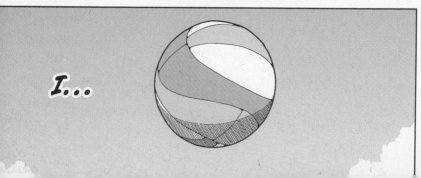

I...

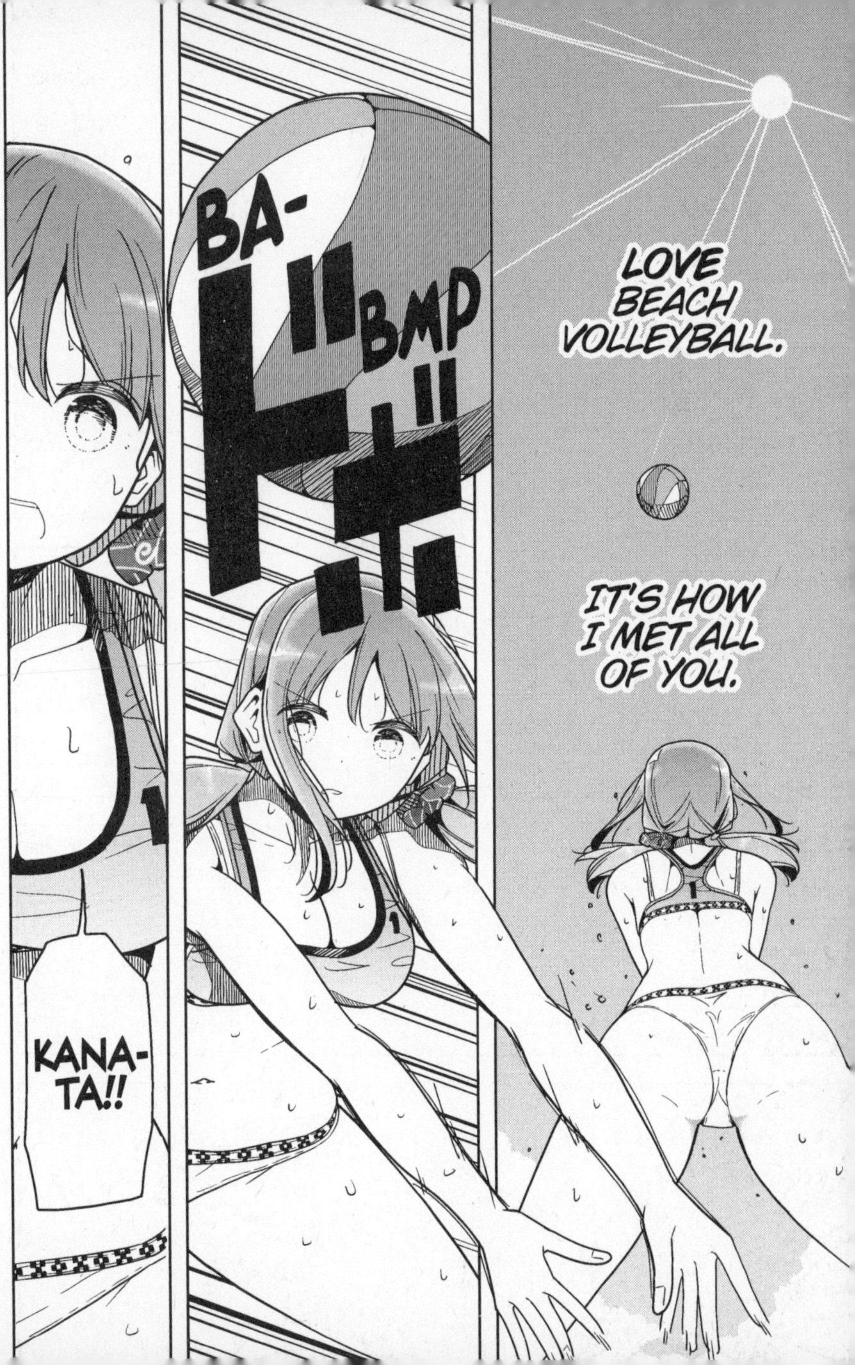
LOVE BEACH VOLLEYBALL.
IT'S HOW I MET ALL OF YOU.
BA-BMP
KANA-TA!!

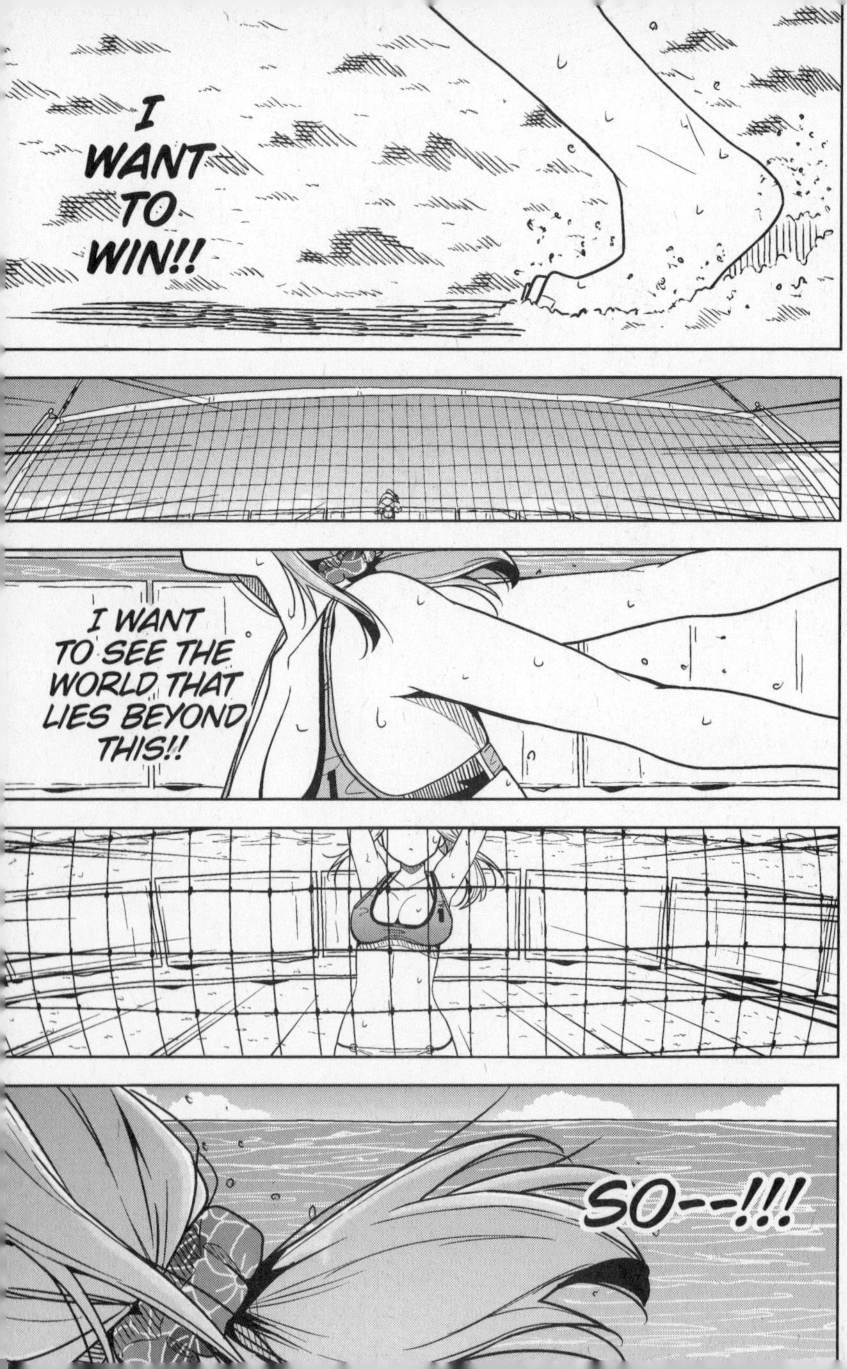
I WANT TO WIN!!
I WANT TO SEE THE WORLD THAT LIES BEYOND THIS!!
SO--!!!

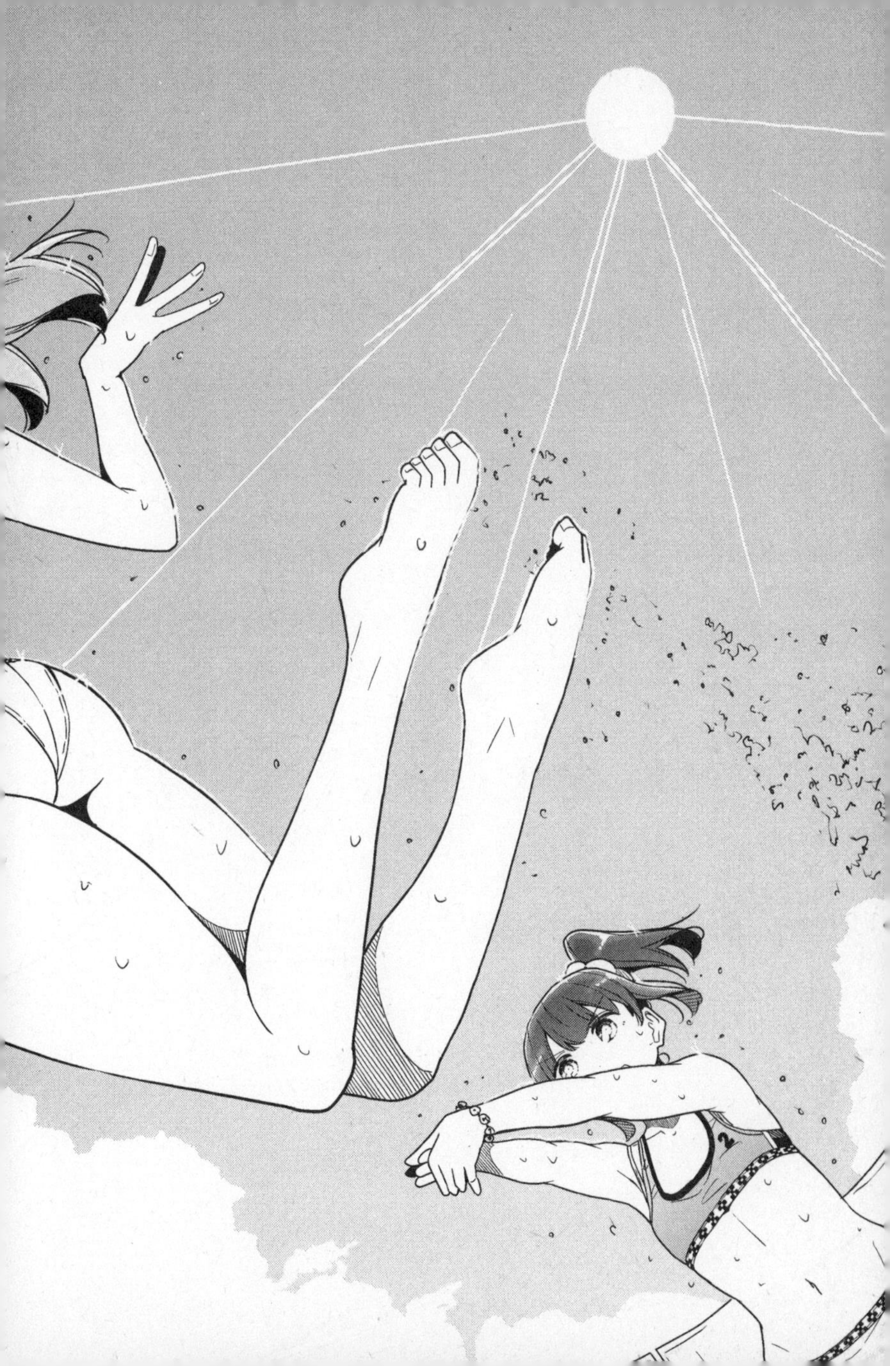

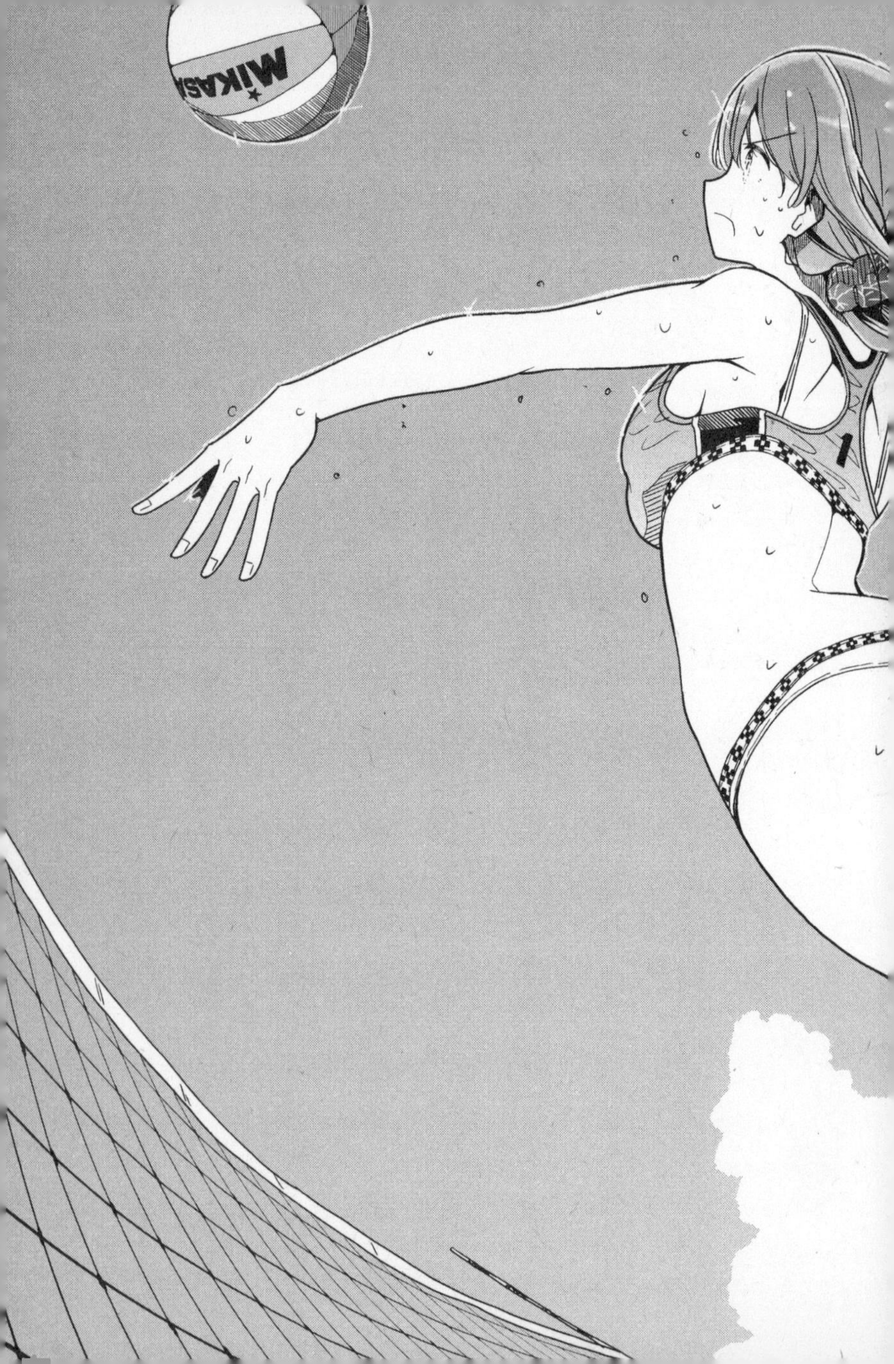
MIKASA

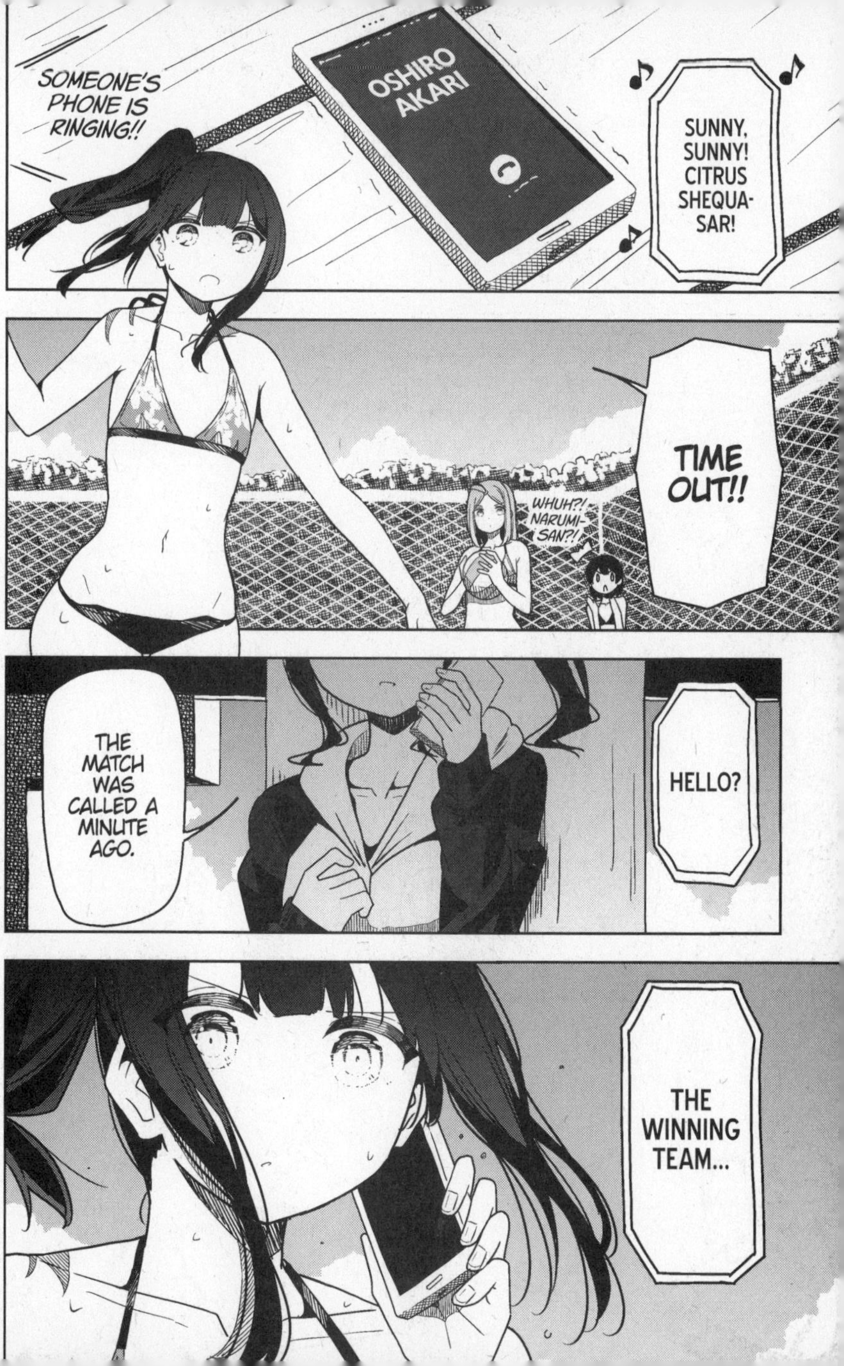
SUNNY, SUNNY! CITRUS SHEQUA-SAR!
OSHIRO AKARI
SOMEONE'S PHONE IS RINGING!!
TIME OUT!!
WHUH?! NARUMI-SAN?!
HELLO?
THE MATCH WAS CALLED A MINUTE AGO.
THE WINNING TEAM...

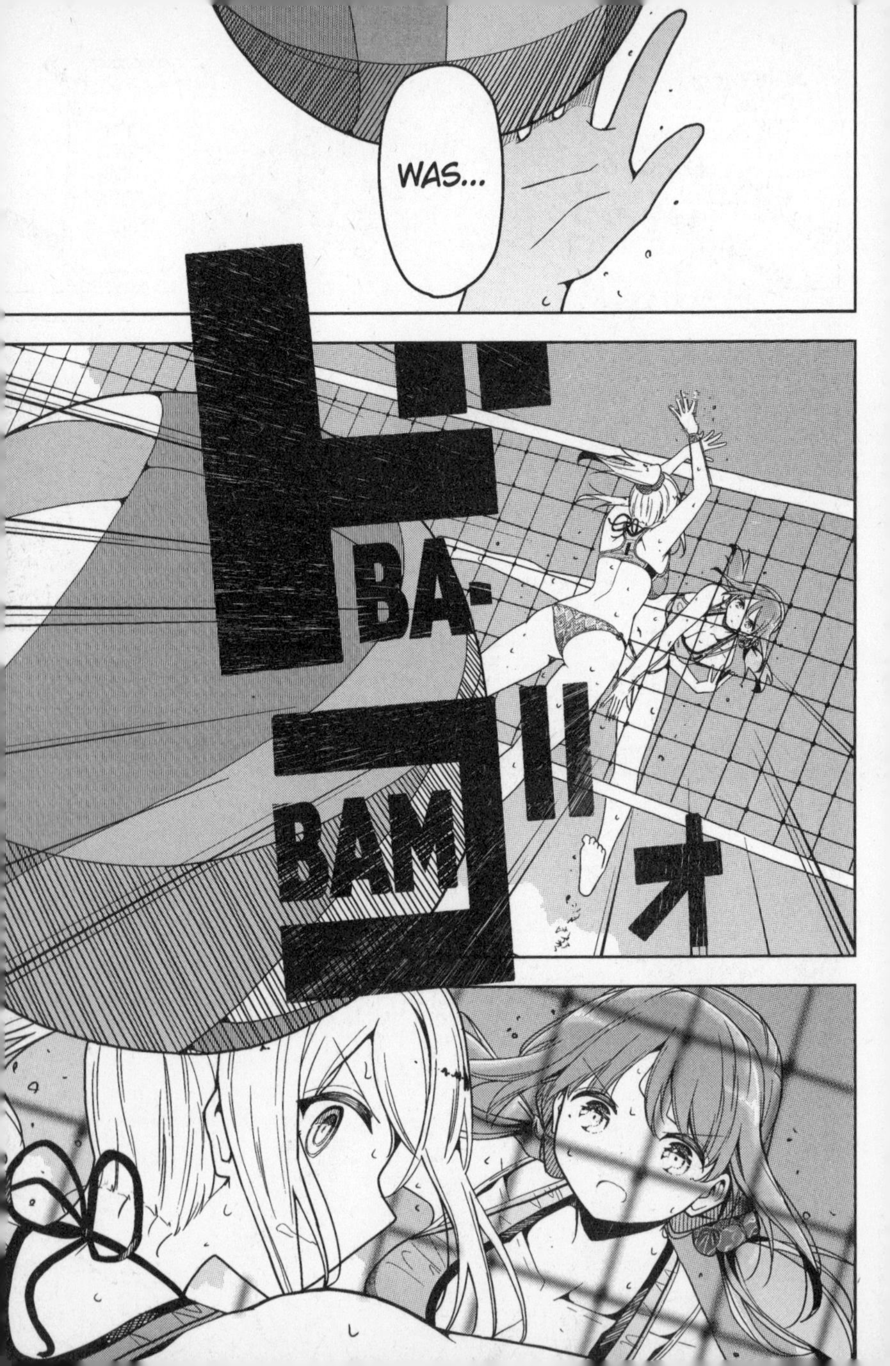
WAS...
BA-
BAM

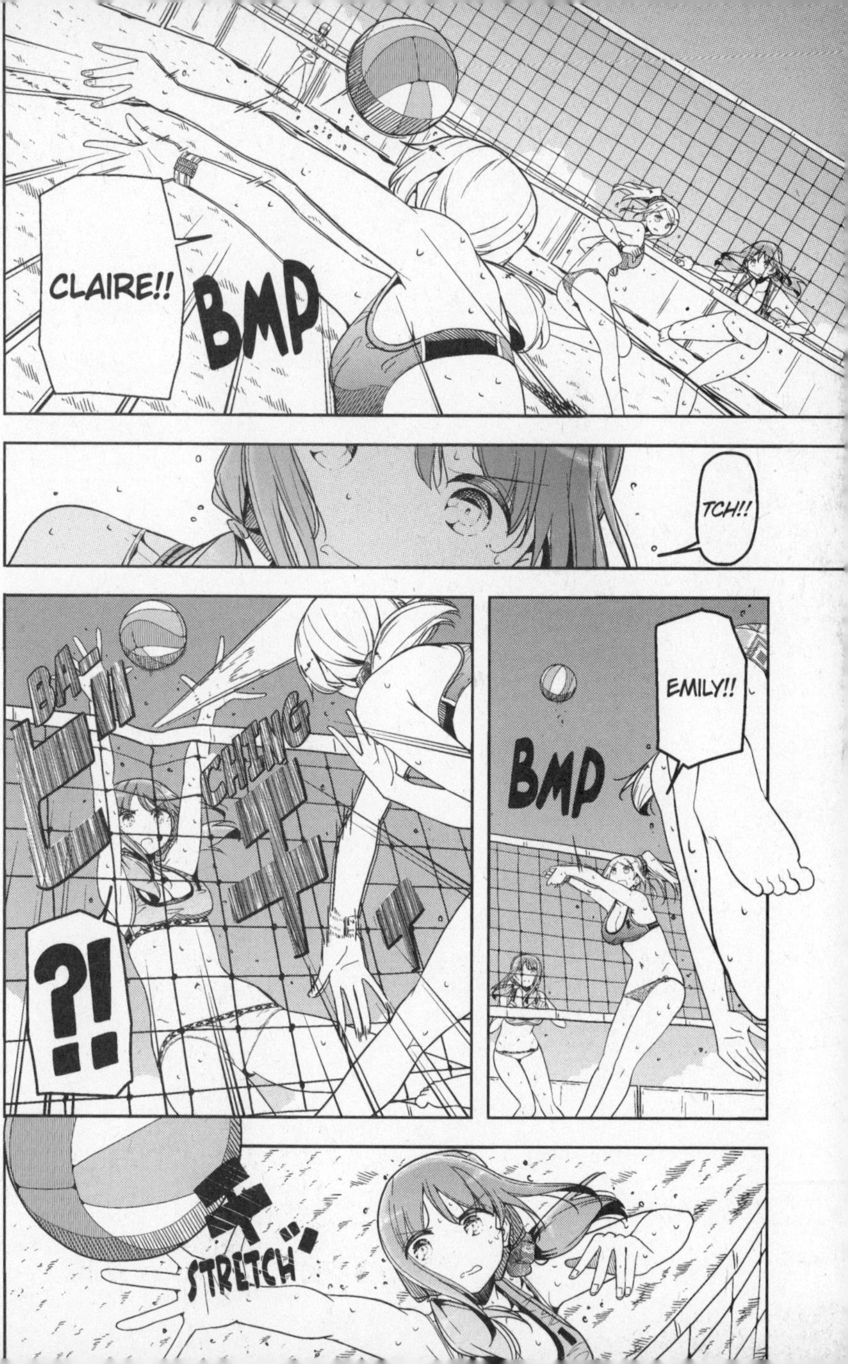
CLAIRE!!
BMP
TCH!!
EMILY!!
BMP
BA
CHING
?!
STRETCH

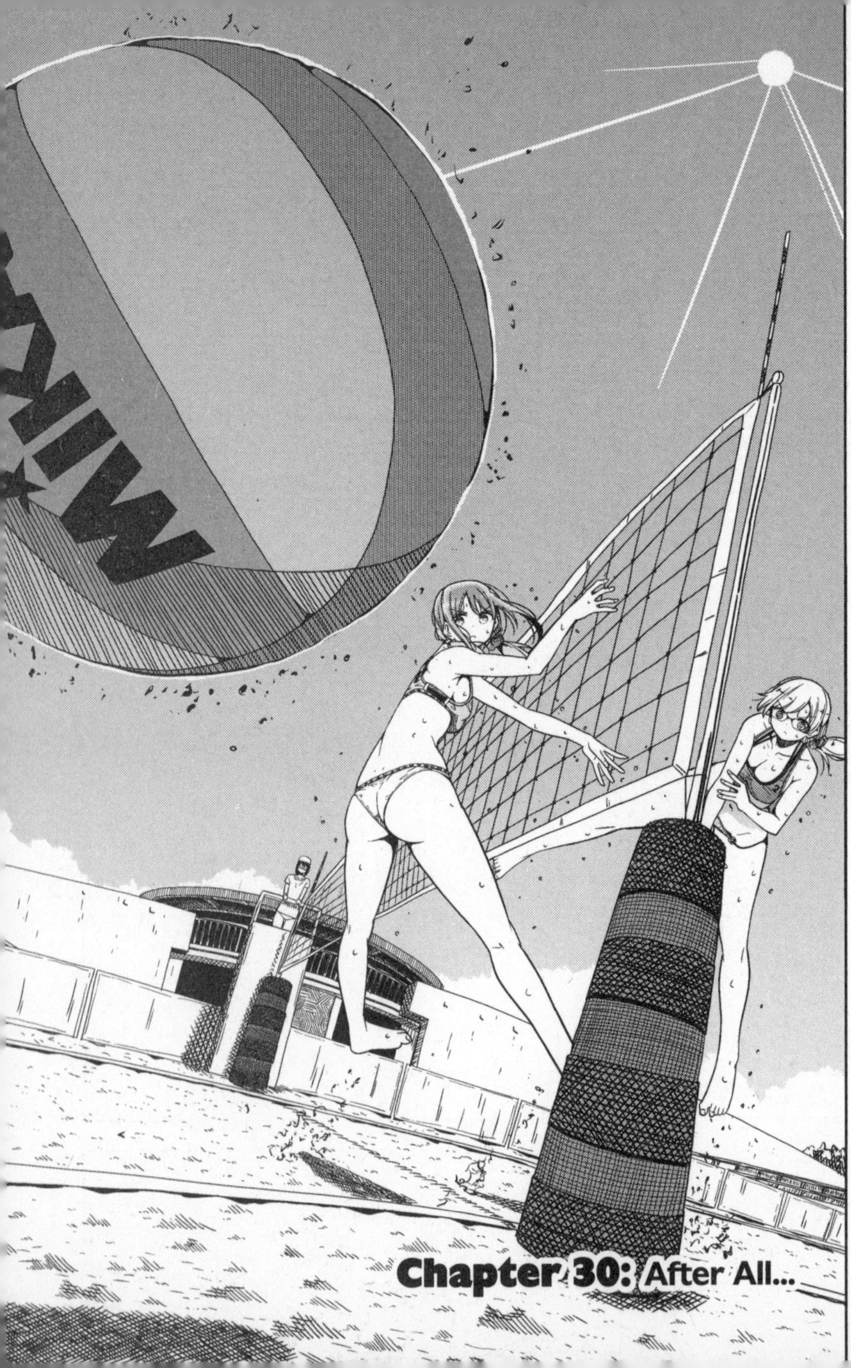

Chapter 30: After All...

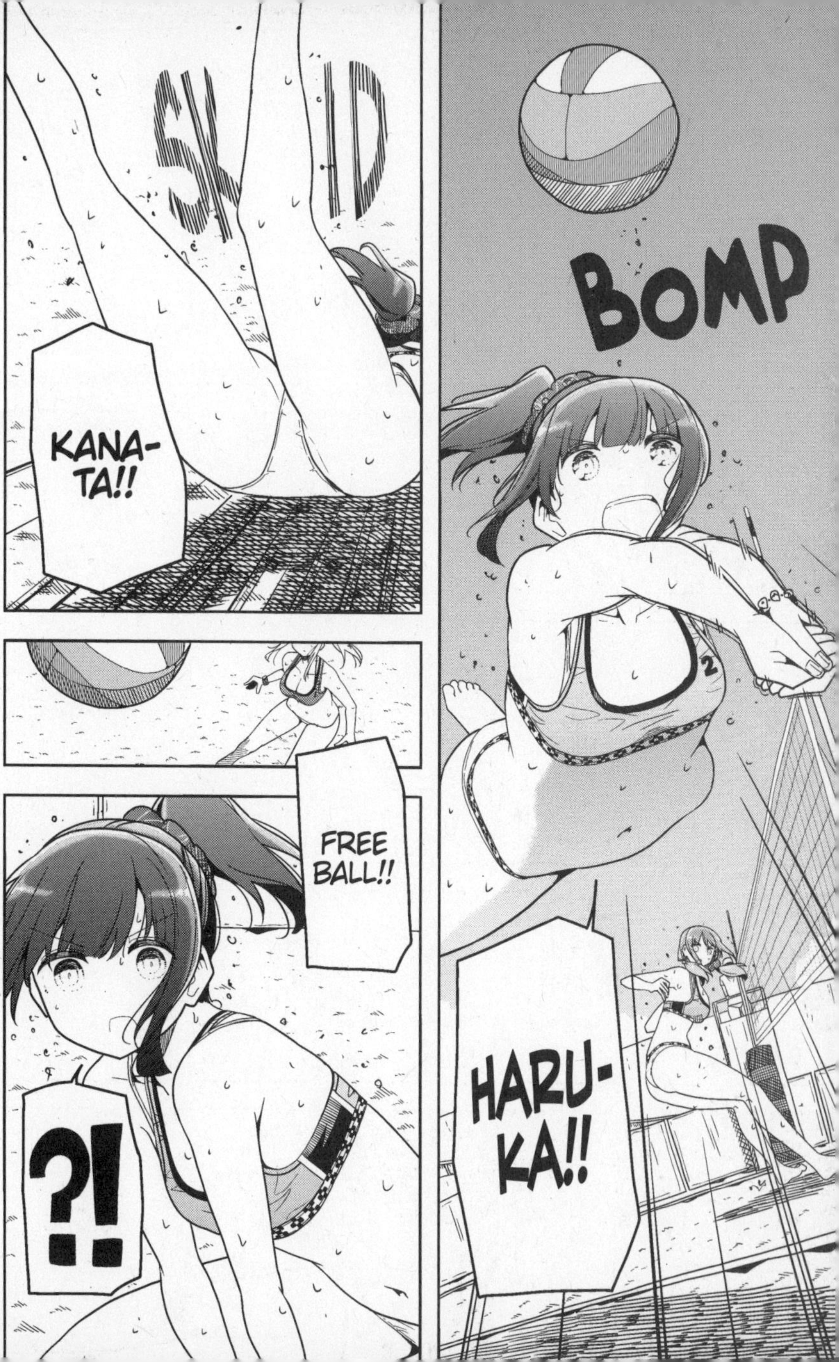
BOMP
HARU-KA!!
SKID
KANA-TA!!
FREE BALL!!
?!

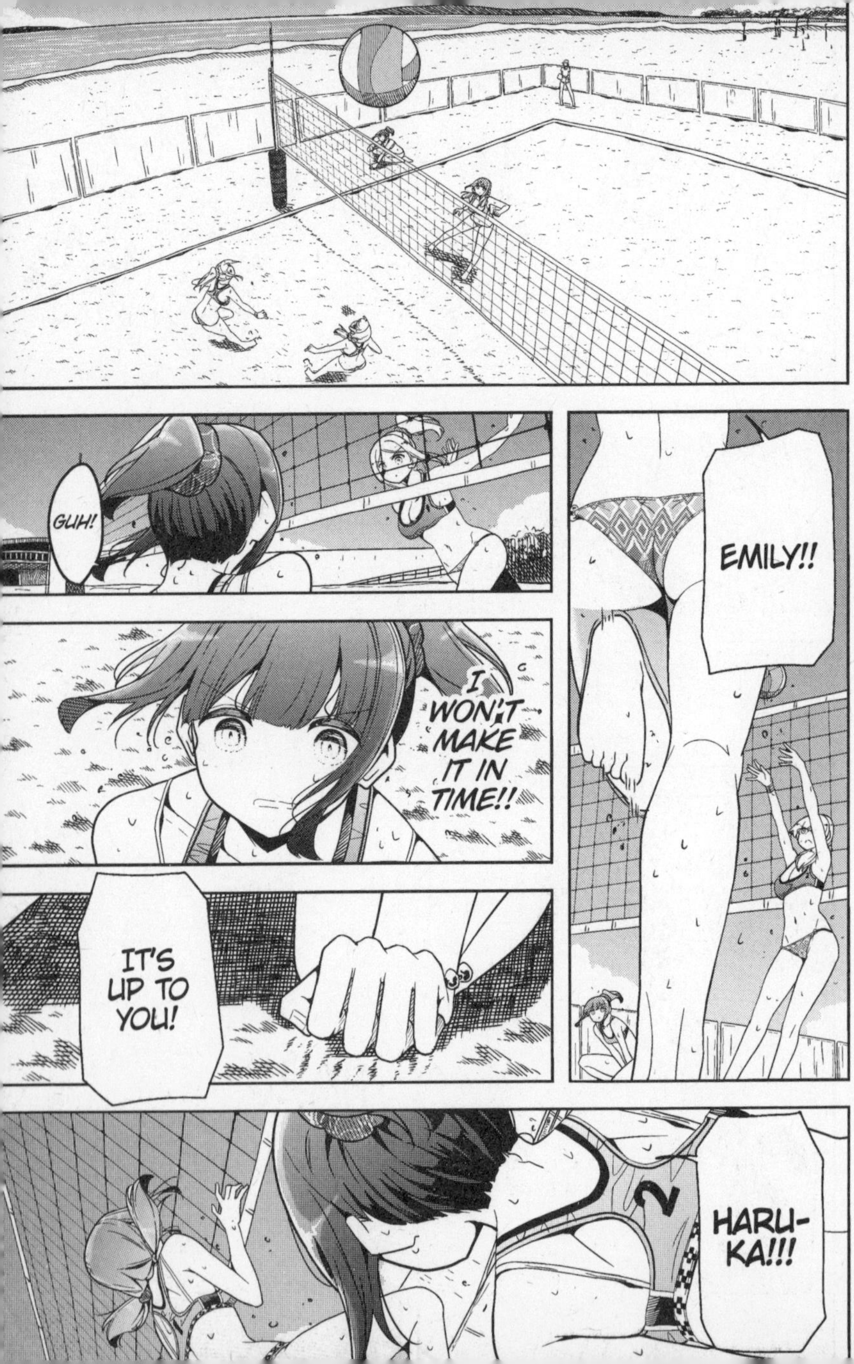
GUH!
I WON'T MAKE IT IN TIME!!
IT'S UP TO YOU!
EMILY!!
HARU-KA!!!

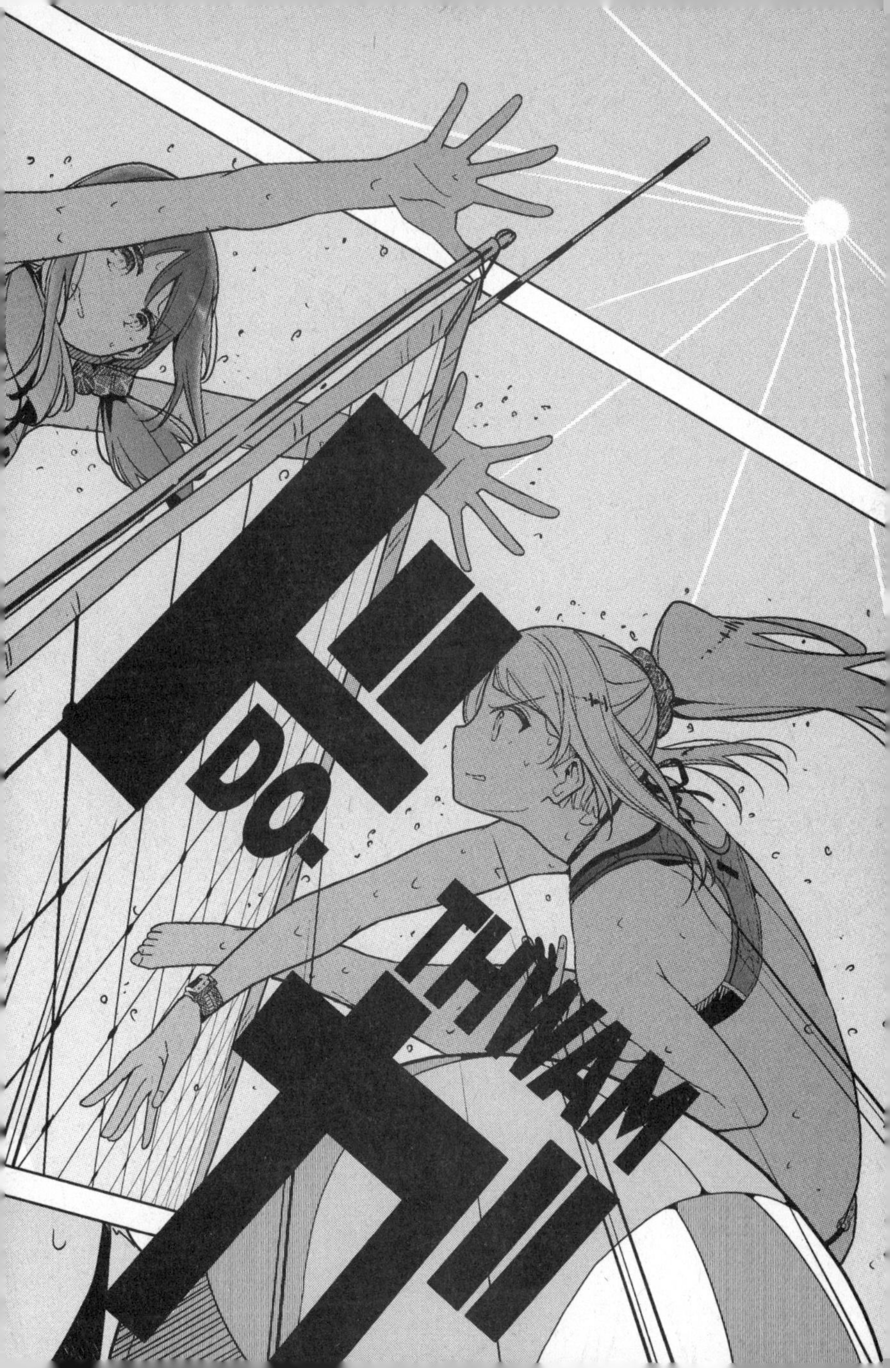
DO.
THWAM

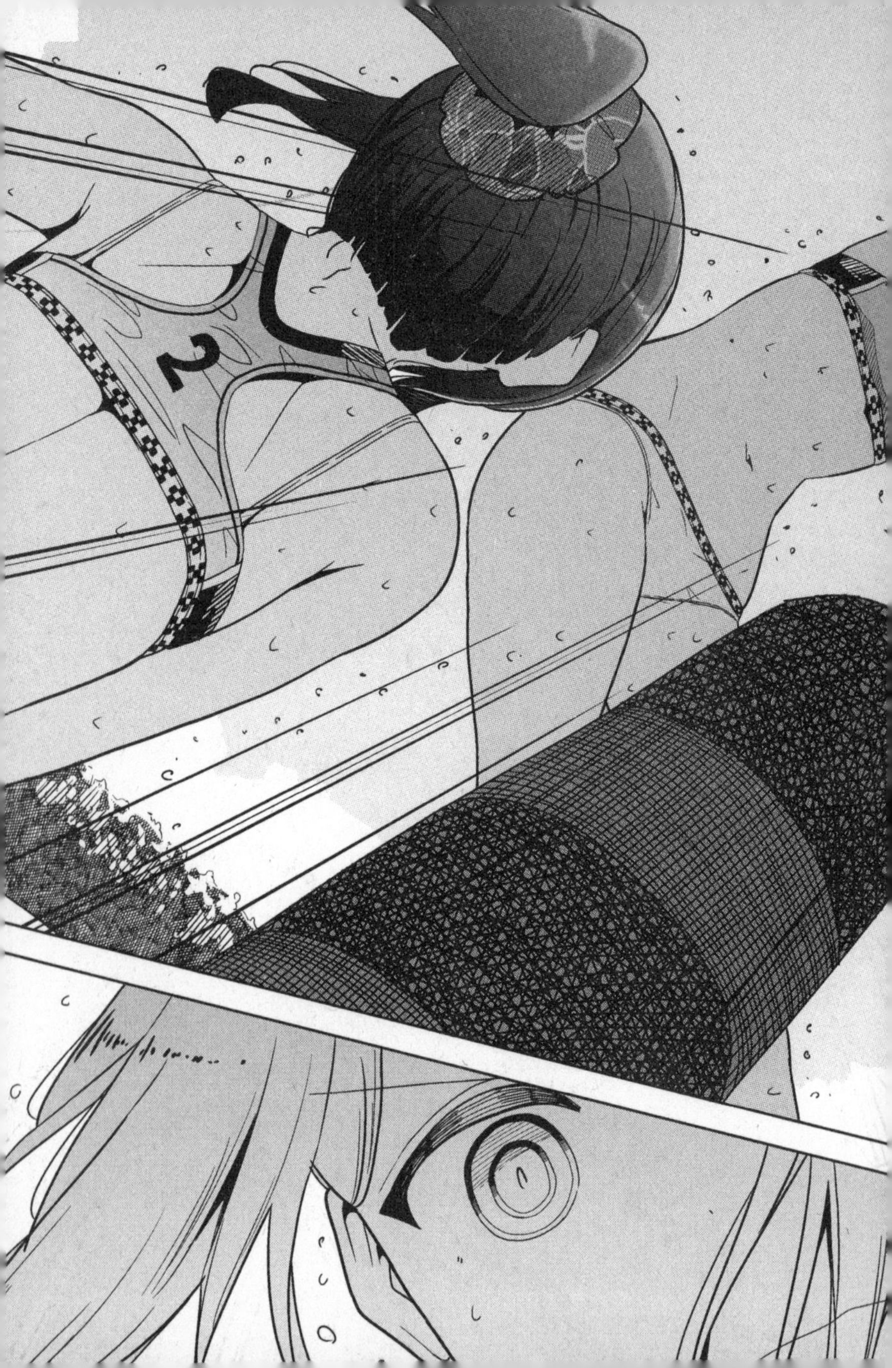

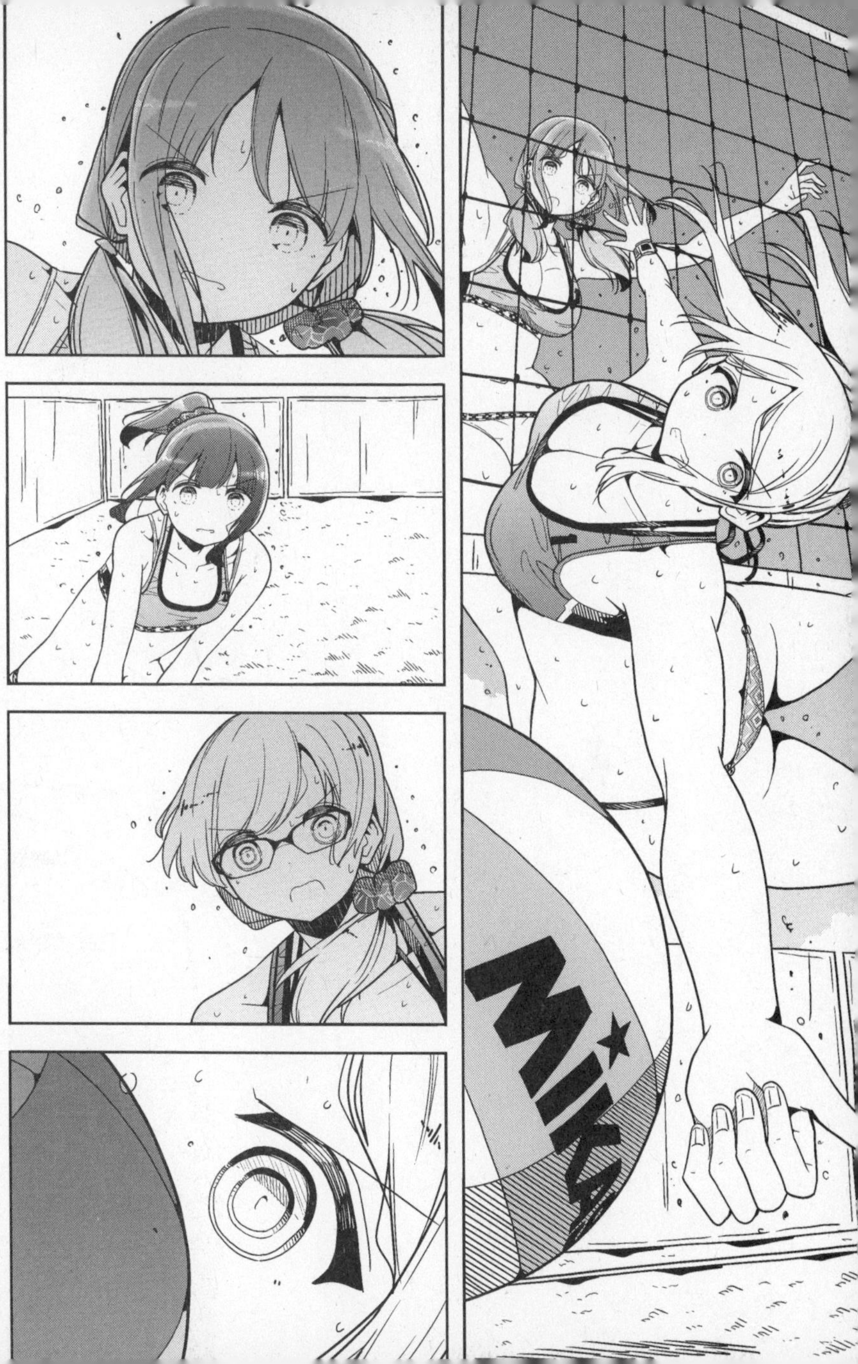

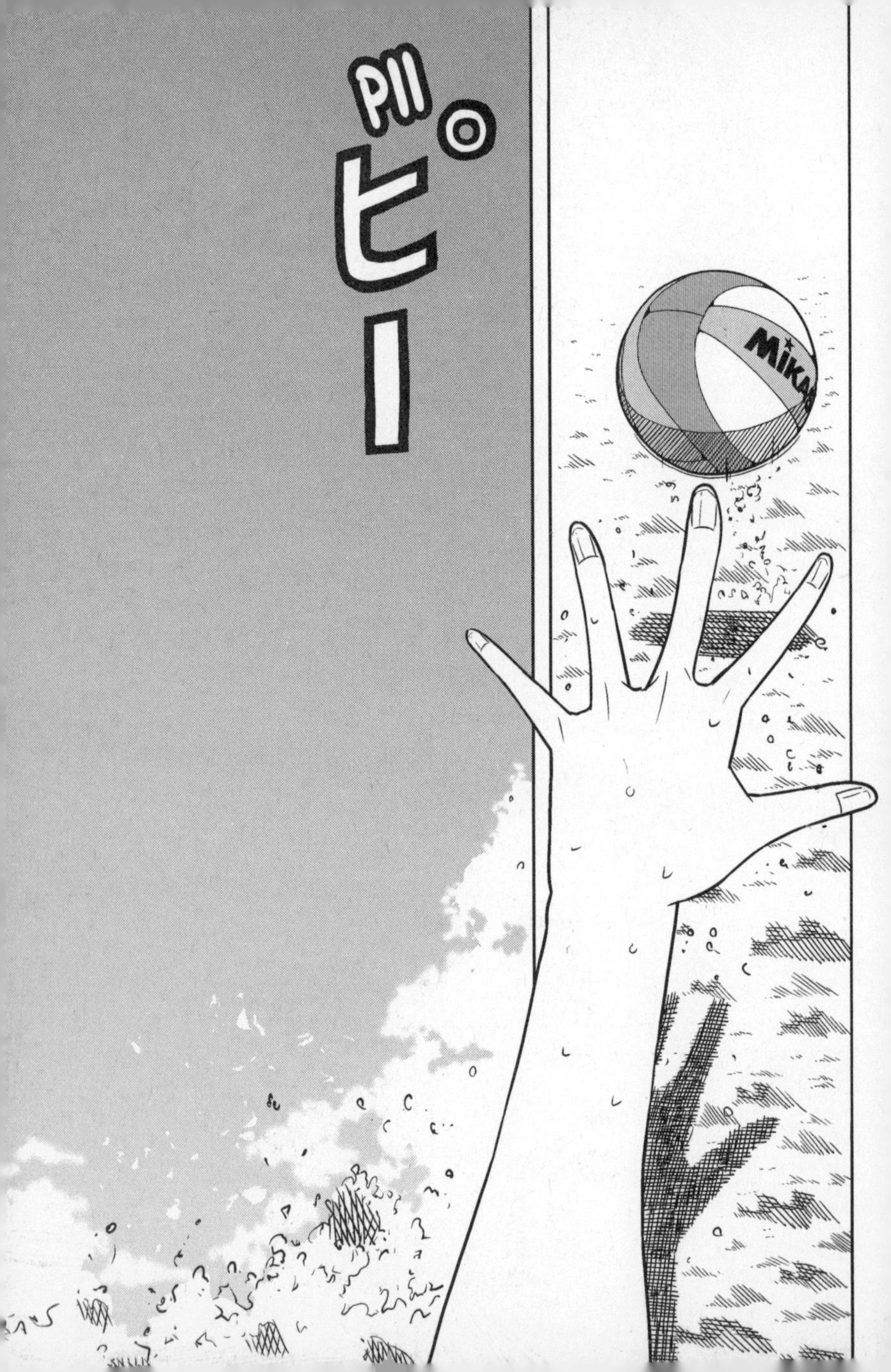

PII
ピー
MIKASA

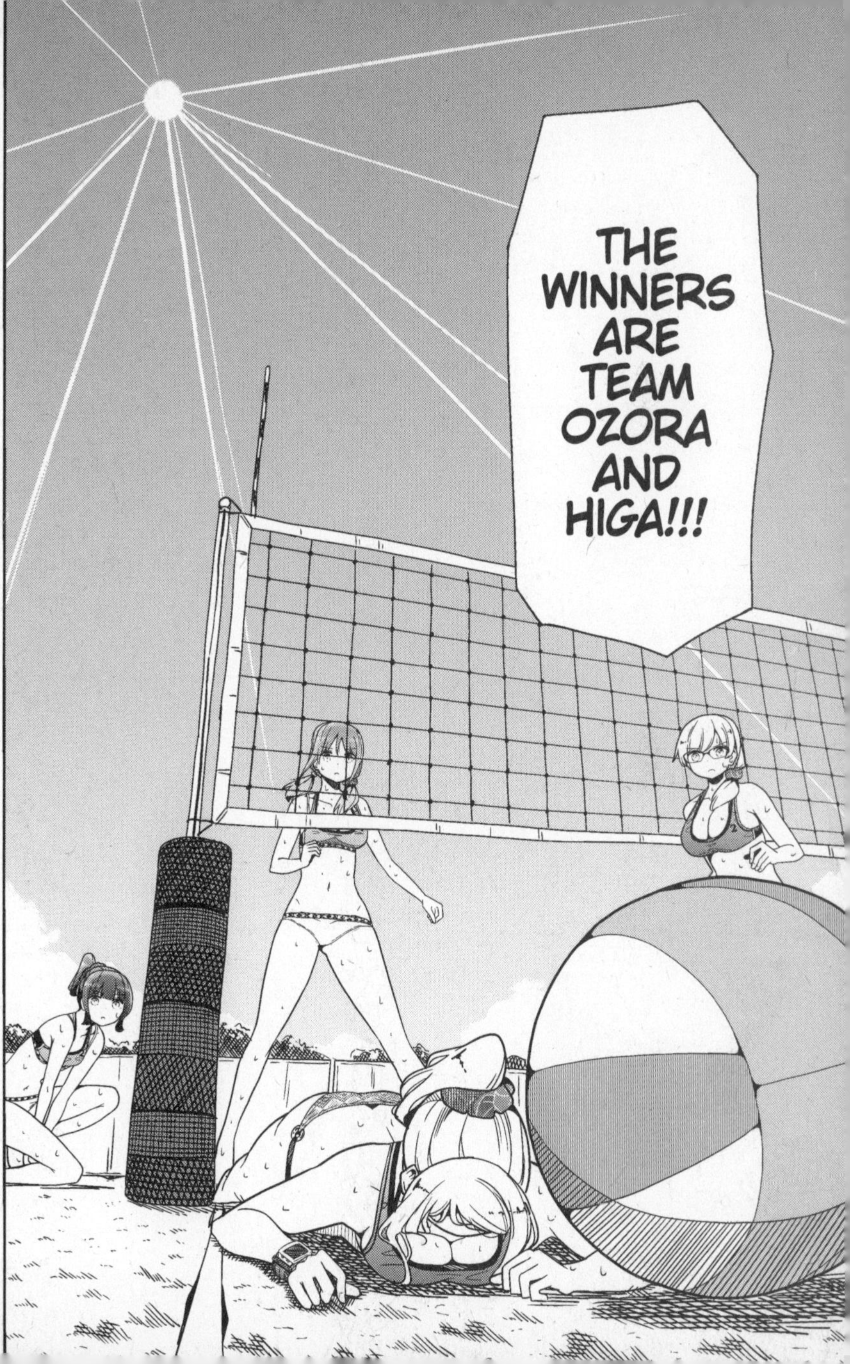
THE WINNERS ARE TEAM OZORA AND HIGA!!!

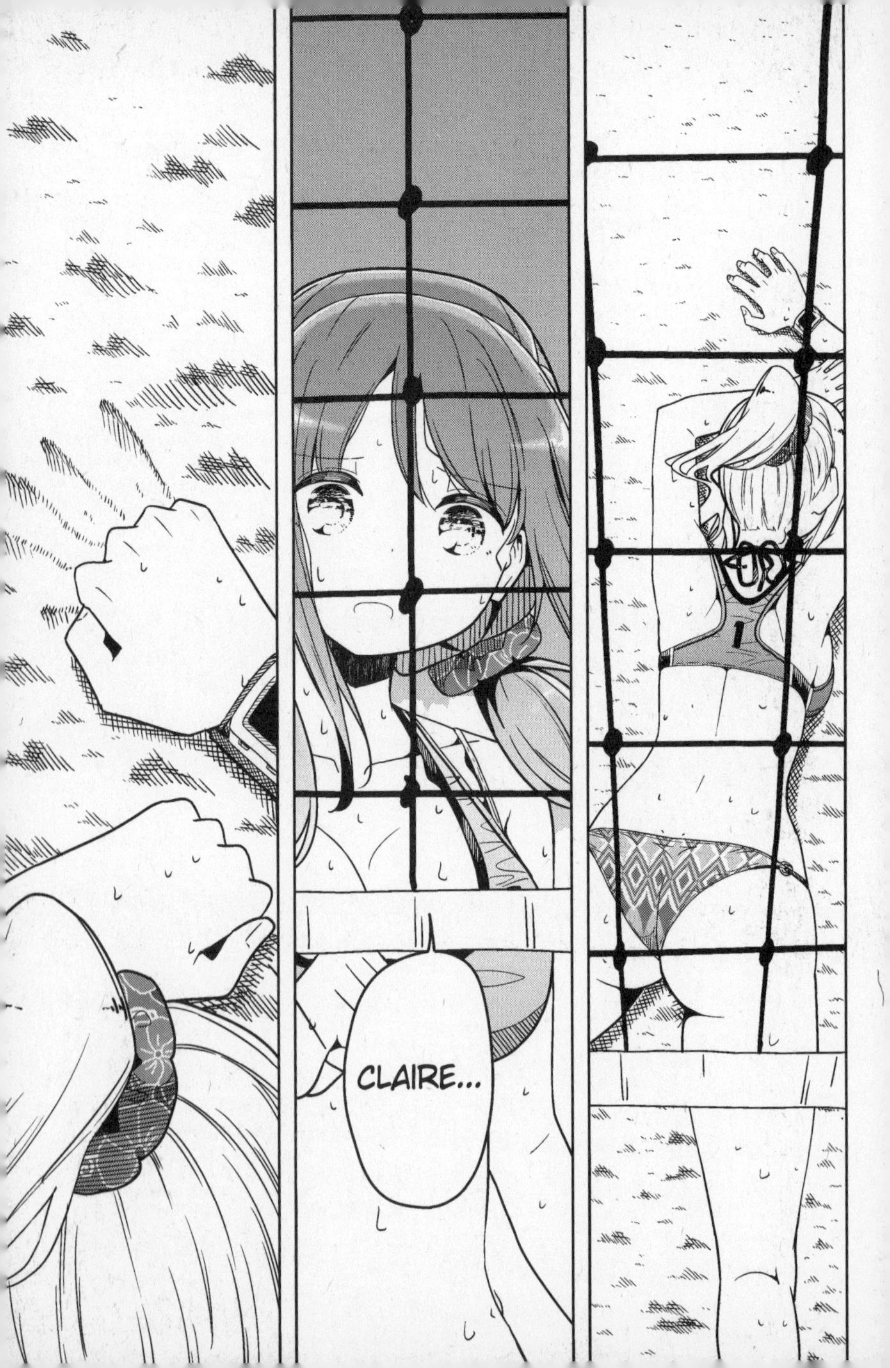
CLAIRE...

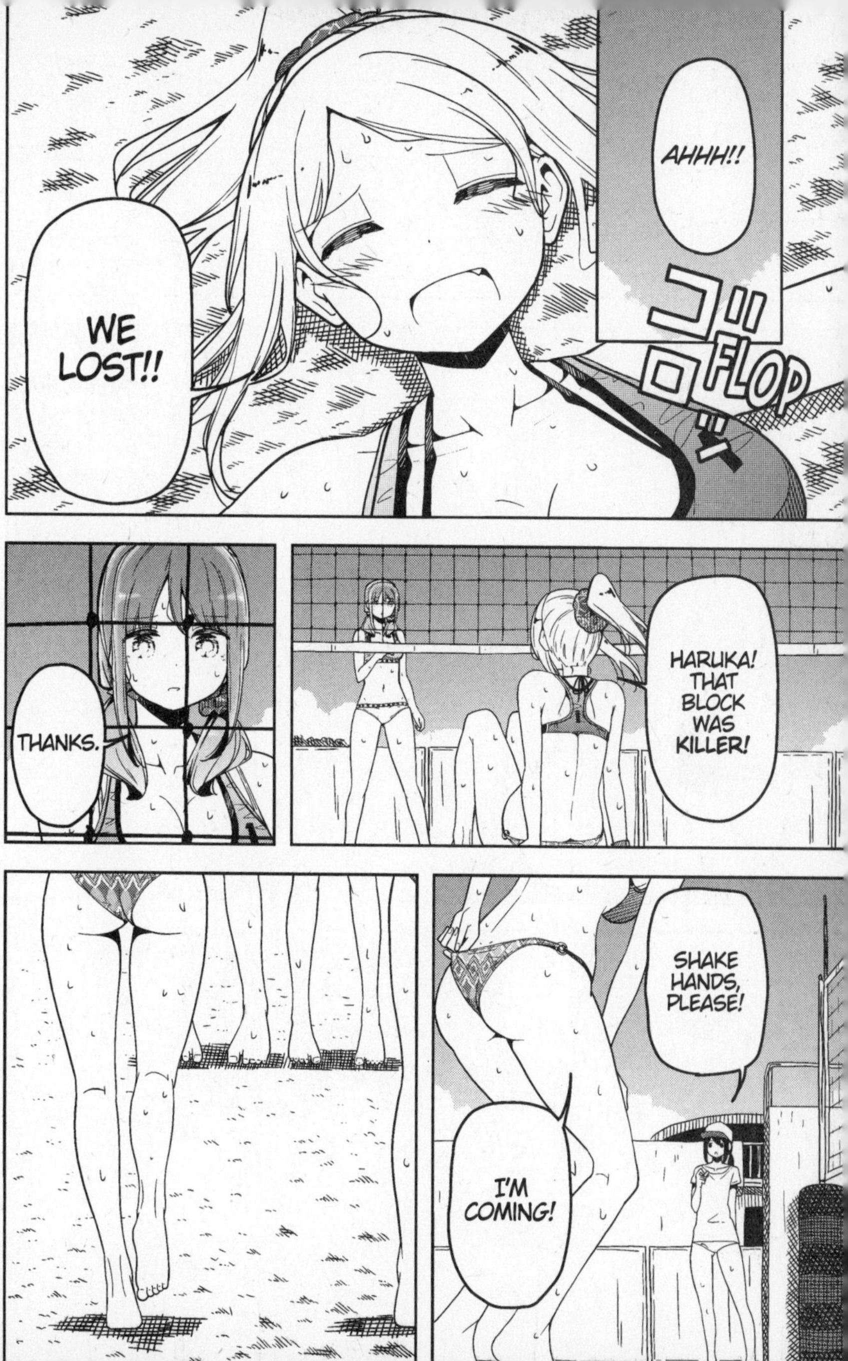
AHHH!!
ゴロッ
FLOP
WE LOST!!
HARUKA! THAT BLOCK WAS KILLER!
THANKS.
SHAKE HANDS, PLEASE!
I'M COMING!

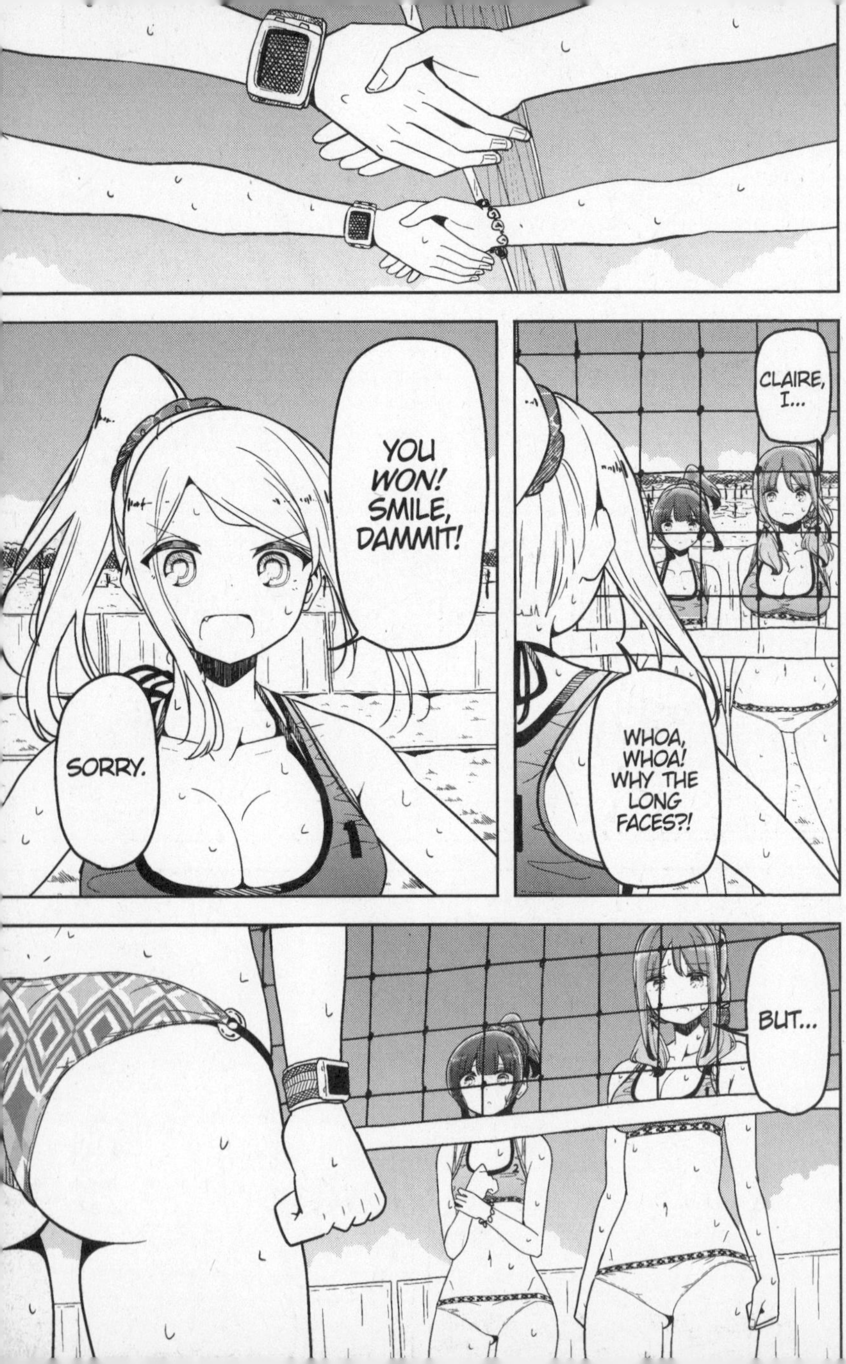
CLAIRE, I...
WHOA, WHOA! WHY THE LONG FACES?!
YOU WON! SMILE, DAMMIT!
SORRY.
BUT...

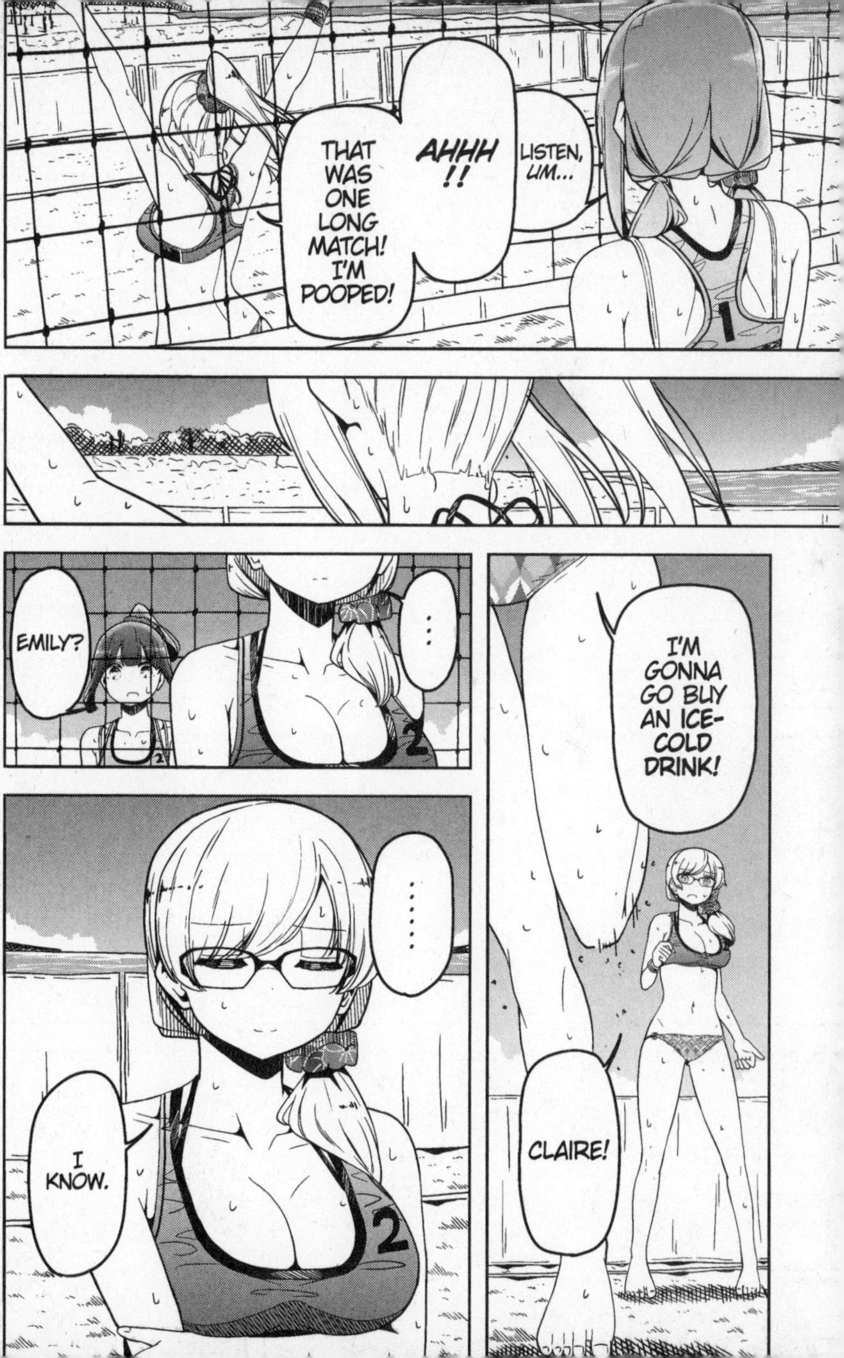
LISTEN, UM...
AHHH!!
THAT WAS ONE LONG MATCH! I'M POOPED!
I'M GONNA GO BUY AN ICE-COLD DRINK!
CLAIRE!
...
EMILY?
......
I KNOW.

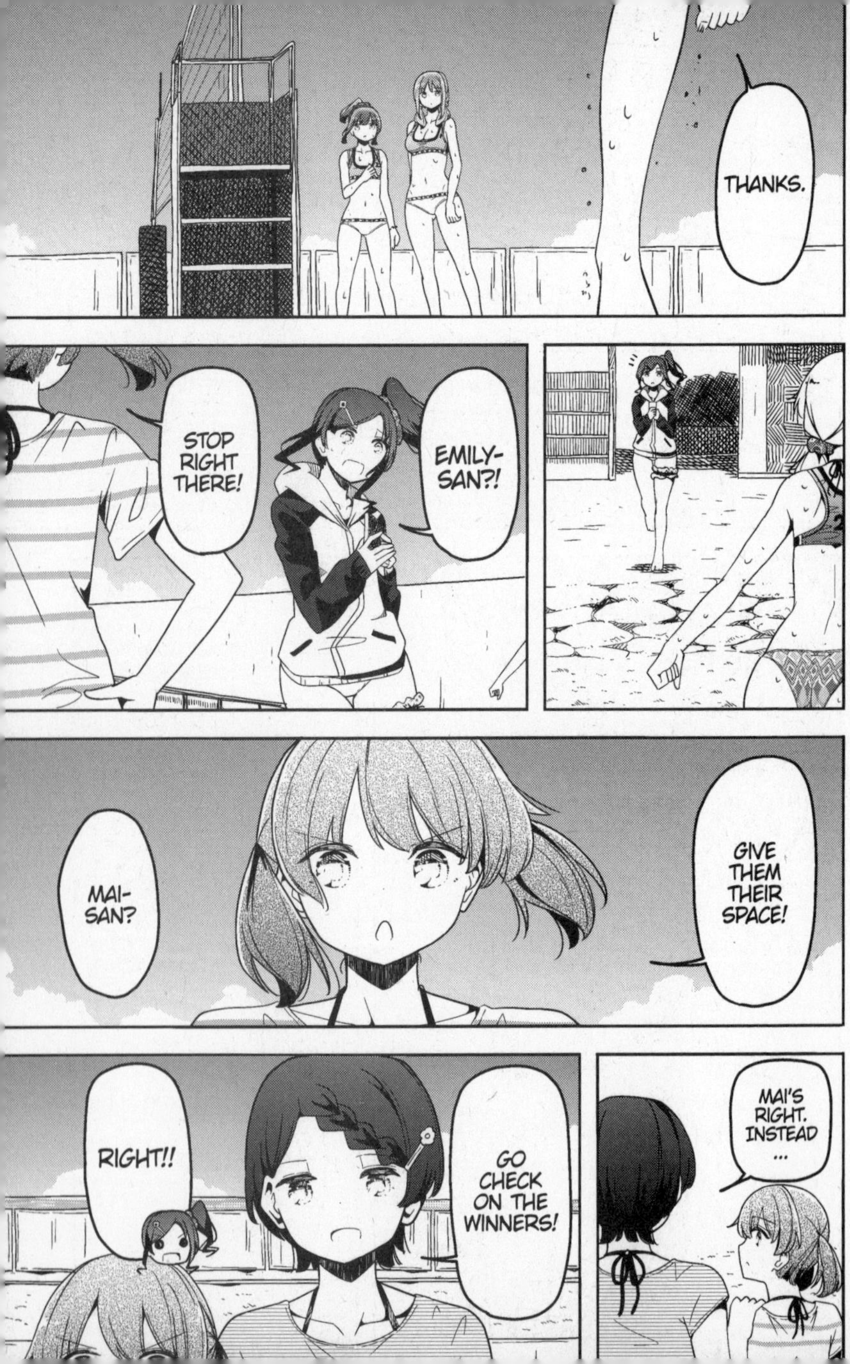
THANKS.
EMILY-SAN?!
STOP RIGHT THERE!
GIVE THEM THEIR SPACE!
MAI-SAN?
MAI'S RIGHT. INSTEAD ...
GO CHECK ON THE WINNERS!
RIGHT!!

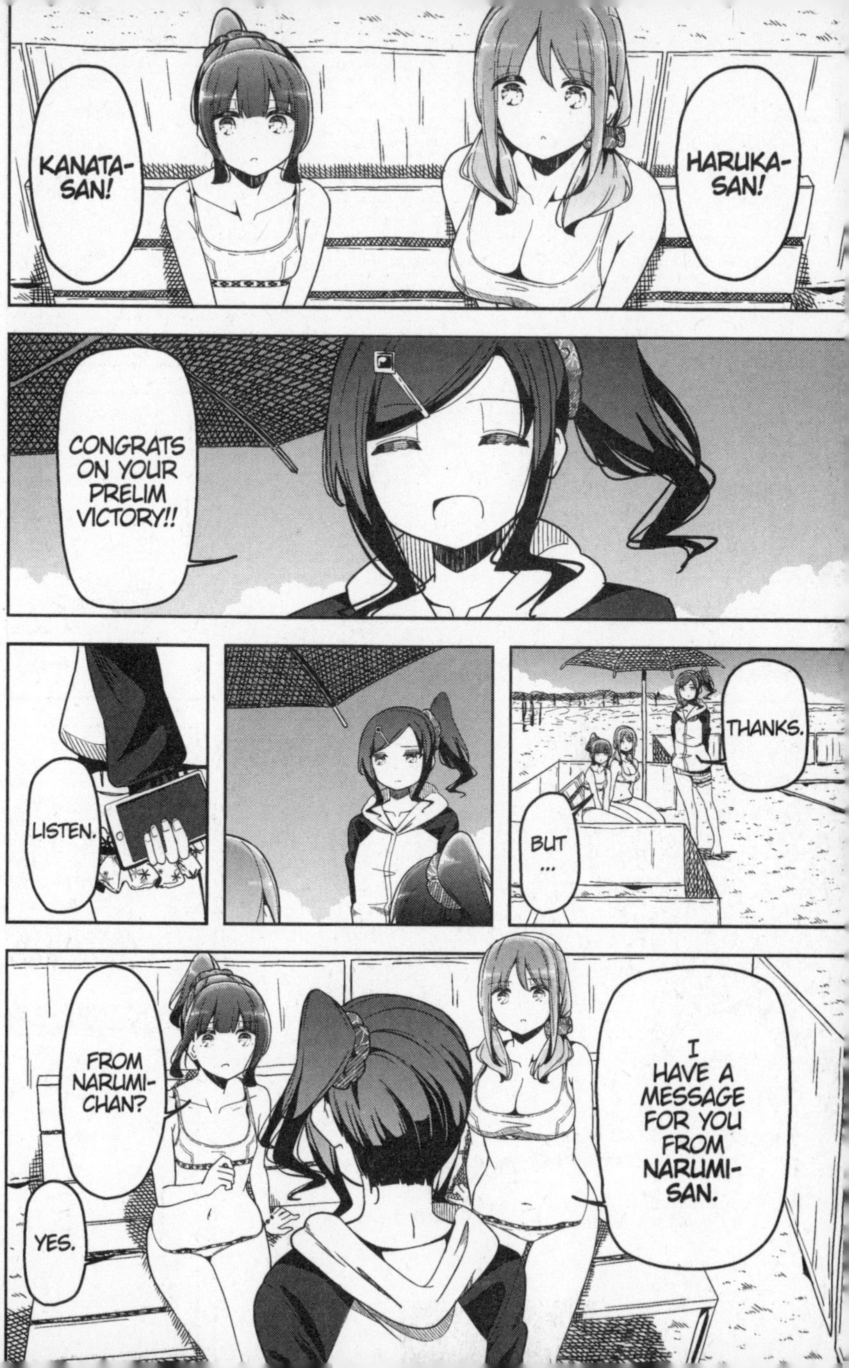
HARUKA-SAN!
KANATA-SAN!
CONGRATS ON YOUR PRELIM VICTORY!!
THANKS.
BUT ...
LISTEN.
I HAVE A MESSAGE FOR YOU FROM NARUMI-SAN.
FROM NARUMI-CHAN?
YES.

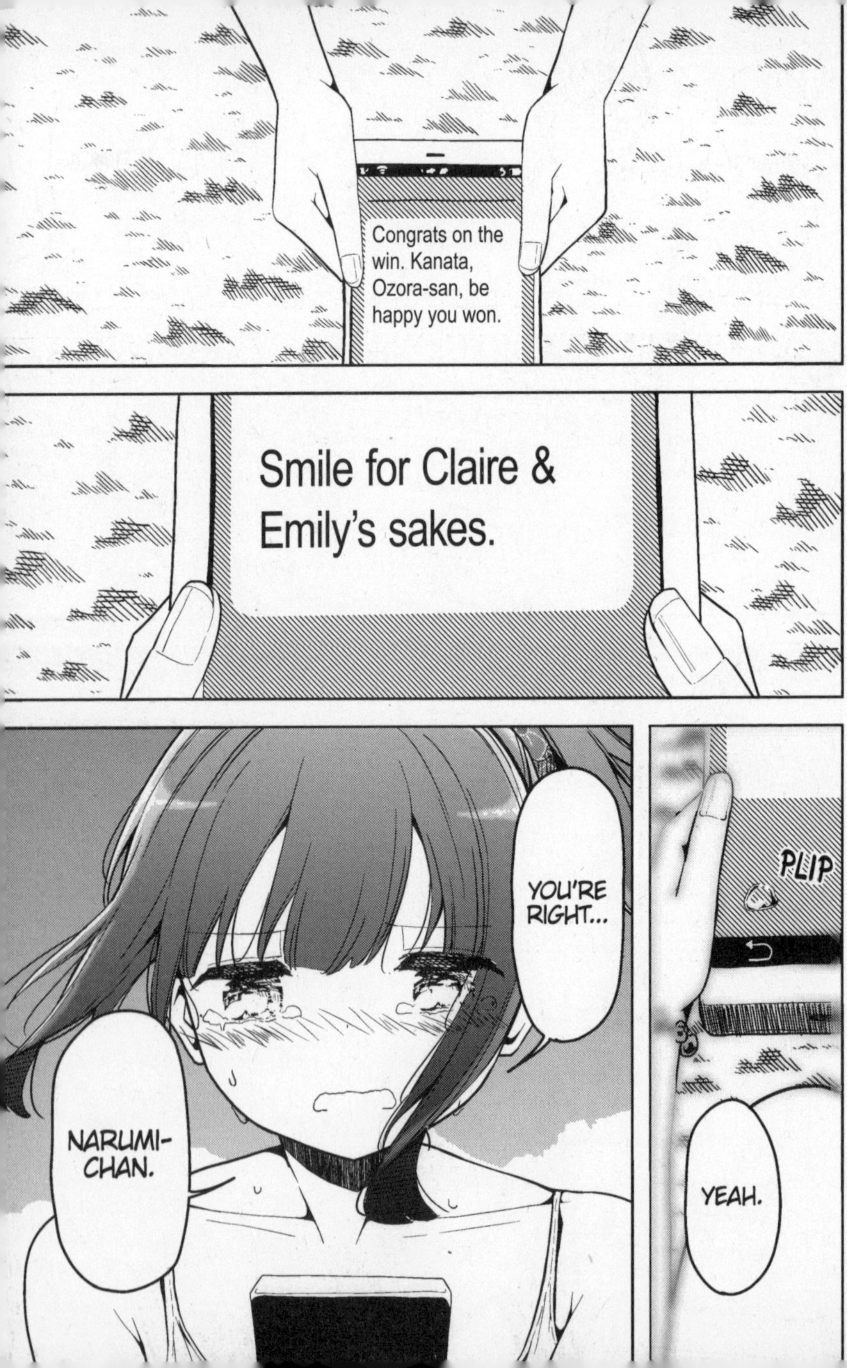
Congrats on the win. Kanata, Ozora-san, be happy you won.
Smile for Claire & Emily's sakes.
PLIP
YEAH.
YOU'RE RIGHT...
NARUMI-CHAN.

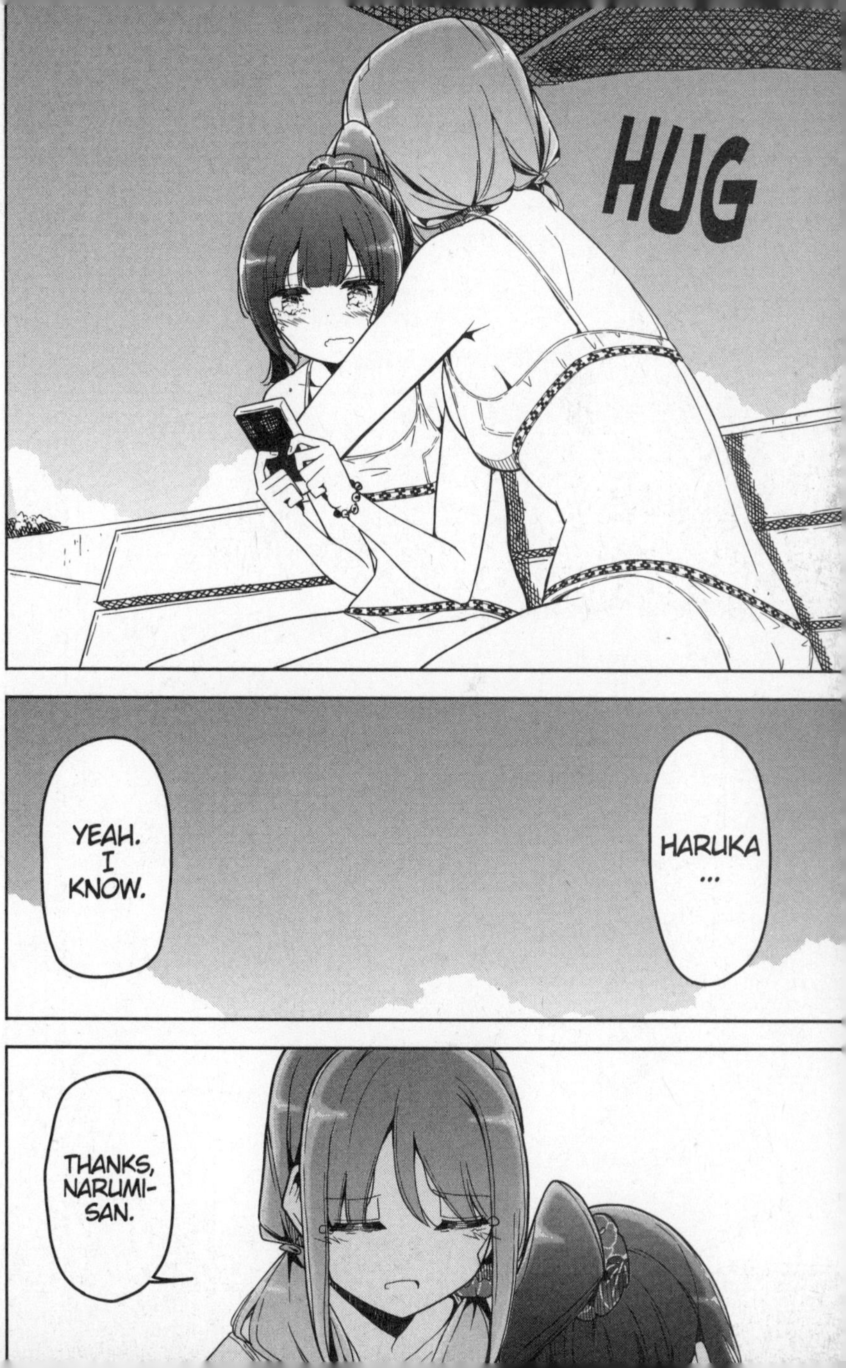
HUG
HARUKA ...
YEAH. I KNOW.
THANKS, NARUMI-SAN.

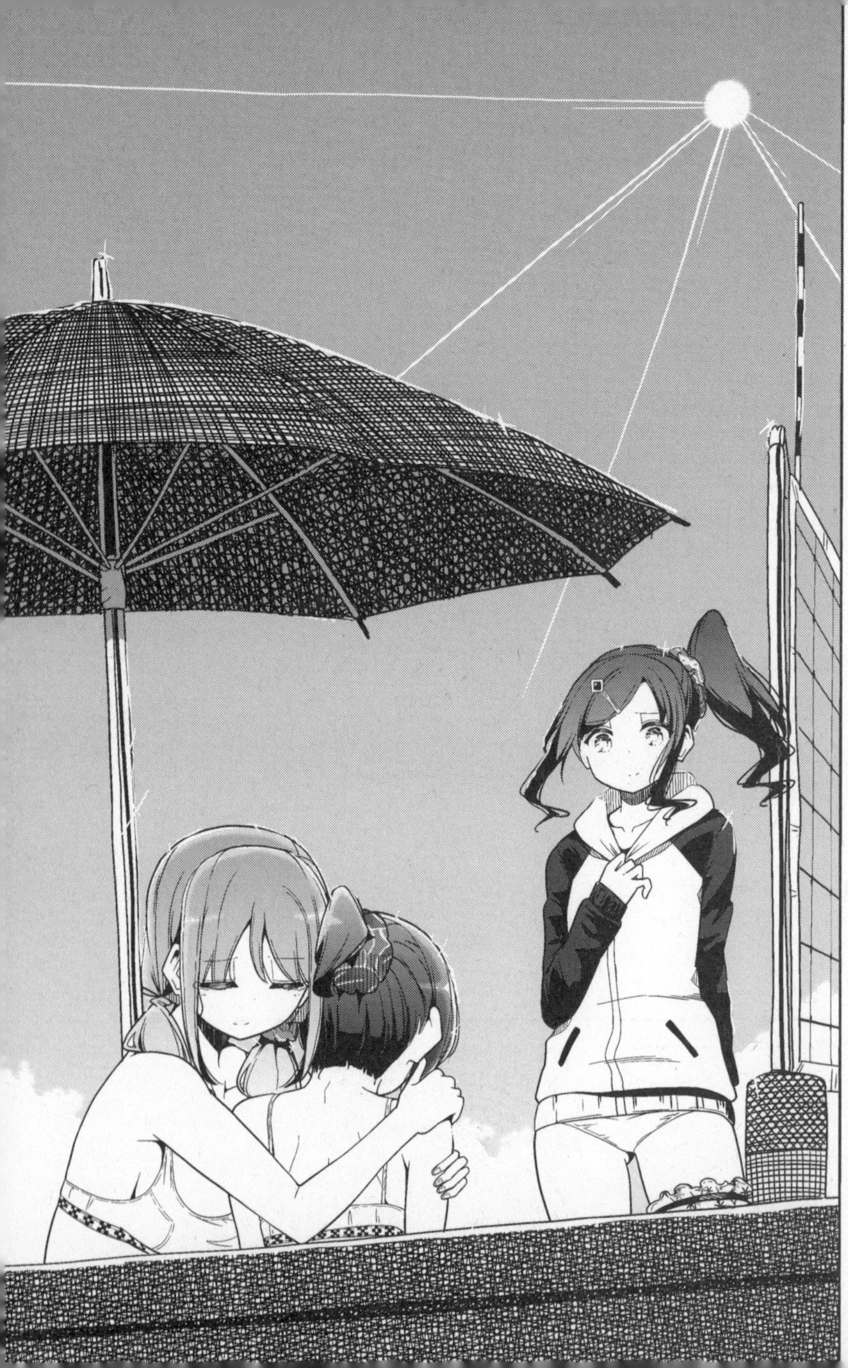

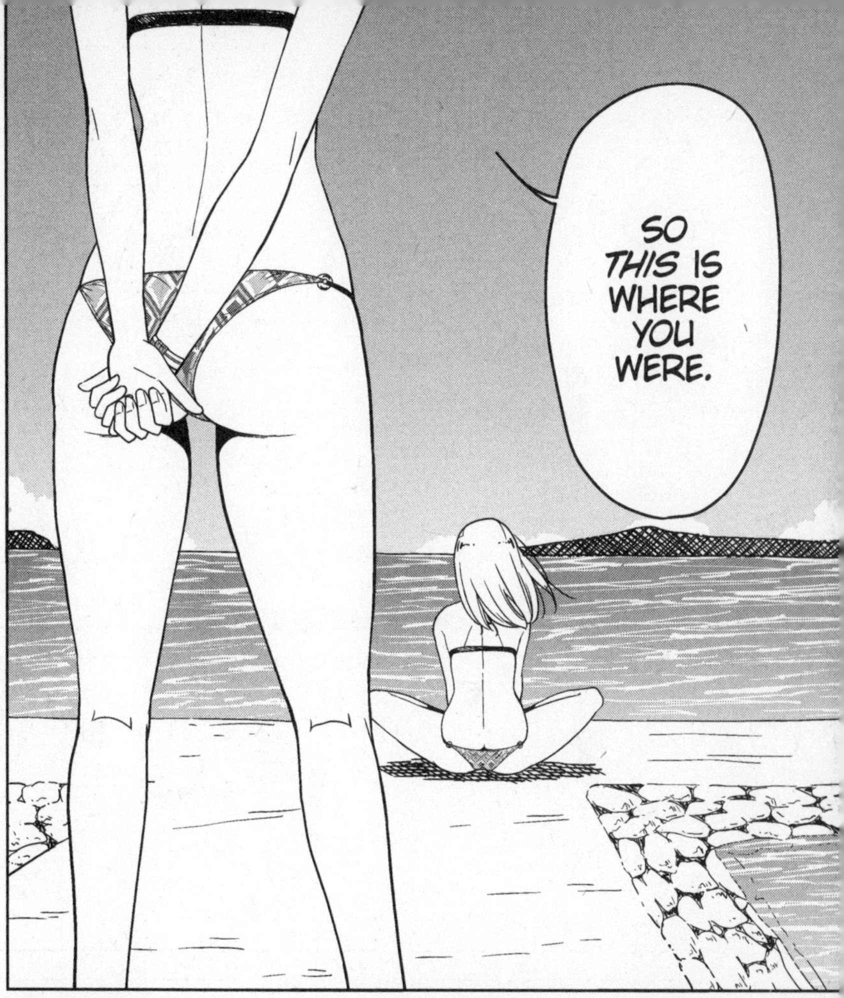
SO THIS IS WHERE YOU WERE.

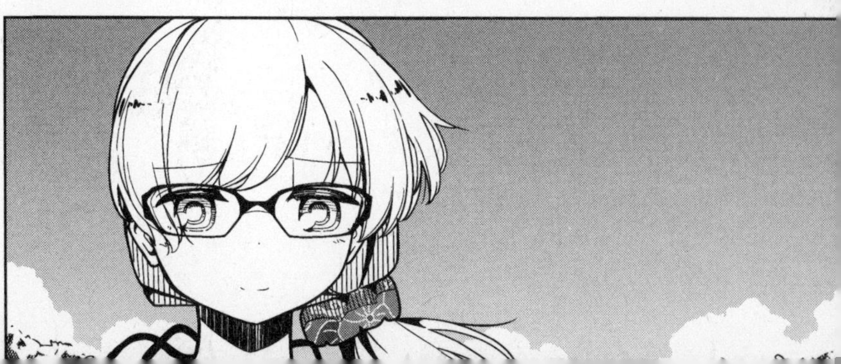

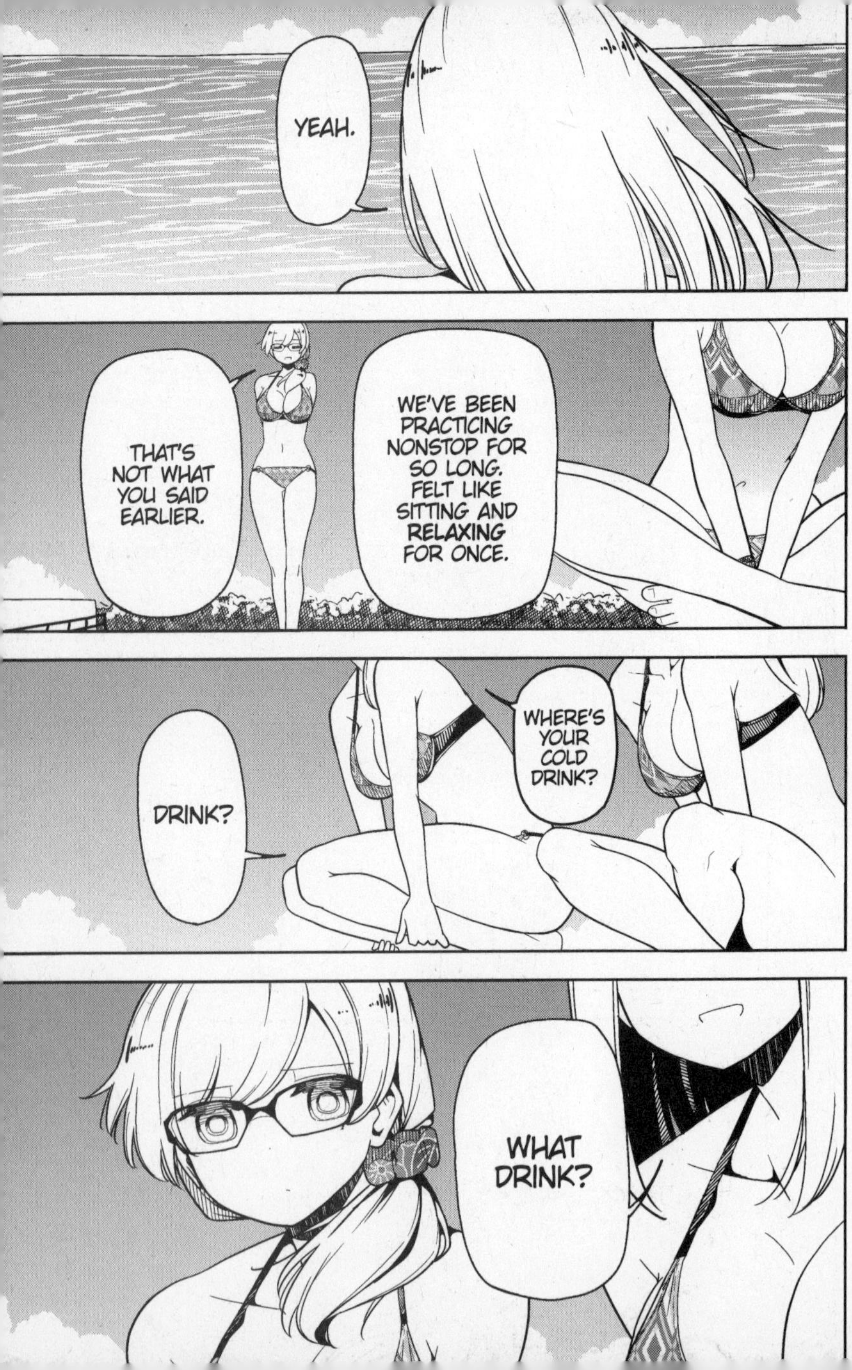
YEAH.
WE'VE BEEN PRACTICING NONSTOP FOR SO LONG. FELT LIKE SITTING AND RELAXING FOR ONCE.
THAT'S NOT WHAT YOU SAID EARLIER.
WHERE'S YOUR COLD DRINK?
DRINK?
WHAT DRINK?

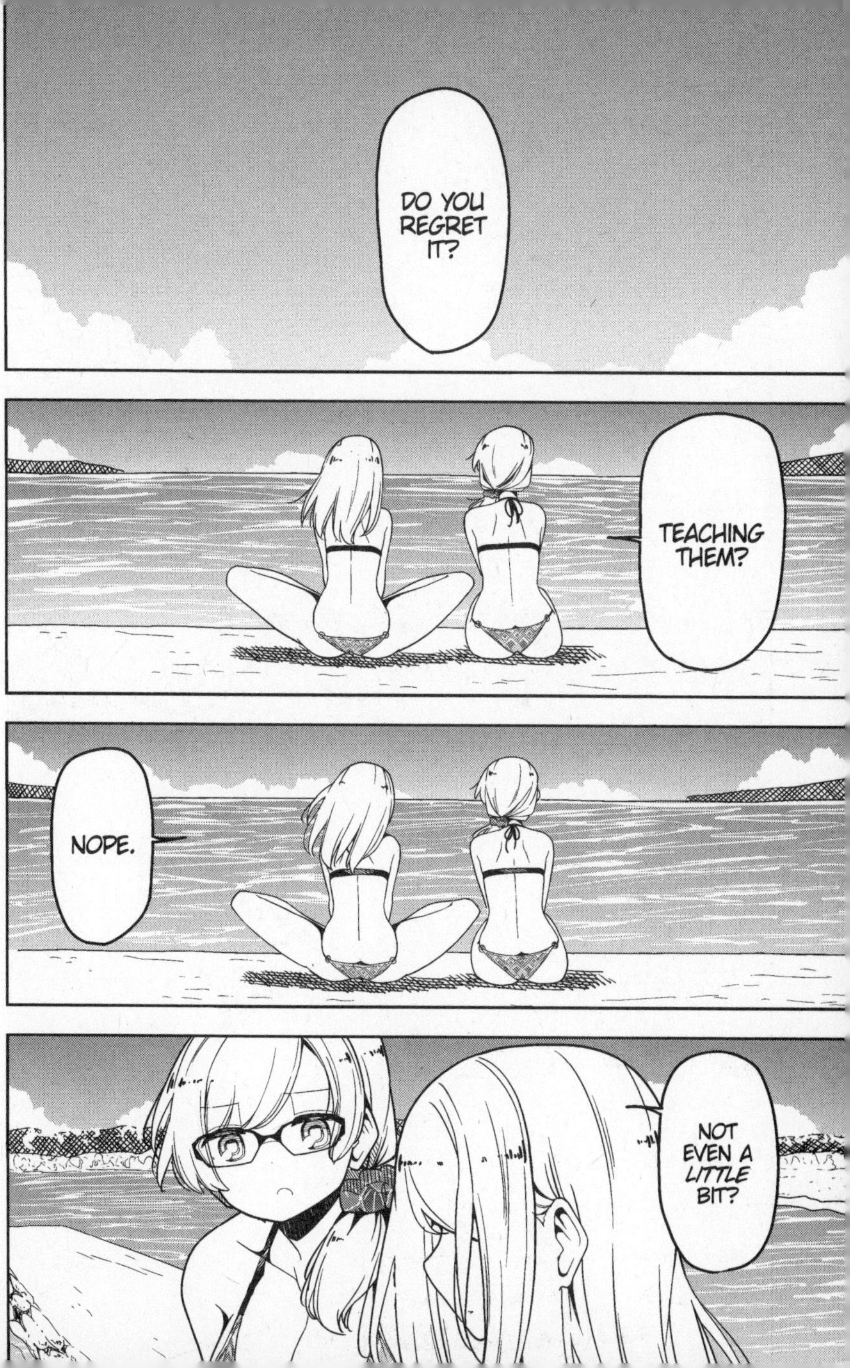
DO YOU REGRET IT?
TEACHING THEM?
NOPE.
NOT EVEN A *LITTLE* BIT?

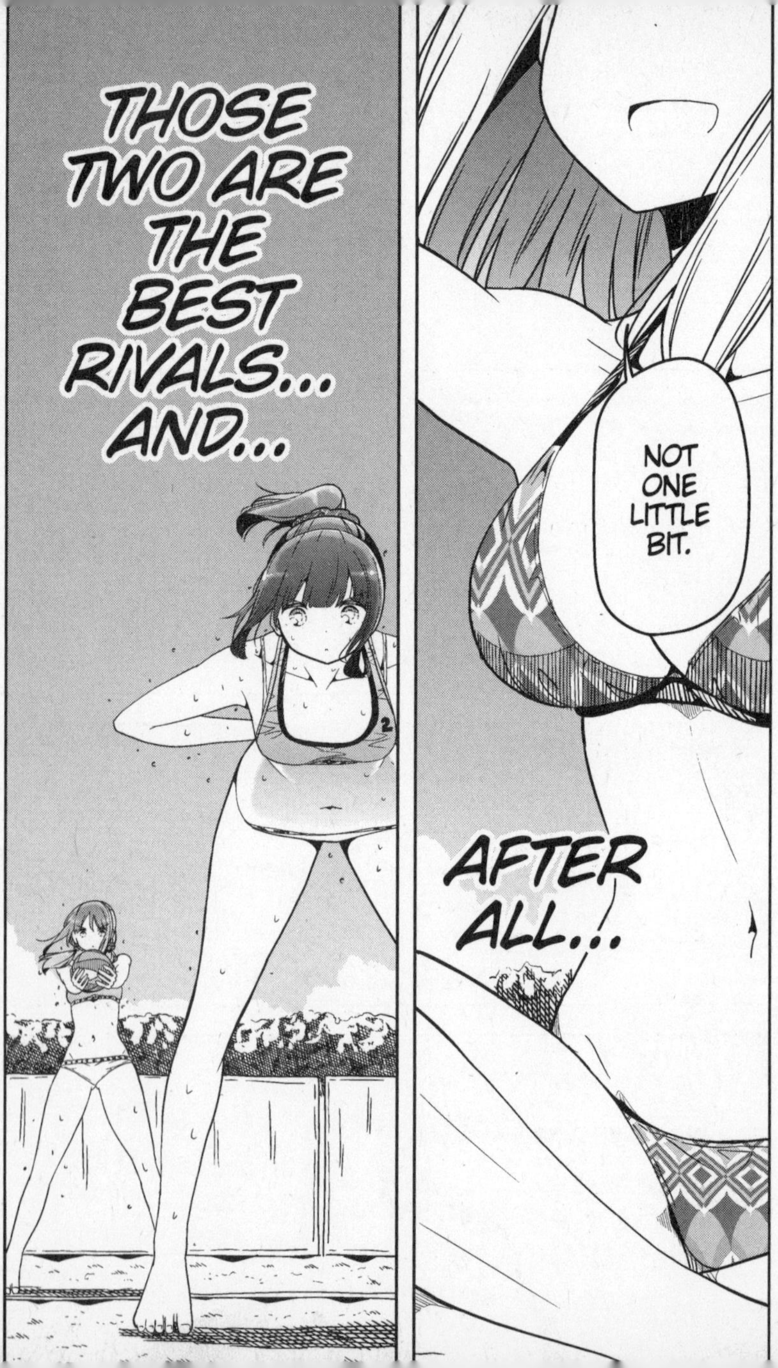
NOT ONE LITTLE BIT.
AFTER ALL...
THOSE TWO ARE THE BEST RIVALS... AND...

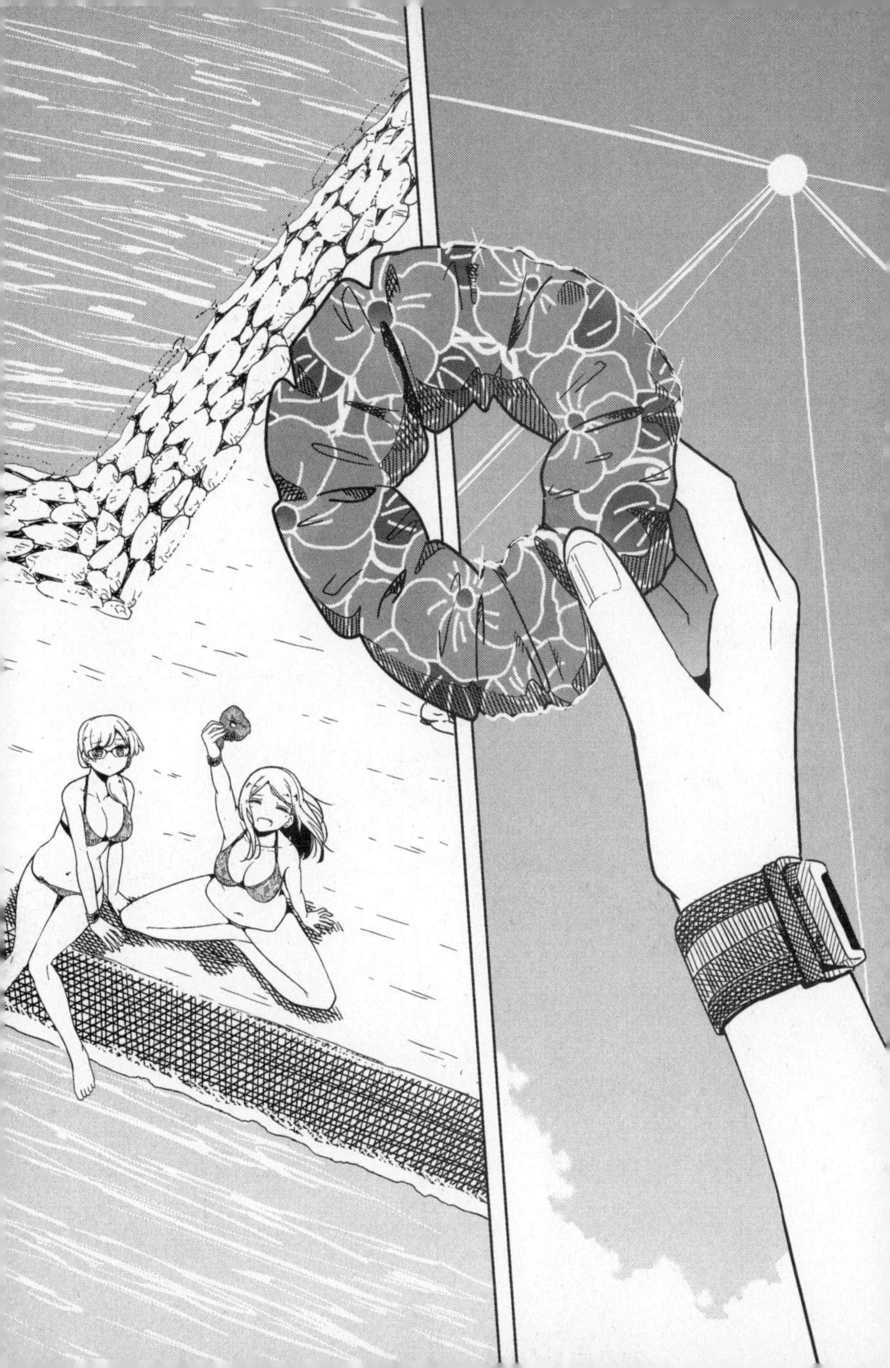

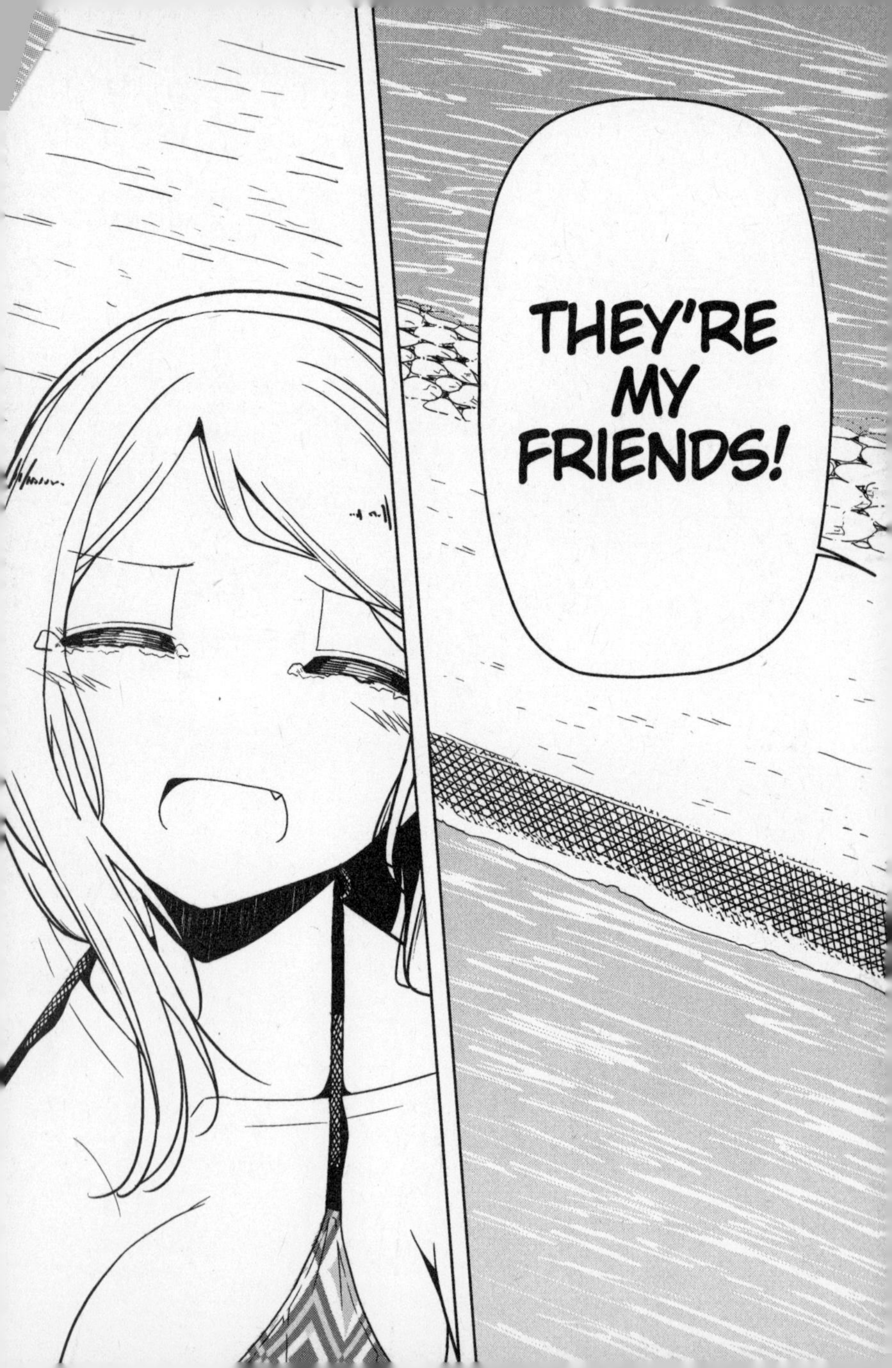
THEY'RE MY FRIENDS!

HONEST-
LY!

YOU
ARE
SUCH A
DUMMY,
SIS.

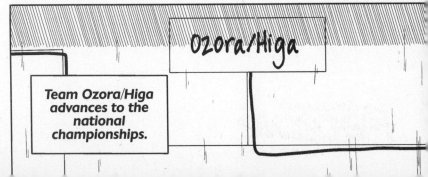

Ozora/Higa

Team Ozora/Higa
advances to the
national
championships.

Presented by Nyoijizai

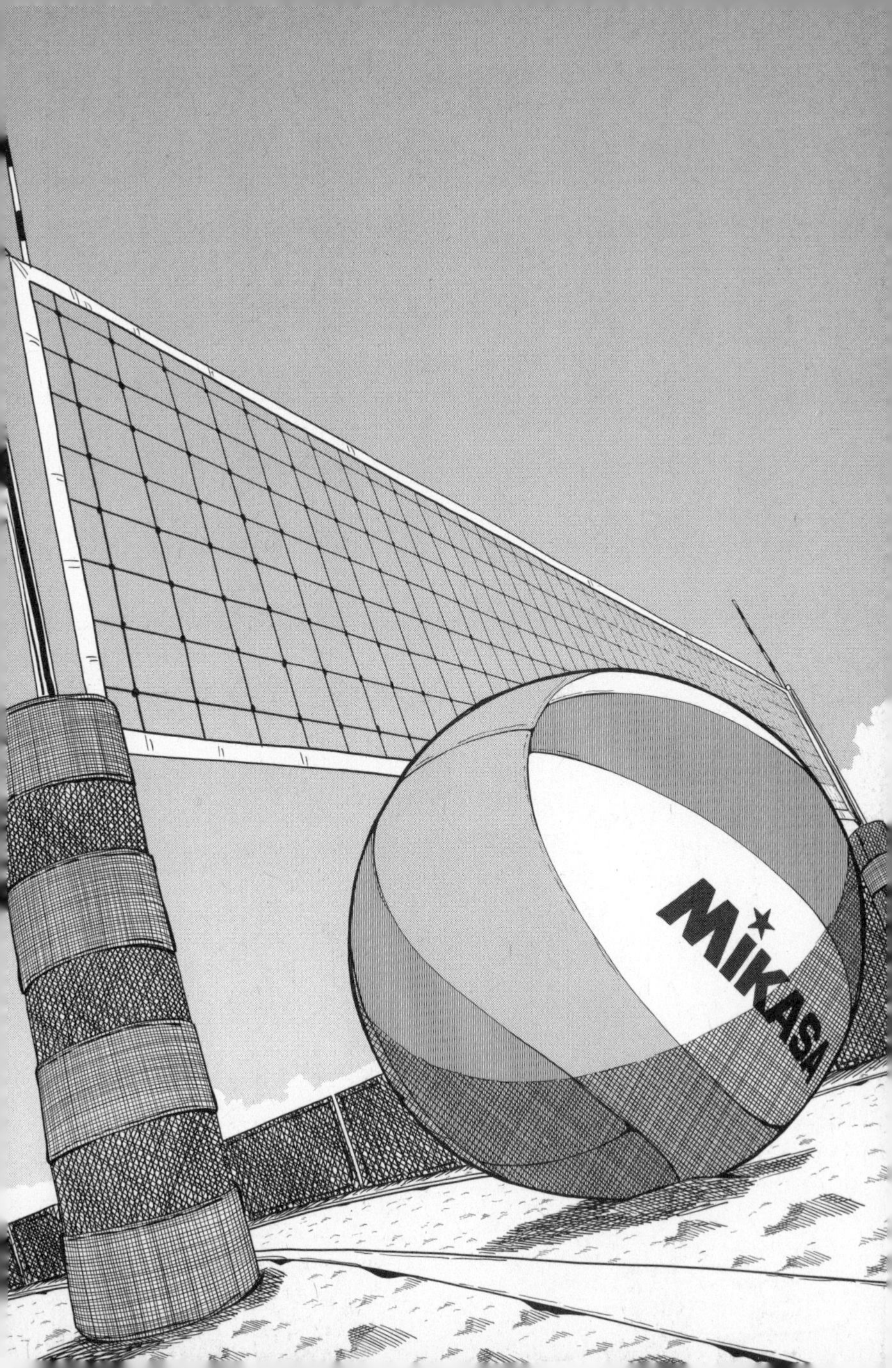
MIKASA

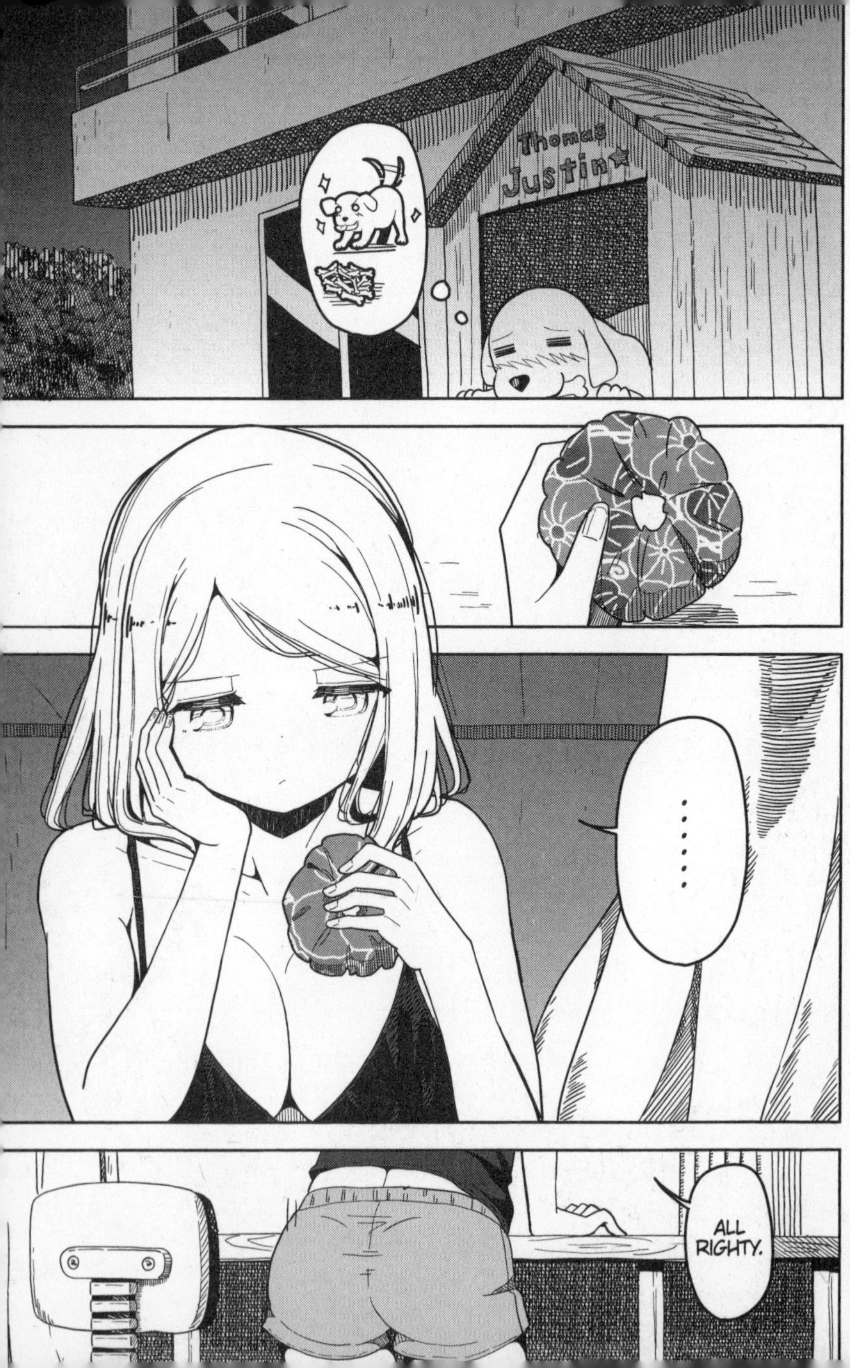
Thomas
Justin☆
......
ALL RIGHTY.

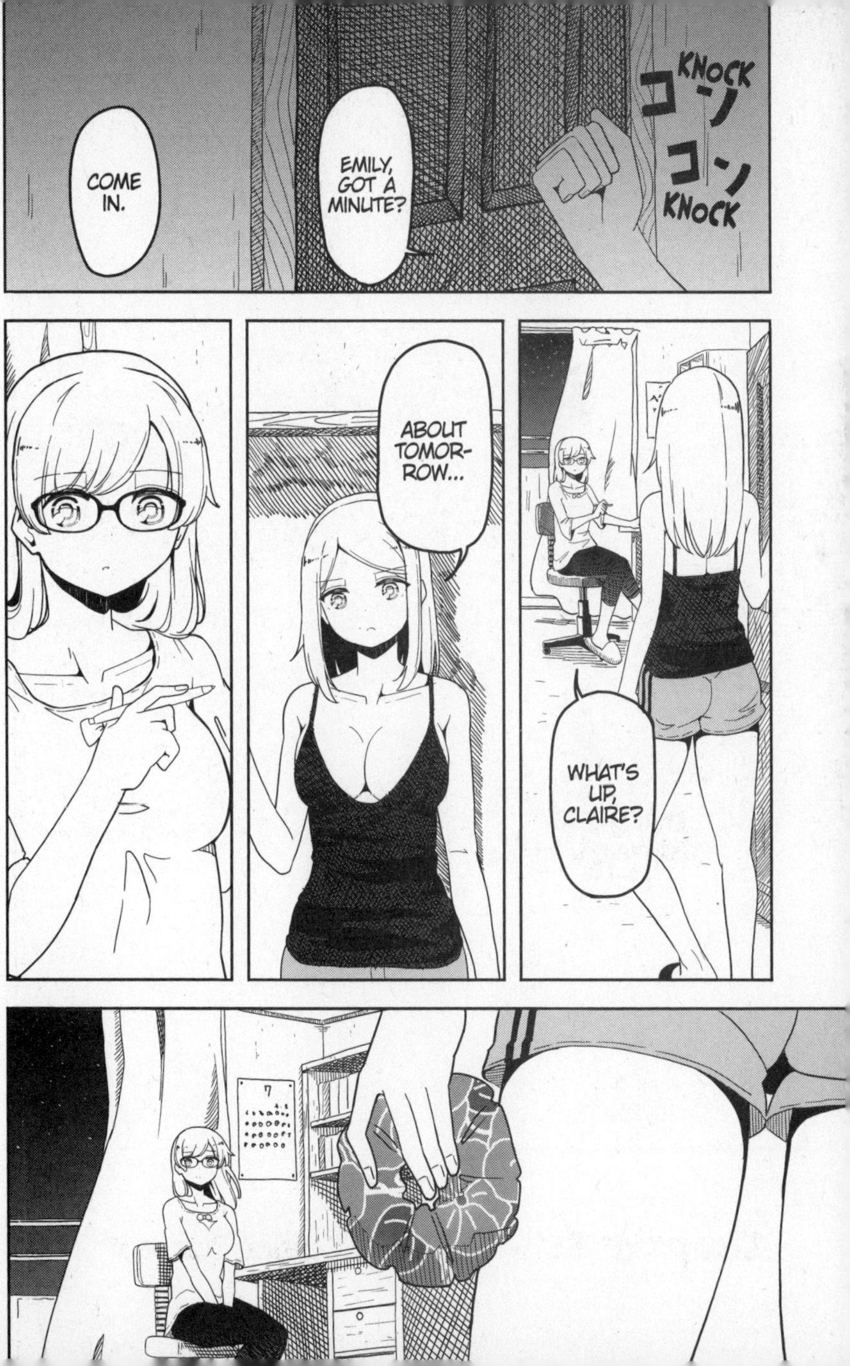
KNOCK
コン
コン
KNOCK
EMILY, GOT A MINUTE?
COME IN.
WHAT'S UP, CLAIRE?
ABOUT TOMOR-ROW...

Chapter 31: We're Only Getting Started!

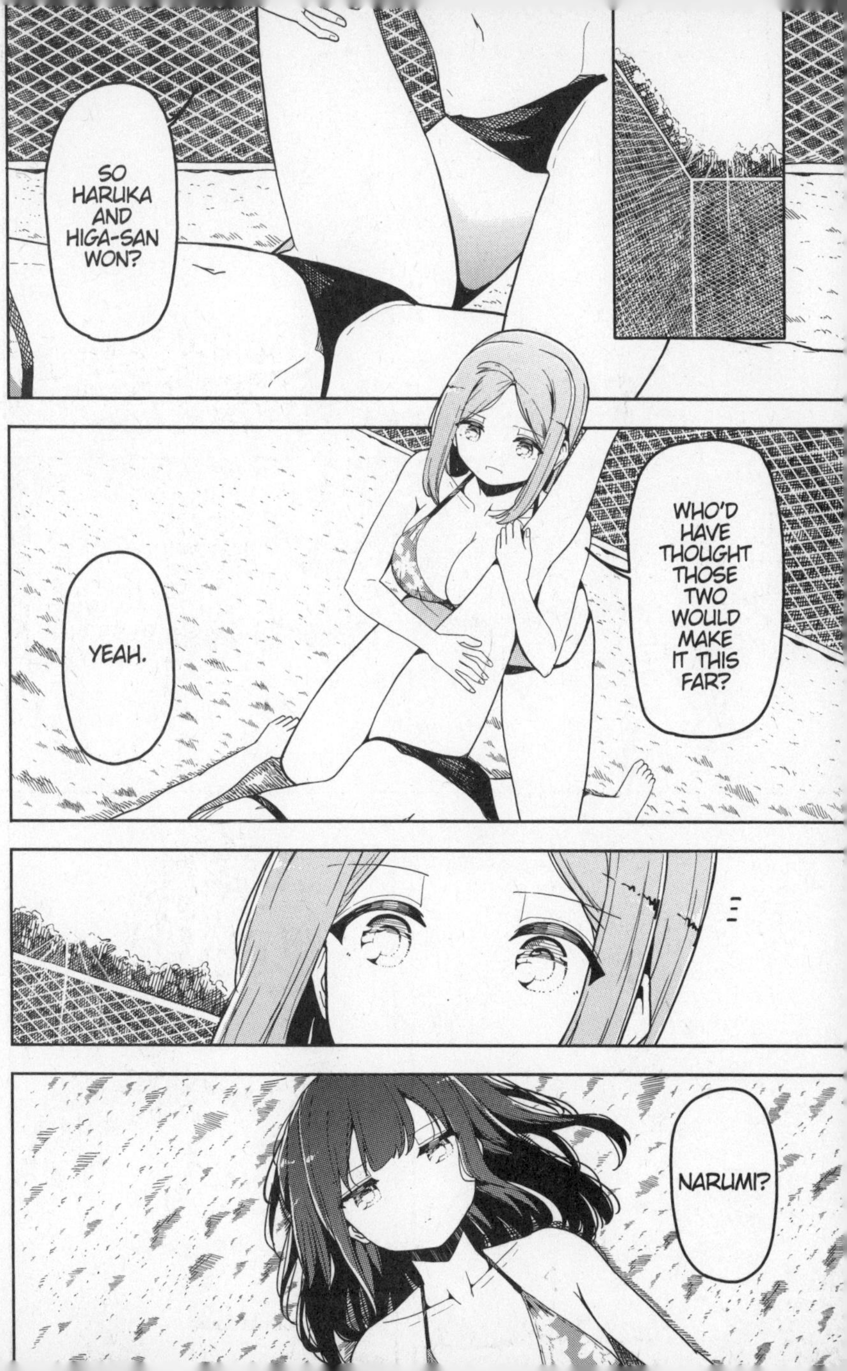
SO HARUKA AND HIGA-SAN WON?
WHO'D HAVE THOUGHT THOSE TWO WOULD MAKE IT THIS FAR?
YEAH.
...
NARUMI?

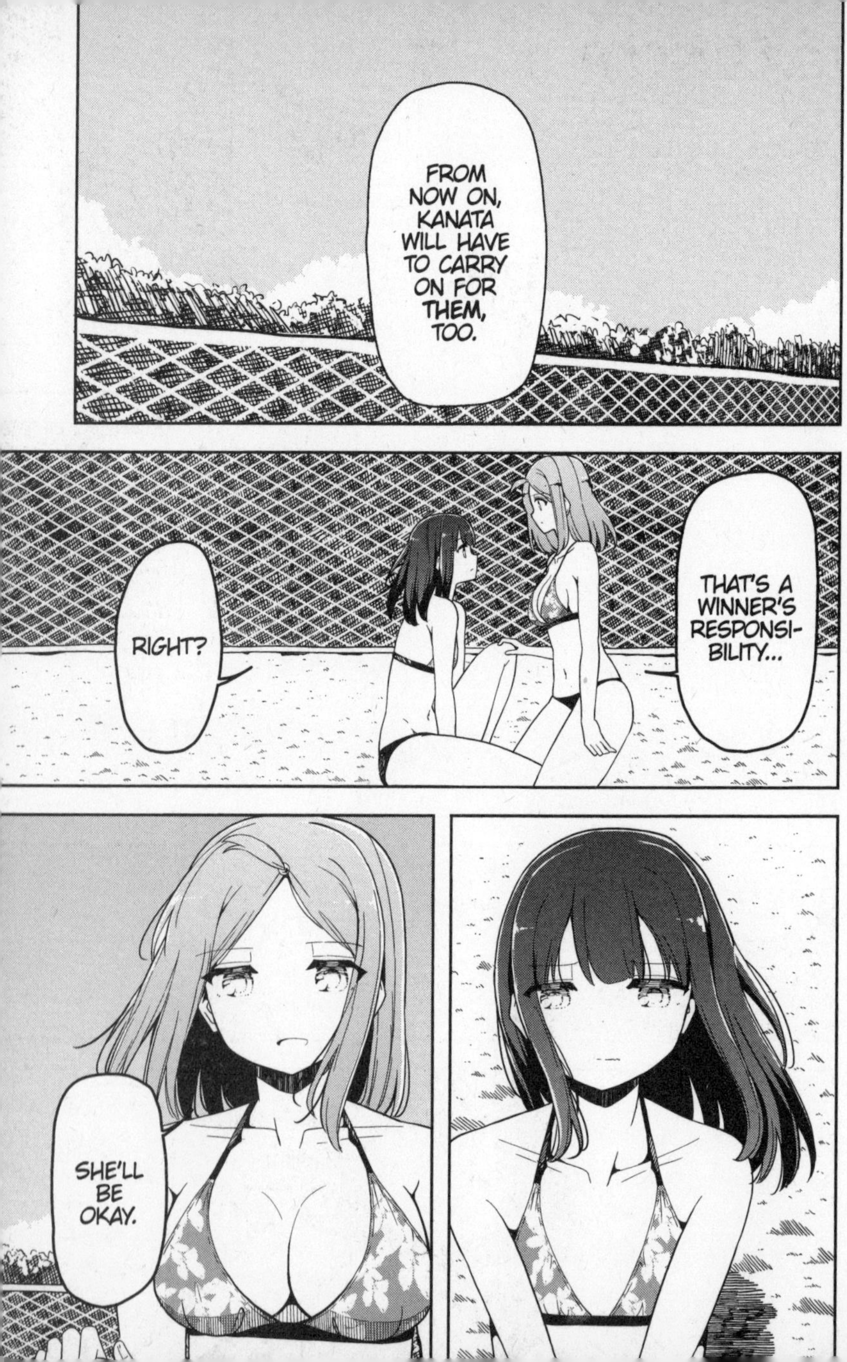
FROM NOW ON, KANATA WILL HAVE TO CARRY ON FOR THEM, TOO.
THAT'S A WINNER'S RESPONSI-BILITY...
RIGHT?
SHE'LL BE OKAY.

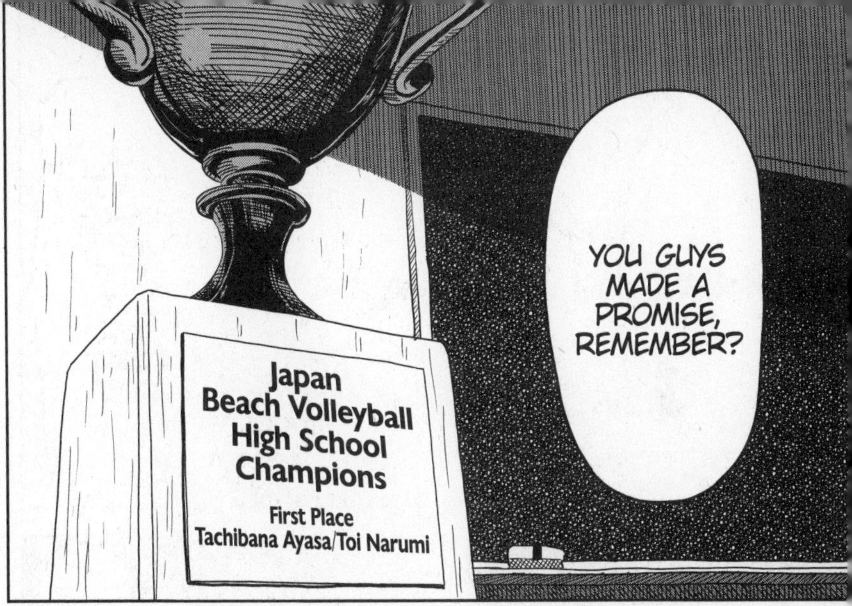
YOU GUYS MADE A PROMISE, REMEMBER?
Japan Beach Volleyball High School Champions
First Place
Tachibana Ayasa/Toi Narumi
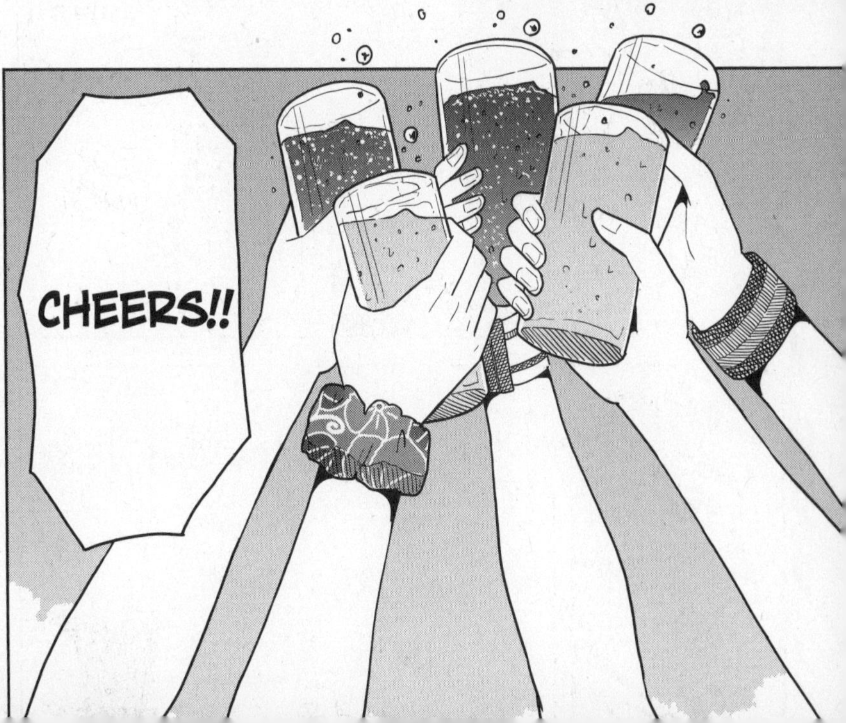
CHEERS!!

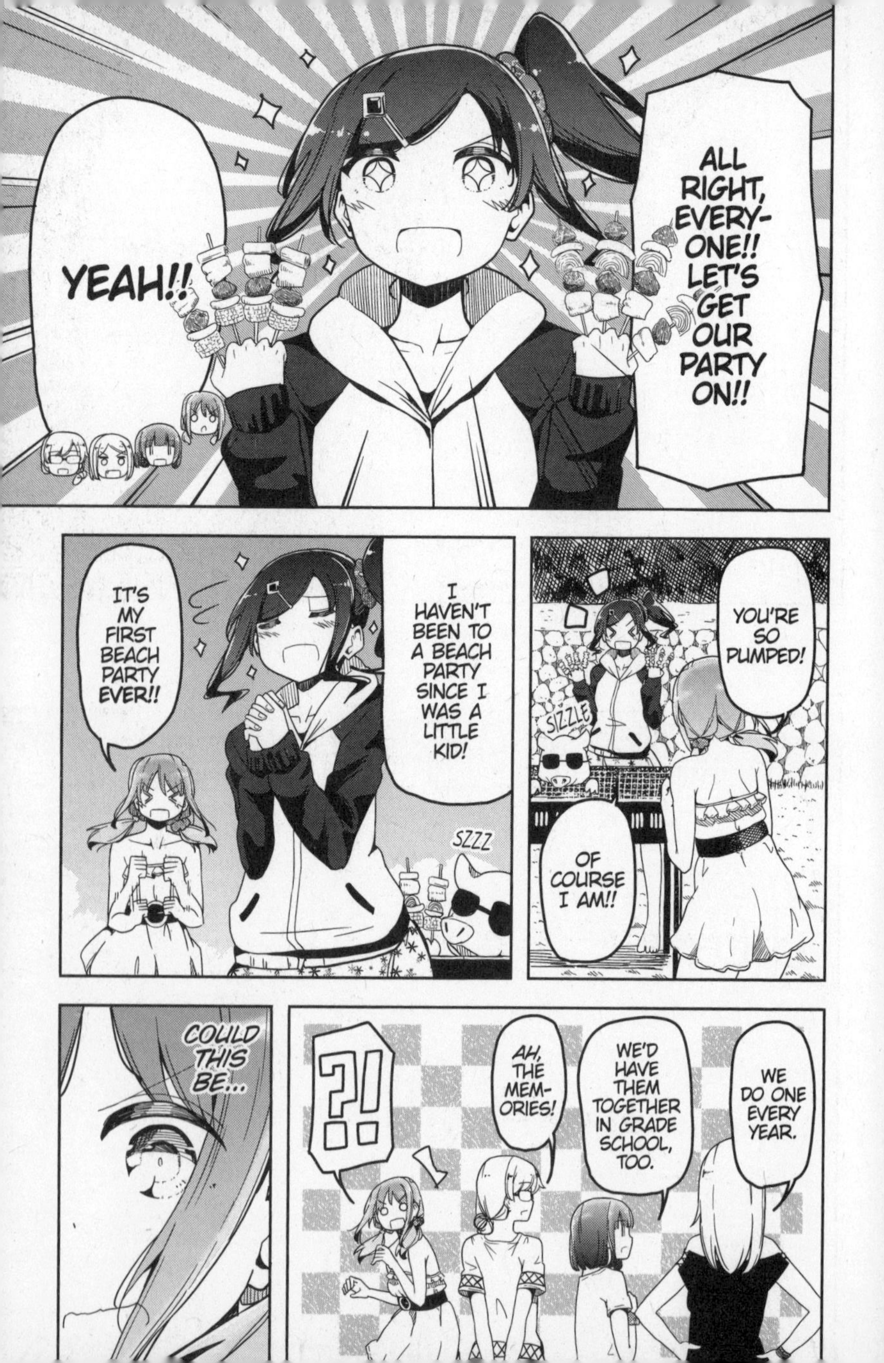
ALL RIGHT, EVERY-ONE!! LET'S GET OUR PARTY ON!!
YEAH!!
YOU'RE SO PUMPED!
SIZZLE
OF COURSE I AM!!
I HAVEN'T BEEN TO A BEACH PARTY SINCE I WAS A LITTLE KID!
IT'S MY FIRST BEACH PARTY EVER!!
SZZZ
WE DO ONE EVERY YEAR.
WE'D HAVE THEM TOGETHER IN GRADE SCHOOL, TOO.
AH, THE MEM-ORIES!
?!
COULD THIS BE...

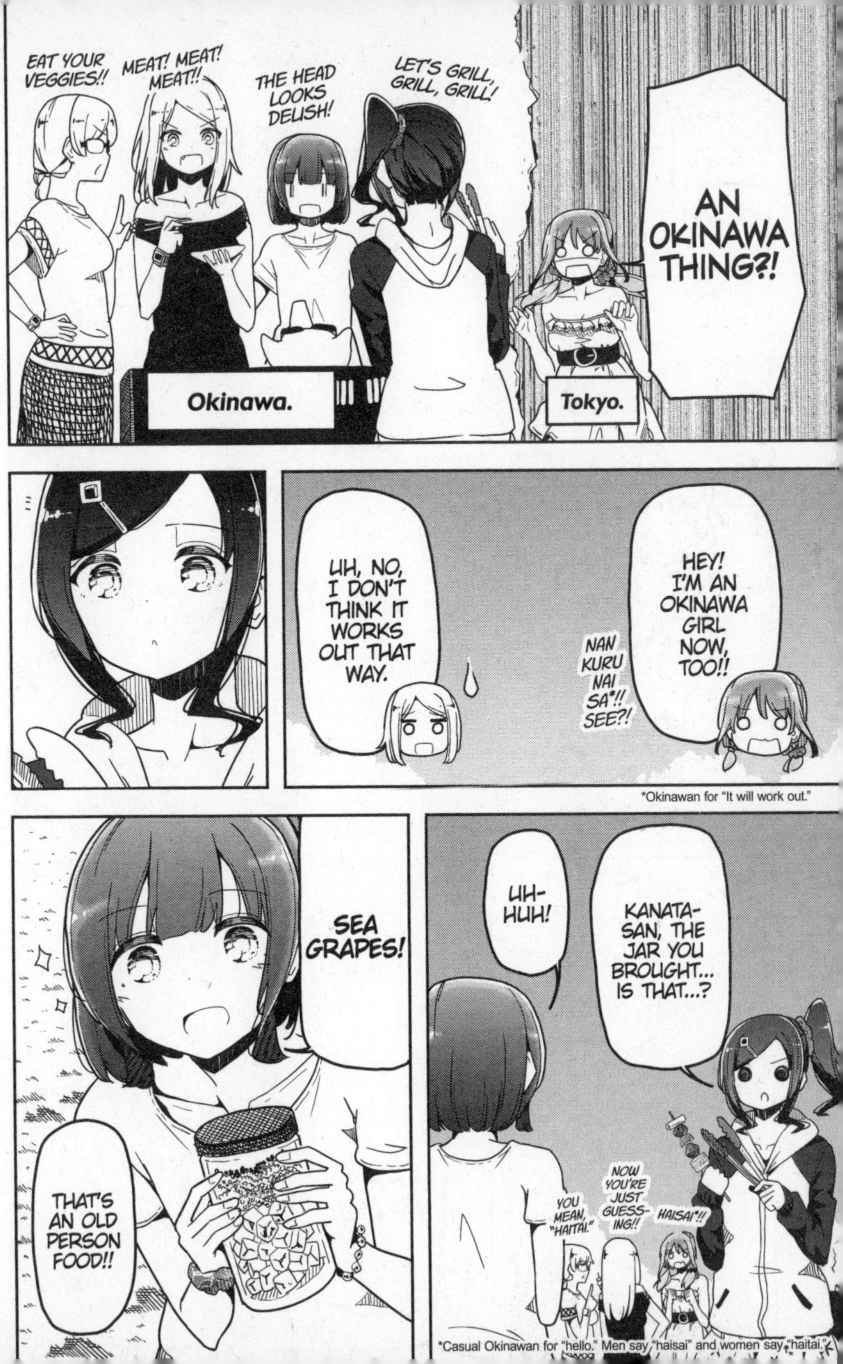
AN OKINAWA THING?!
LET'S GRILL, GRILL, GRILL!
THE HEAD LOOKS DELISH!
MEAT! MEAT! MEAT!!
EAT YOUR VEGGIES!!
Tokyo.
Okinawa.
HEY! I'M AN OKINAWA GIRL NOW, TOO!!
NAN KURU NAI SA*!! SEE?!
UH, NO, I DON'T THINK IT WORKS OUT THAT WAY.
*Okinawan for "It will work out."
KANATA-SAN, THE JAR YOU BROUGHT... IS THAT...?
UH-HUH!
HAISAI*!!
NOW YOU'RE JUST GUESSING!!
YOU MEAN, "HAITAI."
*Casual Okinawan for "hello." Men say "haisai" and women say "haitai."
SEA GRAPES!
THAT'S AN OLD PERSON FOOD!!

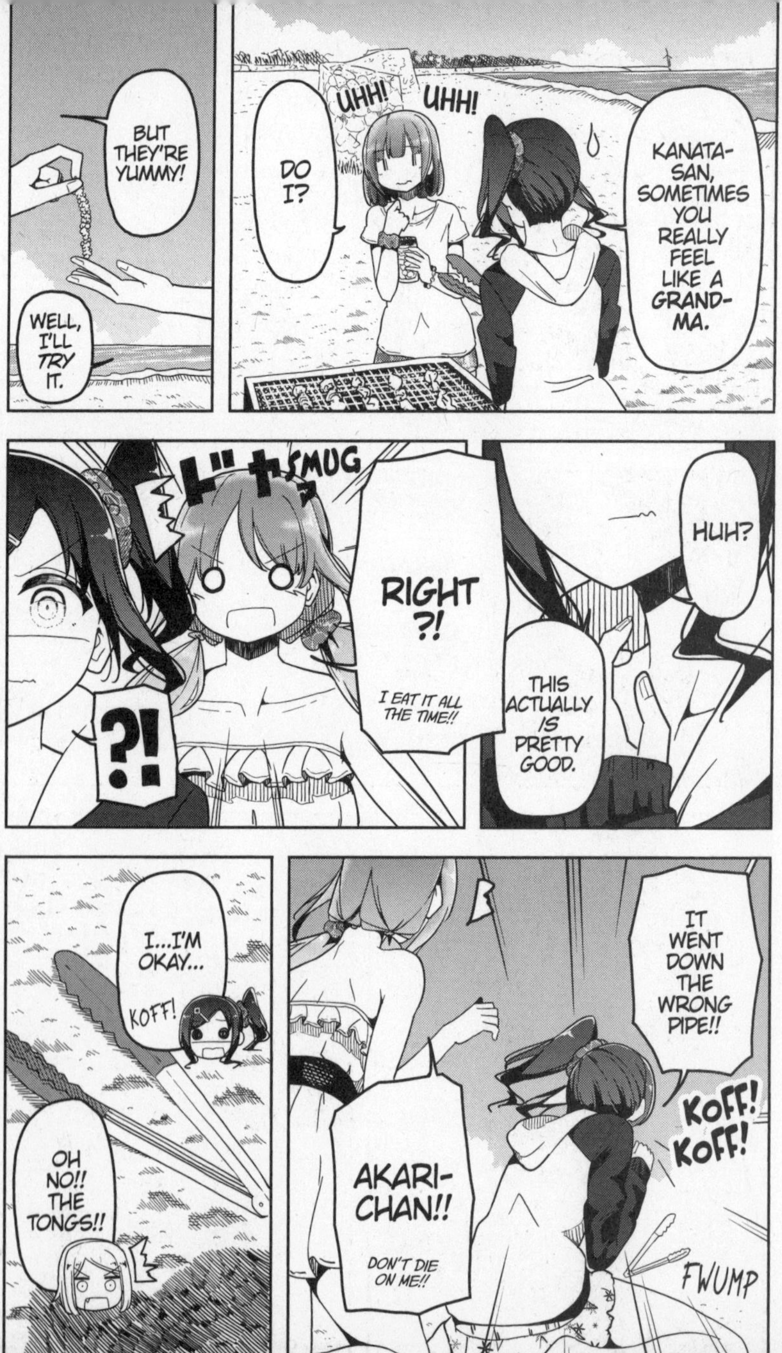
KANATA-SAN, SOMETIMES YOU REALLY FEEL LIKE A GRAND-MA.
UHH! UHH!
DO I?
BUT THEY'RE YUMMY!
WELL, I'LL *TRY* IT.
HUH?
THIS ACTUALLY *IS* PRETTY GOOD.
ドヤ SMUG
RIGHT?!
I EAT IT ALL THE TIME!!
?!
IT WENT DOWN THE WRONG PIPE!!
KOFF! KOFF!
AKARI-CHAN!!
DON'T DIE ON ME!!
FWUMP
I...I'M OKAY...
KOFF!
OH NO!! THE TONGS!!

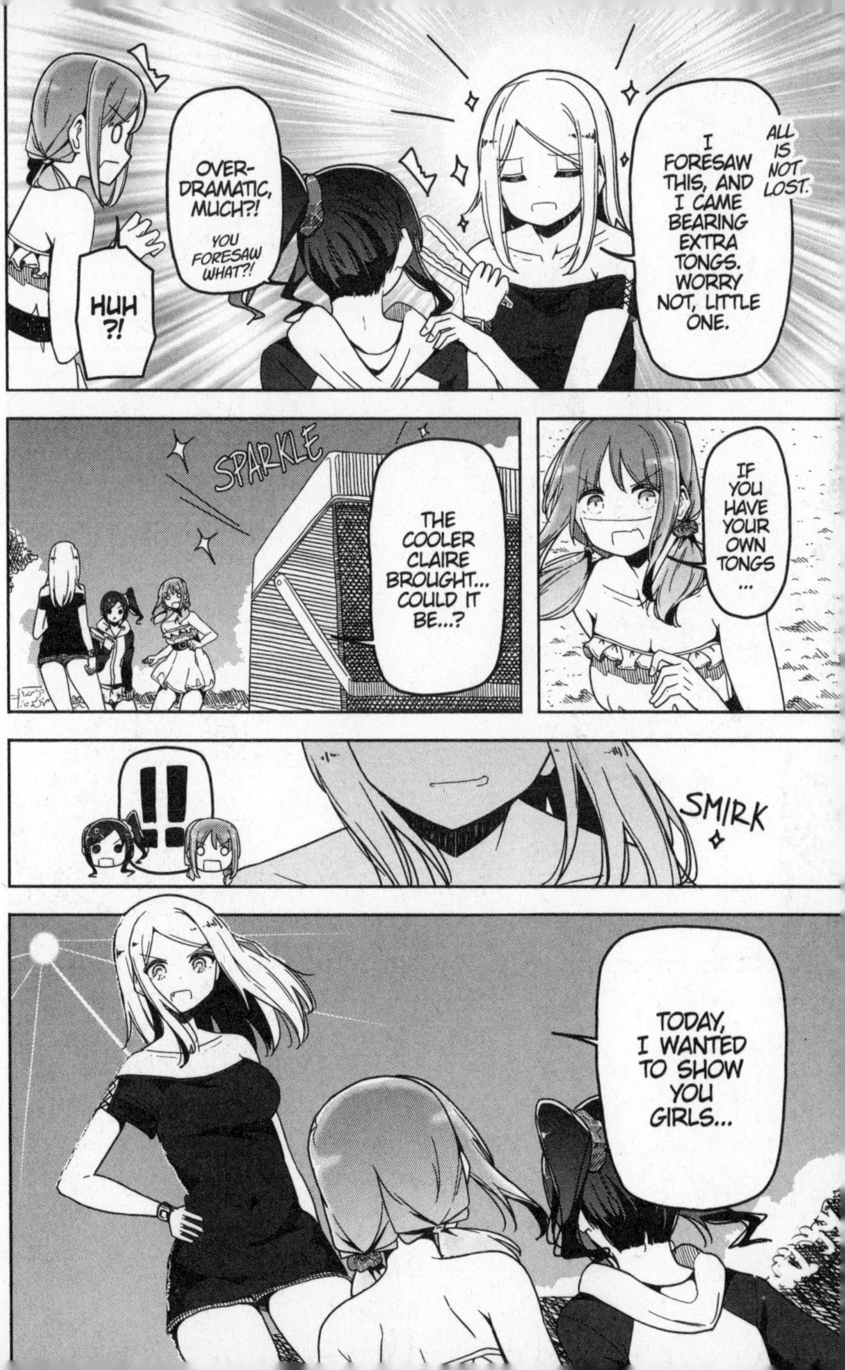

ALL IS NOT LOST.
I FORESAW THIS, AND I CAME BEARING EXTRA TONGS. WORRY NOT, LITTLE ONE.
OVER-DRAMATIC, MUCH?!
YOU FORESAW WHAT?!
HUH?!
IF YOU HAVE YOUR OWN TONGS...
SPARKLE
THE COOLER CLAIRE BROUGHT... COULD IT BE...?
SMIRK
!!
TODAY, I WANTED TO SHOW YOU GIRLS...

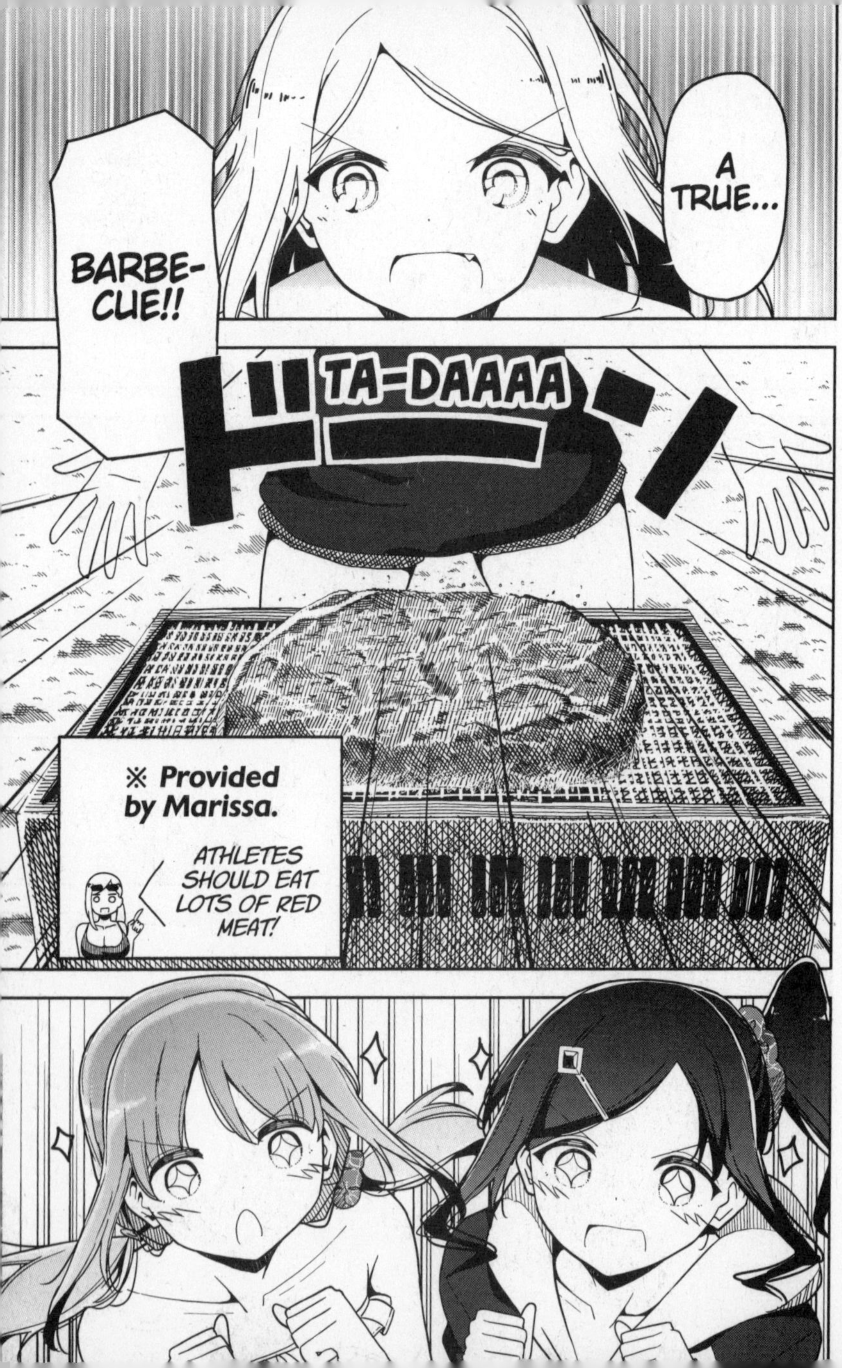
A TRUE...
BARBE-CUE!!
TA-DAAAA
※ Provided by Marissa.
ATHLETES SHOULD EAT LOTS OF RED MEAT!

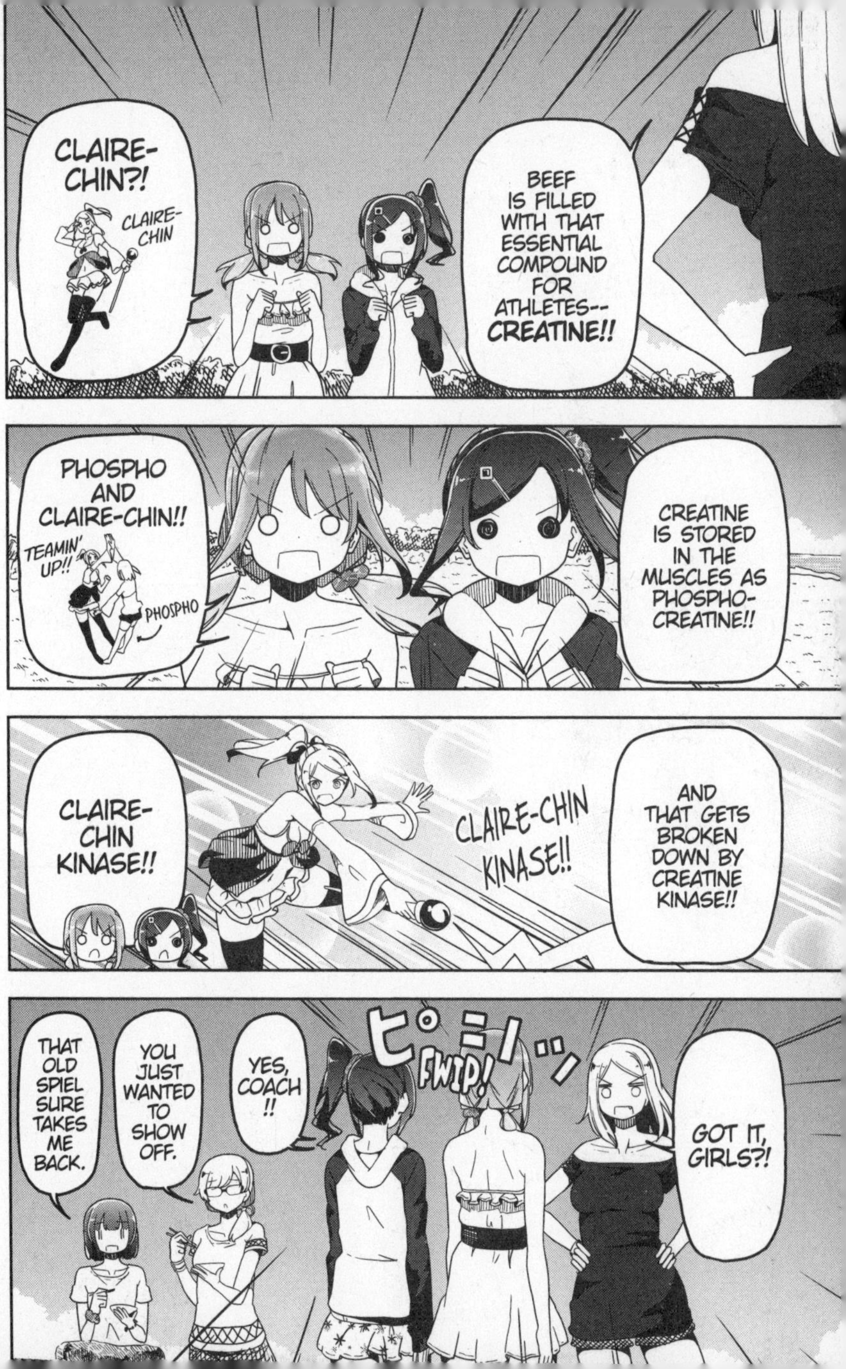
BEEF IS FILLED WITH THAT ESSENTIAL COMPOUND FOR ATHLETES-- CREATINE!!
CLAIRE-CHIN?!
CLAIRE-CHIN
CREATINE IS STORED IN THE MUSCLES AS PHOSPHO-CREATINE!!
PHOSPHO AND CLAIRE-CHIN!!
TEAMIN' UP!!
PHOSPHO
AND THAT GETS BROKEN DOWN BY CREATINE KINASE!!
CLAIRE-CHIN KINASE!!
CLAIRE-CHIN KINASE!!
GOT IT, GIRLS?!
FWIP!
YES, COACH!!
YOU JUST WANTED TO SHOW OFF.
THAT OLD SPIEL SURE TAKES ME BACK.

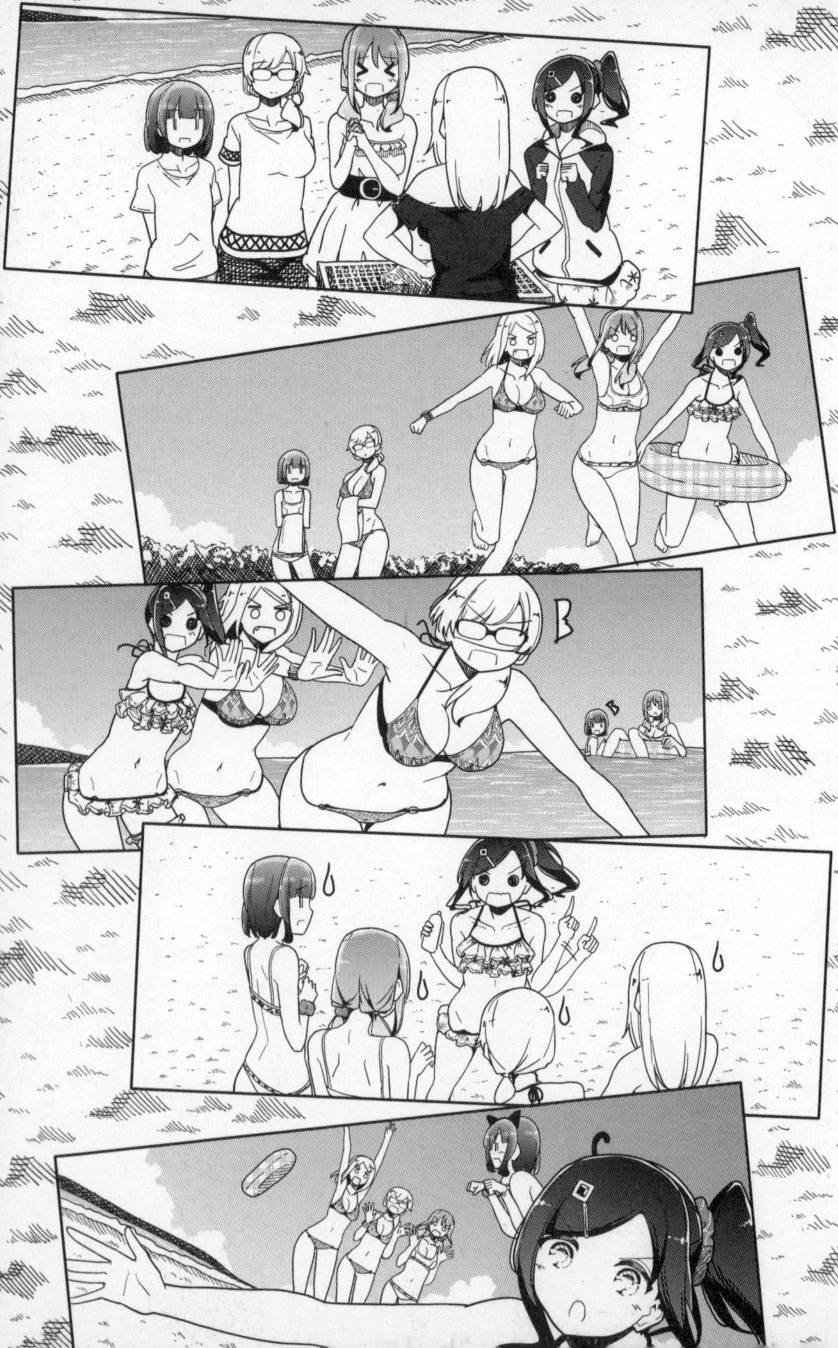

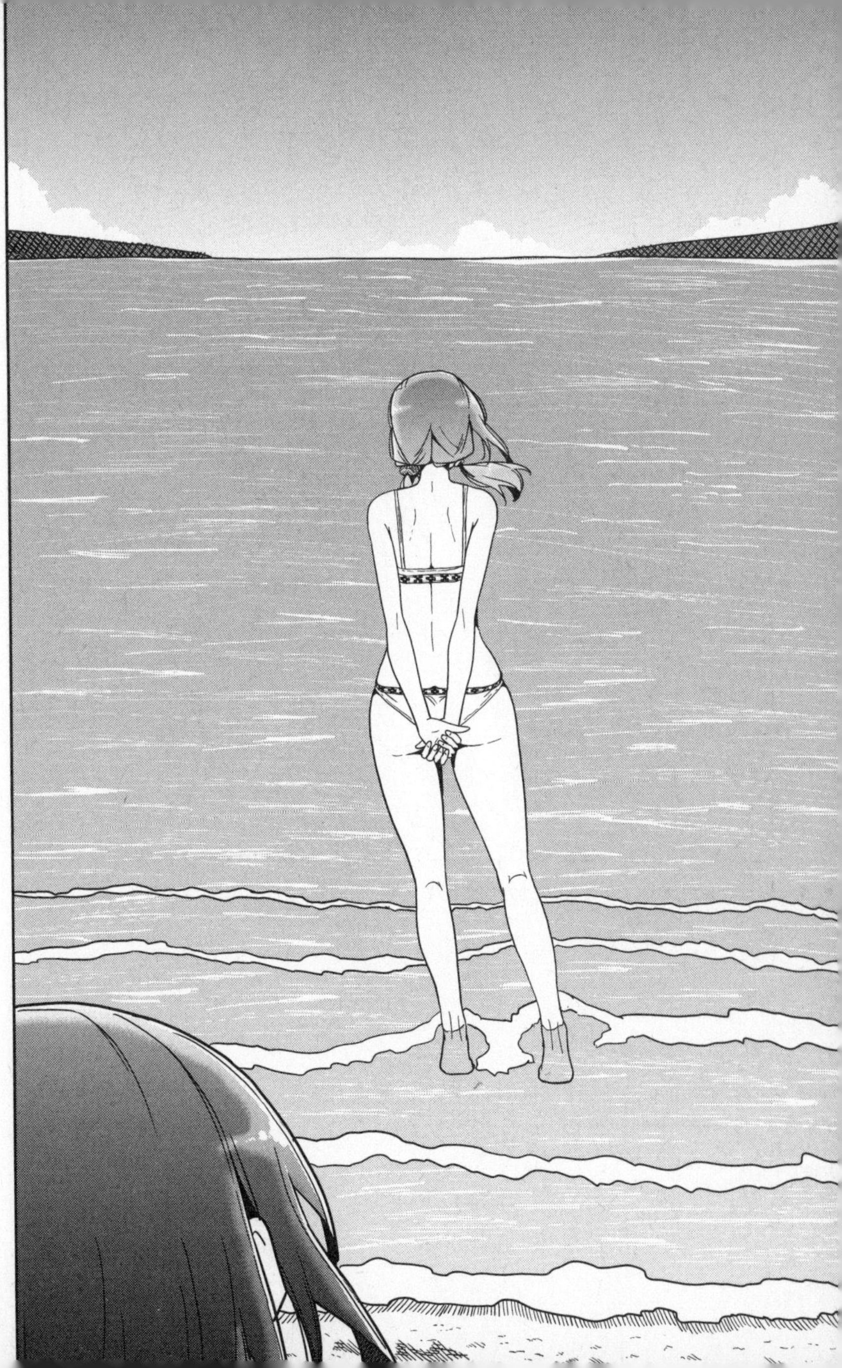

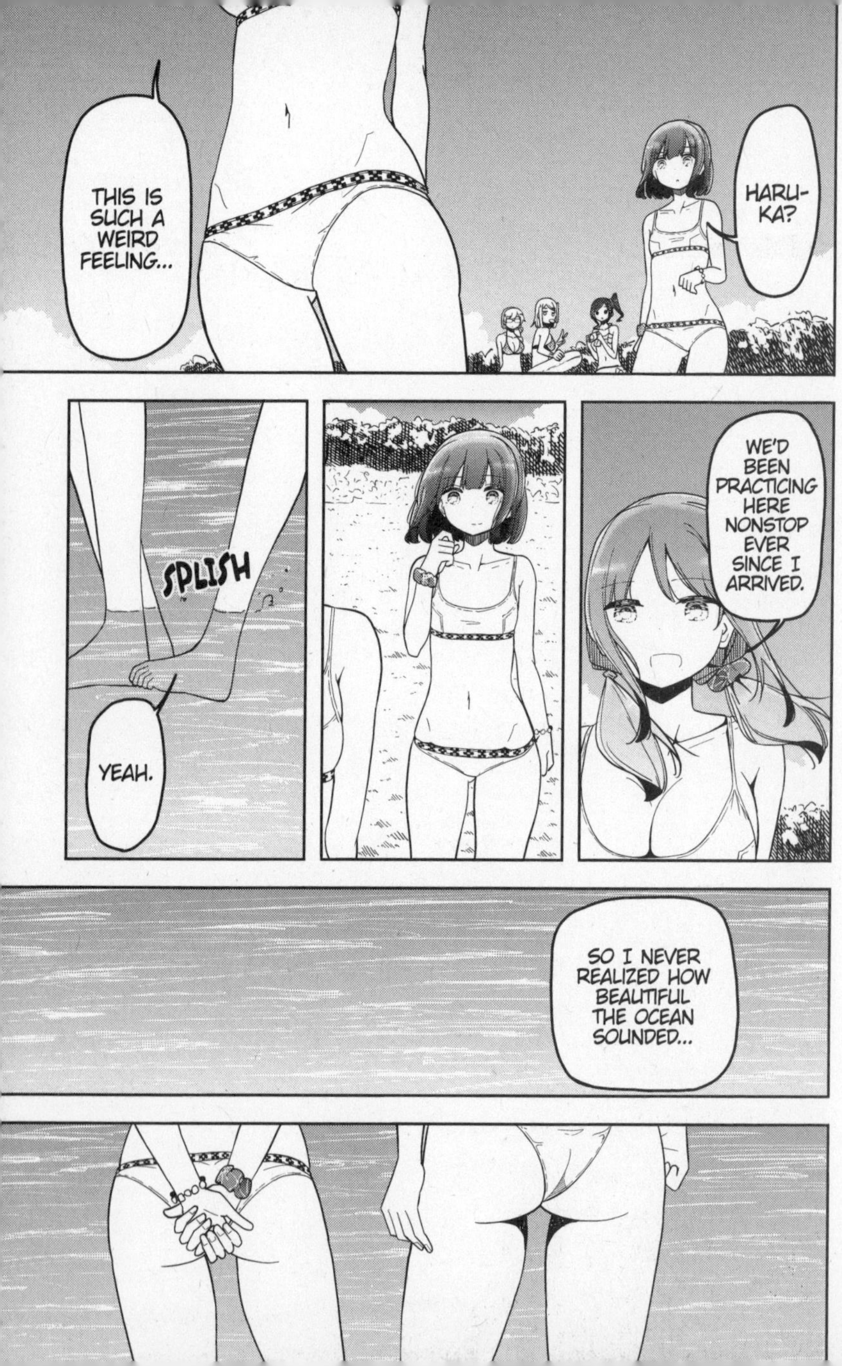
HARU-KA?
THIS IS SUCH A WEIRD FEELING...
WE'D BEEN PRACTICING HERE NONSTOP EVER SINCE I ARRIVED.
SPLISH
YEAH.
SO I NEVER REALIZED HOW BEAUTIFUL THE OCEAN SOUNDED...

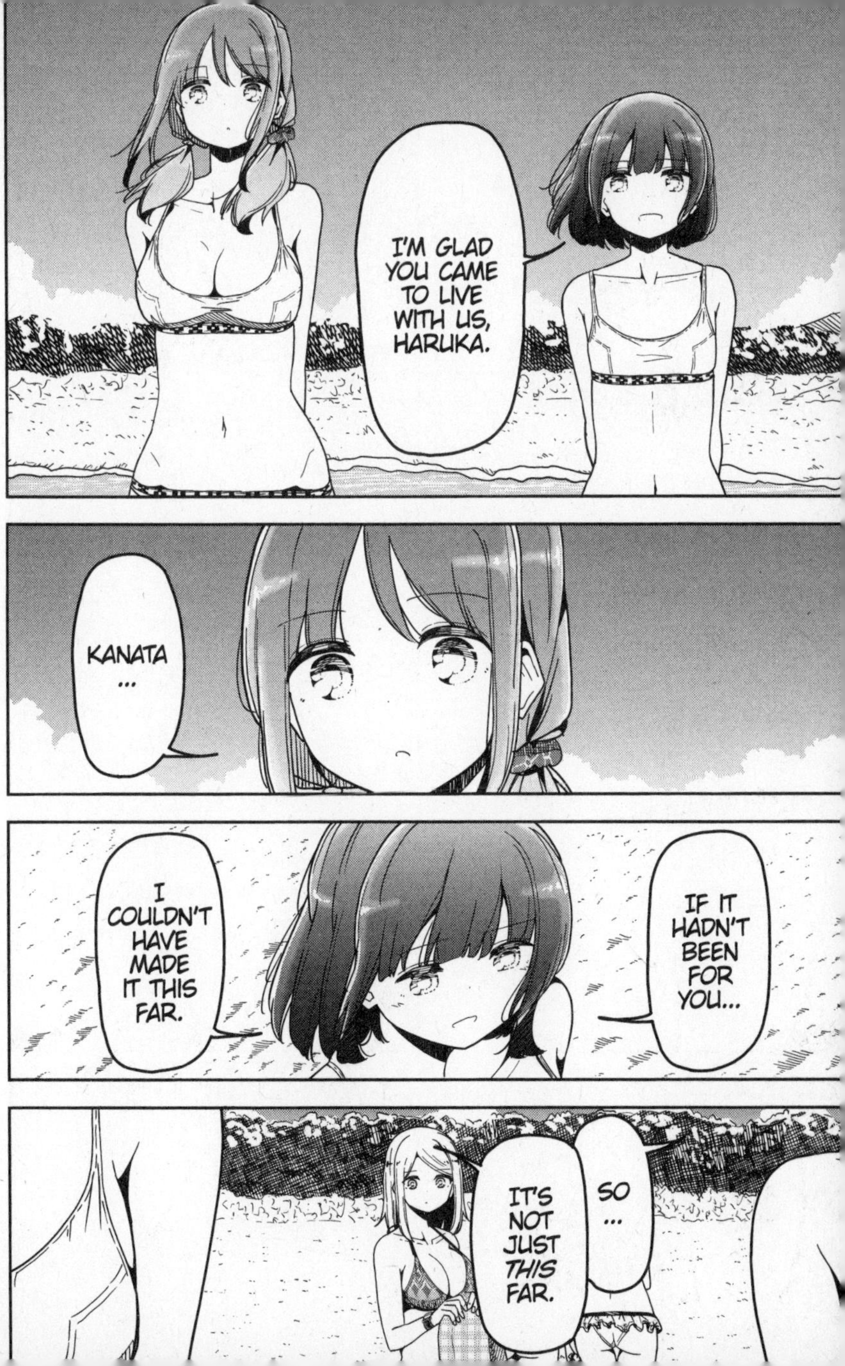
I'M GLAD YOU CAME TO LIVE WITH US, HARUKA.
KANATA ...
IF IT HADN'T BEEN FOR YOU...
I COULDN'T HAVE MADE IT THIS FAR.
SO ...
IT'S NOT JUST *THIS* FAR.

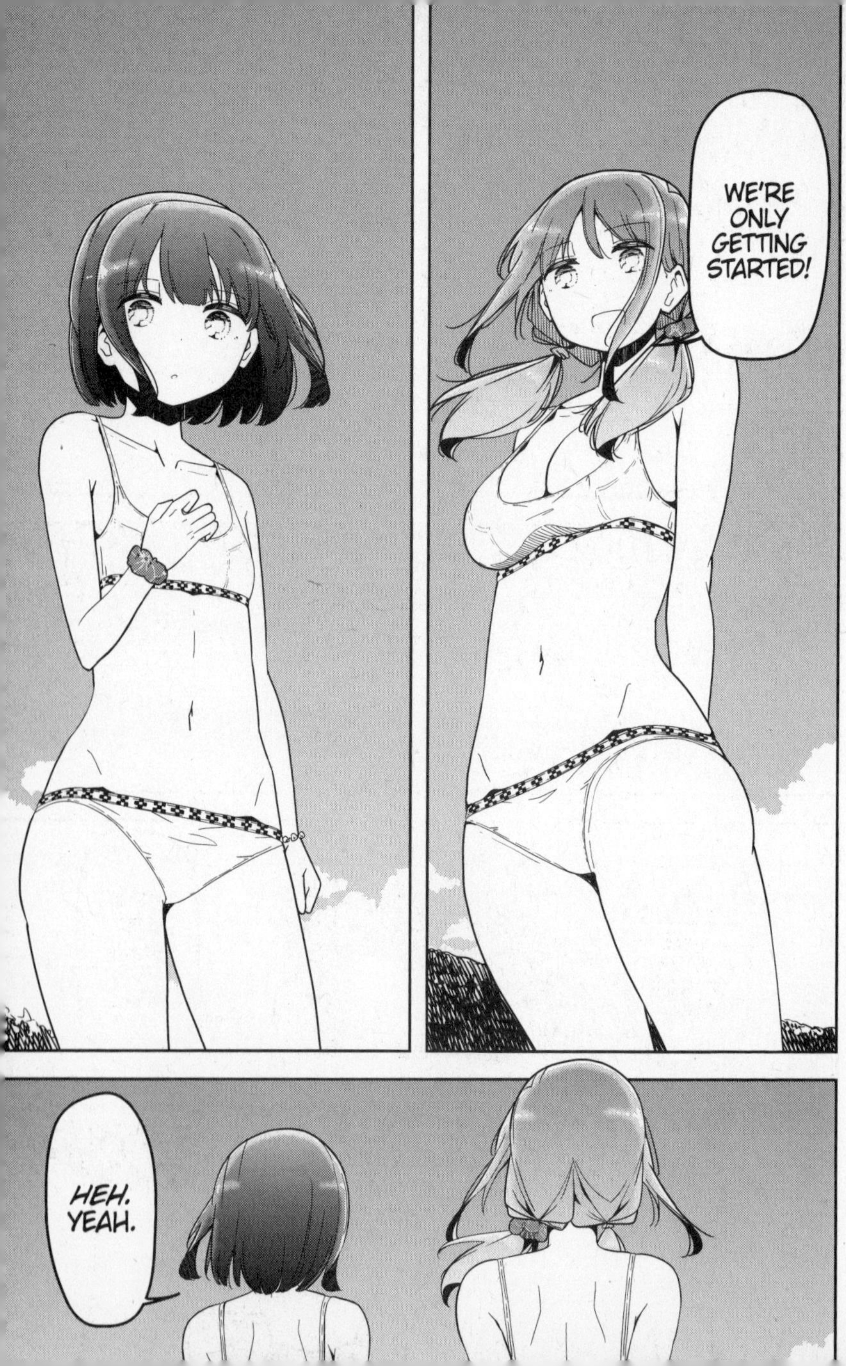
WE'RE ONLY GETTING STARTED!
HEH. YEAH.

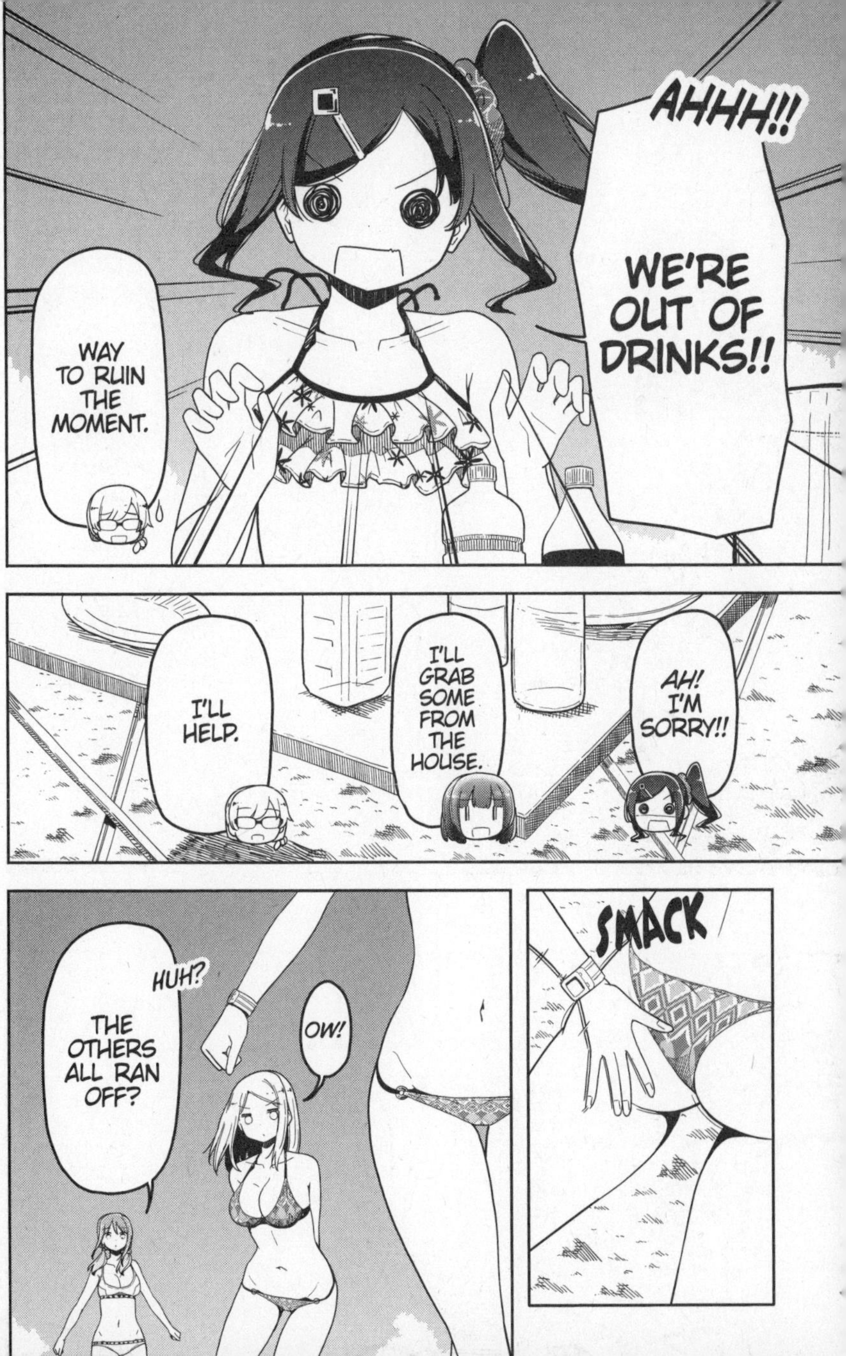
AHHH!!
WE'RE OUT OF DRINKS!!
WAY TO RUIN THE MOMENT.
AH! I'M SORRY!!
I'LL GRAB SOME FROM THE HOUSE.
I'LL HELP.
SMACK
OW!
HUH?
THE OTHERS ALL RAN OFF?

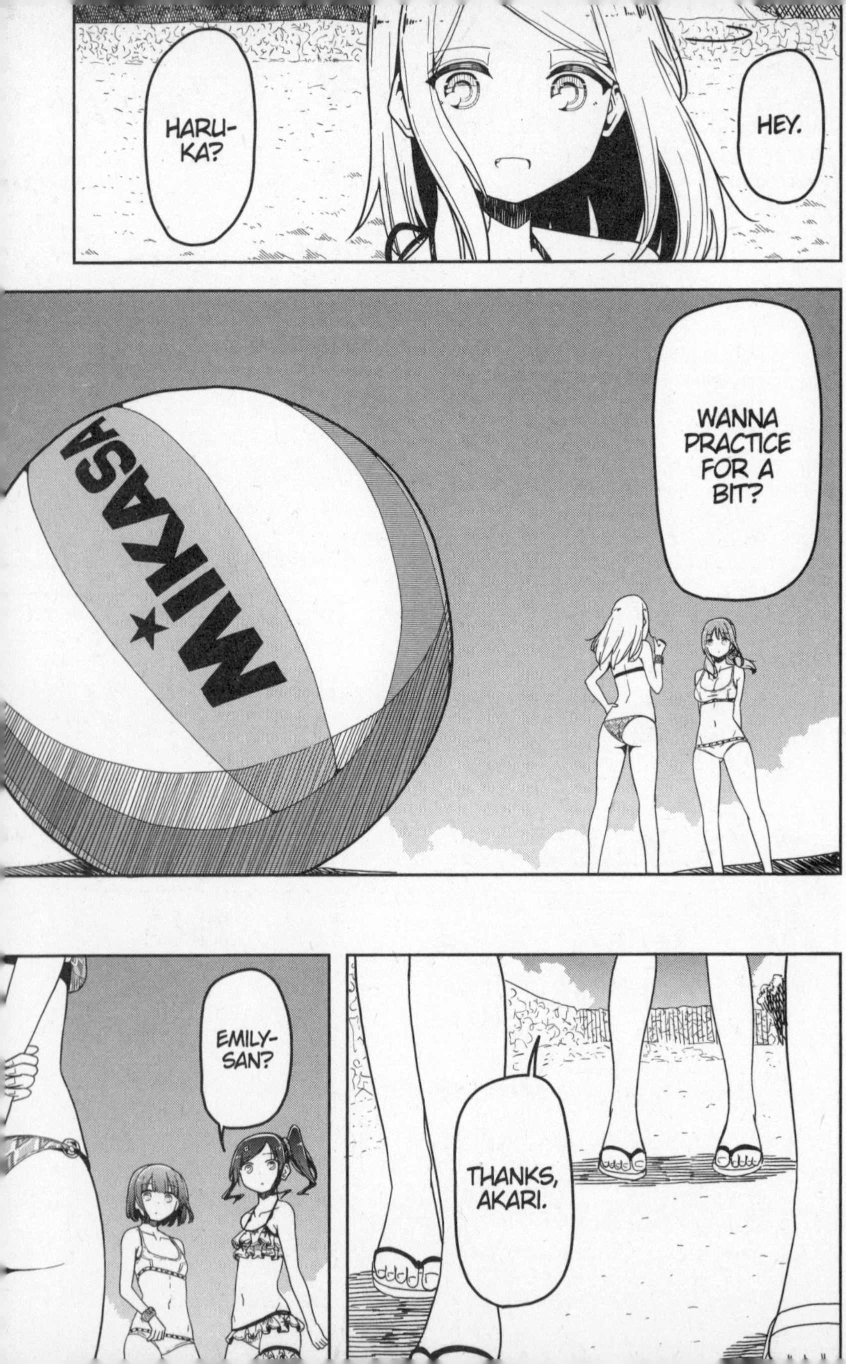
HEY.
HARU-KA?
MIKASA
WANNA PRACTICE FOR A BIT?
THANKS, AKARI.
EMILY-SAN?

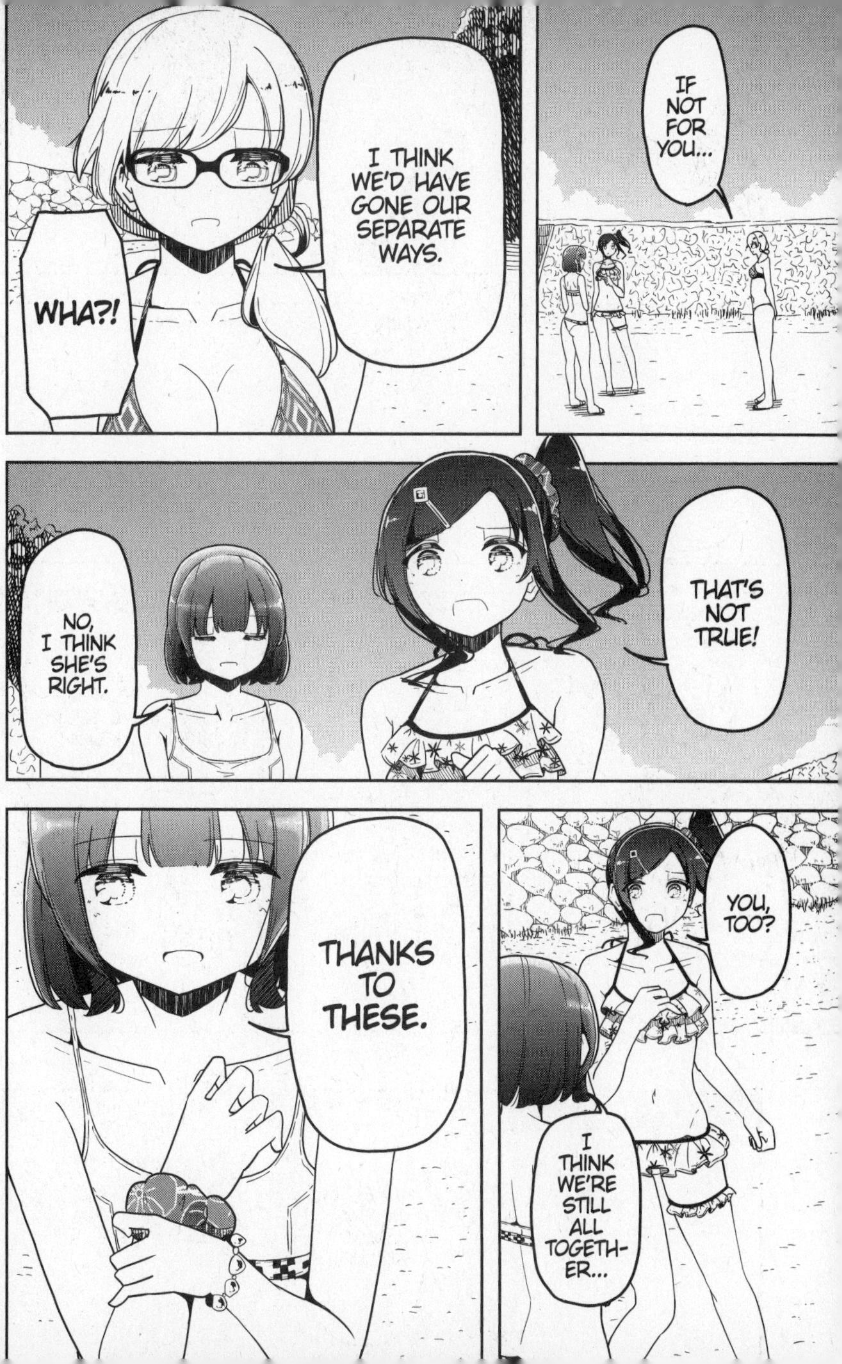
IF NOT FOR YOU...
I THINK WE'D HAVE GONE OUR SEPARATE WAYS.
WHA?!
THAT'S NOT TRUE!
NO, I THINK SHE'S RIGHT.
YOU, TOO?
I THINK WE'RE STILL ALL TOGETH-ER...
THANKS TO THESE.

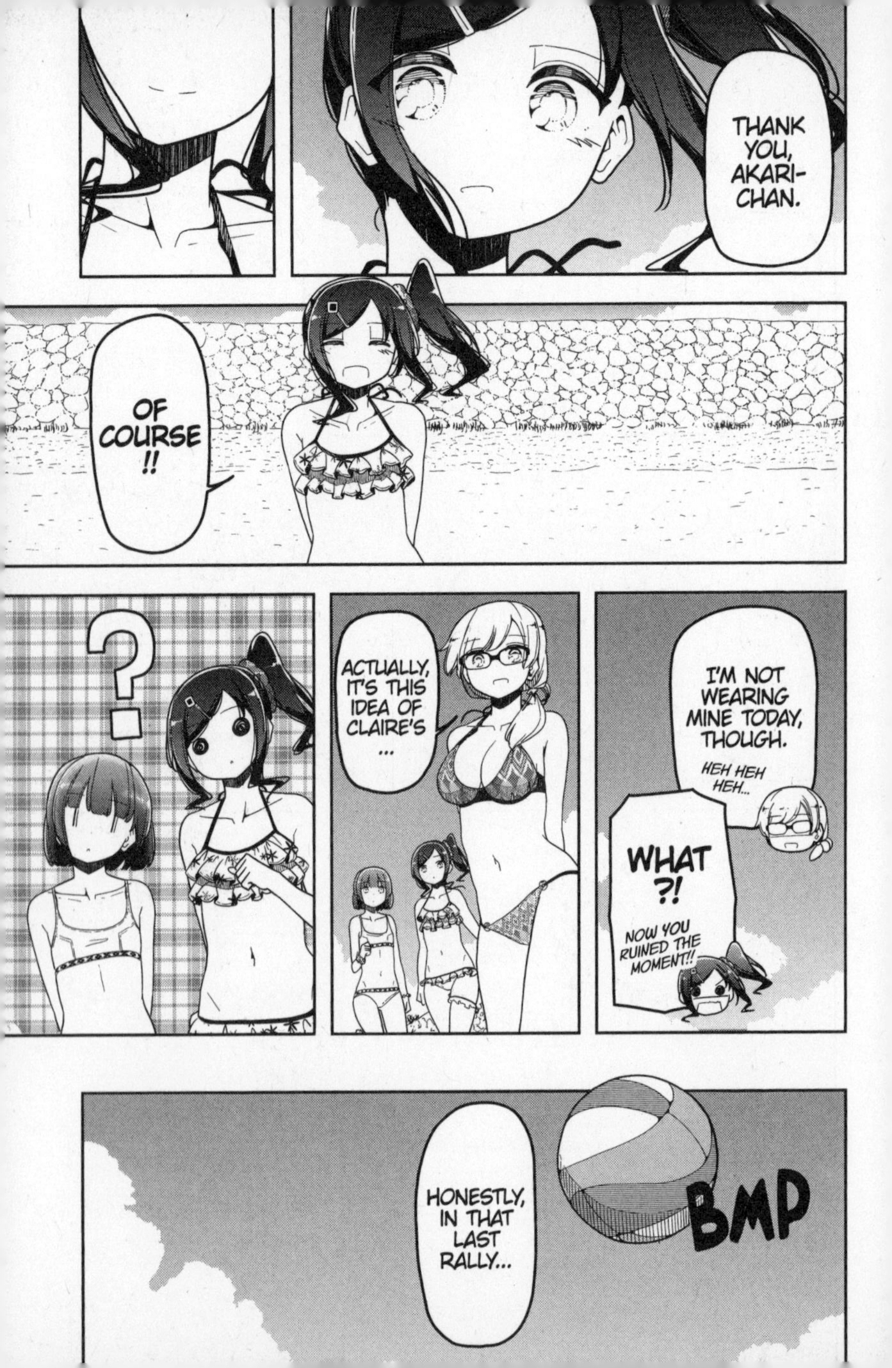
THANK YOU, AKARI-CHAN.
OF COURSE!!
?
ACTUALLY, IT'S THIS IDEA OF CLAIRE'S...
I'M NOT WEARING MINE TODAY, THOUGH.
HEH HEH HEH...
WHAT?!
NOW YOU RUINED THE MOMENT!!
BMP
HONESTLY, IN THAT LAST RALLY...

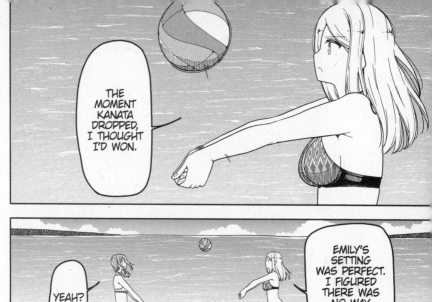

THE MOMENT KANATA DROPPED, I THOUGHT I'D WON.

YEAH?

EMILY'S SETTING WAS PERFECT. I FIGURED THERE WAS NO WAY WE'D LOSE.

WELL, I DIDN'T THINK THAT.

BECAUSE OF THE WIND?

THMP

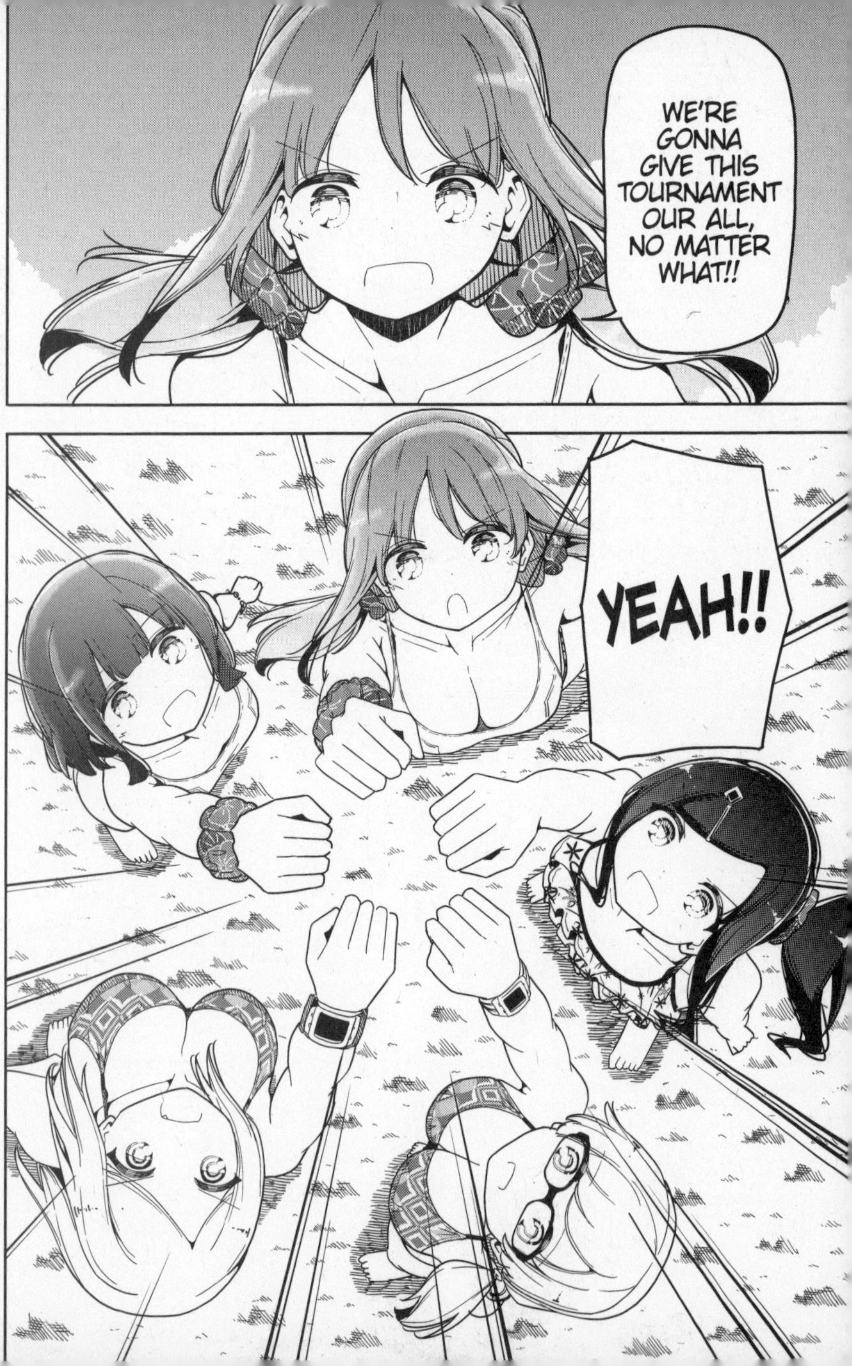
WE'RE GONNA GIVE THIS TOURNAMENT OUR ALL, NO MATTER WHAT!!
YEAH!!

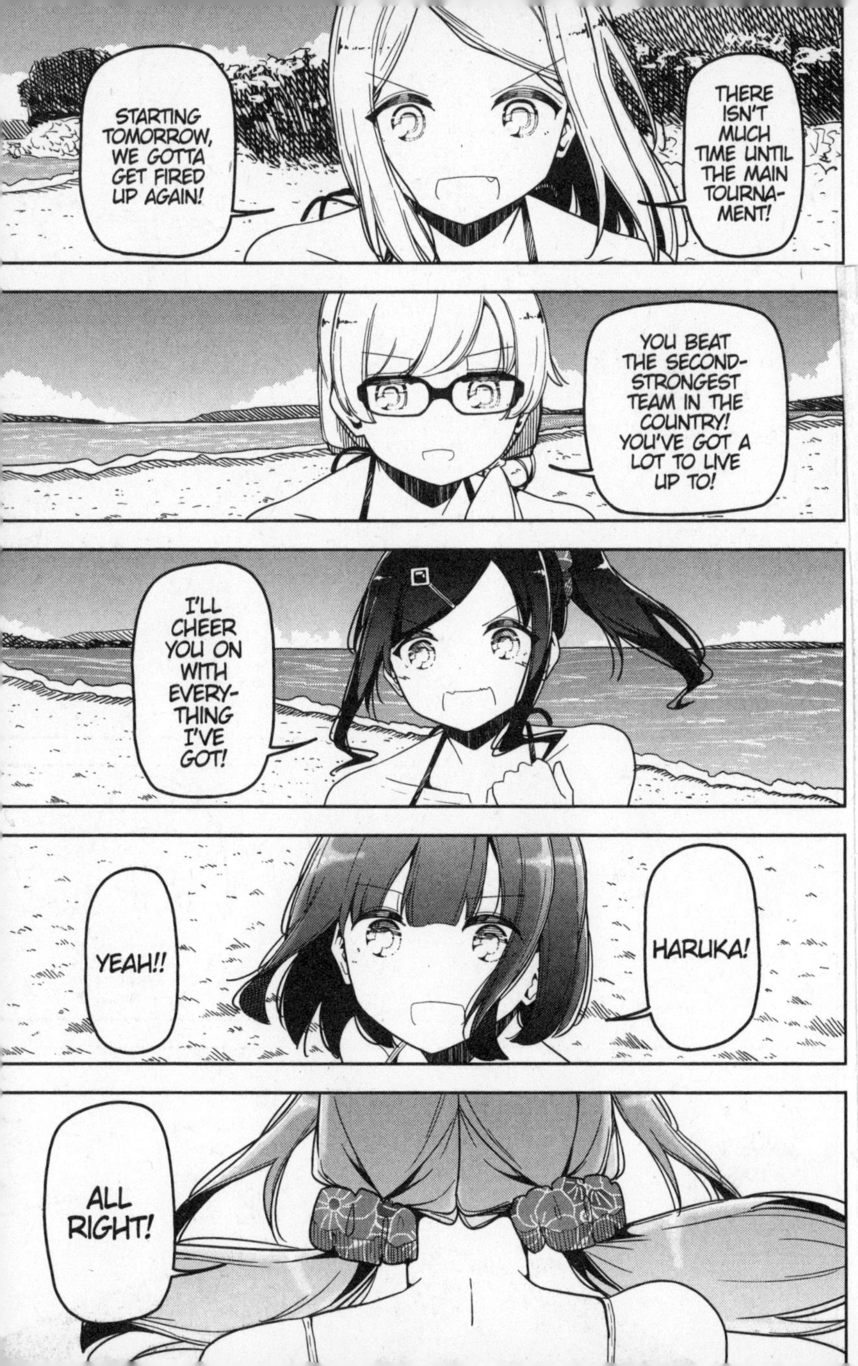
THERE ISN'T MUCH TIME UNTIL THE MAIN TOURNA-MENT!
STARTING TOMORROW, WE GOTTA GET FIRED UP AGAIN!
YOU BEAT THE SECOND-STRONGEST TEAM IN THE COUNTRY! YOU'VE GOT A LOT TO LIVE UP TO!
I'LL CHEER YOU ON WITH EVERY-THING I'VE GOT!
HARUKA!
YEAH!!
ALL RIGHT!

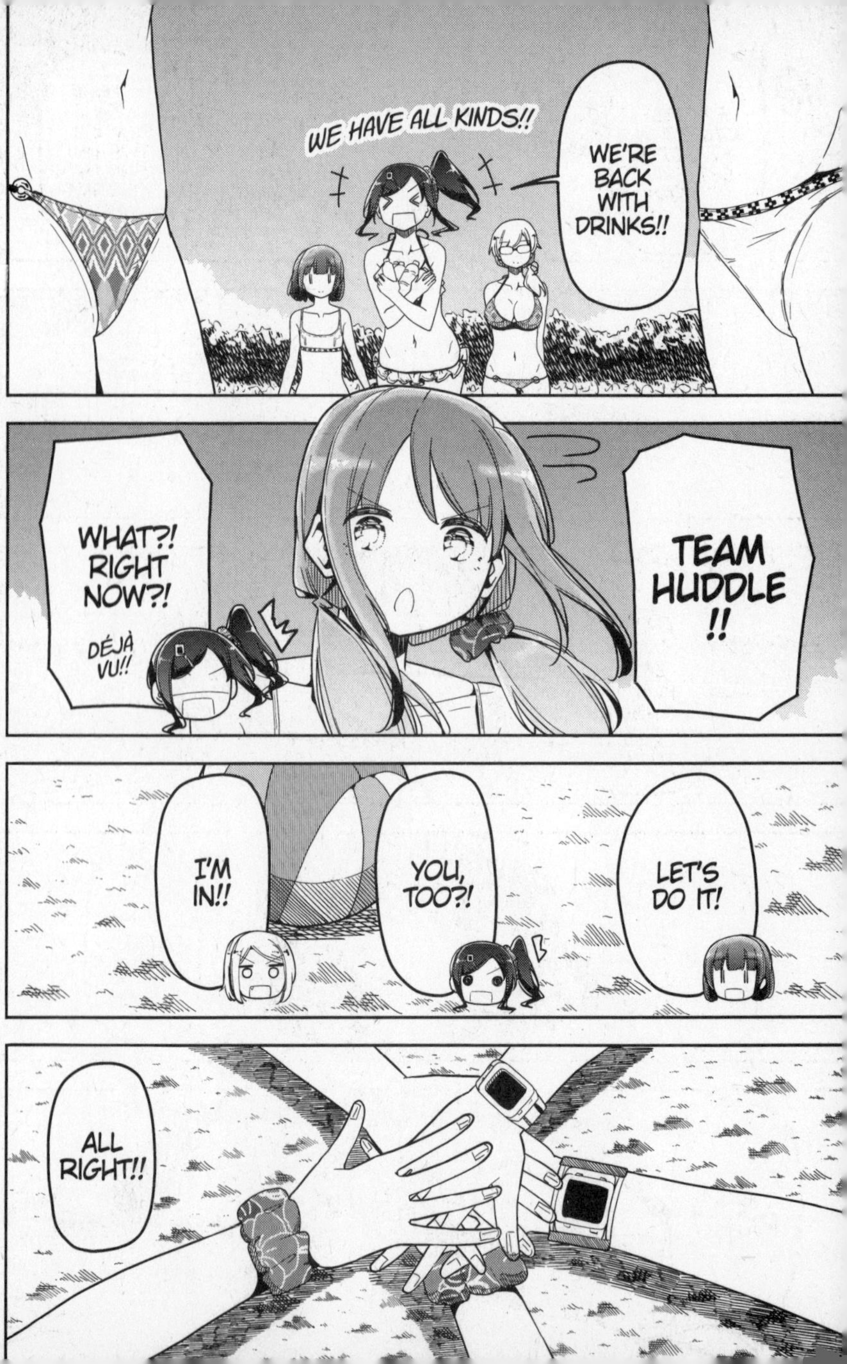
WE'RE BACK WITH DRINKS!!
WE HAVE ALL KINDS!!
TEAM HUDDLE !!
WHAT?! RIGHT NOW?!
DÉJÀ VU!!
LET'S DO IT!
YOU, TOO?!
I'M IN!!
ALL RIGHT!!

WIN, HARUKA!

DO IT FOR US!

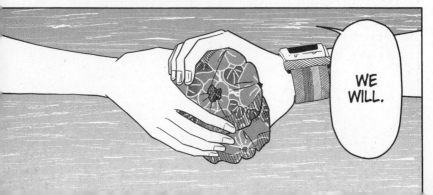

WE WILL.

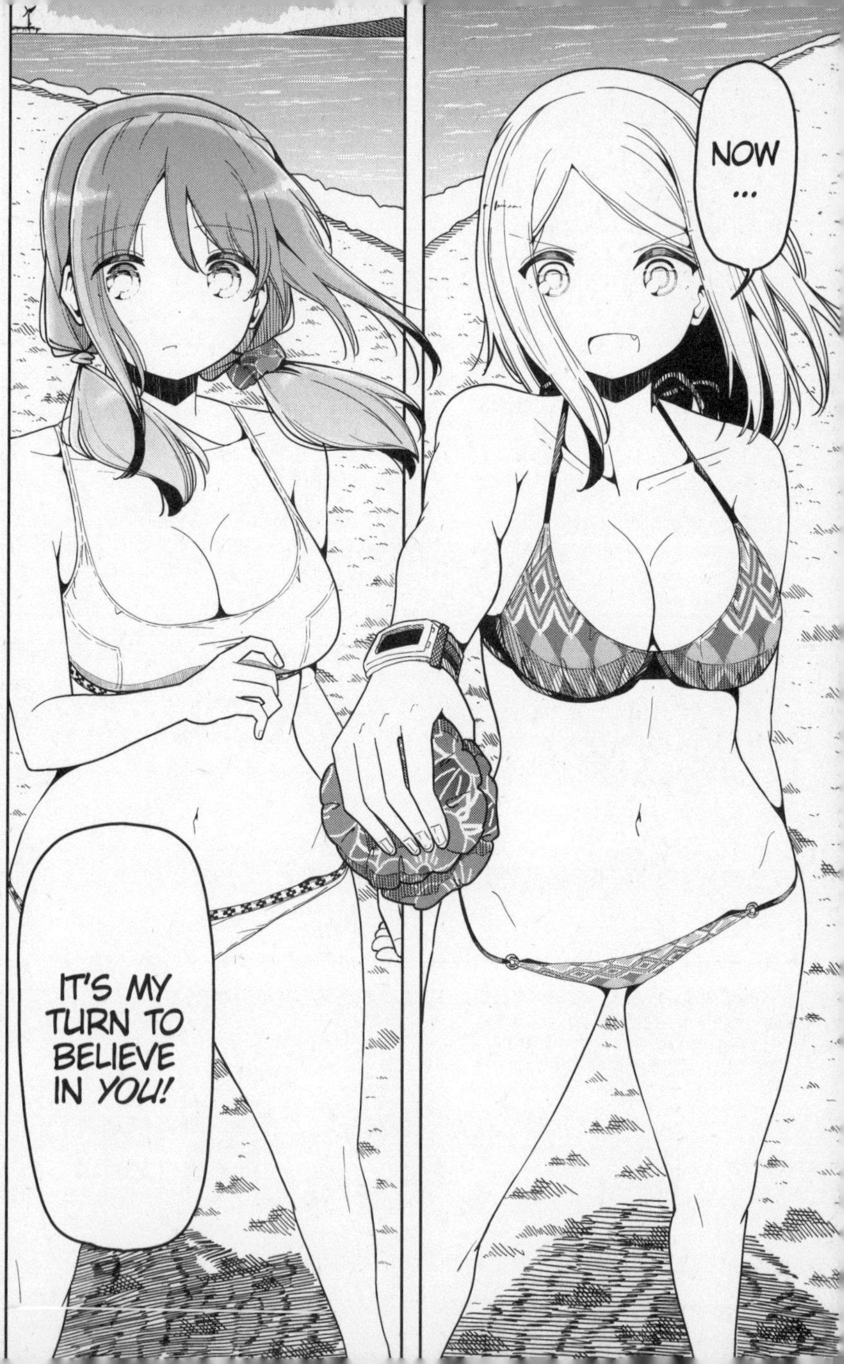
NOW ...
IT'S MY TURN TO BELIEVE IN *YOU!*

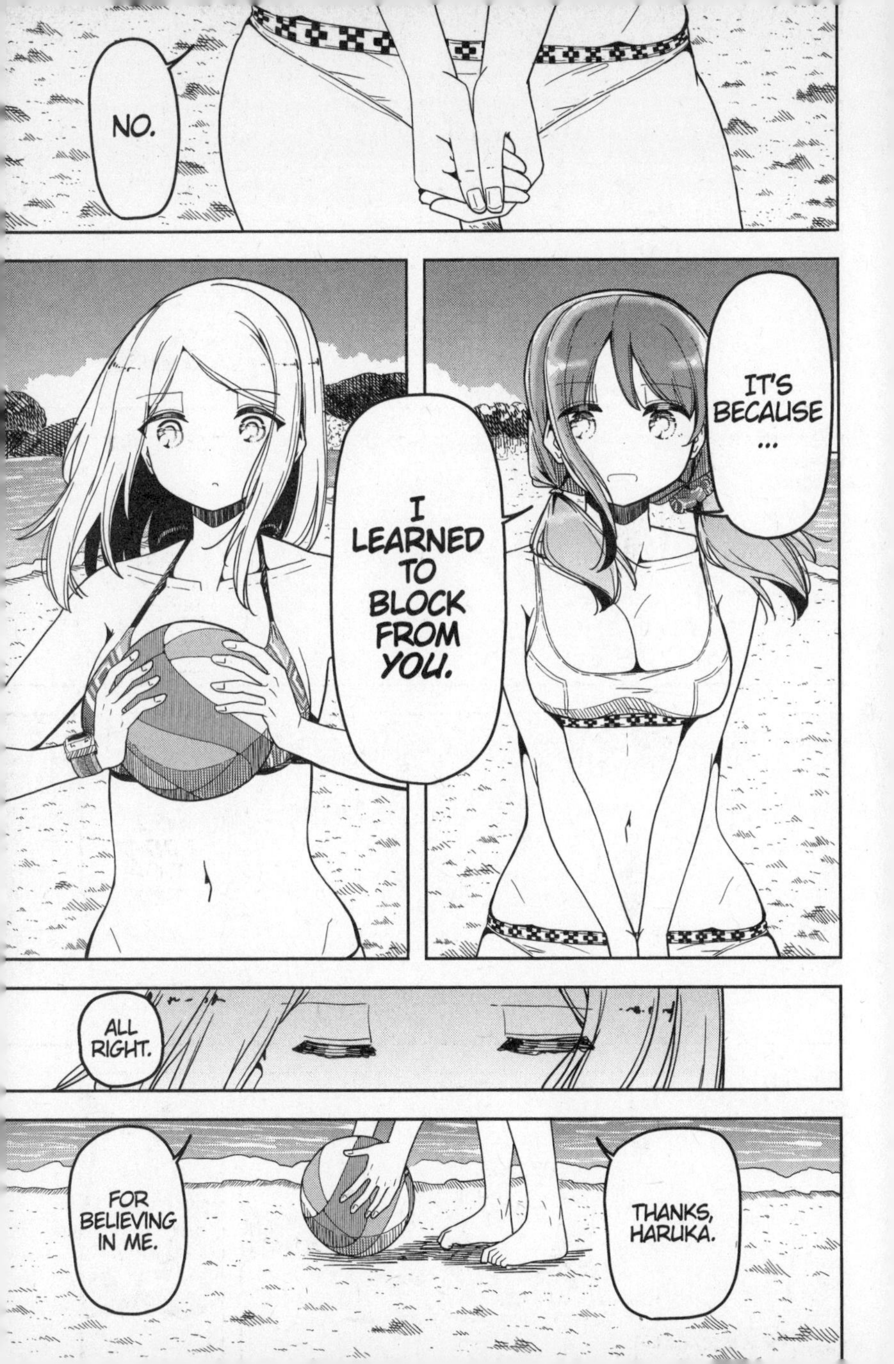

NO.
IT'S BECAUSE ...
I LEARNED TO BLOCK FROM YOU.
ALL RIGHT.
THANKS, HARUKA.
FOR BELIEVING IN ME.

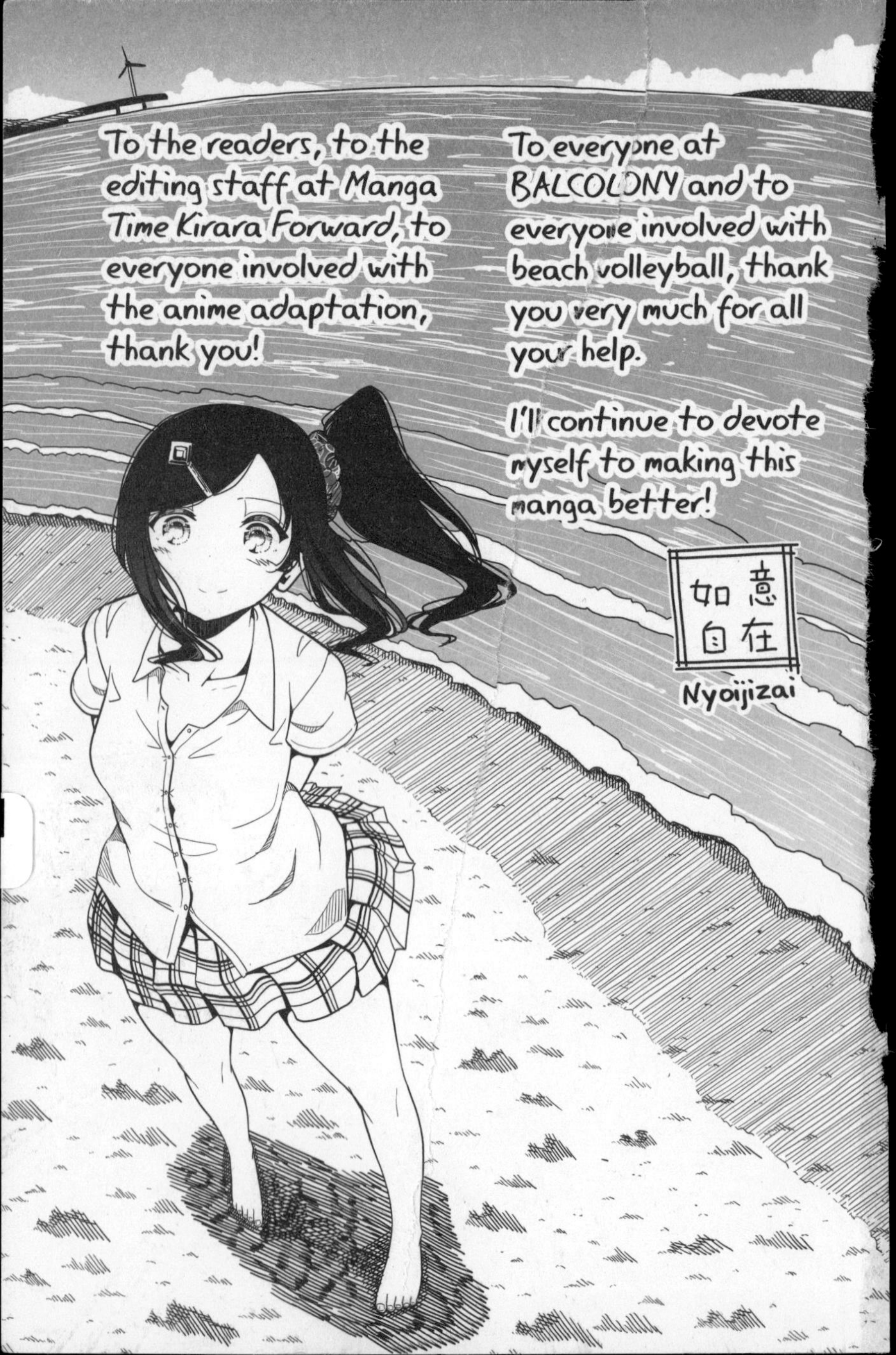
To the readers, to the editing staff at Manga Time Kirara Forward, to everyone involved with the anime adaptation, thank you!
To everyone at BALCOLONY and to everyone involved with beach volleyball, thank you very much for all your help.
I'll continue to devote myself to making this manga better!
如意
自在
Nyoijizai

SEVEN SEAS ENTERTAINMENT PRESENTS

Harukana★ Receive

VOLUME 5

story and art by **NYOIJIZAI**

TRANSLATION
Amanda Haley

LETTERING AND RETOUCH
Ray Steeves

COVER DESIGN
KC Fabellon

PROOFREADER
Kurestin Armada
Stephanie Cohen

EDITOR
Shannon Fay

PRODUCTION MANAGER
Lissa Pattillo

MANAGING EDITOR
Julie Davis

EDITOR-IN-CHIEF
Adam Arnold

PUBLISHER
Jason DeAngelis

HARUKANA RECEIVE VOL. 5
© Nyoijizai 2018
First published in 2018 by Houbunsha Co., LTD. Tokyo, Japan.
English translation rights arranged with Houbunsha Co., LTD.

Seven Seas press and purchase enquiries can be sent to Marketing Manager Lianne Sentar at press@gomanga.com. Information regarding the distribution and purchase of digital editions is available from Digital Manager CK Russell at digital@gomanga.com.

Seven Seas and the Seven Seas logo are trademarks of Seven Seas Entertainment. All rights reserved.

ISBN: 978-1-642756-83-8

Printed in Canada

First Printing: November 2019

10 9 8 7 6 5 4 3 2 1

W9-BBO-297

FOLLOW US ONLINE: *www.sevenseasentertainment.com*

READING DIRECTIONS

This book reads from *right to left*, Japanese style. If this is your first time reading manga, you start reading from the top right panel on each page and take it from there. If you get lost, just follow the numbered diagram here. It may seem backwards at first, but you'll get the hang of it! Have fun!!

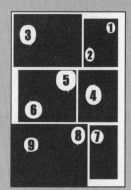